THE CONSERVATION CONSTITUTION

ENVIRONMENT AND SOCIETY

KIMBERLY K. SMITH, EDITOR

The Conservation Constitution

The Conservation Movement and
Constitutional Change, 1870–1930

Kimberly K. Smith

UNIVERSITY PRESS OF KANSAS

Published by the University Press of Kansas (Lawrence, Kansas 66045), which was
organized by the Kansas Board of Regents and is operated and funded by Emporia State
University, Fort Hays State University, Kansas State University, Pittsburg State University,
the University of Kansas, and Wichita State University.

Library of Congress Cataloging-in-Publication Data
Names: Smith, Kimberly K., 1966– author.
Title: The conservation constitution : the conservation movement and
    constitutional change, 1870–1930 / Kimberly K. Smith.
Description: Lawrence : University Press of Kansas 2019. | Series:
    Environment and society | Includes bibliographical references and index.
Identifiers: LCCN 2019007131
    ISBN 9780700628445 (cloth)
    ISBN 9780700628452 (ebook)
Subjects: LCSH: Conservation of natural resources—Law and
    legislation—United States—History. | Constitutional history—United
    States. | Progressivism (United States politics)
Classification: LCC KF5505 .S65 2019 | DDC 344.7304/6—dc23
LC record available at https://lccn.loc.gov/2019007131.

British Library Cataloguing-in-Publication Data is available.

Printed in the United States of America

10 9 8 7 6 5 4 3 2 1

The paper used in this publication is recycled and contains 30 percent postconsumer
waste. It is acid free and meets the minimum requirements of the American National
Standard for Permanence of Paper for Printed Library Materials Z39.48-1992.

Contents

Preface

This book is a response to a problem that has troubled me for several years. Although my primary interest as a scholar and teacher is environmental management, I have also taught constitutional law for more than twenty years. That distinction between "environmental management" and "constitutional law" is the problem: Constitutional law as it is generally taught seems to have nothing to do with environmental management. The standard constitutional law and constitutional history textbooks contain virtually no discussion of the topic.

That oversight is astonishing. One of the primary responsibilities of federal, state, and local governments in the United States is managing public lands and other natural resources, to conserve and protect them for future generations. Constitutional conflict over that management has been endemic in American politics for more than a century. Yet most constitutional histories barely mention the topic. My well-used copy of *The American Constitution*, by Alfred Kelly, Winfred Harbison, and Herman Belz, buries the critical Supreme Court decision *Missouri v. Holland* in a brief discussion of the treaty power. David O'Brien's lengthy *Constitutional Law and Politics* gives *Missouri v. Holland* similar treatment and doesn't mention the Article IV Property Clause at all. (Look for that clause in his index and you'll find this telling entry: "property, *see* private property.") This neglect of environmental management is so common that I hardly noticed it myself for many years. It took some perfectly reasonable questions from my students to alert me to the fact that *I had no idea why Congress has the authority to protect the environment.*

The rationale for this book is therefore straightforward: to fill this gap in the literature and bring environmental management more fully into the story of the American constitution. Happily, this project has turned out to be a lot of fun, in large part because of the people who have helped me along the way. This book owes a great deal to the advice and support of my colleagues George Vrtis, Julie Novkov, and Mark Kanazawa. I also received considerable help from reference librarian Danya Leebaw, research assistant James Harren, the Forest Service staff at the Kaibab National Forest Headquarters, the National Archive staff at College Park, Maryland and Washington, DC, the reviewers for the University Press of Kansas, and grant guru Christopher Tassava. The William Nelson Cromwell Foundation supported my research with a generous grant, and Carleton College provided both grant and sabbatical support. My family provided additional support, mostly by listening to me talk endlessly about obscure nineteenth-century cases and the history of game management. Finally, I want to acknowledge my students, and particularly Marianna Zapanta, Dana Lyons, Joe Haase, and Carly Yu. Their interest in the constitutional dimensions of environmental management inspired this project, and this book is dedicated to them.

CHAPTER ONE

Introduction

From January 2 to February 11, 2016, Americans witnessed the dramatic occupation of the Malheur National Wildlife Refuge in Oregon by armed protestors. The protestors, led by activists Ammon and Ryan Bundy, objected to federal control of the nation's vast public lands. The protest ended with one dead and at least thirteen convicted of conspiracy (several more were acquitted of the conspiracy charge).[1] Meanwhile, in North Dakota, a different conflict was brewing as Native Americans from several tribes gathered to protest the permitting of an oil pipeline near the Standing Rock Sioux reservation. The Standing Rock conflict evolved over several months from a focus on Native American sovereignty to a broader call for federal action in defense of the natural environment. These protestors also risked their physical safety and more than seven hundred were arrested.[2]

It might seem puzzling that protestors would take such risks over ordinary environmental management strategies—operating a wildlife refuge, permitting a pipeline. But the protestors saw these conflicts in more fundamental terms: as a fight over constitutional principles. The standoffs were in fact part of a long-standing constitutional debate over environmental policy, with roots stretching back to the early twentieth century. Many of the Standing Rock protesters were environmental activists promoting the view that the federal government has a duty to protect natural resources and the welfare of those who depend on them, and perhaps even to direct the economy away from fossil fuels altogether. The protestors at the Malheur National Wildlife Refuge, on the other hand, saw in the nation's environmental protection regime a challenge to American constitutional norms. The Malheur protestors would characterize pollution-abatement measures and public land management strategies as potentially infringing on private property rights and undermining the free market. The two groups held radically different visions of the role and acceptable limits of state power.

Such ideological conflict often centers on environmental regulation because managing the natural environment has become a major impetus for state building—for extending government authority over the economy and private behavior. And that ultimately is what protests over federal environmental policy are about. The United States cherishes the ideal of limited government. How do we reconcile that constitutional value with the expansion of state authority over the environment—an expansion that seems both constitutionally problematic and increasingly necessary?

Many Americans observing the standoff at the Malheur refuge (including myself) found it difficult to sympathize with the protestors. As much as we might appreciate the value of private property rights and limited government, the standoff pitted those values against the basic purpose of the refuge: to protect wildlife. That, too, is an important American value. After all, it was not some foreign revolutionary but the very American civil servant Aldo Leopold who, in *A Sand County Almanac*, called on Americans to recognize our membership in a biotic community. But as he well understood, thinking about the political community in this broad, ecologically informed way requires us to rethink our political institutions—to build what some theorists have called "the green state."[3] How do we create a polity that gives recognition and respect to its nonhuman members and protects ecological systems not only for current but also for future generations? How will our political and legal traditions have to change to accommodate this new consciousness? Can a liberal constitution provide an adequate foundation for that project?

The United States is a particularly interesting place to look for answers to those questions. On the one hand, the United States emerged as a leader in conservation policy in the twentieth century. It negotiated the first successful international conservation treaties, pioneered the idea of the national park, and led the world in creating a modern environmental regulatory regime in the 1960s and 1970s.[4] On the other hand, the United States is famously committed to the liberal values of limited government, decentralization, and strong protection of private property rights. These constitutional values make protecting natural resources a challenge:

Establishing that environmental protection is a legitimate responsibility of the national government—justifying the centralization of government power and limits on property rights— required a significant change in the liberal constitutional framework that governed the nation during its first one hundred years. My question, then, is: How has the United States accommodated this expansion of state power over the natural environment in its constitutional framework?

Most scholars trace the modern environmental protection regime to the 1960s, when the United States along with most other OECD states created environmental agencies and national antipollution laws.[5] I don't dispute that time line. But in the United States, the constitutional *foundations* of that environmental regime were laid during the Progressive Era conservation movement. It is not coincidental that the Malheur National Wildlife Refuge was established in 1908 by Theodore Roosevelt—with the thinnest of constitutional justifications. The Progressive Era conservationists advocated, and largely achieved, constitutional changes that allowed for the creation of the modern environmental regime several decades later. Accordingly, this study centers on the Progressive Era: roughly 1900 to 1920, the two decades during which the Progressive movement was a potent political force. However, to understand how conservationists affected the evolution of constitutional doctrine, we will need to begin the story earlier (about 1870) and end later (the 1930s).

This book, then, is a study of constitutional change. Most of the Progressive Era state and federal policies aimed at addressing pollution and conserving wildlife, forests, and water resources would have been considered unconstitutional, or at least of doubtful constitutionality, in the mid-nineteenth century. By 1930, constitutional objections to the new conservation regime had been met, and state and federal authority to manage natural resources was written into constitutional law. How did it become constitutional "common sense"[6]—not uncontested but commonly accepted—that federal and state governments have broad authority to protect natural resources and the integrity of ecosystems in the interests of future generations?

Creating that consensus required conservationists to answer two questions: What is the governmental interest in the natural environment? And what means can the government use to achieve its objectives? Specifically, the modern environmental regime required developing a judicially recognized government interest in the natural environment. It also required courts to approve of broad grants of power away from local and state governments to the federal administrative agencies that implemented most conservation policy. The result of this constitutional transformation was what I call the Conservation Constitution: a set of legal traditions that continue to structure environmental law and policy, providing the foundation for an emergent green state.

Historiography of the Conservation Movement and Constitutional Change

"Constitutional change" usually refers to one of three kinds of transformations. It can refer to broad, enduring changes in the distribution of government power across institutions and among social groups—our "unwritten constitution" (the basic and relatively stable principles, institutions, and practices that govern political life). It can also refer to changes in "the people's constitution": constitutional values as asserted in popular political discourse, whether or not they are written into formal law. And, of course, it can refer to changes in the "constitution of judges": the text and doctrines that judges and lawyers use as a source of law in legal forums. Most of the historical scholarship on the Progressive Era conservation movement focuses on how conservation values became part of our unwritten constitution and the people's constitution. This study focuses on how those values made their way into the "constitution of judges": the transformation of the legal rules defining private rights and responsibilities, the relationship between state and federal power, and the extent of government authority. I aim to explain the transformation of what legal scholar John Leshy calls "constitutional common law," or the values, assumptions, and conceptual models that underlie interpretation of key clauses and legal concepts.[7] In grappling with constitutional questions around conservation policy, how did judges conceptualize the natural environment, its relation to human society, and the public interests at stake? In justifying conservation policies before the courts, how were the state and national interests in the natural environment defined? What options were on the table? Which ones were accepted and which ones rejected? What sort of constitutional legacy are we working with as we try to reform the relationship between the natural world and the political community?

Surprisingly, the substantial historical literature on the Progressive Era conservation movement hasn't addressed these questions of doctrinal change. This literature follows the path marked out by Samuel Hays's seminal 1959 book, *Conservation and the Gospel of Efficiency*, which focuses on how to characterize the ends of the conservation movement. Hays contends that conservationism was led by elite intellectuals concerned with bringing scientific expertise to bear on economic development; it was part of a larger process of industrialization.[8] Later historians have shown that Hays's argument was too narrow; conservationism had broad popular support as well, much of which was inspired by aesthetic and other noneconomic values.[9] Much of this scholarship focuses, reasonably enough, on federal executive and legislative efforts to create conservation policy.[10] Other lines of scholarship focus on state-level conservation[11] and conservation at the grassroots.[12] However, the historical scholarship continues to overlook the courts. The major studies typically recognize certain judicial decisions as important to the movement—such as the Supreme Court decisions in the 1907 case *Kansas v. Colorado* (concerning state and federal authority over water resources) and in the 1920 case *Missouri v. Holland* (upholding federal protection for migratory birds). But none of these studies focus on the role of courts, lawyers, and doctrinal innovation in explaining the movement's goals or outcomes.

To be sure, there is an excellent body of scholarship on the history of environmental law that addresses particular cases and lines of doctrine. But even the broadest of these studies address only one dimension of conservation policy, such as wildlife law, federal regulation of the public domain, or water resources.[13] We lack a synthetic narrative of the constitutional evolution that underpins the twentieth-century conservation regime as a whole. This is my goal.

To create such a narrative, it's useful to begin with a theoretical account of the role that legal institutions play in state building. Happily, this question has received considerable attention in the substantial body of scholarship on American constitutional history. For constitutional scholars, the role of the courts in the Progressive Era is clear: They were obstacles to progressive policy reform. Indeed, legal scholars have dubbed this period (roughly 1890 to 1937) the infamous Lochner era. First-year law students are taught the standard story: In response to the increased pace of industrialization and urbanization at the end of the nineteenth century, Progressive Era reformers campaigned for a host of new social policies, most of which required the expansion of government's role in regulating social relations and the economy. Although the Progressives won many legislative victories, the courts were reluctant to sanction policies that infringed on private property and contract relations, as well as those that threatened state sovereignty and the distribution of power between the legislative and executive branches. This reluctance is epitomized by the 1905 Supreme Court decision, *Lochner v. New York*,[14] which struck down New York's minimum hours legislation for bakeries.

To be sure, this account is too simplistic. Scholars have pointed out that the majority of state and federal laws challenged on constitutional grounds during this era were upheld, and as more Progressives were appointed to the bench, especially after 1910, the courts became more supportive of reform.[15] Nevertheless, courts did frequently use constitutional arguments to block important legislation aimed at improving labor conditions, restraining trusts and monopolies, and imposing national standards on industry. That obstructive role continued until the 1937 case *West Coast Hotel v. Parrish*,[16] which upheld a Washington minimum wage law and marked the court's capitulation to the New Deal and the modern regulatory state.[17]

Explaining why courts opposed progressive reform is a major goal of Stephen Skowronek's seminal work, *Building a New American State*. Skowronek argues that between 1877 and 1920, the American state administrative apparatus was transformed from the state of "courts and parties" to a modern bureaucracy. Courts, under Skowronek's analysis, were principal governing institutions in the nineteenth century, producing a great deal of social policy. For Skowronek, this explains why courts opposed the emergence of the new American state: They could not be expected to undermine the very system that supported their broad policy-making powers.[18] As reformers sought to create new governing institutions, located principally in the federal executive branch, courts defended their prerogatives. They used judicial review to strike down new social policies and to reign in the power of administrative agencies.

Importantly, however, Skowronek also highlights the role of lawyers in creating the administrative state. Lawyers constituted a "special intellectual cadre that maintains an underlying continuity in governmental activity through social and political changes."[19] Significantly, those lawyers were often working in administrative agencies rather than litigating on behalf of private clients. To the extent that Skowronek offers a theory of constitutional change, he emphasizes the intellectual leadership of the legal profession in responding to new social and economic problems by developing the executive branch's administrative capacity. But he doesn't offer us a theoretical account of how or why lawyers were able to overcome judicial resistance to new social policy.[20]

This reigning view of courts as obstacles to social reform is driven by a focus on welfare policy and labor and business regulation. To be sure, Skowronek's book, which covers civil service reform, reform of the military, and business regulation, doesn't neglect natural resource conservation altogether. On the contrary, he cites conflict over the Forest Service's authority to impose grazing fees in the forest reserves as a pivotal episode in developing the American administrative state. (Interestingly, however, that conflict was resolved judicially in the Forest Service's favor, as we will see.) In general, scholars have treated conservation policy as simply another facet of the federal regulatory regime that extended over commerce, transportation, and other sectors of the economy, all of which rested on a new set of constitutional principles regarding government power and state and federal relations. Because they have not focused on the specific constitutional conflicts surrounding conservation, these scholars have overlooked the fact that the doctrinal transformations involved in conservation policy were not the same as those involved in welfare policy or business regulation. Nor did courts play the same role in this policy arena that they did in other arenas of progressive reform.

Indeed, if we shift our focus from welfare, labor, and business regulation to natural resource conservation, a different story emerges. Like other Progressive Era initiatives, conservation policies posed major challenges to private property rights and to states' rights. And like those other initiatives, conservation policies were politically contentious. Conflicts over conservation efforts often led to violence, not only between social groups but directly against government officials.[21] But courts gave more support to conservation measures than they did to other innovative social policies of the era, and most constitutional issues surrounding conservation were settled by 1930. This is not to deny that the courts were a potential obstacle to conservation policy. Three major constitutional battles over conservation policy were waged in the federal courts: over the Forest Service's authority to impose grazing fees, federal protection for migratory birds, and the exemption of federal lands from state game laws. Opposition to these policies, either in the lower courts or by other government actors, was significant. But in all three cases, the conservationists won decisive victories in the Supreme Court. State power to regulate pollution was also confirmed easily by the Supreme Court. The conservation movement suffered only two defeats in the Supreme Court (*Kansas v. Colorado*[22] and *Pennsylvania Coal Company v. Mahon*[23]). But neither of these decisions significantly undermined federal or state conservation efforts.[24] The most ambitious conservation policy of the era—the Tennessee Valley Authority—was upheld in 1936, a full year before the "switch in time" that usually marks the judicial acceptance of other New Deal policies.[25]

Explaining this favorable judicial response to conservation policy requires a more sophisticated understanding of courts and the legal community than Skowronek offers. Daniel Carpenter's important 2001 book, *The Forging of Bureaucratic Autonomy*, is useful in this respect. Carpenter gives natural resource management a more central role than do earlier scholars of American political development (APD). Perhaps as a result of this focus, his argument helps to expand our understanding of the role of legal institutions in political development.

Carpenter is interested in how government agencies achieved autonomy from legislative and judicial control—in other words, how agencies overcame resistance from institutions like the courts. He highlights the importance of competence-based legitimacy: "When bureaucracies in turn-of-the-century American politics gained a lasting esteem for their ability to provide unique services, author new solutions to troubling national dilemmas, operate with newfound efficiency, or offer special protections to the public from economic, social, and even moral hazards, bureaucratic autonomy usually followed."[26] Carpenter identifies the US Department of Agriculture as an agency that effectively marshaled and managed scientists, creating political and social networks that supported the agency's bids for autonomy. It thus gained a network-based reputation for scientific authority, managerial efficiency, and innovative thinking to which Congress and the courts tended to defer.[27] The Department of the Interior, in contrast, was less effective at managing its scientific and administrative work; as a result, it produced less innovative policy, remained under greater control of Congress, and received less deference from the courts.

Thus, Carpenter identifies courts as a potential constraint on bureaucracies, but he also helps us understand how some bureaucracies were able to overcome that constraint: By achieving a reputation for scientific expertise and efficiency, some bureaucracies were able not only to come up with innovative policies but also to win legislative and judicial support for them. Granted, Carpenter's detailed histories of the USDA and the Department of the Interior actually give little attention to the courts and legal conflicts; he focuses more on Congress's relationship to these agencies. But his attention to reputation and networks helps to explain how agency lawyers were also able to overcome judicial resistance to doctrinal innovation.

Importantly, Carpenter's theory underscores the role of professionalization in shaping the behavior of government actors, including judges and lawyers. While legal professionals, like elected officials, often pursue policy preferences, they are also concerned with their professional reputations. Therefore, they pursue policy goals in ways that are consistent with the norms governing the legal profession. In short, because many of the actors involved in state building were legal professionals, legal doctrine and norms of legal reasoning operated as real constraints on their behavior— but that constraint could be overcome by creative lawyering from respected agencies. Constitutional change required doctrinal innovation, and that innovation was more likely from some agencies than from others.

This theoretical framework suggests some hypotheses concerning why courts put up less resistance to conservation policy than they did to many other Progressive policies. My study supports the following claims: First, government authority over natural resources had a broader legal foundation and longer history than its authority over labor and business. Second, conservation policy benefited from the authority of environmental science, backed by the growing scientific reputation of the US Department of Agriculture. Third, the conservation movement had a great deal of help from the creative lawyering of a handful of well-placed lawyers.[28] These factors gave conservationists a decided advantage in persuading courts to accede to new constitutional arguments concerning government's power to protect the natural environment.

It would be a mistake, however, to attribute constitutional change entirely to innovative litigators. Paul Pierson's 2004 work, *Politics in Time*, warns us that focusing on a particular set of actors as catalysts for change can lead us to overlook long-term processes that shaped their options. In our case, long-term developments in ecological science and legal doctrine, the growth of the legal profession, and technological and ecological changes all conditioned the choices available to actors.[29] Moreover, courts are not the only important institutions affecting constitutional doctrine.

Congressional committees, presidents, and executive agencies were often "veto points," preventing constitutional conflicts from reaching the courts. Much doctrinal innovation was aimed at these nonjudicial actors.[30]

Public Law and Doctrinal Change

The theoretical framework offered by the APD literature underscores the importance of doctrinal change to the more general process of constitutional change. Doctrinal change refers to the specific decision rules that judges use to decide constitutional issues, such as whether racial segregation denies "equal protection of the laws" or whether Congress's powers include the power to regulate hunting. The answer to both of those questions, in 1890, was no. Today, the answer to both of them is yes. So constitutional doctrine changes over time, and explaining this evolution is the special focus of the public law literature. This literature assumes that the decisions of judges drive this doctrinal change. But the distinctive character of courts as legal institutions and the professional socialization of legal actors means that the existing doctrinal framework and the norms of legal reasoning are an important constraint on what judges do.

The public law literature on constitutional doctrinal change begins with the observation that although the framers of the original US Constitution created a formal mechanism for changing it—the Article V amendment process—many of the most important transformations in constitutional doctrine have happened outside this formal process. The Constitution of 1789 was quite brief. It did not dramatically alter the existing state governments, which retained their general authority over the welfare and liberty of their citizens, but simply delegated a set of specifically defined powers to the new federal government.[31] For our purposes, it is significant that the federal government was granted authority to raise taxes to provide for general welfare (Article I, Section 8), to regulate interstate commerce (Article I, Section 8), to dispose of and make regulations concerning federal property (Article IV, Section 3), and to make treaties (Article VI). But it was not granted general authority over economic development or natural resources.

The 1789 Constitution also left unanswered many questions about the relationship between federal and state governments, as well as how the federal government's powers would be divided among the three separate but interrelated branches. The formal amendment process being somewhat cumbersome, many of these questions were resolved through public debate, political practice, institutional development, judicial decisions—

and, tragically, armed conflict. The Civil War, for example, resulted in new answers to many questions about federal/state relations, such as the federal government's authority to protect civil rights. (As we will see, the federal government's expanded role in this area would have implications for natural resource management.) Those new answers were formally implemented in the Thirteenth, Fourteenth, and Fifteenth Amendments. But the Civil War was not the only transformative event in American history, nor do transformative events always result in formal amendments.

The seminal work in this field is Bruce Ackerman's 1991 work, volume 1 of *We the People*. Ackerman argues that American constitutional history is marked by important, disruptive "constitutional moments" during which we see dramatic transformation not merely in constitutional doctrine but in the whole constitutional order—the "matrix of institutional relationships and fundamental values that are usually taken as the constitutional baseline in normal political life."[32] Key constitutional moments include the Founding, Reconstruction, and the New Deal. Such dramatic changes require the support of the American public and involve structural changes in a wide range of political institutions. They do not become part of the "constitution of judges," however, until they are confirmed by judicial decisions as part of formal constitutional doctrine. For example, in explaining the constitutional transformation of the New Deal, legal scholar Stephen Griffin points to a set of key Supreme Court decisions[33] concerning industrial relations and social welfare that confirmed the federal government's expanded power to regulate the economy and to spend money to advance the general welfare. Those decisions turned what had been merely accepted practice supported by a political consensus into formal constitutional law, supported by a new interpretation of, but no actual amendments to, the constitutional text.[34]

These scholars thus agree that broad political movements outside of the courts lead to constitutional change, but they emphasize the agency and independence of judges: They are not passively reflecting the broader social movements but actively constraining, catalyzing, or negotiating political order and change. (Indeed, it is not uncommon for legal activists pursuing constitutional change in the courts to become judges when their side wins electoral victory.) Nevertheless, judges are a distinctive kind of political actor. Their behavior is shaped by their extensive professional training and socialization into the norms of the legal community. As public law scholars Ronald Kahn and Ken Kersch explain, this includes "the norm that judges be apolitical, a norm reinforced by the requirement that judges craft their legal rulings according to a 'legal grammar' in which some forms of argument . . . are considered legitimate and others . . . are not."[35] Such norms are not unbreachable, but they are "constitutive of who a judge thinks he is and what he understands himself to be charged with doing."[36] These scholars also emphasize the important role of the legal community: the lawyers who guide litigation, develop new constitutional arguments, staff administrative agencies, and influence judicial appointments.[37] So the pace and direction of doctrinal change—whether and how a new constitutional order becomes entrenched in doctrine—depends a great deal on how lawyers and judges respond to the broader political movement that is driving constitutional change.

Public law scholars have produced subtle and complex studies of how the courts have contributed to American political development in areas such as civil rights and labor policy.[38] But such studies of doctrinal change are lacking in the conservation policy area. And they are needed, because legal doctrine matters. It affects the pace, structure, and success of state development. It is important that the constitutional framework for natural resource conservation was not the same as the framework governing other areas of progressive policy reform. The expansion of government regulation of the natural environment did not follow automatically from the expansion of government regulation of railroads, monopolies, or labor standards. It had to be defended on its own terms, with reference to the distinctive legal principles governing natural resource use.

Several doctrinal bases for both state and federal authority over natural resources were developed during the early years of the twentieth century. The state's police power and federal authority over interstate commerce were significant sources of authority, but property concepts were also important. As other scholars have noted, Article IV, Section 3 (the Property Clause) was a more important and expansive source of power for public lands policy than was the Article I Commerce Clause,[39] and property concepts also played a major role in justifying state game conservation efforts. But I highlight also the special legal rules concerning water resources: Water was conceptualized in the common law as common property, giving states greater authority over it than they typically had over land, and courts extended that common property model to wildlife as well. Moreover, the central place of water in the nation's early transportation system allowed the federal government to extend the commerce power not only over navigable streams but also beyond them, into the hydrological sources of those streams.

In addition to this doctrinal development, I point to the emerging science of ecology as important to the constitutional case for conservation. By "ecology" and "ecological science," I mean the scientific tradition, emerging in the second half of the nineteenth century, focusing on community-level relationships among plants, animals, and inorganic matter in a given geographic area. German scientist Ernst Haeckel coined the term "ecology" in the 1860s to refer to "the investigation of the total relations of the animal both to the inorganic and to its organic environment." By the early twentieth century, that term was increasingly used in the United States to describe a body of research on the relationships among water systems, forests, and wildlife, constituting what Arthur Tansley would in 1935 call "ecosystems."[40] As I will show, this way of thinking about nature—as a system of ecological relationships—provided critical support for the doctrinal transformations sought by conservation advocates.

The Pre-Conservation Constitution

One might argue that the foundations for modern conservation policy were laid even before 1787, as did Theodore Roosevelt in his address to the historic 1908 Conference of Governors on the Conservation of Natural Resources. The Constitutional Convention, he reminded his audience, was motivated in large part by the problem of managing water resources— specifically, the interstate waters of the Potomac River. The events leading to the 1787 constitutional convention began with the 1785 meeting called by George Washington at Mt. Vernon, bringing together delegations from Maryland and Virginia to develop principles of interstate cooperation in fishing, navigation, and commerce on the Potomac River and other tributaries of the Chesapeake Bay. The meeting was successful; both states subsequently ratified the Mt. Vernon Compact, which declared that these waterways would be "forever considered as a common Highway Free for Use and Navigation of any vessel belonging" to the other. That success led to a second meeting, at Annapolis in 1786, to develop further principles for cooperation among the several states. That meeting, of course, produced the famous call for the convention in Philadelphia that produced the Constitution.[41] The point, according to Roosevelt, was that "the Constitution of the United States . . . grew in large part out of the necessity for united action in the wise use of one of our natural resources."[42]

But if the Constitution was meant to facilitate a national, coordinated policy on natural resource use and development, it failed. The 1789 Constitution created a relatively weak, decentralized system that was poorly designed for long-term natural resource management. The federal government was limited to a specific set of powers; state governments retained the broad authority, inherent in the eighteenth-century conception of sovereignty, to regulate private conduct in the interests of the health, safety, and welfare of the community. State authority thus extended over the states' natural resources. But the states had very little institutional capacity to manage those resources and even less capacity to coordinate management with other states. Indeed, the Constitution (in Article I, Section 9) prohibits states from forming compacts with one another (like the Mt. Vernon Compact) without the consent of Congress.

The federal government in turn had virtually no explicit authority over natural resources. To be sure, the federal government was granted authority over interstate commerce, a measure meant to prevent the damaging trade wars that troubled the colonies under the Articles of Confederation. The federal government also had authority (under the Article IV, Section 3, Property Clause) to dispose of and regulate public lands (lands owned by the national government, primarily in the western territories). Many of the delegates to Philadelphia (including Benjamin Franklin, James Madison, Alexander Hamilton, and George Washington) hoped that the federal government would use its authority over interstate commerce and western lands to promote development of waterways and other natural resources.[43] But in practice, attempts to exercise federal authority over the national economy and public lands were met with considerable suspicion throughout the nineteenth century.

To be sure, the federal government's authority to regulate interstate commerce was given a broad interpretation in the 1824 Supreme Court decision in *Gibbons v. Ogden*.[44] The Marshall Court famously read the Interstate Commerce Clause as giving Congress power to regulate "the commercial intercourse between nations, and parts of nations, in all its branches" (including, importantly, navigation).[45] But "commerce" was commonly interpreted to mean the movement of goods in trade; nineteenth-century jurists typically held that the commerce power did not reach to regulation of agriculture, manufacturing, mining, or any of the other economic activities affecting natural resources. And Congress's power to promote economic development through "internal improvements" (such as funding roads, canals, bridges, and dams) was also hotly contested.

The nineteenth-century debate over federal spending on internal improvements is central to our story and requires some explanation. At its center is the clause in Article I, Section 8 of the Constitution, giving Congress authority "to lay and collect Taxes, Duties, Imposts and Excises, to pay the Debts and provide for the common Defence and general Welfare of the United States." This clause might naturally be read to authorize Congress to spend federal tax revenue on policies that promote the "general welfare" of the nation, such as building roads and canals (or, for later generations, irrigation works, wildlife refuges, or forest reserves). But from the earliest days of the republic, important actors advocated for a more limited interpretation of the spending (or general welfare) power. This was in fact one question at issue in the famous 1791 debate over whether Congress could establish a national bank. When President Washington asked his advisors for an opinion on whether the bank bill was constitutional, Thomas Jefferson argued that the "general welfare" clause could not support it; the "general welfare" merely referred to the sum of the enumerated powers of Congress, and its power could not reach beyond those specific ends. Alexander Hamilton disagreed, arguing that the "general welfare" included any object of national rather than local importance. Hamilton won this debate, but the Jeffersonian interpretation continued to find advocates.[46] For example, it was Jefferson's theory that motivated President Monroe in 1822 to veto an act to authorize funds to repair the Cumberland Road, arguing that neither the Commerce Clause nor any other part of the Constitution authorized spending on a "complete system of internal improvement."[47]

The constitutional debate over internal improvements grew only more intense as sectional conflict deepened in the years leading up to the Civil War. The northern and western states initially supported such expenditures, as the West had an interest in roadbuilding and river development and the North could secure in return the western states' support for high tariffs.[48] But that agreement broke down under President Jackson, who forged a new coalition between the West and the South. The South was not geographically positioned to benefit as much from internal improvements, so Jacksonian Democrats typically endorsed a limited reading of the spending power, blocking efforts to engage the federal government in building roads and canals. The Whigs, seeking continued road and canal development, usually advocated for a more expansive view of the spending power, and this expansive view was also embraced by the nascent Republican Party.

Republican ascendancy during and after the Civil War temporarily removed southern interests from the legislative equation, thus opening the door to more federal spending on economic development. During this period, Congress began a program of internal improvements that included supporting railroads and developing water transportation infrastructure, as well as creating in 1862 a Department of Agriculture with a clear scientific and educational mission to promote agricultural productivity. These policies created a foundation (albeit limited and uncertain) for a federal natural resources policy. Thus federal spending on such internal improvements increased as the nineteenth century drew to a close. Nevertheless, it still faced challenges from states' rights advocates in Congress. Most conservation policies would have to be defended against this resistance.

Similar states' rights sentiments limited the federal government's power over public lands, and nineteenth-century federal policy focused simply on disposing of those lands as quickly as possible. Indeed, southern lawmakers, worried about the fate of slavery in the West, even challenged federal authority to govern the territories. For example, Justice Taney in *Dred Scott v. Sandford*[49] insisted that the Article IV Property Clause (giving Congress power "to dispose of and make all needful rules and regulations respecting the Territory or other Property of the United States") did not apply to most of the western territories, concluding that it referred only to the Northwest Territories that were held by the United States in 1789. That narrow interpretation of the Property Clause was rejected along with the rest of *Dred Scott*. Nevertheless, during most of the nineteenth century, public policy in general favored private ownership of natural resources, regulated (lightly) by state governments.

This, then, is the constitutional context in which Americans attempted to develop an administrative state capable of managing the natural environment in the interests of future generations. Agitation for what today we would call "environmental reform" began quite soon after the Civil War, starting with wildlife conservation and broadening to include conservation of forests, water, and public lands generally. "Conservation" was in fact a broad term and could be used to describe what we would now call economic development projects, such as building irrigation systems and hydroelectric dams. Indeed, much of the constitutional conflict over conservation was due precisely to the fact that managing natural resources could be conceptualized as economic development policy. In addition, a separate but related movement within the Progressive coalition addressed urban environmental problems, campaigning against pollution and for urban planning. These campaigns, too, are part of our story.

Conservationists typically began their efforts at the state level, since states traditionally had constitutional authority over wildlife, forests, and water resources. State-level conservation policies faced challenges under the new Fourteenth Amendment (as an infringement on civil rights) or under the Interstate Commerce Clause (as a restriction on interstate commerce). Those challenges led conservationists to develop more explicitly the constitutional rationale for government action in this area. When state conservation programs proved inadequate, conservationists moved the fight to the federal level. Justifying federal conservation policy raised different constitutional problems and therefore brought new constitutional arguments into play. We see this process play out first in the arena of wildlife conservation, the subject of the next two chapters, and then in forest conservation and management, and finally in pollution control, where reformers encountered the limits of constitutional change.

In general, as conservation proponents turned from the general public to legal institutions, the arguments they offered for these policies changed. Aware that constitutional doctrine limited state and federal governmental power, conservation advocates in legal forums focused on a narrower set of policy rationales for their measures. They also developed new ways to conceptualize natural resources, drawing on emerging ecological science. Specifically, the need to fit new conservation policies into the existing constitutional framework led proponents to emphasize what today we call an "ecosystem services" concept of natural resources. Increasingly, in the course of defending wildlife and forest conservation, proponents would move away from the concept of natural resources as a collection of commodities; instead, they would draw on arguments from the nascent ecological sciences to paint a picture of complex, interdependent ecological systems that provide important services to the national economy. That conception of the natural world was critical to several key constitutional debates—over federal protection of migratory birds, over federal authority to manage public lands, and even over federal authority to acquire forest reserves. Congress and the executive branch were important arenas in which this conception developed, but it was strongly endorsed by the courts as well. Indeed, by the 1930s, a judicial consensus took shape that (1) several legitimate governmental interests could be served by protecting wildlife and forests, including recreational, scientific, and commercial interests; (2) natural resource conservation was a matter of not only local but also national concern; and (3) natural resources could be treated not only as commodities but also as complex, interdependent ecological systems that are integral to the national economy. This constitutional "common sense," along with judicial interpretations of key doctrines, supported the expansion of both state and federal power to protect natural resources, forming the legal foundation of the contemporary environmental protection regime.

Astute readers will note that my story leaves out an important piece of conservation policy: the expropriation of natural resources from the prior inhabitants of the continent. Conservation policy assumes the extinguishment of Native American title to the land. But those claims were not extinguished in 1870, or 1930, or even today. On the contrary, the protests at Standing Rock and the Malheur National Wildlife Refuge that began this chapter are also part of this ongoing story of Native American land loss. The Standing Rock protest was first and foremost an assertion of tribal sovereignty, and Malheur National Wildlife Refuge never would have been established without the forced removal of the Northern Paiute from the Lake Malheur region to a reservation in the Washington territory in 1879.[50]

The federal courts played an important role in legitimating efforts by the federal government to acquire title to Indian land throughout the late nineteenth and early twentieth centuries, producing a complex set of rulings concerning tribal sovereignty, treaty rights, and access to natural resources. That line of doctrine is typically treated by the legal community as sui generis, on the grounds that tribes have a legally anomalous status requiring special legal rules.[51] I think that treatment makes sense, and with one important exception (*Ward v. Race Horse*[52]), I will not be delving into Indian law in this study. This is not say, however, that judicial decisions concerning Native Americans are irrelevant to the story I am telling. Conflicts between state and tribal governments, especially over hunting and fishing rights, generated some important litigation in the conservation area (including *Ward*). Moreover, key legal actors were often fighting over conservation policy and Native American sovereignty at the same time. For example, Justices Edward White and Willis Van Devanter made significant contributions to decisions undermining tribal sovereignty and supporting conservation policy.[53] It is plausible, even likely, that some judicial decisions about natural resource conservation were taken with an eye toward expanding federal power over Indian territory—or vice versa. However, this book is long enough as it is, so I must leave it to future scholars to investigate the relationship between conservation policy and Indian law during this critical period.

CHAPTER TWO

State Wildlife Conservation

Creating a consensus that the government has constitutional authority to protect natural resources required conservationists to define the governmental interest in the natural environment. The nineteenth-century wildlife conservation movement devoted considerable attention to this question: What is state government's interest in wildlife? Nineteenth-century law provided a straightforward answer: States have an interest in protecting their citizens' food supply. The legal framework for protecting that interest—public trust doctrine—was less straightforward. Public trust doctrine, derived from the rules concerning water inherited from English common law, established wildlife as common property of citizens of a state. That foundation supported a set of constitutional doctrines very much at odds with the rest of the American constitutional tradition—more supportive of state authority and more hostile to private property rights.

But in the years from 1900 to 1920, as conservation efforts moved from the state to the federal level, we see a major shift in legal discourse. Conservation advocates moved from characterizing wildlife as a source of food and the common property of citizens of a state to a more complex understanding of the social and economic value of wild animals to the nation as a whole. This chapter reviews the nineteenth-century constitutional framework for wildlife conservation and the beginnings of its transformation: the emergence of a judicial consensus that several legitimate state interests could be served by wildlife protection and that these interests are better conceptualized as general welfare interests protected by the state's police power (the general regulatory power to protect the welfare and safety of the community) rather than as common property interests.

This constitutional change occurred not through formal constitutional amendment but through changes in judicial interpretation of doctrine. As the next chapter will demonstrate, those doctrinal developments would support the gradual judicial recognition that the nation as a whole may be interested in local populations of wildlife. This recognition would in turn prove to be critical to the Conservation Constitution.

The Wildlife Conservation Movement

The American conservation movement has its roots in the growing scientific and popular concern about the state of the country's wildlife and forests in the decades after the Civil War. Worries about the depletion of fish and game were voiced periodically and with increasing regularity throughout the nineteenth century by sportsmen, commercial fishermen, and naturalists; after 1890, they were joined by a chorus of women involved in the Progressive reform movement.[1] This lament about disappearing wildlife drew on the moral discourse of civilizational decline, but it correctly diagnosed an ecological reality with serious economic consequences: Habitat loss and the commercial exploitation of fish and game over the course of the nineteenth century had led to the population crashes, and in some cases the extinction, of several species of wild birds, fish, and mammals by 1900.[2]

To address these threats, conservationists sought closed seasons, bag limits, and restrictions on hunting methods, as well as some efforts to improve habitat quality (particularly for freshwater fisheries). Such regulations were not unprecedented; several states had imposed closed seasons on deer and other game since the early years of the republic.[3] But they were not uncontroversial. On the contrary, restrictions on hunting and fishing generated a good deal of litigation throughout the nineteenth century. As states expanded conservation efforts after the Civil War, constitutional issues were increasingly raised in state and (taking advantage of the new Fourteenth Amendment) federal courts.

In addition, conservationists during this period targeted the growing interstate trade in game. By the 1890s, conservationists had concluded that the interstate trade in feathers, hides, and game meat was a major barrier to effective game conservation. The market for game created an economic incentive that overwhelmed the states' rudimentary capacity to enforce game laws.[4] Accordingly, many states started to attack this interstate trade by prohibiting the sale of any game during the closed season (even if it was taken, legally, in another state). Some states even prohibited exporting game out of state. A few conservationists wanted to go further and make the sale of game illegal altogether. Unfortunately, all of these policies potentially conflicted with federal authority over interstate commerce. Thus, wildlife conservation advocates had to make a constitutional case for these regulations, explaining the source of state power to regulate hunting and fishing, the public interest served by this use of government power, and the relationship between state and federal authority in this area.

In addressing the general public and policy makers, conservationists forwarded a variety of arguments for government protection of wildlife. Prominent among those arguments was an economic case emphasizing the commodity value of fish and game. In the 1870s and 1880s, a major argument for game laws was that they were necessary for protecting a valuable food source, particularly for the poor. Historian John Cumbler documents the frequent use of this argument in mid-century legislative debates; the idea of protecting fishing as a recreational sport did not become common until the very end of the century.[5] But conservationists also recognized that the market for fish and game provided economic benefits to the state. Thus the US Fish Commission, established in 1871 to study the causes of declining fish populations, focused on fish that were popular food sources and had significant commercial value.[6] Indeed, the commodity value of bison was a major theme in conservationist William Temple Hornaday's important 1889 book, *The Extermination of the American Bison*. His detailed descriptions of the bison may have aroused popular sentimental and scientific interest in the threatened mammal, but his explicit argument for bison preservation relied almost exclusively on statistics concerning the economic value of bison meat, hides, and other products.[7]

Support for wildlife conservation came also from the growing animal welfare movement, led by Henry Bergh, who founded the American Society for the Prevention of Cruelty to Animals in 1866. Bergh gave most of his attention to protecting domestic animals, but humane societies did attempt to end some of the more egregious hunting practices by prosecuting hunters under the new anti-cruelty laws.[8] They also participated in the fight to end the feather trade, countering the view of birds as commodities with an ethic of kindness toward animals as a basis for legislative restrictions on hunting. Congressmen Lacey and Cummings, for example, defended the 1900 Lacey Act (prohibiting interstate trade in wild birds and game) by appealing to "the love of birds," which Lacey thought a proper sentiment that "ought to be taught in every school." Cummings appealed to his fellow legislators' affection for birds by reminding them that the capitol used to be filled every April with song birds and that the trees were "alive with music."[9] Such humanitarian arguments resonated with sportsmen's campaigns against "unsportsmanlike" hunting practices, as well as naturalists' aesthetic and scientific interest in animals.[10] Hornaday's later work, *Our Vanishing Wildlife* (1913), reflects this broader range of arguments, characterizing wild animals as our "friends" and advocating an ethic of humanitarian concern.[11]

A final important thread in the popular case for wildlife protection focused on the valuable services that wild animals, and particularly birds, offered to farmers. This was a frequent topic of discussion in magazines directed at farmers. Historian Richard Judd notes that farmers who contributed to these magazines recognized that birds played an important role in farming.[12] Scientists, particularly at the US Department of Agriculture (USDA), promoted and informed this popular discourse. Since the 1850s, a small group of scientists working in the Division of Agriculture within the Patent Office had been studying the role of birds and other predators in agriculture. Concerned that farmers typically viewed birds simply as a nuisance that ate their crops, they gathered data to demonstrate that many birds provided a valuable service to farmers by eating destructive insects. The USDA took up this research in the 1880s. C. Hart Merriam, head of the new Division of Economic Ornithology and Mammology within the USDA, was particularly concerned to educate farmers and legislators on the valuable role of predators like hawks, owls, weasels, minks, and coyotes in agriculture. The division produced numerous bulletins and reports identifying insectivorous birds and estimating their economic impact. The USDA thus became a strong advocate for repealing bounties on predators and for laws protecting nongame birds—and its case rested almost entirely on the economic value that insectivorous birds and other predators provided to agriculture.[13] Although this was ultimately an economic argument, it differed from the arguments about food security in that it rested on ecological science and focused on wildlife as providers of what today we would call "ecosystem services." As we will see, that argument proved to be particularly important in making the constitutional case for federal wildlife protection.

In sum, conservationists developed a broad (and often conflicting) set of arguments for wildlife protection, appealing to a variety of different interests. But when we turn to litigation over fish and game laws, we see a much more limited set of arguments being forwarded. In court, defenders of game laws had to adapt their arguments to the existing legal framework for justifying government regulation. That framework privileged economic arguments, and particularly arguments about property rights. Thus the dominant rationale for state protection of wildlife in the nineteenth century rested on property concepts: Judicial decisions characterized wildlife as common property, owned collectively by the people of the state for their use as a food source. That property right constituted the chief foundation for state game laws.

Nineteenth-Century Legal Framework: Public Trust Doctrine

Litigation over fish and game laws predates the wildlife conservation movement by many decades. Courts dealt with challenges to laws that required dam owners to create fish ladders,[14] conflicts over restrictions on fishing in public waters,[15] and restrictions on methods of fishing.[16] In adjudicating these conflicts, courts drew on two common law principles.

First, there are no private property rights in wildlife until the animal is captured. This rule was announced in the 1805 New York case, *Pierson v. Post*.[17] Post was in hot pursuit of a fox when he trespassed onto Pierson's land. Pierson shot the fox and took possession. Post sued, claiming the fox was his, and lost. The court held that private property rights in wild animals can be acquired only "by occupancy," interpreting "occupancy" to mean that the animal is captured (or killed). That decision was not particularly revolutionary. Far more significant would be the extension of that reasoning to conclude that landowners do not have any property rights in the wild animals living on their land. That conclusion drew on a second principle, public trust doctrine.

Public trust doctrine has its origins in the distinctive rules surrounding ownership of water that American colonists inherited from England. In applying English common law to American conditions, courts concluded that public waters (usually defined as "navigable waters") are held in trust by the state for the benefit of the people—and so, by extension, are the inhabitants of those waters. The leading case is the 1821 decision by the New Jersey Supreme Court in *Arnold v. Mundy*.[18] Arnold owned property in Perth Amboy on the Raritan River, which included an oyster bed, planted by Arnold, extending below the ordinary low-water mark. Mundy brought a small fleet of skiffs and gathered the oysters, and Arnold sued for trespass.

The court was thus presented with the question of how far a riparian property owner's control over the riverbed extended. After a lengthy review of English precedent, Judge Kirkpatrick summed up the winning argument: The oyster bed did not belong to Arnold. "The air, the running water, the sea, the fish, and the wild beasts" are all part of the "common property" of the nation. Title to this property is "to be held, protected, and regulated for the common use and benefit. But still, though this title, strictly speaking, is in the sovereign, yet the use is common to all the people."[19] In other words, the sovereign holds title to the "common property" as a trustee for the people of the state. Kirkpatrick further suggested that this property cannot be sold by the sovereign; its enjoyment by the public is a "natural right which cannot be infringed or taken away."[20]

This reasoning was adopted by the US Supreme Court in *Martin v. Waddell*[21] in 1842. That case also arose in Perth Amboy and concerned oystering in Raritan Bay. Waddell's lessee instituted the suit to eject Martin and others from one hundred acres of submerged lands in Raritan Bay, to which he claimed he had an exclusive right to establish an oyster bed. Chief Justice Taney, however, accepted the principle that "the dominion and property in navigable waters, and in the lands under them," are held by the sovereign as a public trust for the common benefit and denied the lessee's claim.[22] Importantly, both decisions rested on the distinction between navigable and unnavigable waters, which would become a basic principle in American law: Unnavigable waters can be privately owned, but navigable waters are held in trust by the sovereign and cannot be alienated.

Public trust doctrine did not go unchallenged, but most of the controversy concerned whether the legislature could grant exclusive rights to fish or establish oyster beds in public waters.[23] The degree to which the legislature could alienate or otherwise infringe on the public's common property right in navigable waters remained a contentious point (and arguably still is).[24] But that controversy shouldn't distract us from the main purpose of public trust doctrine in these cases: The goal was not to limit the legislature's power but to protect the public's common right to navigation and fishing against *private* property owners. In fact, because fish did not respect property lines, the public's right to fish in navigable waters ended up *extending* the state's regulatory power into privately held waters. For example, the Massachusetts Supreme Court held in the 1808 decision *Stoughton v. Baker*[25] that a riparian owner's grant to build a dam was subject to an implied condition that he build a fish passageway on his own property, "to protect the rights of the public to the fishery."[26] That ruling was confirmed repeatedly in American law throughout the nineteenth century, despite the judiciary's generally favorable attitude toward dam owners.[27] Under public trust doctrine, the legislature could regulate both public and private property to protect the public's common property right in the fish inhabiting the state's navigable and unnavigable streams.

Public trust doctrine thus had its origins in water law. But its logic seemed to apply to game animals as well. Hunting, like fishing, was a favored activity in the early republic. In stark contrast to Europeans, Americans treated hunting as a common right of citizenship; in some states, the people's right to hunt had constitutional protection.[28] Nevertheless, extending public trust doctrine to terrestrial game was not automatic. Judge Kirkpatrick had cited wild animals as part of the common property of the people, but that rule didn't resolve the question of how far the legislature could intrude on private property rights to protect wild animals. English law, for example, granted landowners constructive possession of all animals on their property, which allowed landowners to control hunting on their land.[29] That principle had a good deal of support in the United States as well and was often asserted against state efforts to restrict hunting on private land.[30] For example, a correspondent in the November 25, 1880, issue of *Forest and Stream* (one of the major sportsmen's magazines and a leading voice in the conservation movement) insisted that all restrictions on trapping game on one's own land are unconstitutional, because the landowner is the true owner of the game animals on his land.[31] The editors, however, respectfully disagreed with that position. They endorsed the competing view: that restrictions on hunting to protect private property were anti-republican and that the public as a whole was the true owner of game animals.

Social practice generally supported the second view. Trespass laws in the early part of the century were weak and difficult to enforce, so it was challenging for landowners to prevent others from hunting on their land.[32] Some legal commentators of the era suggested that there was an "implied license" to hunt on unenclosed land.[33] At least on the frontier and in the early years of settlement, private landowners had little ability to enforce property rights over the game animals on their land. As a result, American communities treated game animals as the responsibility of the community as a whole, and courts generally followed suit, upholding regulation of hunting as a traditional function of the state. But not until late in the nineteenth century did courts begin to cite the public trust doctrine as the rationale for such legislation.

State v. Magner,[34] an 1881 case from the Illinois Supreme Court, is an important precedent extending the public trust rationale from fish to game. Magner, a game dealer, sold a box of quail that had been killed in Kansas and transported into Illinois. Illinois's game laws prohibited the sale of game during the closed season for such game—a regulation put in place to make it easier to enforce the closed season laws. Magner argued that the law unconstitutionally interfered with interstate commerce. The judge disagreed, on the grounds that "no one has a property in the animals and fowls denominated 'game,' until they are reduced to possession." Instead, "whilst they are untamed and at large, the ownership is said to be in the sovereign authority"—the people of the state. The judge goes on to assert that regulating hunting is within the police power of the state. But he adds, "It is, perhaps, accurate to say that the ownership of the sovereign authority is in trust for all the people of the State, and hence, by implication, it is the duty of the legislature to enact such laws as will best preserve the subject of the trust and secure its beneficial use, in the future, to the people of the State."[35]

That rationale appears with greater frequency in the 1890s. For example, in the 1894 decision *Minnesota v. Rodman*,[36] the Minnesota supreme court rejected the argument that a game law (prohibiting possession of game during the closed season) violated the Due Process Clause of the Fourteenth Amendment. This post–Civil War amendment prevented state governments from depriving persons of "life, liberty, and property" without due process of law. Originally intended to protect the rights of freedmen, it was quickly seized upon by enterprising lawyers to challenge a wide range of state regulations that arguably infringed on liberty or property rights—such as the law at issue in *Rodman*. The court dismissed the claim by denying that Rodman had any property right in wild game:

> We take it to be the correct doctrine in this country that the ownership of wild animals . . . is in the state, not as proprietor, but in its sovereign capacity, as the representative, and for the benefit, of all its people in common. The preservation of such animals as are adapted to consumption as food, or to any other useful purpose, is a matter of public interest; and it is within the police power of the state . . . to enact such laws

as will best preserve such game, and secure its beneficial use in the future to the citizens.

The court goes on to conclude that these regulations do not infringe anyone's property rights "because he who takes or kills game had no previous right of property in it, and, when he acquires such right by reducing it to possession, he does so subject to such conditions and limitations as the Legislature has seen fit to impose."[37]

Public Trust and Constitutional Doctrine

Some commentators see public trust doctrine as unnecessary for supporting wildlife conservation; the same regulations could be and often were upheld simply as an exercise of the police power, aimed at protecting a general community interest in wildlife.[38] But characterizing that community interest as an expression of a common *property right* served three important purposes for nineteenth-century jurists, with significant implications for the constitutional principles regarding wildlife.

First, as other commentators have recognized,[39] a collective property right could serve as a significant counterweight to the private property rights that were threatened by restrictions on fishing and hunting. It was well-established in common law that riparian owners had the right to fish on their property, and the norm of open, unrestricted hunting reinforced the same principle with regard to the right to hunt. So, enforcing closed season laws on persons fishing and hunting on their own land was problematic. State ownership doctrine helped to justify restrictions on fishing and hunting against these private landowners. Given the important constitutional status of property rights during the nineteenth century, simply asserting that private property rights were limited by the police power might have sounded less persuasive than weighing those private rights against a *common* property right.

This was not a merely hypothetical problem; private landowners often did complain that efforts by the state to protect fish populations violated their property rights. In the 1835 Massachusetts case, *Cottrill v. Myrick*,[40] for example, a landowner on the Damariscotta River complained that fish wardens from the town of Newcastle had come onto his land and broken a dam, to open a passage for fish. The river was not navigable and therefore constituted private property, and the landowner complained that the legislative acts allowing the town to destroy such dams was unconstitutional (under the Massachusetts Constitution), characterizing it as a taking of property without compensation. But the court rejected that reasoning. The judge agreed that under the common law in England, fisheries in unnavigable streams belong to the riparian owner. But Massachusetts had modified that rule: "It was deemed most conducive to the public good, to subject the salmon, shad and alewive fisheries to public control, whenever the legislature thought proper to interpose. They were much relied upon, as among the means of subsistence, afforded by the common bounty of Providence, and some regulation became necessary for their preservation."[41]

Such decisions show courts' concern to articulate a clear and weighty public interest that could justify governmental intrusion on private property rights, and the public trust concept offered such an interest. An article in the May 7, 1874, issue of *Forest and Stream* illustrates the point: The author (an "eminent jurist") discussed at length whether restricting landowners from fishing and hunting on their own land violated the Due Process Clause of the Fourteenth Amendment by infringing on property rights without adequate justification. The article concluded that it did not. Because fish and game are owned collectively by the state, landowners do not actually own the animals on their land; therefore, these laws do not actually invade any property right.[42]

In addition to supporting restrictions on private landowners, public trust doctrine helped to justify restricting fish and game rights to residents of the state and restricting the interstate trade in game. The first kind of restriction ran into objections raised under the Privileges and Immunities Clause of Article IV of the US Constitution, and the second came up against the Commerce Clause (Art. I, Sec. 8).

Both clauses were at issue in the 1823 decision *Corfield v Coryell*.[43] The plaintiff, who was not a resident of New Jersey, was dredging for oysters in Delaware Bay, which lay within the territorial waters of New Jersey. The state of New Jersey seized the plaintiff's vessel, citing a state law that prohibited nonresidents from dredging oysters in state waters. That provision, according to the plaintiff, violated both the Commerce Clause (by interfering with interstate commerce) and the Privileges and Immunities Clause of the US Constitution, by discriminating against an out-of-state resident. He accordingly sued the state for trespass in federal circuit court.

Justice Bushrod Washington delivered the court's opinion. Rejecting first the Commerce Clause argument, he reasoned that when the state ratified the Constitution, it granted to Congress the right to regulate commerce on its navigable waters. But this grant did not include the "jus privatum which a state has in the soil covered by its waters." That property right includes fisheries, which remain "common to all the citizens of the state to which it belongs."

> If then the fisheries and oyster beds within the territorial limits of a state are the common property of the citizens of that state, and were not ceded to the United States by the power granted to congress to regulate commerce, it is difficult to perceive how a law of the state regulating the use of this common property . . . can be said to interfere with the power so granted.[44]

The court insisted that oysters do not become articles of trade until they are lawfully harvested; while they are still in their beds, they are common property and subject to the police power of the state.

The US Supreme Court endorsed this logic in the 1896 decision *Geer v. Connecticut*,[45] which upheld an explicit restriction on interstate commerce: a Connecticut law prohibiting anyone from transporting certain game birds into or out of the state—even if the birds had been lawfully killed in the state. Such laws were becoming popular in the 1890s, as conservationists realized that the greatest danger to wildlife was the interstate market in game. These restrictions on selling game out of state were state-level attempts to destroy those interstate markets. They would therefore seem to be an obvious infringement on Congress's authority over interstate commerce. Indeed, Geer's attorney cited a decision to that effect from the Kansas Supreme Court.[46] Nevertheless, the Supreme Court upheld Connecticut's law, using the public trust logic. Reasoning that wildlife is held by the state in trust for the benefit of the people of the state, Chief Justice White pointed out that "the sole consequence of the provision forbidding the transportation of game, killed within the State, beyond the State, is to confine the use of such game to those who own it, the people of that State." Geer's attorney had insisted (not unreasonably) that "there is no such shadowy, uncertain, indefinable state wherein an article is for some purposes an article of commerce, and for others is not."[47] But Justice White concluded otherwise, holding that

> in view of the authority of the State to affix conditions to the killing and sale of game, predicated as is this power on the peculiar nature of

such property and its common ownership by all the citizens of the State, it may well be doubted whether commerce is created by an authority given by a State to reduce game within its borders to possession, provided such game be not taken, when killed, without the jurisdiction of the State.[48]

He went on to assert that even without the public trust logic, the police power of the state was sufficient to justify this "incidental" restriction on interstate commerce: "The source of the police power as to game birds (like those covered by the statute here called in question) flows from the duty of the State to preserve for its people a valuable food supply."[49] As I will discuss below, by 1890, the rationale that the state could protect wildlife as a valuable food supply had become an uncertain basis for regulation. The common property right rationale provided a stronger basis for the restriction (although not strong enough to persuade either Justice Field or Justice Harlan, both of whom dissented).

Finally, the public trust argument was important to defending conservation laws against claims under the Privileges and Immunities Clause. That clause, providing that the citizens of each state are entitled to all the privileges and immunities of citizens in the several states, was intended to prevent discrimination against nonresidents. Accordingly, the plaintiff in *Corfield* objected that New Jersey's prohibition on nonresidents dredging oysters in state waters violated the Clause. But the *Corfield* court concluded that oystering was not a privilege of citizenship; it was a property right, albeit a common property right shared equally by all citizens of the state:

A several fishery . . . is as much the property of the individual to whom it belongs, as dry land, or land covered by water; and is equally protected by the laws of the state against the aggressions of others, whether citizens or strangers. Where those private rights do not exist to the exclusion of the common right, that of fishing belongs to all the citizens or subjects of the state. . . . They may be considered as tenants in common of this property; and they are so exclusively entitled to the use of it, that it cannot be enjoyed by others without the tacit consent, or the express permission of the sovereign who has the power to regulate its use.[50]

This logic was adopted by the US Supreme Court in *McCready v. Virginia*[51] in 1876, in a decision upholding Virginia's restrictions on nonresidents using the oyster beds in Ware River. Chief Justice Waite wrote, "The right which the people of the State acquire [to use state fisheries] comes not from their citizenship alone, but from their citizenship and property combined. It is, in fact, a property right, and not a mere privilege or immunity of citizenship."[52]

Given the importance of fishing and hunting rights in the nineteenth century, it may seem surprising that courts were so willing to deny that they were privileges of citizenship and to sanction blatantly discriminatory laws. But the ability to discriminate against out-of-state hunters and fishers was highly valued and well-rooted in social practice. As early as the 1820s, the decline in fish and game was leading towns to petition state legislatures for hunting and fishing restrictions on "foreigners." State legislatures were largely supportive, treating the regulation of fishing and hunting as a local community responsibility.[53] Fish and game management was very much a local affair, and discrimination against outsiders was a popular management strategy.[54] It was not uncontroversial, however. That the constitutionality of such laws was not entirely settled by judicial decision is illustrated by a lively debate in the pages of *Forest and Stream* about the constitutionality of a New Jersey law requiring nonresident hunters to pay a fee.[55] But such complaints notwithstanding, the *McCready* decision remained good law at least until the 1948 case *Toomer v. Witsell*.[56] In fact, such restrictions on out-of-state hunters persisted even in the face of Supreme Court disapproval.[57]

In sum, characterizing the state's interest in fish and game as a common property right was an important legal foundation for early conservation policies. It supported against constitutional objections legislative efforts to restrict hunting and fishing and to protect habitat, even on private lands; to restrict the hunting and fishing rights of out-of-state residents; and to destroy the interstate markets in game. It supported, in fact, a degree of local community control over wildlife that contrasts quite strikingly with the laissez-faire ideology that was increasingly influencing other areas of law.[58]

The Food Security Rationale for Wildlife Conservation

Judicial deference to fish and game regulations was not driven purely by precedent and legal reasoning. Judges frequently brought up policy considerations as well—or, to be precise, one overriding policy consideration: Wild fish and game populations were considered a major source of food, especially for the poor. As mentioned above, this food security rationale was by far the most common argument for conservation in the nineteenth century among reformers and government officials. And it is the only policy argument that consistently shows up in judicial decisions. The *Cottrill* court, for example, supported Massachusetts's protection of salmon, shale, and alewives on the grounds that "they were much relied upon, as among the means of subsistence."[59] Similar language can be found in cases from others states[60] and Supreme Court decisions. For example, the 1873 US Supreme Court case *Holyoke v. Lyman,* which concerned the legislature's authority to require that a dam owner build a fish passageway, began with a strong reminder that "rivers, though not navigable even for boats or rafts, and even smaller streams of water, may be and often are regarded as public rights, subject to legislative control, . . . as the source for furnishing a valuable supply of fish, suitable for food and sustenance."[61]

The food security argument may have been popular with judges in part because it fit into constitutional doctrine quite easily. Several cases supported using the police power to protect food purity, by establishing inspection laws and prohibiting the sale of unwholesome or adulterated products. Justice White's decision in *Geer,* for example, cited *Plumley v. Massachusetts,*[62] which upheld a state law prohibiting the sale of colored oleomargarine. Justice White thought that the Connecticut law fell squarely within the principle governing *Plumley:* "the power of a State to protect by adequate police regulation its people against the adulteration of articles of food, . . . although in doing so commerce might be remotely affected, necessarily carries with it the existence of a like power to preserve a food supply which belongs in common to all the people of the State."[63] White also cited *Kidd v. Pearson,*[64] which upheld an Iowa law prohibiting the manufacture and exporting of alcohol. (Alcohol, of course, was also being brought under greater state regulation, using strategies similar to those that conservationists were bringing to bear on the market in game.)

In short, treating fish and game regulations as food regulations allowed conservationists and sympathetic judges to draw on some favorable precedents. Unfortunately, by the 1890s, this food security argument was creating difficulties for the conservation effort. Leading conservationist George Bird Grinnell had concluded by 1894 that markets in game were a major factor in the decline of wildlife and that the conservation movement should therefore abandon the notion that hunting and fishing could provide a regular, cheap source of food. Historian John Reiger points to an important editorial in *Forest and Stream* in which Grinnell argued that "for the vast and overwhelming multitude of the people of the continent game is no longer in any sense an essential factor of the food supply." On the contrary, it has become a luxury: "The day of wild game as an economic factor in the food supply of the country has gone by." This was, as Reiger notes, a revolutionary shift in conservation strategy. Grinnell called for states to prohibit selling game altogether—a complete destruction of the market in game meat.[65] The 1894 case *Minnesota v. Rodman* reflects this turn away from the food security argument. The court carefully extended the argument, writing that "the preservation of such animals as are adapted to consumption as food, *or to any other useful purpose*, is a matter of public interest." That language suggests a growing recognition among judges of the other arguments for protecting wildlife.

It's worth noting that both the food security argument and Grinnell's attack on it had a firm foundation in reality. Throughout the first half of the nineteenth century, fish and game did in fact constitute an important part of the ordinary American diet. All historians agree that Americans during the nineteenth century ate a great deal of meat, and most of that meat was pork or beef.[66] But fish and game also contributed to the American diet, especially during the settlement period of a region. Historian Reginald Horsman describes how American diets changed during western migration: the general pattern was that the earliest settlers would eat the food they brought with them. While establishing farms and communities, though, they also relied heavily on game—venison, ducks, turkeys, and out West, bison and bears.[67] As the region became more thickly settled, the supply of large game diminished, but settlers continued to eat small game, such as squirrels and rabbits. Commercial hunters also provided fish and game to cities. There's little data on how much the urban dwellers relied on wild fish and game, but there are some reports that it was sometimes cheaper than beef (the preferred meat of most Americans). James Tober reports that in the 1870s, there were thriving markets in game in large cities such as Chicago, New York, and St. Louis. Game could be quite cheap; in St. Louis in 1874, one could buy venison for three cents per pound, which was considerably less than pork or beef. It appears that for most of the nineteenth century, Americans did not regard fish and game as luxury items, as they were in Europe.[68]

In the 1870s, however, several factors converged to diminish the importance of fish and game to the American diet. First, most areas were sufficiently settled that the supply of fish and game was noticeably declining. Second, the growth of large urban markets, the extension of the rail network, improvements in refrigeration and other preservation technologies, and the opening of the western cattle lands all contributed to greater availability of domesticated meat—especially beef, which most Americans preferred over pork and game.[69] Meanwhile, game was becoming more expensive. While venison was selling for 3 cents per pound in St. Louis in 1874, it was selling for 25 cents per pound in New York.[70] For comparison, a May 10, 1874, article in the *Chicago Tribune* was complaining about the high price of beef, which the commentator thought should not retail at more than sixteen cents per pound.[71] In cities, at least, game was increasingly becoming a luxury item. Poor rural communities had less access to the markets in domesticated meats, of course, and they continued to suffer nutritional deficiencies during the late nineteenth century. But, as historian Harvey Levenstein notes, supplying those deficiencies with fish and game in places like the southern Cotton Belt would have been challenging. Sharecroppers routinely worked twelve-hour days and had little time for hunting or fishing.[72] In any case, the chief nutritional deficiency suffered by the poor was typically not lack of protein but lack of fresh produce.[73]

In sum, it appears that Grinnell was correct. By the 1890s, it would have been disingenuous to argue that wild fish and game were an important food source for the poor. By this time, however, there were other policy arguments that might have been used in court to defend conservation measures. As mentioned above, the animal welfare movement participated in the campaign to restrict bird hunting, and they managed to persuade a few courts to apply anti-cruelty laws to hunting practices. The rationale for anti-cruelty laws was that the police power can be used to preserve public morals by punishing acts of cruelty. In the 1896 case *Waters v. People*,[74] for example, the Colorado Supreme Court upheld the defendant's conviction for shooting captive doves for sport. The defendant was charged under Colorado's anti-cruelty statute, and the question was whether the statute covered hunting activities. The judge noted that most courts had held that such statutes do not, but the Colorado statute was broad enough to cover the killing of animals merely for sport (and not for food). Concerning the rationale for the statute, the court stated:

> It is common knowledge that within the past few years, as incident to the progress of civilization, and as the direct outgrowth of that tender solicitude for the brute creation . . . laws . . . have been enacted by the various states having the common object of protecting these dumb crea-

tures from ill treatment by man. Their aim is not only to protect these animals but to conserve public morals, both of which are undoubtedly the proper subjects of legislation.[75]

This humanitarian rationale supported quite a lot of anti-cruelty laws protecting domesticated animals.[76] Such arguments also appeared in the congressional debates over the Lacey Act, as mentioned above. It is thus imaginable that our wildlife conservation regime, like our protections for domestic animals, might have come to rest upon this "public morals" rationale. But the occasional application of anti-cruelty laws to hunting proved to be anomalous. Most courts concluded that these laws protected only domestic animals, and the animal welfare movement in general remained largely independent of the wildlife conservation movement. Humanitarian arguments thus would not be a major theme in the judicial discourse concerning wildlife conservation during the Progressive Era (or after).

A second argument, however, did become more prominent in public and policy discourse as the constituency for conservation changed toward the end of the nineteenth century. Increasingly, conservationists focused on serving sportsmen—the wealthier segment of society that hunted and fished for sport. That focus led them to highlight the value of recreational fishing and hunting to the state's economy.[77] This new conception of wildlife as a source of recreation quickly found its way into judicial reasoning over state-level wildlife policy, displacing the food security rationale.

Evolution of the State Interest in Wildlife Conservation

In the wake of *Geer v. Connecticut*, states expanded their efforts to protect fish and game. As historian Ann-Marie Szymanski explains, during the nineteenth century, states generally lacked the means to enforce game laws. They often relied on local officials, private sportsman clubs, or local wildlife protection societies to enforce such laws. But by 1909, forty-one states had game commissioners, wardens, or other state officers with enforcement powers. These state game commissioners were a political force. The National Association of Game and Fish Wardens and Commissions, formed in 1902, became the International Association of Fish and Wildlife Agencies in 1917, which had a significant voice in major wildlife legislation. Game commissioners' power was enhanced by the widespread adoption of state licensing laws. By 1912, thirty-six states required hunting licenses of residents and forty-six required them of nonresidents. License regimes provided the state agencies with a reliable source of income.[78] At the same time, fishing and hunting interests were becoming more organized. Industries were developing around recreational hunting and fishing, along with new national associations like the Izaak Walton League, serving the interests of sportsmen.

This shift in the constituency for wildlife conservation influenced judicial reasoning over state wildlife policy, but this line of doctrine was also affected by a general trend toward more expansive interpretations of the state's police power—in particular, the courts' willingness to sanction the use of state regulatory authority to protect aesthetic and other "quality of life" values.[79] As the reach of police power expanded, reliance on public trust doctrine to support wildlife conservation diminished in importance. Thus, during the first decades of the twentieth century, courts increasingly upheld state wildlife laws as valid exercises of the police power aimed at regulating access to opportunities for fishing and hunting. However, we also see a gradual recognition by courts that fishing and hunting are not the only interests served by wildlife—that states have interests, as well, in protecting nongame species.

Because state authority over wildlife was so well-established by 1900, there are few cases from the Progressive Era discussing the nature of the state's interest in protecting wild animals. Indeed, even while other state regulatory efforts were being successfully challenged under the Due Process and Equal Protection Clauses (as in the notorious *Lochner* case[80]), state wildlife regulations continued to receive deference from the courts. But the New York Supreme Court did address the nature of the state's interest in wildlife in the 1917 case *Barrett v. State of New York*,[81] which would become an important precedent affirming the state's regulatory authority over wildlife.

Barrett grew out of a successful effort to reintroduce beavers to the Adirondacks. Hunted nearly to extinction in the nineteenth century, only one small colony of beavers remained in New York by 1895. Conservationists interested in forest preservation in the Adirondacks included among their goals preserving the native wildlife; accordingly, in 1895, they pressed for protective legislation. By 1900, hunting of beavers in New York had been banned altogether. Conservationists then followed up that successful effort in 1904, persuading the New York Fish and Game Commission to adopt a program to reintroduce several native mammals to the region: elk, moose, and beavers. The introduced elk and moose didn't survive, but the beavers thrived. The state released twenty-one beavers and private individuals brought in fourteen more. By 1908, observers estimated that the beaver population had risen to 150, and by 1912 it was estimated at 600.[82]

The beaver reintroduction program was initially well-received by the public. But by 1916, the landowners in the Adirondacks began to report that beaver dams were affecting trout streams, killing valuable timber, and spoiling the landscape. Barrett was one of a group of landowners on the Fourth Lake of the Fulton Chain in the Adirondacks. These landowners complained that the beavers had destroyed several poplar trees, diminishing the attractiveness of the area and thus its value. Barrett argued, first, that the law protecting beavers was unconstitutional—that it was an unreasonable exercise of the police power because the state had no legitimate interest in protecting a destructive animal. Second, he sought compensation for the damage done by the beavers.

The New York Court of Appeals (the highest court) rejected both claims. In explaining why the government had a legitimate interest in the beaver, the court faced an interesting and somewhat novel problem: Since the beavers could not be hunted for recreation, food, or their pelts, it could not draw on any of the usual rationales for state wildlife policy. What was the state's interest in protecting an animal from being used by humans?

The court first drew on public trust doctrine for the principle that "the general right of the government to protect wild animals is too well established to be now called in question."[83] Moreover, courts should defer to the legislature in this policy domain. Of course, protected animals might harm individuals:

Deer or moose may browse on his crops; mink or skunks kill his chickens; robins eat his cherries. In certain cases the legislature may be mistaken in its belief that more good than harm is occasioned. But this is clearly a matter which is confided to its discretion. It exercises a governmental function for the benefit of the public at large and no one can complain of the incidental injuries that may result.[84]

But what is that public benefit? According to the court, "The police power is not to be limited to guarding merely the physical or material interests of the citizen. His moral, intellectual and spiritual needs may also be considered. The eagle is preserved, not for its use but for its beauty." And: "The same thing may be said of the beaver. They are one of the most valuable of the fur-bearing animals of the state. They may be used for food. But apart from these considerations their habits and customs, their curious instincts and intelligence place them in a class by themselves. Observation of the animals at work or play is a source of never-failing interest and instruction."[85] In short, the court endorses the absolute prohibition on hunting beavers because they are particularly interesting. Natural history—the opportunity to study their habits—is enough of a public benefit to justify the state law.

The court went on to reject the claim for damages. While an individual might be liable for acts that result in property damage, the state is not always subject to the same rule: "In liberating these beaver the state was acting as a government. As a trustee for the people and as their representative it was doing what it thought best for the interests of the public at large."[86] *Barrett* is most often cited for this rule against landowners seeking damages from the government for destruction caused by protected animals. But I would suggest that it is even more significant for affirming the government's interest in protecting animals simply for their beauty and scientific interest.

As *Barrett* suggests, by the 1920s, courts accepted that states had a range of legitimate interests in protecting wildlife. Chief among those state interests was the recreational benefit provided by game species, but the states' interests could be extended to cover nongame species that provided scientific or aesthetic value to citizens. The federal interest in wildlife, however, was not so readily apparent, either to courts or to other key actors in the policy arena. In pursuing federal wildlife protection, the conservation movement would have to develop even further the government's interest in wildlife to include the value of the ecosystem services provided by wildlife to the national economy.[87]

CHAPTER THREE

The Road to *Missouri v. Holland*

The nineteenth-century legal framework concerning wildlife ensured that state-level authority to protect wildlife would run into relatively few constitutional difficulties. Achieving federal wildlife conservation was more difficult. The Constitution delegates a set of powers to the federal government, and protection of natural resources is conspicuously absent from that list. Conservationists were well aware of this problem. But they had the good fortune to include among their number some innovative lawyers who developed arguments that would eventually win the support of key actors in Congress, the executive branch, and (critically) the federal courts. These actors sought to expand constitutional doctrine by offering novel arguments about the national government's interest in wildlife. The most successful of these arguments drew on the science of ecology and focused on the value of wildlife not as commodities but as elements of what we today would call complex ecosystems that provided critical services to the national economy. That concept of wildlife would be affirmed in the 1920 Supreme Court decision *Missouri v. Holland*,[1] upholding federal legislation protecting migratory birds. But the road to *Missouri* was a long one, beginning with the earliest efforts to protect fisheries.

Fisheries and the State Failure Argument

As early as the 1870s, conservationists were raising questions about the efficacy of state-level wildlife conservation efforts. The problem was clear to those concerned with fish conservation: Although several states had created fish commissions that aimed to increase the supply of fish, they were less motivated to protect boundary waters or interstate streams. Why would they work to protect fish that might be taken by citizens of other states? Such interstate conflicts were already becoming problematic in New England, where interstate cooperation was notably failing to protect the Connecticut, Merrimack, Penobscot, and Kennebec Rivers.[2] Proponents of fish conservation and propagation therefore called on Congress to address this problem by taking charge of the great river systems and the Great Lakes. However, that call raised a constitutional objection: Regulating fish and game was traditionally the function of state government, and no provision of the federal Constitution explicitly authorized federal action in this sphere. Federal regulation would seem to violate the principle of federalism.

Importantly, this objection was not being raised in court. In the 1870s, there was virtually no federal legislation on wildlife conservation that could be challenged in court.[3] But constitutional arguments concerning federal authority to protect fish and game appeared regularly in the letters to the major sportsmen's magazines, and constitutional concerns would also be asserted by key actors in the executive branch and by congressional representatives contemplating federal regulation. Many actors outside the judiciary could exercise an effective constitutional veto over federal legislation, from presidents and congressional representatives to lawyers for federal agencies (whose opinions were often sought on legislation). Constitutional arguments concerning federal authority over fish and game were accordingly raised and widely debated among the Washington elite long before they ever ended up in court.

The conservation movement actively shaped this constitutional debate. True, the movement did not seem to have a nationally coordinated litigation strategy during the 1870–1900 period. Unlike the animal welfare movement, which did bring lawsuits explicitly intended to develop doctrine in favorable directions, conservationists apparently did not initially bring test cases. But the leading periodicals frequently reported on important cases and published letters on the constitutional dimensions of conservation laws. Moreover, the movement's leaders included a lot of legal talent. The Boone and Crockett Club, established in 1887 to promote fish and game conservation, included among its members not only Theodore Roosevelt but William Hallett Phillips, a Supreme Court lawyer, and Elihu Root, a major architect of American foreign policy during this period. Phillips would have a hand in creating the first federal wildlife conservation legislation, and Root would be involved with negotiating the first international conservation treaties.[4] Accordingly, creative constitutional arguments for federal wildlife conservation were not long in coming.

Constitutional defenses of federal protection of wildlife appear very early in the movement's history. In 1872, for example, Congressman Robert Roosevelt of New York (Theodore Roosevelt's uncle) proposed that Congress fund the artificial propagation of fish in major American rivers. Recognizing the doubtful constitutionality of extending federal power into this area, he told Congress,

> It is essentially a national matter; the state alone cannot take charge of it and manage it efficiently. . . . Rivers run through different states, or are the boundaries between them, and the law made for part or for one shore might not be identical with those made for other places. Unity of action is essential, for it is useless to protect in one locality if wanton destruction is permitted in another.[5]

Roosevelt's proposal concerned the federal spending power (the power to "lay and collect taxes . . . to provide for the common Defence and general Welfare of the United States") rather than its regulatory power. But his reasoning was echoed by US Fish Commissioner Spencer Baird in the Commission's 1871–1872 report arguing for federal regulation. Baird suggested that the federal government should be able to regulate fishing on the "common waters" of the United States, including the great river systems and the Great Lakes. He recognized that such efforts would be opposed on states' rights grounds, but if the states could not effectively protect fish, that fact alone should be grounds for the federal government to act.[6]

Roosevelt and Baird offered one of the earliest statements of the "state failure" argument, which would become a major theme in conservationists' arguments for federal action. This argument is more commonly associated with civil rights: Civil rights activists asserted that under the Fourteenth Amendment, the federal government had the authority to enact legislation to protect civil rights where the state had systematically failed to do so. Historically, the state failure argument has been unpersuasive; it did not usually prevail even in the civil rights realm, even though the Fourteenth Amendment included an explicit grant of authority to Congress to enforce its provisions.[7] There was no such grant of authority to Congress to protect natural resources.

However, Roosevelt's and Baird's argument rested also on Congress's authority over the "navigable waters" of the United States, which in turn derived from Congress's authority to regulate interstate commerce. The interstate commerce power included the power to regulate transportation on navigable waters, as confirmed in the 1824 Supreme Court decision, *Gibbons v. Ogden.*[8] This power, called the federal "navigation servitude," includes the authority to remove obstacles to navigation and to improve navigation by dredging and building canals (at least, when such efforts could overcome resistance to federal spending on "internal improvements"). But whether the navigation servitude authorized Congress to enact fishing regulations was unsettled, at best. Decisions such as *Corfield v. Coryell*[9] suggested that it did not and that states retained ownership (in trust) of the beds and fisheries of navigable waters. That decision was affirmed by the Supreme Court in 1855 in *Smith v. Maryland,*[10] which upheld a Maryland prohibition on dredging oysters in Chesapeake Bay against a Commerce Clause challenge. However, the court in that case declined to decide a host of questions concerning the limits of the state's authority and the extent of the federal government's powers in coastal waters.[11] The fishing public apparently considered the constitutional question unresolved. A *Forest and Stream* article in 1881 noted that the US Fish Commission received a good deal of correspondence on this constitutional issue.[12] Despite frequent calls from fish commissioners for a judicial ruling, it remained unaddressed throughout the nineteenth century. In practice, the federal government generally left fishing regulations to the states, in keeping with the narrow interpretation of the Commerce Clause that prevailed in Congress through most of the nineteenth century.

Some guidance on this question finally came in 1912 in *The Abby Dodge.*[13] The federal government enacted a law to protect sponges in the Gulf of Mexico, and the Supreme Court held that while it could do so under its power to regulate foreign commerce, the statute could apply only outside of state territorial waters. The decision could be read to hold that Congress did not have the authority to protect fish within state territorial waters. But the court expressly noted that it was concerned only with sponges (which remain attached to the soil), not with "running fish." Thus the case explicitly left unaddressed whether the state or the federal government had authority over fish whose migratory routes crossed political boundaries.[14] Still, given these precedents, the federal navigation servitude was a weak constitutional basis for fish conservation. But there was another potential basis for federal authority taking shape during the final decades of the nineteenth century: the treaty power.

The Treaty Power

Article II, Section 2 of the Constitution grants the president the power "by and with the Advice and Consent of the Senate, to make Treaties." That power, combined with the Article VI Supremacy Clause ("This Constitution, and the Laws of the United States which shall be made in Pursuance thereof; and all Treaties made, or which shall be made, under the Authority of the United States, shall be the supreme Law of the Land"), constitutes a potentially broad grant of federal power to override state laws. The treaty power emerged as a potential counterweight to state authority over wildlife as early as the 1880 case of *In re Ah Chong*[15] from the District Court of California. Ah Chong was arrested for violating a California law prohibiting Chinese aliens from commercial fishing. Ah Chong complained that the law violated the Equal Protection Clause of the US Constitution and also the Treaty of Burlingame, which promised Chinese residents the same privileges enjoyed by citizens of the "most favored nation." The state relied on *McCready v. Virginia*,[16] and the court agreed that *McCready* did allow states to discriminate against out-of-state citizens. But it reasoned that while the right to fish and hunt was a property right for citizens of the state, for nonresidents it was a mere privilege that could be granted or withheld by law. Denying Chinese persons a privilege that was enjoyed by many other nonresidents amounted to treating them differently from other nonresidents. This violated the Equal Protection Clause—but it also violated the treaty, which (according to the court) overrode state fishing laws.[17]

In re Ah Chong was an intriguing precedent, but the ability of treaties to override state laws was (and is) controversial. That controversy erupted in 1906, when the San Francisco Board of Education enacted a measure to send Japanese and Chinese children to segregated schools. This move violated the 1894 treaty between the United States and Japan, guaranteeing Japanese residents the same rights and privileges as US citizens. San Franciscans complained bitterly about this federal interference with their local laws. In response, Secretary of State Elihu Root published an article in the *American Journal of International Law* asserting that there was no question of states' rights involved. "The treaty power," he insisted, "is . . . all vested in the national government" and "in international affairs there are no states; there is but one nation, acting in direct relation to and representation of every citizen in every state."[18] In other words, when negotiating treaties, the federal government acts on behalf of the states and can therefore act on matters normally under state authority. Under his reasoning, if a subject is a legitimate matter for international negotiation, it can be reached under the treaty power. That logic was reiterated by Chandler Anderson, counselor for the State Department, in an article published in the same issue of the *American Journal of International Law*. Anderson's article specifically referenced the *Ah Chong* case and insisted that treaties could override state game laws. The opinions of Anderson and Root are particularly noteworthy, because at the time that these articles were published, they were both deeply involved in negotiating the country's first international conservation treaty: the Inland Fisheries Treaty with Great Britain, concerning fishing in waters along the Canada-US border.

International conservation treaties were only just beginning to appear. In 1900, France, Germany, the United Kingdom, Italy, Portugal, and the Congo Free State agreed to the Convention for the Preservation of Wild Animals, Birds, and Fish in Africa, the first international conservation effort.[19] The convention never went into effect, however, and the same fate awaited the Inland Fisheries Treaty of 1908. The treaty was under negotiation in 1906, when the controversy with the San Francisco school board erupted. It was finalized in 1908, but Congress never passed implementing legislation, in part because of constitutional objections over federal interference with state fishing laws.

Indeed, Chandler Anderson's public assertion that treaties could override state game laws contrasted with his own private misgivings about using that power to interfere in state matters.[20] Throughout the negotiations with Canada over the Inland Fisheries Treaty, Anderson raised concerns over states' rights with the American lead negotiator, David Starr Jordan. Jordan (an ichthyologist, not a lawyer) dismissed these concerns, and Elihu Root also assured the skeptical British ambassador Sir Mortimer Durand that treaties could override and annul state laws.[21] However, by the time the treaty was finalized, Root had left office. President Taft and his new secretary of state, Philander Knox, endorsed a stricter interpretation of the Constitution, one less favorable to expansive uses of the treaty power.[22] Commercial fishermen and state fish commissioners also raised constitutional objections to the regulations proposed under the treaty.[23] With little support from the president and strong objections from their constituents, Congress declined to enact the proposed regulations into law.

David Starr Jordan did not give up on the treaty without a fight, however. As historian Kurkpatrick Dorsey reports, in 1910, Jordan wrote to Chandler Anderson (who still worked for the State Department), offering a novel constitutional argument for federal protection of West Coast salmon fisheries: Federal regulation of international salmon fisheries could not violate states' rights, he argued, because salmon spent most of their time in international waters. Therefore, the public trust doctrine shouldn't apply; they could not belong to either a state or any Canadian province. Nor could the federal government claim ownership of a fish that spent only a few weeks of the year in inland waters. Thus these regulations should not be seen as transferring a property right in the fish from state to federal authority. Rather, they are merely regulations of international waters.[24]

In retrospect, Jordan's rejection of property concepts as a foundation for wildlife regulation seems promising, although it is problematic that his reasoning applies only to fish that spend most of their lives in international waters. But a shift away from public trust doctrine would require a more extensive reconsideration of the constitutional foundations of wildlife law. The driving force behind that reconsideration was a new broad-based movement for bird protection, which changed both the policy and the legal debates around wildlife conservation.

From Fish to Fowl

The story of the campaign for federal migratory bird conservation is well-known. The movement included the influential members of the Boone and Crockett Club, but it was not merely the province of a small group of well-placed elites. Of all the Progressive Era conservation efforts, bird protection had the broadest appeal, enjoying both mass support and leadership from public officials at the state and federal levels.[25] The movement, led by sportsmen, naturalists, and a strong contingent of women engaged in progressive reform, targeted commercial bird hunting and the feather trade and advocated for closed seasons and restrictions on hunting methods.[26]

The campaign resulted in the 1900 Lacey Act, which supported state-level game laws, and then the Weeks-McLean Act of 1913, which authorized the secretary of agriculture to establish national closed seasons on migratory birds. As we will see, the Weeks-McLean Act was declared unconstitutional in several (but not all) cases in the lower courts. The State Department, however, was also working on a treaty with Great Britain to protect migratory birds, and conservationists thought that this treaty would allow Congress to legislate in this area. The treaty was concluded on December 8, 1916. Congress enacted the Migratory Bird Treaty Act in July 1918, supplanting the Weeks-McLean Act, and the Supreme Court upheld the new federal law in *Missouri v. Holland* in 1920.

The bird conservation movement marked an important shift in the principal policy arguments for wildlife conservation. Deemphasizing the argument that game should be preserved as a cheap source of food for the poor, bird protectors sought to decommodify wildlife: Many of the bird conservationists appealed to humanitarian principles, offering the ideal of animal friendship and appreciation for the beauty of birds as an alternative to the hunter/prey relationship. These humanitarian appeals show up frequently in popular discourse and even legislative arenas. But by far the most common policy argument in legislative and judicial discourse was the claim that birds provided economically valuable services to the country by eating insects that can damage agriculture and forests.

As mentioned in chapter 2, establishing the economic value of birds to agriculture was a long-standing research project in the USDA. As a result, the growing scientific literature on the economic value of insect-eating birds became standard fare in congressional hearings and debates over bird protection legislation.[27] For example, in the 1913 congressional debate over the Weeks-McLean Act, Senator McLean read into the record the report of the House Committee on Agriculture, which concluded that the economic rationale for the bill was twofold. First, it mentioned that "the game birds yield a considerable and an important amount of highly valued food, and if given adequate protection will be a constant valuable asset." But it had a great deal more to say about the insectivorous migratory birds, which

> destroy annually thousands of tons of noxious weed seed and billions of harmful insects. These birds are the deadliest foe yet found of the boll weevil, the gypsy and brown-tailed moths, and other like pests. The yearly value of a meadow lark or a quail in a 10-acre field of cotton, corn, or wheat is reckoned by experts at $5. The damage done to growing crops in the United States by insects each year is estimated, by those who have made the matter a special study, at about $800,000,000.[28]

McLean also included a long excerpt from the Senate Committee report that went into much greater detail about the economic value of insectivorous birds. That report relied heavily on the USDA research and concluded with this interesting statement about the ecological relationships among plants, birds, and insects that the bill was trying to protect:

> All of the foregoing evidence goes to demonstrate the existence of a natural economic relation between these three orders of life. There is a sort of interdependence, and the existence of each one is dependent upon the existence of the others. But for the vegetation the insects would perish, and but for the insects the birds would perish, and but for the birds the vegetation would be utterly destroyed by the unchecked increase of insect destroyers.[29]

Proponents of the bill in the House debates also relied heavily on research showing the economic value of birds to farmers, such as an entire article by Professor de Loach of the University of Georgia titled "The Economic Value of Birds to the Farmer."[30] By the time the federal law reached the courts, the argument that birds were critical to checking destructive insects was commonplace.

Despite this scientific support, however, the constitutional case for federal bird protection was even more problematic than the case for federal fish protection; there was nothing in the Constitution comparable to the federal navigation servitude that could support federal regulation of birds on the wing. Several novel constitutional arguments would be developed, tested, and rejected on the road to *Missouri*.

The Lacey Act

The first success in the campaign for federal bird conservation was the 1900 Lacey Act, which provided that game taken in violation of state law could not be shipped in interstate commerce.[31] The Act benefited from the talents of Supreme Court lawyer W. H. Phillips, as well as the expertise of Congressman Lacey himself (also a lawyer).[32] It was modeled on the Wilson Act, a prohibition statute that allowed "dry" states to regulate the possession and sale of liquor entering or passing through their jurisdictions.[33] The Lacey Act deftly avoided all constitutional problems: It respected state authority over game and confined its prohibitions to game shipped in interstate commerce. This effort to conform to constitutional principle apparently worked; the Lacey Act never encountered serious constitutional difficulties in the courts. The few cases considering the act in the decade after its passage were favorable.[34] It was sustained against direct constitutional challenge by a federal court in *Rupert v. United States* (1910),[35] and in 1912 the Arkansas Supreme Court upheld a conviction under the act in *Eager v. Jonesboro, Lake City & Eastern Express Company.*[36]

The Lacey Act accelerated the general trend toward more state game laws. By 1913, thirty-nine states had passed the Ornithological Union's model law protecting nongame birds. But state laws in general still suffered from lack of uniformity and poor enforcement, and conservationists continued to campaign for a federal law, especially for game that crossed state borders.[37] Any additional federal wildlife conservation efforts, however, would require some creative constitutional arguments.

New Arguments for Federal Jurisdiction: Inherent Power, Property, and Commerce

Bills to protect migratory birds were introduced in Congress every year from 1904 to 1913, supported by three new constitutional arguments.[38] First, conservationists frequently combined the state failure argument with what has come to be known as the "inherent powers" argument. Christopher Tiedman offers a good statement of this doctrine in his 1890 treatise *The Unwritten Constitution of the United States.* Tiedman argues that the federal government has broad implicit power to promote the general welfare, reasoning that "a right to exercise a given power, which falls within the legitimate scope of governmental authority, must be vested in some branch of government." That is, any power ordinarily exercised by sovereign nations must be vested somewhere in the US governmental system. If such power is not expressly forbidden to the United States or expressly reserved to the states, it must be considered an inherent power of the federal government.[39] That view was not particularly popular in 1890, nor would it ever win much support from the courts. It did have one important advocate, however: Theodore Roosevelt.

One of the best articulations of Roosevelt's views on inherent powers is a 1906 speech celebrating founding father James Wilson and his "theory of governmental action." Wilson's theory begins with the proposition that sovereign power lies with the people of the nation collectively, not in the states qua states or in the separate polities of each state.[40]

He developed . . . the doctrine . . . that an inherent power rested in the nation, outside of the enumerated powers conferred upon it by the Constitution, in all cases where the object involved was beyond the power of the several States and was a power ordinarily exercised by sovereign nations. . . . That is, whenever the States cannot act, because the need to be met is not one of merely a single locality, then the National Government, representing all the people, should have complete power to act.[41]

This speech was focused on the regulation of corporations, but Roosevelt's First Annual Message to Congress in 1901 applied similar reasoning to conservation, justifying federal irrigation projects in the western arid lands:

Great storage works are necessary to equalize the flow of streams and to save the flood waters. Their construction has been conclusively shown to be an undertaking too vast for private effort. Nor can it be best accomplished by the individual States acting alone. Far-reaching interstate problems are involved; and the resources of single States would often be inadequate. It is properly a national function.[42]

Under this theory, the conservationists' complaint that the states are unable to protect wildlife during this period could be read to be asserting, at least implicitly, the federal government's "inherent power" to do so. Importantly, this argument led conservationists to characterize wildlife protection as an important *national* interest and, therefore, an appropriate subject for federal regulation.

This theory of inherent power supported one of Roosevelt's more controversial wildlife conservation strategies: establishing wildlife refuges on public land. The 1891 General Revision Act[43] authorized the president to create forest reserves by holding back certain lands from homesteading, but Roosevelt went further, creating the Pelican Island National Wildlife Refuge by executive order in 1903. No statute authorized him to reserve public lands for wildlife refuges. But as he explained in his 1913 *Autobiography*, he took the view (first formulated by the chief law officer of the Forest Service, George Woodruff) that the president could do anything to protect the public domain that was not explicitly prohibited by the Constitution.[44] His critics, of course, objected to this expansive interpretation of executive power. Wyoming Congressman Frank Mondell, for example, complained that the preserves violated state sovereignty and the state's right to control game in its territory (as established by *Geer v. Connecticut*[45]). While courts had upheld the power of the president to dedicate public lands to public uses (such as military bases or lighthouses),[46] Mondell contended that preserving game could not be a public use, because authority over game lay with states and not with the federal government. Mondell in fact questioned whether even Congress had the authority to create game refuges on public lands, at least when such lands lay within the borders of a state. Chapter 7 will explore that debate in depth. Despite these objections, however, Roosevelt stood on his inherent power theory and created fifty-one bird refuges by executive order. Congress supported him with the 1906 Game and Bird Preserves Protection Act, prohibiting hunting of birds or collecting eggs in violation of federal regulations on any lands "which have been set apart or reserved as breeding grounds for birds by any law, proclamation or executive order." This Act, while intended to apply only to the refuges that existed in 1906, was interpreted by Roosevelt and others as authorizing the president to create additional refuges (much to Mondell's annoyance).[47]

Nevertheless, the inherent power argument was anathema to states' rights advocates and won little sympathy from the courts. A more promising defense of federal bird conservation was the Interstate Commerce Clause.[48] For example, Congressman George Shiras III (the son of George Shiras, Jr., Supreme Court justice from 1892 to 1903) introduced a bill in 1904 to protect migratory game birds, defending federal authority by analogizing it to federal laws preventing the spread of disease on interstate railroads. He argued that wild birds, like animals on railroads, might be ownable, but they were not owned by any particular state while in transit between states. Therefore, they should be treated as articles of interstate commerce under the Commerce Clause.[49] Unlike David Starr Jordan's argument about salmon, Shiras's logic does not quite challenge the conceptualization of wildlife as property. He merely points out that, given the difficulty of identifying the owners of this migratory sort of property, it's best for the national government to serve as custodian of it. However, his reasoning does rest on a problematic analogy: The federal authority over animals being shipped in interstate commerce rests on federal authority over the instrumentalities of interstate commerce—the ships, highways, and railroads. Birds do not use any of those instrumentalities.

Shiras would not have the chance to try his argument in court, since his bill never came to the floor. His argument, however, resurfaced during the litigation over the Weeks-McLean Act, as we will see below. Indeed, a version of this argument would be accepted by the Seventh Circuit in 1937, in *United States v. Cochrane*,[50] and would reappear occasionally in later decisions. But it has failed to win broad acceptance in either courts or the legal community more generally.

As will be discussed below, characterizing migratory game as articles of commerce posed some conceptual difficulties that might have made government lawyers unwilling to put too much emphasis on this line of reasoning. A more elegant approach rested on the Property Clause. Article IV, Section 3 of the Constitution provides that "the Congress shall have Power to dispose of and make all needful Rules and Regulations respecting the Territory or other Property belonging to the United States." This provision already supported efforts to conserve forests and wildlife on federal property—forest reserves and national parks. The innovation offered by wildlife conservationists was to assert federal property rights in wildlife that crossed state lines. This property argument started gaining ground when Congressman John Weeks of Massachusetts took up the cause of migratory bird protection in 1912. His bill would extend federal protection to all migratory birds, and a key provision stated:

> All wild geese, wild swans, brant, wild ducks, snipe, plover, woodcock, rail, wild pigeons, and all other migratory game and insectivorous birds which in their northern and southern migrations pass through or do not remain permanently the entire year within the borders of any State or Territory, shall hereafter be deemed to be within the custody and protection of the Government of the United States, and shall not be destroyed or taken contrary to regulations hereinafter provided therefor.[51]

The bill clearly tried to modify the common law rule that wildlife was common property of the people of the several states. If migratory birds were classified as common property held in trust by the United States, they ought to be under federal jurisdiction and subject to federal game laws.

Predictably, opponents in Congress objected to this provision. They argued—not unreasonably—that the bill was an unconstitutional attempt to take the property of the people of each state and transfer it to the federal government.[52] Judging by the debate in Congress, the law's supporters did not have a very persuasive response to this objection. They cited the economic value of birds to agriculture and insisted that cooperation between national and state governments should be considered the normal relationship between the two sovereigns.[53] But they couldn't explain how Congress could unilaterally alter property rights (which were normally defined by state law) in this novel fashion.

The bill's other sponsor, Senator George McLean, rested his defense of the bill on the shaky ground of inherent powers. McLean actually went so far as to introduce a constitutional amendment in 1911 that would have granted Congress explicit power to protect migratory birds.[54] By 1913, however, he had concluded that an amendment was not necessary and gave a lengthy explanation of his reasoning in the Senate on January 14, 1913. This speech illustrates the difficulty bird conservationists were having with the constitutional issue: First, he acknowledged that some of the bill's defenders thought it could rest on the interstate commerce power or on the spending power (the government's authority to spend money for the general welfare). He rejected both of those arguments, however. He instead began with the federal government's authority to protect fish in coastal waters. To support that authority, he pointed to the recently concluded Inland Fisheries Treaty and referenced also *The Abby Dodge*, pointing to language in that case limiting its holding to sponges, which stayed put, and reserving the question of who had authority over running fish, which crossed political boundaries.

Concluding that the federal government probably had some authority to protect fish in navigable waters, McLean drew an analogy between migratory fish and migratory birds: If Congress can protect fish that cross state boundaries, it should be able to protect migratory birds as well. That was questionable reasoning, since federal regulatory authority over fish, if it existed at all, rested on the federal navigation servitude. But McLean's main argument was that states could do little to protect fish and game that routinely crossed state lines. Since protecting wildlife was generally considered a sovereign power, the power to do so must rest somewhere. He concluded:

My contention is that Congress has the implied power as a natural and necessary attribute of its sovereignty to provide for the common defense and promote the general welfare of the Nation whenever the need is general and manifest, and the subject is such that no State, acting separately, can protect and defend itself against the threatened danger or secure to itself those benefits to which it is justly entitled as a part of the Nation.[55]

In response, Senator Borah raised an obvious objection: The fact that the states have failed to exercise their power to protect migratory wildlife effectively does not mean they lack the power to do so: "Simply because the States neglect to use their reserved powers constitutes no reason why the National Government should assume to exercise unconstitutional powers."[56]

The Weeks-McLean Act

Despite its weak constitutional rationale, however, the Weeks-McLean Act passed and was signed into law in 1913. Implementing the law, however, proved problematic. To begin, the law did not provide for an effective enforcement mechanism. It gave the USDA responsibility for establishing open and closed seasons on migratory birds and provided that violation of the regulations would be a misdemeanor carrying a fine of up to one hundred dollars or ninety days in jail. It did not explicitly identify who was to enforce the law, but the statutory language was incorporated into an omnibus appropriations bill under the section devoted to the Bureau of Biological Survey, and the Wilson administration designated that bureau as the principal enforcement agency. Unfortunately, the bureau, which was primarily devoted to research (and eradication of predators) did not have the funds or personnel to implement a nationwide game law. It therefore decided to focus on publicity and education.[57] The bill's proponents may have assumed that state game wardens would embrace the federal regulations and either bring state game laws into conformance with them or, in the absence of state laws, enforce the federal laws. But that plan assumed that states were cooperative; in reality, many states objected to the federal government usurping their authority over game.[58]

The other federal agency in a good position to enforce the law was the Forest Service, which was already enforcing grazing and other regulations in the vast national forests. The Forest Service was willing, but its power to enforce the act was limited—or so advised Robert W. Williams in the solicitor general's office. In response to an inquiry by Associate Forester A. F. Potter, Williams concluded that in the absence of an explicit grant of power, forest service officers had no more power to arrest people for breaking the law than did private citizens. And private citizens could not arrest people for committing misdemeanors; they could only ask a US judge or commissioner for a warrant.[59] Williams was an expert on game laws, and, as we will see in chapter 7, he would play a key role in supporting federal power over wildlife. But his opinion on this topic proved nearly fatal to the

Forest Service's efforts to enforce the law. Forest Service officers confronted with lawbreakers had to go through a cumbersome process of gathering evidence (including witnesses, since possession of the bird was not sufficient to prove guilt), presenting the case to the nearest US Commissioner (who might take days to reach), getting a warrant for arrest, and asking a US marshal to arrest the offender—or turning their evidence over to the US attorney general's office in the hopes that they would bring charges.[60]

Williams advised the Forest Service to ask Congress to authorize Forest Service officers to make arrests without a warrant (as they could in the case of forest regulation violations). But apparently enthusiasm for the policy in Congress had waned after passage of the bill; further enforcement funds and authority were not forthcoming. Lack of support for the policy was likely due in part to the constitutional doubts about the act; even Secretary of Agriculture David Houston expressed concerns and was reluctant to seek judicial review of the law.[61]

Nevertheless, some arrests were made. The USDA reported 1,132 violations of the law from 1913 to 1918, although only a handful of those violations led to prosecutions.[62] And those who were prosecuted were quick to challenge the law's constitutionality. The Act faced seventeen legal challenges in its first year, and twenty cases were pending by 1916. Federal district courts in several states did uphold the law, in unreported cases (in Oregon, California, South Dakota, Nebraska, Minnesota, and Michigan).[63] But it was struck down in two high-profile federal cases and two reported state cases. These decisions rejected all three of the constitutional arguments that had been developed to support it.

In *United States v. Shauver*,[64] the defendant was indicted for killing migratory birds in violation of USDA regulations. Shauver argued that the Weeks-McLean Act violated the Tenth Amendment, invading the powers reserved to the states. The government's counsel argued in response that Congress had power to protect migratory birds under the Property Clause and also offered the state failure/inherent power argument.[65] Judge Trieber dismissed this second argument easily. A similar argument had recently been made and rejected in the 1907 Supreme Court decision *Kansas v. Colorado*,[66] concerning federal authority over unnavigable rivers. There, Justice Brewer pointed out that "the proposition that there are legislative powers affecting the nation as a whole, which belong to, although not expressed in, the grant of powers, is in direct conflict with the doctrine that this is a government of enumerated powers."[67] Trieber also rejected the property argument, citing the long line of cases affirming that ownership of wildlife lies in the state.

The US government, apparently using *Shauver* as a test case for the statute, made a motion for a rehearing, and Assistant Attorney General Marvin Underwood argued the case.[68] In the hearing on the motion, he raised a new argument: that the act was valid under the commerce power because migratory birds were articles of interstate commerce. Specifically, the United States argued:

A migratory bird, from one state into another, passes from the owner-ship of the former into that of the latter state. If this be true, a thing recognized by the courts as an article of commerce, when passing be-tween individuals, passes from the ownership of individuals in their collective capacity to other individuals in their collective capacity, the ownership of the state being merely ownership in trust for their respec-tive citizens.[69]

Judge Trieber insisted that *Geer v. Connecticut* disposed of that argument, since it held that one attribute of state ownership of wildlife was that states could prohibit it from entering into interstate commerce. He denied the motion for a rehearing.

Trieber's terse rejection of the Commerce Clause argument is not par-ticularly lucid, but he was probably troubled by the conceptual difficulty it raised. The problem with the argument as stated is that it both relies on and contradicts the state ownership theory: It assumes that migratory birds are owned by each state as they pass through—but the purpose of the argument is to deny the states' power to protect those birds, which is the entire point of the state ownership theory. It's hard to see how the argu-ment could be made compatible with *Geer*.

The United States, undaunted, appealed to the Supreme Court. The case was argued twice (the first time before six justices, then a rehearing before the full bench was ordered). The government's argument on appeal was similar to its argument before Judge Trieber.[70] The brief elaborated the Property Clause argument, asserting that the precedents establishing state ownership of game animals either concerned nonmigratory species or, if migratory animals were involved, did not explicitly consider the possibility of federal ownership. The government argued that the sovereign's trusteeship of wild animals rested on its ability to control and protect them for the benefit of all. States lacked the ability to do so—in part because they lacked the authority to make the international treaties necessary to protecting migratory animals. In other words, the government reasoned that in adopting the Constitution, the people had expressly granted the federal government the treaty power and, with it, the power to protect migratory animals. Therefore, trusteeship should rest with the national government. Emphasizing the economic value of birds (both as a food source and for the ecological services they provide), the government insisted that the law was a valid exercise of the authority granted in the Property Clause.

The brief also addressed the Commerce Clause argument but added nothing new to its claim that birds passing over state lines under their own powers should be considered articles of commerce. Whether these arguments would have persuaded the Supreme Court is unknown. They postponed deciding the case (apparently at the urging of Justice White, a proponent of bird protection) until after the Migratory Bird Treaty and its implementing legislation was passed. At that point, the court dismissed the government's appeal, since the Weeks-McLean Act had been superseded by the new federal legislation.[71]

The second case striking down the Weeks-McLean Act was the 1915 case *United States v. McCullagh.*[72] George McCullagh was prosecuted under the act for shooting wild ducks in April, which was an open season on ducks in Kansas but a closed season under the federal regulations. The US attorney relied again on the Property Clause and the Commerce Clause. The brief did not spend much time on the Commerce Clause argument, and neither did Judge Pollock. If migratory birds were articles of interstate commerce, he reasoned, then the states had no regulatory authority over them. Similarly, if migratory birds are in the custody of the United States, then the logic of *Geer* is undermined: They cannot be owned by the state, and the state cannot keep them out of interstate commerce.[73] Thus, the only real question in the case is whether the birds covered by the Weeks-McLean Act, simply by virtue of their migratory habits, escaped state custody and became the property of the United States.

Judge Pollock concluded they did not. Here he relied, somewhat oddly, on the 1896 decision *Ward v. Race Horse.*[74] *Ward* is one of series of decisions eroding tribal sovereignty, and it reflects the anomalous nature of cases concerning Indian treaties during this period. But it also became a key decision supporting state authority over wildlife, as we will see in chapters 5 and 7. The defendant, a member of the Bannock Indian tribe, exercised his right to hunt on any unoccupied federal lands—a right explicitly protected by the tribe's treaty with the United States but in conflict with Wyoming game laws. The Supreme Court upheld the conviction, reasoning that when Wyoming entered the union, the hunting rights in the treaty were implicitly repealed.[75] We will encounter this case again in chapters 5 and 7, with reference to debates over federal forest reserves. But whatever the force of its logic with respect to public land, it hardly answers the United States' argument in *McCullagh*. *McCullagh* concerned not whether the federal government can control hunting *on* its own property but whether it can control the hunting *of* its own property. Pollock's conclusion, however, was echoed by both the Maine and Kansas Supreme Courts in 1915. In *Maine v. Sawyer*[76] and *Kansas v. McCullagh and Savage*,[77] defendants were convicted of violating state game laws and argued in defense that the state law was rendered inoperative by the Weeks-McLean Act. Both courts held the Weeks-McLean Act to be unconstitutional, tersely rejecting the commerce, property, and inherent powers arguments.[78]

Interestingly, the Supreme Court did have a chance to consider the Weeks-McLean Act, in *Carey v. South Dakota*[79] in 1919. This case reached the court after the Migratory Bird Treaty had been concluded and the Weeks-McLean Act superseded by the Migratory Bird Treaty Act. But the defendant had been charged with violating a South Dakota law prohibiting shipping game out of state in 1915, before the new statute was passed. In his defense, he raised the same argument that Sawyer and McCullagh offered: that the law had been rendered void by the Weeks-McLean Act. Justice Brandeis did not address the constitutionality of the federal law, however; he merely concluded that the act did not abrogate the state law.

The *Carey* decision may indicate that the Supreme Court would have looked more favorably on the Weeks-McLean Act than did the lower courts. Nevertheless, by 1915, the constitutional weakness of the Weeks-McLean Act was evident to its supporters, and the source of the constitutional difficulty was becoming clearer: Property concepts couldn't easily be applied to things that moved around under their own power, and the governmental interest in these creatures lay less in their value as commodities than in their value in providing ecosystem services. The property framework simply wasn't appropriate, given the nature of the creatures being regulated and the nature of the government's interest in those creatures.

From Property to Ecosystem Services

In light of these judicial defeats, it's not surprising that conservationists were starting to move away from conceptualizing wildlife as property. For example, in 1916, William Temple Hornaday was pressing Congress to pass a bill allowing the president to establish game refuges in forest reserves. This was a long-standing goal of the wildlife conservationists, as we will discuss in chapter 7. The bill was unsuccessful, but it prompted both Henry Graves, head of the Forest Service, and Aldo Leopold, who was working for the Forest Service on game management in the Southwest, to weigh in on the idea of federal ownership of wildlife. Early in 1916, Leopold wrote a memo on the Forest Service's approach to managing the game refuges that he anticipated would be created if Hornaday's proposal were enacted. In his view, "We must . . . provide ways and means for an adequate patrol of these refuges." And "in choosing ways and means to this end, we will have to guide our efforts in the light of a very important question: namely, the ultimate federal ownership of National Forest game." Leopold granted the point that states currently did own wildlife. But he suggested that the states might be encouraged to give up their ownership *voluntarily*, if the Forest Service "prepared the way" for federal ownership. Specifically, the Forest Service should take on exclusive enforcement of state game laws in national forests. If they did a good job of it, he predicted that the states and, importantly, game protective associations, might come to support federal ownership. He concluded on this point:

> It might seem doubtful that the Forest Service is really in a position to influence the development of the question in either direction, but it has been our experience that in this District the development of the question will depend primarily on the attitude of the Game Protective Associations, and these, in turn, have invariably taken their cue from the Forest Service on all matters of general policy.[80]

This memo constitutes a bold call for the agency to take the lead in shaping the law, even on constitutional principles, rather than merely following it. Such boldness reflected the confidence and assertiveness of the Forest Service during these years, as later chapters will demonstrate.

Leopold's memo was popular. It was endorsed by his supervisor, District Forester Paul Redington, and by A. F. Potter in the Washington Office, who sent it to Forest Service Chief Henry Graves. Graves, however, was not convinced. He, too, had been giving deep thought to the problem of game management, and I think Graves had a better grasp of the issue than did Leopold. Graves agreed that there should be a national policy on wildlife but dismissed the question of ownership. What was needed, he argued, was a "single coordinated administration of the game under a single direction"—an approach that was working well with respect to fire prevention. He suggested that the Forest Service could make cooperative agreements with the states to manage game in federal forests on their behalf, without requiring the states to give up any sovereign rights.[81] The diversity of interests and ecological conditions worked against any government having exclusive jurisdiction over wildlife in federal forests. The federal and state governments would necessarily have to cooperate, and the question of property rights wasn't helpful in achieving that cooperation.

Supporting this move away from conceptualizing wildlife as property, legal scholar Edward S. Corwin published in 1916 a defense of the Weeks-McLean Act in the *Michigan Law Review*, offering an entirely new kind of Commerce Clause argument. Although he defended the property, commerce, and inherent powers theories, he also offered a more ambitious argument: He cited the Supreme Court decision *United States v. Rio Grande Irrigation Co.*,[82] which affirmed that the federal navigation servitude authorized Congress to "secure the navigability of all navigable streams within the limits of the United States." Corwin correctly noted that this power, when combined with recent advances in ecological science, could authorize extensive congressional regulation of the natural environment. The principle had already been used to support a bill establishing the Appalachian and White Mountain forest reserve, a measure intended to protect the forests at the headwaters of several rivers (to be discussed in chapter 6). That bill rested on a significant weight of scientific evidence—well-accepted if not uncontroverted—that forests helped to protect streamflow and reduce erosion. Corwin reasoned, "It may very well be questioned whether there is any more intimate relation in fact between the preservation of the navigability of streams and that of the forests at their headwaters than there is between the preservation of forests and that of the bird life of the country."[83] That is, if the Commerce Clause supports federal forest conservation, it should also support efforts to preserve the birds who (according the House and Senate committee reports and a host of scientific authorities) preserved forests by eating destructive insects.

The reasoning may seem a bit strained, but it represents a significant conceptual shift: Corwin suggests that instead of thinking of wildlife as articles of property, we should see these creatures as part of a natural system. They contribute to the national economy not as commodities but through their actions, by helping to maintain forests. Not only is this a different way of thinking about wildlife (as active workers rather than static objects), it represents a different way of thinking about nature: not as a collection of things but as a system composed of activities and relationships. The *Rio Grande* decision shows that this way of thinking was already beginning to influence judicial decisions in the realm of forest conservation. It would be influential in *Missouri v. Holland* as well.

But bird lovers had another, more promising, constitutional strategy, which bypassed the issues of property and commerce altogether: the treaty power. Of course, the power was limited by the fact that one needed a treaty, and therefore a willing foreign government, to bring it into effect. It might not support a general federal conservation regime, but the bird conservation movement had limited objectives. They were willing to settle for protecting migratory birds.

The first public proposal to use the treaty power on behalf of the birds came from Elihu Root. Elected to the Senate in 1909, Root supported the Weeks-McLean Law but clearly had doubts about its constitutionality. Accordingly, during the congressional debate on January 14, 1913, he offered a resolution to the Senate urging the president to negotiate a treaty with other North American countries to protect migratory birds, suggesting that such a treaty would obviate the constitutional difficulty.[84] This suggestion was taken up not by President Taft (who was leaving office) but by the Canadians.[85] President Woodrow Wilson, who took office in March 1913, supported the idea and set international negotiations in motion. The treaty would be ratified in December 1916, and legislation implementing it—the Migratory Bird Treaty Act—was passed in July 1918.[86] The Act prohibited the hunting, killing, sale, and shipment of birds covered by the treaty, unless in accordance with regulations created by the USDA. (Importantly, it also explicitly gave any employee of the USDA power to make arrests without a warrant.) This was the law at issue in *Missouri v. Holland*, which case allowed the Supreme Court to weigh in on the various constitutional theories supporting federal wildlife conservation.

MBTA in the lower courts

The Migratory Bird Treaty Act (MBTA) came up in several federal cases before *Missouri v. Holland* reached the Supreme Court. Judge Trieber had one of the first opportunities to consider the effect of the treaty on federal wildlife conservation authority in *United States v. Thompson*[87] in 1919. This case was important enough to the Justice and Agriculture Departments to warrant the attention of not only Assistant Attorney General Underwood but also the solicitor general of the USDA.[88] Thompson was charged with violating the MBTA and argued in defense that the act was unconstitutional because the treaty power did not extend federal authority over migratory birds. As Judge Trieber concisely put it, Thompson's argument was that "a treaty or convention between the United States and a foreign nation is of no higher grade than an act of Congress, and if an act of Congress regulating migratory birds is beyond the constitutional powers of Congress a treaty on the same subject is also void."[89] Trieber, however, held that the treaty power was not subject to the same limitations that Congress faces when legislating on domestic matters. His opinion is lengthy, but his argument can be summarized briefly: Quoting an opinion of the US Attorney General,[90] Trieber asserts that "in the matter of foreign negotiation, the states have conferred the whole of their power—in other words, all the treaty powers of sovereignty—on the United States."[91] Accordingly, "even in matters of a purely local nature, Congress, if the Constitution grants it plenary powers over the subject, may exercise what is akin to the police power, a power ordinarily reserved to the states."[92] He therefore upheld the MBTA.

The *Thompson* case was decided on June 4. On July 14, a federal district judge in Texas, citing *Thompson*, also upheld the act (*United States v. Selkirk*[93]). And Montana district court Judge Bourquin reached the same conclusion in August 1919, in *United States v. Rockefeller*.[94] Bourquin expanded on Trieber's reasoning, explaining why natural resource conservation was a proper subject for international negotiation:

Fisheries have been the subject of treaties always, and the principles and objects thereof are equally applicable and desirable in relation to migratory birds and other game. So doubtless of air and water, their protection from pollution, their conservation, apportionment, and use. The object of all thereof is to peacefully share those natural resources which are the property of no one till reduced to possession, from which all may take when within their territory, which are alternately found within the territory of the several nations and in places common to all as the high seas, which may be wholly seized and exterminated by one to the great and irreparable damage of all, which in accord may be preserved and enjoyed a blessing to all, but in discord may be annihilated to the injury of all, and which may become legitimate causes for war, to obviate which is of the most ancient and important objects of treaties.[95]

He suggested further that it would be impractical for states to attempt to protect migratory birds on their own, making reference to the state failure argument. That argument, while it may not be sufficient grounds for Congress to act under its ordinary legislative powers, was sufficient grounds for the federal government to act under the treaty power.

These victories encouraged the USDA to enforce the act vigorously. The USDA received 110 convictions during the first year of the act and 393 during the second.[96]

Missouri v. Holland

Missouri v. Holland arose out of the arrest of two Missouri citizens, Samples and DeLapp, for violating federal game regulations. The defendants argued that the law was an unconstitutional infringement on the powers reserved to the state under the Tenth Amendment, and the state of Missouri intervened as well, asking the court to enjoin the federal game warden, Ray Holland, from enforcing the act. Judge Van Valkenburgh heard the case.

Van Valkenburgh's opinion in the lower court case, *United States v. Samples*,[97] closely tracks the reasoning in the previous cases, upholding the act under the treaty power. Drawing an analogy from fish to migratory birds, he notes:

Seals go regularly to their breeding and feeding grounds. Fishes migrate during the spawning season. Migratory birds nest in the north and feed in the south with the regularity of the seasons. The movements of all these forms of life may be computed almost with mathematical precision. . . . If this be true, what distinction can we draw between the fish which swims through one of the great natural elements and the bird which flies through another?[98]

Seals, it should be noted, were already the subject of the 1911 North Pacific Fur Seal Convention, and fish were of course the subject of the Inland Fisheries Treaty. The judge concluded that migratory birds were a proper subject for international negotiations.

Missouri appealed to the Supreme Court and was joined in its brief by Kansas. An amicus brief was also filed by the Association for the Protection of the Adirondacks, supporting the US government's position. The arguments offered in these briefs reflect not only the progress of constitutional reasoning on wildlife conservation but also important developments in two other areas of constitutional doctrine concerning natural resources: The federal government's authority over public lands (and particularly forests), and the parens patriae doctrine, concerning state governments' right to bring suit in federal courts to protect their natural resources. Those developments will be discussed in more depth in later chapters. It is enough here to note that this case represents an emerging synthesis of new ideas about the government's interest in and power over natural resources.

The Missouri, Kansas, and US briefs focused on the treaty argument. But before reaching that argument, Missouri had to explain why it had standing to intervene in the case at all. As the United States noted in its brief, normally states do not have standing to challenge the constitutionality of a federal law in an ordinary criminal case. However, Missouri argued that it had a right to enjoin enforcement of a federal law if it threatened the state's property rights or the state's interest as a "quasi-sovereign" in protecting the natural environment for the benefit of its citizens. The first argument depends on public trust doctrine, but the second depends on parens patriae doctrine, a series of decisions holding that states have a judicially cognizable interest in protecting the natural environment—decisions with obvious importance for environmental policy. We will discuss this doctrine in more detail in chapter 9. The key point here is that when the state is acting as parens patriae—the guardian or protector of its citizens—the state does not need to show that its *property* rights are at risk. Rather, it is protecting its interest in environmental integrity, which is conceptually distinct from property rights. In *Missouri v. Holland*, the state of Missouri had quite a lot to say in its brief about the state's property interest in wildlife, but its reference to the parens patriae doctrine suggests that its standing, at least, depended on a different kind of interest in the natural environment.

However, Missouri and Kansas both devoted most of their briefs to arguing that the treaty power was limited by the Tenth Amendment, and those arguments relied heavily on public trust doctrine, establishing the state's property rights in wildlife. If authority over wildlife is ordinarily reserved to the states, then (according to Missouri and Kansas) the federal government cannot regulate wildlife under the treaty power. Neither brief bothered to address the Property or Commerce Clause arguments.

In response, the United States (represented by Assistant Attorney General William Frierson and Solicitor General Alex King) rehearsed the winning arguments concerning the treaty power in *Thompson, Rockefeller*, and Van Valkenburgh's opinion in the lower court. It included its brief in the *Shauver* appeal as an appendix, but it added nothing new to the Property and Commerce Clause arguments it developed in that case. More interesting for our purposes, the treaty power argument was supported by the argument, now well-developed, about the nature of the federal government's economic interest in migratory birds—the national interest that made migratory birds a proper subject for international negotiation. The brief asserted that "game birds are valuable as furnishing food supply," but it also included in a long appendix a collection of USDA reports and other authorities on the value of migratory game and especially insectivorous birds to agriculture and to forests.[99]

This argument about the value of birds would play an important role in the court's decision. The brief cited statistics from the USDA estimating losses to crops from insect damage, as well as the cost of efforts to fight insect pests such as gypsy moths. It then asked,

> Who or what is it that prevents these ravening hordes from overrunning the earth and consuming the food supply of all? It is not man. . . . Neither is it disease, or the weather, or animals, or fungi, or parasitic or predaceous insects within their own ranks. However large may be the share of these particular natural agencies in keeping insects in check, experience has shown that it is lamentably insufficient. Then what is it? The bird.[100]

The brief goes on to suggest that an insectivorous bird eats at least one hundred insects per day. If there are five insectivorous birds per acre (an estimate based on research in Massachusetts), then birds are devouring about twenty-one thousand bushels of insects per day, at least during the growing season. Birds are therefore a "natural check" on injurious insects, and they maintain "equilibrium" in forests as well.[101] Indeed, "birds attain their greatest usefulness in forests. . . . Forests have their natural insect foes, to which they give food and shelter, and these insects in turn have their natural enemies among the birds, to which the tree also gives food and shelter. Hence it follows that the existence of each one of these forms of life is dependent on the existence of the other."[102] The brief also reported the estimated value of "game resources" to the state (coming up with "hundreds of millions of dollars"), although it's unclear from the short discussion whether the estimate represents the revenue from hunting or the estimated food value of the game birds.[103] The commodity value of game birds received much less attention in the brief than did the ecological value of insectivorous birds, reflecting the changing rationale for federal wildlife protection.

The legal implications of this ecological argument were developed in greater detail in the brief submitted by the Association for the Protection of the Adirondacks, written by the civil rights activist Louis Marshall. Marshall's brief developed an argument similar to Edward Corwin's 1916 Commerce Clause argument. Marshall used similar logic but based his argument on the Property Clause. He argued that Congress had authority to protect birds under the Property Clause, not because the birds were property of the United States but because protecting birds was essential to protecting public lands, including the vast national forest reserves. There was no question that Congress had plenary authority to make "needful rules and regulations" with respect to the public domain.[104] To support that claim, Marshall referenced two key Supreme Court cases affirming the authority of the secretary of agriculture to make and enforce regulations to prevent damage to the forest reserves,[105] as well as the more recent *Utah Power and Light v. United States*,[106] which held that the United States had something akin to the police power on public lands.

Of course, extending federal protection to all migratory birds would be a considerable extension of this power into nonpublic lands. But there was a relevant precedent: Marshall cited *Georgia v. Tennessee Copper Co.*[107] (the same case Missouri relied on for standing) for the proposition that the federal government could prohibit a smelter or factory on private lands near public forests, to prevent their noxious fumes from damaging the trees. By the same logic, he insisted, Congress could regulate or prohibit the killing of the "natural guardians of the prairie and the forest": insectivorous birds.[108] He analogized birds to government agents, appointed to protect the forests. If the federal government had authority to protect federal agents, surely it had the power to protect these feathered guardians—a "police agency supplied by the Creator for the preservation of vegetable life."[109] Marshall's argument, of course, rests on the idea that birds are essential to the health of the forest. He accordingly devoted fourteen pages to scientific authorities on that point, ranging from USDA scientists and university professors to William Temple Hornaday.

Finally, addressing the state's role as trustee of wildlife within its borders, Marshall asserted that this state power was limited by federal authority to protect the public domain.[110] The states, he agreed, had concurrent power to protect wildlife, but their regulations could not supersede federal law.

In sum, these briefs in *Missouri v. Holland* reflect the constitutional "common sense" that there was a strong governmental interest in protecting wildlife. While they disagreed about whether that responsibility lay with the state or federal government, everyone assumed that the government had a sovereign (or quasi-sovereign) interest in wildlife. Their chief disagreement (beyond the central question of the limits of the treaty power) was in how they conceptualized this governmental interest. The attorneys for Missouri and Kansas relied on the nineteenth-century legal framework that characterized wildlife as property. But Missouri's parens patriae argument, Marshall's Property Clause argument, and the United States' claim that protecting wildlife was a valid subject of international negotiation all depend on an emerging understanding of wildlife as dynamic and important elements of what we today call ecosystems. That understanding is reflected, as well, in Justice Holmes's opinion for the court.

The central holding of Holmes's opinion was that the MBTA was a valid exercise of the treaty power. But Holmes also took advantage of this case to weigh in on some of the elements of the arguments in favor of a federal conservation power.

First, Holmes accepted Missouri's argument that it had standing to intervene in the case due to its quasi-sovereign interest; he mentioned but offered no opinion on its pecuniary interest in the birds. As we shall see, he consistently refused to endorse the conception of birds as property. But first he addressed the treaty power: The power to make treaties is expressly delegated to the federal government, so the only question is whether there is some implicit limitation on that treaty power. Whatever such limits may be, Holmes opined, they are not the same as the limits on Congress's authority to legislate in domestic matters: "It is obvious that there may be matters of the sharpest exigency for the national well being that an act of Congress could not deal with but that a treaty followed by such an act could, and it is not lightly to be assumed that, in matters requiring national action, "a power which must belong to and somewhere reside in every civilized government" is not to be found."[111] Holmes then offered one of his more famous quotes, reflecting his view that the Constitution must be interpreted in light of the contemporary context:

> With regard to that we may add that when we are dealing with words that also are a constituent act, like the Constitution of the United States, we must realize that they have called into life a being the development of which could not have been foreseen completely by the most gifted of its begetters. It was enough for them to realize or to hope that they had created an organism; it has taken a century and has cost their successors much sweat and blood to prove that they created a nation. The case before us must be considered in the light of our whole experience and not merely in that of what was said a hundred years ago.[112]

Holmes's decision doesn't depend on this organic conception of the Constitution, but this language does help to lay the groundwork for his reliance on new developments in ecological science. The founders could not have foreseen how settlement of the continent would affect the ecological foundations of American society; the Constitution must be read in light of this new experience.

Holmes goes on to conclude that because the treaty did not contravene an express prohibition in the Constitution, the only question was whether "it is forbidden by some invisible radiation from the general terms of the Tenth Amendment."[113] Does the treaty invade state authority, as Missouri claimed? Here he questioned the nineteenth-century framework governing wildlife conservation:

> No doubt it is true that as between a State and its inhabitants the State may regulate the killing and sale of such birds, but it does not follow that its authority is exclusive of paramount powers. To put the claim of the State upon title is to lean upon a slender reed. Wild birds are not in the possession of anyone; and possession is the beginning of ownership. The whole foundation of the State's rights is the presence within their jurisdiction of birds that yesterday had not arrived, tomorrow may be in another State and in a week a thousand miles away.[114]

In other words, he questions the State's claim to own the wildlife in question, just as the United States brief had asked him to. But further, he suggests that the United States can't assert a property right in wildlife either. Indeed, he seems to be saying that migratory animals cannot be owned at all.

With the states' property rights dismissed, we are left with only the state's regulatory authority at stake:

> We cannot put the case of the State upon higher ground than that the treaty deals with creatures that for the moment are within the state borders, that it must be carried out by officers of the United States within the same territory, and that but for the treaty the State would be free to regulate this subject itself. As most of the laws of the United States are carried out within the States and as many of them deal with matters which in the silence of such laws the State might regulate, such general grounds are not enough to support Missouri's claim.[115]

Holmes cited several cases holding that treaties overrode state laws and concluded with a strong statement of the national interest in this treaty:

> Here a national interest of very nearly the first magnitude is involved. It can be protected only by national action in concert with that of another power. The subject-matter is only transitorily within the State and has no permanent habitat therein. But for the treaty and the statute there soon might be no birds for any powers to deal with. We see nothing in the Constitution that compels the Government to sit by while a food supply is cut off and the protectors of our forests and our crops are destroyed.[116]

Thus, without actually discussing the Property or Commerce Clause arguments in the United States brief, or even mentioning Marshall's argument in the amicus brief, Holmes concisely undermines the nineteenth century legal framework on which the Missouri and Kansas briefs depended: The state's authority over wildlife rests on its regulatory authority rather than on the state's property interest; the governmental interest in wildlife rests not only on its commodity value but also on its critical role in protecting agriculture and forests; and that economic interest concerns the nation as a whole. The guiding principle underlying the whole opinion is the emerging conception of nature not as property but as a system that supports the national economy. Indeed, the parens patriae argument suggests that the natural environment could carry other, noneconomic, values in which state governments, at least, had an interest. But at the very least, Holmes's opinion suggests that the economic value of nature reached well beyond its commodity value. Under a proper understanding of ecological science, the natural environment must be considered a vital part of the national economy and therefore a proper subject for international negotiation.

Justices Van Devanter and Pitney dissented from the decision (without an opinion). Nor were they alone; *Missouri v. Holland* has received substantial criticism over the years. Virtually all the criticism concerns whether there are implicit limits on the treaty power.[117] But Holmes's treatment of the *Geer* doctrine has received less attention.

It's important to note that in rejecting the notion that the government's interest in wildlife is a property right, Holmes was not rejecting the underlying principle that state governments have a strong interest in protecting natural resources. In previous decisions, he had affirmed that states can keep natural resources from becoming articles of interstate commerce and can discriminate against nonresidents.[118] However, Holmes's theory was not based on the idea that (static, unchanging) common law principles define the state's property interest in natural resources. Rather, he reasoned that the state *creates* property rights in natural resources and therefore can put any conditions on those rights that it sees fit, including preventing those resources from entering into interstate commerce.[119]

Legal scholar Sheldon Novick contends that the Supreme Court ultimately declined to follow this reasoning; over the course of the twentieth century, it extended the federal interstate commerce power, gradually chipping away at the state's authority to keep natural resources out of the stream of commerce. Indeed, *Geer v. Connecticut* itself was specifically overruled in 1979, by *Hughes v. Oklahoma*.[120] But critical elements of Holmes's reasoning remain central to constitutional doctrine concerning state authority over natural resources: The state defines property rights and can alter them;[121] the state has an interest in protecting natural resources that cannot be reduced to its interest in protecting its own property;[122] and the state may interfere with interstate commerce to protect its interest in environmental integrity.[123] More generally, *Missouri v. Holland* reflects a new and enduring constitutional "common sense" that both state and federal interest in the natural environment lies not simply in protecting public property for its commodity value but in maintaining the integrity of ecosystems, so that they may continue to provide ecosystem services to the national economy.

However, the actual holding in *Missouri v. Holland* was quite narrow: It upheld federal authority over migratory birds only, and only on the basis of the Migratory Bird Treaty. It did not explicitly provide for the broad federal authority over wildlife desired by conservationists and important actors in federal land management agencies. Nor did it settle a host of constitutional questions involved in conserving forests and water resources or addressing pollution.

CHAPTER FOUR

Forest Conservation in the States

It should be clear from the previous chapters that the story of wildlife conservation is intertwined with the story of forest conservation. But the doctrinal foundations of forest policy are distinct from the foundations of wildlife policy and are less friendly to government intervention. Arguments for forest conservation therefore had to rely heavily on ecological science to find a public interest in forests that the government could legitimately protect. And the most constitutionally useful scientific theory supporting forest conservation was the relationship between forests and water systems. Government regulation to protect the commodity value of forests might have seemed sensible to voters and policy makers, but to courts that goal was constitutionally suspect. In contrast, the government's interest in protecting streamflow in major river systems—a key component of the nation's transportation system—had a stronger constitutional foundation. Protecting watersheds would thus become a primary legal rationale for forest conservation during this period.

The story of forest conservation also provides more insight into the process of constitutional change. While the wildlife conservation movement focused on working within and gradually extending judicial doctrine, forest conservationists working at the state level often sought to amend the text of state constitutions directly. As we will see, however, textual amendment did not in itself guarantee the constitutionality of forest conservation. Securing the legitimacy of forest programs required both creative legislative action and supportive doctrinal interpretations from the courts. As was the case with wildlife conservation, however, the courts did not pose a major obstacle to state-level forest conservation efforts. Constitutional objections were usually debated in legislative arenas before cases came to court, and judges were largely (but not unanimously) supporting players in the forest conservation movement.

The Forest Conservation Movement

The forest conservation movement, like the wildlife conservation movement, developed in the decades after the Civil War, reflecting both popular and scientific concern about the state of the country's forests.[1] Throughout the nineteenth century, farmers were encouraged to maintain woodlots and cultivate individual trees for both their economic and their aesthetic values. This perspective was promoted by the American Forestry Association, founded by John Warder in Ohio in 1875. As historian Samuel Hays notes, this organization was composed of botanists, landscape gardeners, and estate owners. They promoted planting trees (supporting, for example, the creation of Arbor Day as a national holiday) but were not initially focused on forest management.[2]

Joining this aesthetic interest in trees were economic concerns driven by the growing market for wood after the Civil War. Demand for wood increased dramatically during these decades, putting considerable pressure on the nation's forests.[3] Historian Michael Williams estimates that the nation's total consumption of wood was about 3.76 billion cubic feet per year in 1859 and had nearly doubled by 1879 to 6.84 billion cubic feet per year. It continued to rise to 13.38 billion cubic feet/year by 1907, stabilizing at 10–11 billion cubic feet/year throughout the rest of the twentieth century.[4] Thus, once a seemingly inexhaustible resource, by the 1870s the nation's forests were a subject of considerable anxiety among timber industry experts and policy makers. This economic concern with maintaining a supply of wood and other forest products brought the forest conservation movement into conversation with these industry and business interests.

But scientists, too, were promoting forest conservation. The scientific basis for the movement was developed in detail by George Perkins Marsh's 1864 masterpiece, *Man and Nature*. One of the most influential books in American conservation history, Marsh's book focused on the importance of forests to a healthy agriculture, with particular attention to their effects on the hydrological cycle. Drawing on a wealth of scientific authority, he argued that forests help to preserve and regulate streamflow—a relatively uncontroversial proposition at the time—and may also increase rainfall. This second claim was less well-accepted, but after reviewing the evidence for and against it, Marsh concluded that "both theoretical considerations and the balance of testimony strongly favor the opinion that more rain falls in wooded than in open countries."[5]

The evidence in favor of the effect of trees on rainfall was enough to persuade Franklin Hough, of the American Association for the Advancement of Science, that planting trees was the key to a prosperous agriculture, especially in the arid West. In 1873, after reading *Man and Nature*, he delivered a paper titled "On the Duty of Governments in the Preservation of Forests" and followed up by urging Congress to create a national forestry commission. The cause was taken up by Congressman Mark Dunnell of Wisconsin, whose home state had recently been devastated by the Great Peshtigo forest fire of 1871. In 1876, he succeeded in persuading Congress to create a forest commission to study the nation's forests, and Hough was appointed to lead it.[6] In 1881, Hough would become chief of the new Division of Forestry in the USDA (the predecessor of the Forest Service). In that capacity, he issued several reports advocating changes in federal forest policy.

Institutional development was proceeding at the state level as well. The first meeting of the American Forest Congress in Cincinnati in 1882 produced a burst of activity at the state level, as delegates returned to their respective states and began campaigning for forest conservation. As a result, several states created forest commissions during the 1880s and 1890s.[7] Both the state and federal commissions focused primarily on educating the public and policy makers about forest management issues. But some of the state commissions did attend to forest management directly, for example, by organizing fire-suppression patrols and building lookout stations. In fact, taking advantage of wildlife conservation successes, some local authorities deputized game wardens as fire wardens.[8] A few states showed even more ambition. New York, a leader in the field, created a forest commission in 1885 with the authority to hire a forest warden, inspectors, and clerks; appoint fire wardens; and prosecute people for trespass on state forest lands. Pennsylvania, too, created a Department of Agriculture with a Division of Forestry in 1895. In 1897, the Pennsylvania legislature authorized the creation of forest reserves, raised the Division of Forestry to department status, and hired a professional state forester in 1901. It established the Pennsylvania State Forest Academy in 1906.[9] But funding for these state efforts was usually quite limited, and state foresters often lacked authority, even the authority to regulate cutting or suppress fires.

Like protecting wildlife, protecting the nation's forests would require the expansion of state authority.

Policy Rationales for Forest Conservation

The commodity value of forests was more obvious to nineteenth-century policy makers than was the commodity value of wildlife, and the economic consequences of diminishing forest resources was a major theme in public discourse about forests. The movement also enjoyed support in some states from populist critics worried about the timber industry's monopolizing of public lands.[10] Nevertheless, there were few precedents in nineteenth-century policy for prohibiting the economic development of forested land, and late-nineteenth-century laissez-faire ideology didn't support direct intervention by government to conserve natural resources. To persuade reluctant legislators that such policies were justified, conservationists offered several additional arguments.

One of the most successful of these was the value of preserving "natural wonders." Indeed, this rationale constituted California senator Conness's entire argument in favor of granting Yosemite Valley and Mariposa Big Tree Grove to California in 1864, to create a state park. As he explained to the Senate, the valley and grove of giant sequoias constitute "one of the greatest wonders of the world." Although he acknowledged that such a grant of federal land to a state for the purposes of creating a park was "unprecedented," this action was warranted by the extraordinary nature of this landscape. The Mariposa Big Tree Grove contains "magnificent monarchs of the forest," estimated to be at least three thousand years old. His colleagues in the Senate and the House were impressed and passed the measure with little further discussion.

Although its critics often described this policy rationale as a concern with mere "scenery," several values were thought to be served by preserving (or creating) natural beauty. The economic, recreational, and public health value of parks had become a major focus of urban communities, particularly with the construction of Central Park in New York City in 1857. Central Park was not only supposed to provide recreational opportunities and increase land values in Manhattan; it was meant to maintain social order by easing stress and improving the health of urban dwellers.[11] As historian William Irwin notes, similar "quality of life" arguments would support the creation of parks outside of city limits, such as Niagara Falls. Indeed, the 1880s movement to create a state park at Niagara Falls captures some of the complexity of the economics of natural beauty: Although the movement, led by the nation's premier landscape architect Frederick Law Olmstead, appealed to natural beauty, patriotism, and other high-minded ideals, it was also supported by business owners in Niagara. They were seeing their summer tourist trade fall off because private ownership of land around the Falls had created a landscape of tawdry tourist traps—appealing to day visitors, but not to the resort trade. In other words, the business community was beginning to understand that to maintain their economic value, natural wonders had to be managed carefully, ideally by a public authority *not* concerned with short-term profit.[12]

The campaign to preserve the Adirondacks forests, which began in the 1860s, similarly cited the economic benefits of tourism to the region. But advocates also emphasized the public health benefits of providing urban dwellers with access to green space and fresh air. The Adirondacks had gained a reputation as a healthy location to recover from tuberculosis, and by the 1880s, the health tourism trade had become an additional reason to preserve the forested mountains.[13] Much of the same rhetoric appeared in arguments for national parks in the West. The *New York Times*, for example, described Yosemite as both a "pleasure ground" and a "sanitarium," implying that it would offer health benefits similar to those of the Adirondacks.[14]

Nevertheless, restricting land from private development was always controversial, and it was important to Senator Conness's argument that the Yosemite Valley had little economic value other than tourism. That point also supported the effort to create Yellowstone National Park in 1872. This proposal received more attention in Congress than did the Yosemite bill, since it proposed that the federal government retain control of the park and would therefore have to manage it. The primary rationale for Yellowstone Park was the same as that offered for Yosemite: the land had no other obvious economic use, and it contained natural wonders, including (in Congressman Dawes's words) "sublime scenery" and "the most wonderful geysers ever found in the country."[15] Yellowstone Park also received support from the wildlife conservation movement, as it was intended as a wildlife sanctuary; hunting and fishing were prohibited.[16] In the Senate, however, the bill did get some criticism: Senator Cole opined that there was no good reason to set aside land in the Rocky Mountains as a public park, when much of the mountainous region would not be suitable for settlement anyway. If the proposed park was not suited to agriculture, he thought protection was unnecessary; if it was suited to agriculture, then it should be open to settlers.[17] The bill was passed over his objection, and subsequent national parks met with very little objection. But most public parks during this period were created within forest reserves—on lands *already* reserved from settlement. Cole's skepticism about Yellowstone reflected not so much a reluctance to protect rare natural wonders as a growing resistance in Congress to reserving large tracts of public lands from settlement.

That resistance required forest advocates to develop stronger arguments, and the conservation movement responded by drawing on environmental science—specifically, the arguments surveyed in *Man and Nature* concerning forests' connection to rainfall and streamflow. As mentioned above, Franklin Hough was persuaded that forests could promote rainfall, but that controversial claim was not as influential as Marsh's other hydrological hypothesis: Forests protect streamflow. This claim proved to be critical to influencing skeptical policy makers.

Marsh explained in some detail what today we would call an ecosystem service provided by forests: "It is well established that the protection afforded by the forest against the escape of moisture from the soil, insures the permanence and regularity of natural springs. . . . As the forests are destroyed, the springs which flowed from the woods, and, consequently, the greater watercourses fed by them, diminish both in number and in volume."[18] He cited a number of factors that account for this dynamic, but the primary one is that the roots of trees and leaf litter increase the soil's ability to absorb and retain precipitation, making it like a "sponge."[19] As we will see, by the early twentieth century, the scientific consensus reported by Marsh would begin to break down. But during most of the late nineteenth century, the weight of authority and popular opinion supported Marsh's streamflow argument.[20]

Given the nation's dependence on waterways for transportation, streamflow was a subject of broad economic concern. The argument that forest reserves were necessary to protect streamflow would play a central role in the New York campaign to protect the Adirondacks in the 1880s, and the streamflow argument also became prominent in congressional debates over forest policy. For example, a lengthy debate over the boundaries of Yellowstone Park in 1892 showed that congressional resistance to national parks was growing. Senator Berry confessed that he didn't understand how the park benefited anyone other than a few wealthy tourists. Senator Call, in response, made an eloquent case for securing equal access to natural wonders for all Americans but also emphasized the value of preserving "the timber and the rainfall, which is a scientific fact now demonstrated."[21] (It is worth noting that Yosemite and Yellowstone are both located at the headwaters of important river systems: Yosemite protects the Merced River headwaters and Yellowstone protects the headwaters of several great rivers.) As we will see, the streamflow argument would become even more important as resistance to forest reservations grew in the 1890s and early twentieth century.

In sum, like the wildlife conservation movement, forest conservationists developed several (sometimes conflicting) arguments for protecting forests. And as long as the movement was focused on state conservation efforts, most of the policy arguments for forest conservation were accepted by courts as legitimate objects of governmental action. This is in part because most of these arguments were rooted in economic development and public health, traditional functions of state government. But it was also because forest conservation was pursued primarily through governmental acquisition of land, rather than through restricting the activities of private individuals. Although state intervention in the forest economy sometimes crossed constitutional lines, in general, forest conservation advocates faced few constitutional barriers to state efforts to preserve forests. As the movement shifted its focus to the federal level, however, constitutional problems would multiply, and ecological science would become even more central to justifying forest conservation.

Nineteenth-Century Constitutional Framework for Forest Conservation

Franklin Hough's first report to Congress on federal forest policy recognized the constitutional dimension of forest management in the United States: Most forested land in the United States, he asserted, is privately owned. Unlike Europe, where forests are often owned by government or communes, forests in the United States are typically held by a private owner who has "no other obligation to others, further than to bear his just share of the expenses of government for the general protection of property and the maintenance of good order."[22]

Of course, strictly speaking, this claim was true only in the eastern United States. As of 1867, when the federal government acquired the Alaskan territory, the public domain constituted about 81 percent of the nation, and much of it was forested.[23] But Hough was correct in a more general sense: The federal government's policy was to turn the public domain over to settlement, and if it proceeded as planned, most of the nation's forests would soon be in private hands. The constitutional norm in the United States was private, not public, ownership of natural resources.

And American government, as a constitutional matter, seemed to have little authority to protect these privately held forests. True, states have the police power: the general power to regulate private conduct to protect the health and safety of the community. But Hough apparently did not believe that the police power would extend to regulating private forest management. The only useful constitutional authority that he could identify was the eminent domain power: the power to take private land, with compensation, for public purposes.[24] Both state and federal governments enjoyed eminent domain authority. But in general, Hough opined that the state governments were probably limited to educating private forest owners on good management techniques.

Hough recognized that the federal government did have authority (under the Property Clause, Article IV, Section 3) to manage its own forests.[25] But he also demonstrated a good grasp of the distance between law on the books and law on the ground:

> Whatever may be the legal rights involved, it cannot be denied that timber growing upon government lands in the newer States and in the Territories, is often loosely regarded as applicable to the wants of the settlers. . . . Such native growths appear to be regarded, like wild fruits, a proper object for use wherever found, and it is not until timber is planted and cared for by an owner that it comes to be regarded as the property of the soil.[26]

Hough thus identified precisely the constitutional problem of forest conservation. As discussed in chapter 1, the government's authority over wildlife derived from the legal rules concerning water, and water (under English common law) was usually treated as a commons to which individuals had only use-rights. That somewhat anomalous foundation gave rise to a unique set of constitutional principles, allowing states greater authority to regulate wildlife than our constitutional traditions would normally allow. Land, in contrast, is usually privately owned by holders who enjoy extensive rights to manage it in any way they choose (as long as they don't interfere with others' property rights). Government restrictions on the use of private forests would therefore be a striking departure from American constitutional traditions. Indeed, even the government's authority to manage its own lands was uncertain, as settlers had come to regard public lands as open-access resources, like "wild fruits," available to anyone who cares to use them.

Hough also correctly identified eminent domain as one of the principle legal devices that would be used to overcome this limited governmental authority over private lands. But the eminent domain power was also limited; it allowed land to be taken only for "public use." In short, the government's authority to protect forests was less clear than its power to protect wildlife.

Of course, one way to ensure that legislatures have constitutional authority to protect forests is to write that authority into the constitution. Several states did just that. While it was far more common for states to address water resources in constitutional reform (especially in the arid western states), several states specifically provided that their legislatures could engage in forest conservation, including most famously New York,[27] but also Utah,[28] Ohio,[29] Massachusetts,[30] Louisiana,[31] Minnesota,[32] and Wisconsin.[33] These efforts, however, did not always represent or lead to a significant advance in forest conservation. For example, Colorado was the first state to include a forest conservation provision in its constitution, at the urging of Frederick Ebert, a professional forester who participated in the 1875 Colorado constitutional convention. Ebert is responsible for Article XVIII, Section 6 of the Colorado Constitution: "The General Assembly shall enact laws in order to prevent the destruction of, and to keep in good preservation, the forests upon the lands of the state, or upon lands of public domain, the control of which shall be conferred by Congress upon the State." But Ebert's interest in forest conservation wasn't widely shared, and the legislature did not actually create a forest program until 1891. The very short-lived program died when the federal government put most of the state's forests into federal reserves.[34] Utah and Ohio also failed to follow through on the conservation sentiment that led to their constitutional amendments.[35] On the other hand, several states, such as Pennsylvania, pursued ambitious forest conservation programs without explicit constitutional authorization.[36]

This history underscores the point made in the introduction, that constitutional change in the United States does not always, or even typically, happen through the formal amendment process. More commonly, constitutional change is a process in which legislatures and courts interact to produce new policies and new doctrines (or new interpretations of constitutional principles) to support them. That process is illustrated, for example, in the New York campaign to protect the Adirondack forest. This was perhaps the most ambitious state-level forest preservation policy, and it involved constitutional amendment, legislative and administrative action, and influential decisions out of the New York Court of Appeals and the US Supreme Court—all of which worked to establish forest preservation as a "public use."

The Adirondack Campaign and Public Use Doctrine

The vast forest of the Adirondacks became a focus of a New York–based forest conservation movement in the 1870s. The Adirondacks forest was mostly privately owned and had been subject to continual logging from its first settlement by Europeans. The pace of logging picked up in the post–Civil War Era, when demand for wood was increasing rapidly. Unfortunately, that was the same time that the Adirondacks became a favorite resort locale for New York elites. The *New York Times* in 1864 was already suggesting that some parts of the Adirondacks should be protected from logging so that they could be enjoyed for their natural beauty, healthy air, and recreational opportunities.[37] But as historian Frank Graham recounts, the winning argument in the campaign for conservation was developed by the movement's primary leader, Verplanck Colvin, a naturalist from Albany. Colvin explored Mount Seward in the Adirondacks in 1870 and made a report to the New York State Museum of Natural History, which was included in its annual report to the state legislature. Colvin's report added, at the end, the following argument for preservation:

> The Adirondack wilderness contains the springs which are the sources of our principal rivers, and the feeders of our canals. Each summer the water supply for these rivers and canals is lessened, and commerce has suffered. . . . The immediate cause has been the chopping and burning off of vast tracts of forest in the wilderness, which have hitherto sheltered from the sun's heat and evaporation the deep and lingering snows, the brooks and rivulets, and the thick, soaking, sphagnous moss. . . . It is impossible for those who have not visited this region to realize the abundance, luxuriance and depth which these peaty mosses—the true sources of our rivers—attain under the shade of those dark, northern, evergreen forests.[38]

Colvin would continue to press this argument that protecting the forests was necessary to preserve streamflow (and commerce), and the legislature was eventually persuaded to appoint a commission of state parks, including Colvin and the indefatigable Franklin Hough. The commission's 1873 report emphasized the importance of the forest to protecting the watershed that fed the Erie Canal, which opened the New York Harbor and Hudson River to western lands.

Of course, this hydrological argument was not the only policy rationale for protecting the Adirondacks; other groups would join the movement, including sportsmen worried about the disappearing fish and game, business owners worried about the tourist trade, and an influential group of wealthy New York elites who favored the Adirondacks as a resort. But the legislature was ultimately convinced by Colvin's theory that forest preservation was necessary to protect streamflow in the all-important Hudson-Erie system.[39] In 1883, as Frank Graham points out, New York experienced a severe drought that reduced water levels in the state's principal rivers. This event focused the attention of New York City's business community on the issue of streamflow. Legislative action on the Adirondacks, which had been stalled since 1873, finally responded to this economic threat. The legislature prohibited the sale of state lands in ten Adirondacks counties, authorized the state comptroller to acquire disputed titles, and designated certain lands as a "Forest Preserve."[40]

Much of the land within the Forest Preserve remained privately owned, however, and even state-owned land was not well-protected from forest fires and illegal logging. Thus, conditions in the Adirondacks continued to deteriorate, and forest conservationists continued to agitate for protection. They were able to generate enough support during the 1894 New York constitutional convention to amend the state constitution, providing: "The lands of the state, now owned or hereafter acquired, constituting the Forest Preserve as now fixed by law, shall be forever kept as wild forest lands. They shall not be leased, sold or exchanged, or be taken by any corporation, public or private, nor shall the timber thereon by sold, removed, or destroyed."[41] This is the famous "Forever Wild" provision of which the forest conservation movement is quite proud. But it may not be clear why supporters thought a constitutional amendment necessary. After all, the provision merely establishes a policy concerning how the State will manage land it already owns. The state legislature already had full constitutional authority to hold on to the Forest Preserve lands that it owned and to prohibit logging them. This constitutional provision did not affect the scope or distribution of government power at all.

This point underscores a chief difference between state and federal constitutional politics. It was fairly common throughout the nineteenth century for legislative policies to end up in state constitutions. Easier to amend than the federal Constitution, state constitutions were often used to set long-term policy—in this case, to protect forests against powerful interests (the lumber industry) pursuing short-term gains.[42] Because it was not actually expanding government authority, the "Forever Wild" provision should not have raised any constitutional problems. But in fact, legislative action under that provision did face a constitutional challenge almost immediately. *New York v. Adirondack Railway Company*[43] is worth reviewing in some detail, because it illustrates the prevailing constitutional framework for state-level forest conservation.

The controversy began in 1897, when the legislature authorized the forest preserve board to acquire land within the Adirondacks park, either through voluntary purchase or through eminent domain. The board accordingly arranged to acquire an extensive tract of land within the park, known as the Totten and Crossfield purchase. Unfortunately, the Adirondack Railway Company had plans to build a railroad over that land. It had progressed as far as conducting a survey and filing a map and profile of the planned route in the affected counties but had not yet negotiated purchase of the land.

The railway company managed to persuade a judge that, based on its map and profile filing, it had some sort of lien on the land in question. The judge accordingly issued an injunction against the owners of the land, preventing them from completing the sale to the forest board. The forest board, unable to persuade the judge to vacate the injunction, accordingly initiated condemnation proceedings to acquire the land. On the same day (but later in the afternoon), the railway company also started its own proceedings to condemn the land in question. (The legislature had granted the company this eminent domain power when the company was first formed, a common practice to facilitate the construction of railroads.)

The state sought an injunction to stop the railroad company's condemnation proceeding, and that is the case that ended up in New York's highest court in 1899. The state won in the trial court, but that judgement was reversed on appeal. The New York Court of Appeals reversed the intermediate appellate decision, giving judgment to the state.

The railway company's principal argument was that it had a property right in the Totten and Crossfield land and that the state's condemnation proceeding therefore violated the Due Process Clauses of the state and federal constitutions by infringing on this property right. It also complained that, even if the condemnation proceeding were valid, it should get some compensation for the land it intended to acquire. Neither argument prevailed. Judge Vann rejected the fundamental basis of the railway's claim, concluding that it had not acquired a vested interest (that is, a legally recognized right) to the land in question simply by filing notice of its plans. But Judge Vann also addressed the constitutionality of the forest board's actions in some detail, beginning with the due process claim.

We have encountered due process arguments before, challenging state regulations on hunting and fishing. Such arguments typically focus on the state's use of the police power, its general regulatory power to protect its citizens' welfare. In this case, however, the railway company was challenging the state's use of its eminent domain power. The judge pointed out that the power to take property for public use differs from the police power. While the due process clause requires that the use of the police power must be "reasonable," the eminent domain power is subject to only two limitations: The property must be taken for a public use and just compensation must be paid.

The railway had apparently not pressed the argument that creating a park was not a legitimate public use, but the judge addressed the question anyway, perhaps because there was in fact some doubt about the question. As legal scholar Errol Meidinger points out, several legal authorities, in the nineteenth century and earlier, had expressed doubt that property could be condemned for mere "ornamental" or aesthetic purposes.[44] But Meidinger also points out that as of the 1890s, there was "no developed doctrine, nor even sharply defined rationale, to support this opinion."[45] Actually, the more controversial use of the eminent domain power was authorizing a private corporation to use eminent domain to develop some for-profit service, like a mill dam or a railroad.[46] That may be why the railway didn't pursue this argument; creating a park that was intended to be open to "use by the public" looked more like a traditional use of the eminent domain power than did the railroad's use of the power to further its private enterprise. In any case, Judge Vann had no difficulty in determining that the forest board was taking the land for a public use: "The object of the legislature was to create a great public park for the promotion not only of health and pleasure, but of commerce as well. The statute declares that it is 'for the free use of all the people for their health and pleasure,' as well as 'the preservation of the head waters of the chief rivers of the state, and a future timber supply.'"[47] Thus, the judge embraced almost all the usual rationales for forest reservations, leaving out only wildlife conservation: health, pleasure, streamflow protection (essential to commerce), and future timber supply. He cited for support several cases upholding the use of eminent domain to create parks in cities.[48]

The railway appealed to the US Supreme Court, but that court agreed with Judge Vann on all points, including his takings clause analysis. Chief Justice Fuller noted:

> The lands taken for the park were thereby dedicated to a public use regarded by the State as of such vital importance to the people that they were expressly put by the [state] constitution beyond the reach of any other destination. The general rule is that the necessity or expediency of appropriating particular property for public use is not a matter of judicial cognizance but one for the determination of the legislative branch of the government, and this must obviously be so where the State takes for its own purposes.[49]

Far from treating the park as merely "ornamental," Fuller was clearly impressed that the people of New York had thought it of "vital importance," warranting constitutional status. But he also emphasized that the court played a very limited role in evaluating the legitimacy of the state's purpose in taking property.

This deferential attitude toward the "public use" requirement of the Takings Clause supported the use of eminent domain to protect forests and other environmental amenities during this period. Moreover, it also helped state legislatures establish aesthetics, recreation, and other "quality of life" goals as legitimate state purposes justifying the use of the police power. Indeed, the constitutional status of the Adirondacks forest preserve helped to justify extending the police power, as we see in the 1917 *Barrett v. New York*[50] case, discussed in chapter 2. That case upheld the use of the police power to protect wildlife in the Adirondacks forest, even at the expense of property rights. But notice also the important place that "protecting commerce" played in justifying this forest program. Even though judges consistently supported efforts to create parks for purely aesthetic and health reasons, policy makers continued to press (and judges continued to endorse) the commodity and ecosystem services rationale for forest conservation.

The New York case is a good example of how the legislature's authority to protect forests can become "constitutional common sense" through formal amendment, legislative policy, administrative action, and judicial decision. But not all states enjoyed such broad institutional support for forest conservation. As the forest conservation movement pursued more ambitious restrictions on private use of forests, state forest programs encountered more difficulties on the path to constitutional status. Nevertheless, the experience of the states throughout this period demonstrates a general trend: Despite some misgivings, judicial opinion in general was moving in favor of forest conservation.

Constitutionalizing Forest Conservation

Two prominent opinions, out of Maine and New Jersey, illustrate the potential constitutional difficulties with regulating private forests. The Maine legislature had created a forest commissioner in 1891 whose primary responsibility was to prevent forest fires but had not given him the funding or administrative support to accomplish much.[51] Disastrous fires in 1903 and 1908 finally prompted the legislature to act, and in the 1908 session it considered a "Bill for the Preservation of Forests and Water Supply." The bill would prevent the cutting of spruce and pine less than twelve inches in diameter (with exceptions for landowners cutting wood for their own use). Such a direct restriction on private lumber companies was (as far as I can tell) unprecedented; most states had limited their conservation measures to protecting state-owned land and educating private landowners about good forest management. This measure aimed to halt the clear-cutting practices of the large lumber companies that owned most of the Maine forests. Unsurprisingly, it ran into fierce opposition. The House had already tabled it when the Senate asked the Maine Supreme Court for an advisory opinion[52] on the measure's constitutionality.

The Supreme Court advised the Senate that the measure was clearly constitutional. Although the Maine Constitution didn't explicitly authorize the legislature to protect forests, it did grant the legislature the general police power.[53] Regulations enacted under this power are valid "however inconvenienced, restricted, or even damaged particular persons and corporations may be," unless specifically prohibited by some constitutional principle. The obvious candidate for such a principle was the Due Process

Clause of the Fourteenth Amendment of the US Constitution, which was commonly used to strike down "unreasonable" regulations, or the Maine Declaration of Rights, which explicitly protected property rights. But the Maine judges thought these clauses no bar to a state's ability to "increase the industries of the state, develop its resources and add to its wealth and prosperity."[54] (Notice how they characterize forest preservation as a kind of economic development—a point we will return to later in the discussion of Wisconsin's forest preservation efforts.)

The Court also considered whether this regulation took property without just compensation. It acknowledged that some courts did think a regulation of property might constitute a "taking" of property for public use. But it endorsed the reasoning of the eminent Massachusetts jurist Justice Shaw: "We think it a settled principle, growing out of the nature of well ordered civil society, that every holder of property . . . holds it under the implied liability that his use of it shall be so regulated that it shall not be injurious to the equal enjoyment of others . . . nor injurious to the rights of the community."[55] The Court agreed with those cases holding that private property can only be said to have been taken for public use when the public is given well-defined rights to its use—as when the state creates a highway, ferry, or railroad.[56] Turning to the regulation in question, the court noted that property in land "is not the result of productive labor" but was acquired through a grant from the original owner—the state. Moreover, land is "incapable of increase," and "if owners of large tracts can waste them at will without state restriction, the state and its people may be helplessly impoverished." The regulation, although it may interfere with the owners' profits, would nevertheless "leave him his lands, their product and increase, untouched. . . . He would still have large measure of control and large opportunity to realize values."[57]

The opinion sounds like a resounding victory for forest conservation; indeed, President Roosevelt quoted it approvingly at the National Governors' Conference that same year, in support of his national forest conservation efforts.[58] But it had little impact on forest conservation in Maine. The Senate did not act on the bill, and the measure died. Instead, private landowners in Maine came up with an innovative alternative: They created a Fire Control District, and landowners within the district *voluntarily* assessed themselves and turned the revenue over to the Forest Commissioner, to implement fire control strategies. Judicial opinion notwithstanding, the powerful timber industry—the most important industry in the state and owner of almost all the forest land—ensured that in Maine, protection of forests would remain a matter of voluntary measures.

New Jersey's attempt to control forest fires, while more successful, also ran into constitutional difficulties. Unlike Maine, New Jersey was thickly settled, and its primary difficulty was managing forests, and especially preventing forest fires, near human settlements. It created its forest program in 1905, establishing a Forest Park Reservation Committee with the power to acquire and manage lands and to appoint fire wardens.[59] The state was particularly concerned with the Pine Barrens, which were vulnerable to devastating fires. It pursued several policies to reduce this threat, none of which were particularly controversial until the legislature passed the Railroad Fire Line Law in 1909. This law required railroads that passed through woodlands to create a fire barrier under the direction of the Forest Commission. The Forest Commission ruled that fire barriers must be 110 feet wide, which meant that if there was forest on both sides of the track, the fire barrier would have to be at least 225 feet wide. The railroads complied, which led to the complaint from James Vreeland, who owned land through which the Erie Railroad passed. Vreeland objected that the law was unconstitutional because it took his land without compensation, and in 1913, the New Jersey Court of Appeals (the highest court) unanimously agreed with him.

The Forest Commission argued that this law was merely an ordinary exercise of the police power—a restriction on property to protect the public welfare. But the court held that completely clearing the land down to the bare earth would "deprive the complainant of all beneficial use of the land involved."[60] It continued,

> The sole purpose of the statute is to protect the public from a nonexistent, but possible condition, if sparks of fire should be thrown from the engines of the defendant railroad company, running over land adjacent to that of the complainant, and for that purpose authorizes the appropriation of private lands lying adjacent to railroads for the purpose of preventing the spread of fires, caused by the railroad company, for the benefit of property other than that of the owner of the land taken.[61]

In short, this measure was not a regulation of use of the property by the owner; it looked more like taking it from the owner altogether. If the state wants to do this, it must use the eminent domain power and compensate the owner.

The *Vreeland* case demonstrates that there were limits to the police power, even against as great a threat to human welfare as forest fires. But New Jersey's regulation was extreme, and the decision didn't prevent the state from pursuing a variety of other forest protection measures. A broader challenge to forest conservation came from the Wisconsin Supreme Court in 1915. This decision highlights one of the constitutionally problematic aspects of relying on economic rationales for conservation. While basic forest conservation usually looked like a simple restriction on economic development to protect public values (like the New Jersey fire line law), the more ambitious programs could look like a form of state-directed economic development that competed with private initiatives. The more a state forest preserve looked like an economic enterprise, the more constitutionally suspect it was, as the Wisconsin case illustrates.

Wisconsin and "Internal Improvements"

A 1924 amendment to the Wisconsin Constitution authorized the legislature to use money from the treasury or raised through taxes for "the purpose of acquiring, preserving and developing the forests of the state." One might think that by 1924, there would be little need to clarify that state governments could use the eminent domain and police power to protect forests. But this amendment proved to be necessary to overcome another provision in the state's constitution, a specific prohibition on state government contracting debt to fund works of "internal improvement" unless specifically authorized by the state constitution. Legal scholar Jack Stark offers a helpful explanation of the context for the "internal improvement" provision: Several states in the mid-nineteenth century sought to replicate New York's success with the Erie Canal by attempting their own large-scale public works projects. Unfortunately, many of those projects failed, leaving the states with crippling debt. The 1847 Wisconsin Constitutional Convention sought to guard against such decisions with this prohibition. Only a few kinds of internal improvements—public roads, for example— were allowed.[62]

While this prohibition on "internal improvements" was motivated by concerns over state debt, it was also part of a larger nineteenth-century constitutional debate over the role of government (state or federal) in economic development. As mentioned in the introduction, at the federal level, spending for internal improvements such as roads, canals, and railroads was a central issue in sectional conflict. Within states, too, critics charged that state support for large-scale public works would displace private initiative and unfairly tax those citizens who were not in a position to benefit from them.

This debate over internal improvements was central to efforts to protect public lands, as we see in *State ex rel. Owen v. Donald.*[63] This 1915 decision by the Wisconsin Supreme Court held that many aspects of the state's forest conservation program constituted "internal improvements," so the state could not contract debt to fund it. The case arose out of an attempt by the state forester to purchase land to add to the state's forest preserve. The forest program, enacted in 1911, was one of Wisconsin's major Progressive initiatives, and it granted the state forester broad authority to buy land to create the preserve. Importantly, it also provided that the preserve would be partially self-funded by the revenues generated by the sale of forest products. The state accordingly purchased about 90,000 acres of cutover land from various lumber companies, including the G. F. Sanborn Company. Most of the purchases were in the form of land contracts, with payments to be made in installments.

By 1915, $20,000 was still due on the Sanborn contract. But the Progressives were no longer in power, and the new governor opposed the forest program. The secretary of state refused to pay the final installment, claiming it violated several provisions of the state constitution. The attorney general (on behalf of the Sanborn Company) asked the court to order the secretary of state to honor the contract.[64] The petition came to the Wisconsin Supreme Court, which denied it.

Judge Roujet Marshall found three constitutional difficulties with the forest program: It violated a provision putting restrictions on the state's ability to contract debts exceeding $100,000,[65] the program included lands that were designated to be set aside for educational purposes, and the program violated a specific prohibition in Article VIII, Section 10, on contracting debt for internal improvements. This last issue is most interesting for us, since it implicates a broader constitutional question about the state's role in the economy. More specifically, it raises the question of how to categorize conservation for constitutional purposes: Is it economic development or a restriction on economic development?

The Attorney General, defending the forest program, argued the latter. He reasoned that normally improving forested land means clearing it. Allowing the forest to grow would be leaving the land in a state of nature, and thus unimproved. Moreover, he argued that the expression "internal improvement" nearly always implies facilitation of transportation—roads, canals, turnpikes, railroads, and so on. But Judge Marshall read the "internal improvement" prohibition more broadly, as encompassing "those things which ordinarily might, in human experience, be expected to be undertaken for profit or benefit to the property interests of private promoters, as distinguished from those other things which primarily and preponderantly facilitate the essential functions of government."[66] He relied on an earlier decision (*State ex rel. Jones v. Froehlich*[67]), in which the same court held that constructing and strengthening the levee system around the Wisconsin River constituted an internal improvement.

Marshall insisted that the mere fact that the forest program served public purposes did not mean it wasn't an internal improvement. He acknowledged that forest preservation could indeed provide a host of benefits to the general public, including improving climatic conditions, protecting and regulating streamflow in rivers whose sources are in the reserve area, preserving and cultivating the animal life of forests and streams, and conserving facilities for hunting, fishing, and otherwise enjoying life on wild unsettled lands (thus endorsing the usual ecosystem services rationales for forest conservation).[68] But these public benefits notwithstanding, the forest preserve program looked to Marshall like a for-profit forestry enterprise.[69] Many of the environmental benefits of forest conservation accrued to the landowner directly, by improving the quality of the land and increasing its usefulness for producing waterpower, game, and wood products. Since private landowners should have sufficient economic incentive to pursue these ends, this program would seem to be the kind of thing normally left to private enterprise. And the prohibition on using debt to fund "internal improvements," he believed, was meant to restrict precisely this sort of state-funded economic development.

In reaching this conclusion, Marshall was clearly concerned about the self-financing part of the scheme. Instead of providing general revenues for the state, the money generated by the preserve would go back into the preserve. In contrast, if the land were turned over to private development, it ought to produce considerable general tax revenue. The program therefore constituted a "permanent removal of a vast property acquired at public expense from the field of opportunity for any return to the taxpayers of the present or even of the future."[70] He apparently did not consider the idea that environmental benefits of the forest preserve might also constitute a valuable return on the land to taxpayers.

This ruling alone would have been sufficient to defeat the attorney general's case. But the judge decided to take this opportunity to weigh in on a much broader question: "Is it competent for the legislature to burden the people with taxation to raise money to purchase land for a large forest reserve, the anticipated benefits of which will, necessarily, be postponed to some indefinite time in the distant future, and to likewise burden the people with the expense of cultivating such lands for public benefit?"[71] That is, could the legislature use ordinary tax revenue to pursue forest conservation? The counsel for the secretary of state contended that such appropriations are *not* legitimate expenses of state government—that is, forest conservation is simply not within the police power at all. Marshall, however, was not quite willing to go that far.[72] However, he did agree that using tax money to create a perpetual forest reserve was constitutionally problematic. Although other states were creating forest reserves (he considered efforts in New Hampshire, Maine, Minnesota, Michigan, Pennsylvania, and New York), he thought it significant that those programs involved lands already owned by the state or donated for conservation purposes, or else they were authorized by a specific constitutional amendment. This program, in contrast, involved using tax revenue to buy land, and the tax power, he argued, was inherently limited to "public purposes."[73] Taxes must benefit the public—but even further, there must be some *reciprocal* advantage to the taxpayer: "The taxing district obtains the contribution to the public treasury and the contributor, in return, receives a legal consideration of a pecuniary or protective nature to his person or his property or both."[74] This language captures the social contract idea in American constitutional thought: Government was created by the citizens to protect their rights (including their property rights). How to square this principle with a program that imposes "large public burdens upon the people of the present without any hope of return to them . . .—burdens imposed with the avowed purpose of accumulating benefits for generations yet unborn" he found "somewhat puzzling."[75]

Nevertheless, Marshall was forced to admit that "where reasonably necessary the conservation of forests and conservative reproduction of them has been, time out of mind, one of the well recognized ways of promoting the public welfare," and so the goal intended by the program does lie within the police power.[76] But he reminded us (citing several decisions interpreting the due process clause) that "the means [used by the state] must be reasonably adapted to the particular end and must not be so burdensome as regards private rights as to outweigh any reasonably probable benefit from the interference." Moreover, "what would be reasonable in any particular field would depend upon circumstances."[77] Thus, "Reforestation activity, in an old and thickly settled country where necessity, in the near future, for increase of fuel supply and for storing and equalizing the flow of natural waters is apparent, would be quite reasonable, the degree of activity and weight of public burden being in some rational degree proportionate to the exigencies of the case."[78] That describes pretty well the situation of the eastern states, such as New Hampshire, Maine, New York, and Pennsylvania, where state forest conservation programs were most advanced and where the streamflow rationale was a dominant theme in forest preservation. However,

> In a country, more than half its territory unseated lands, in the whole sparsely settled and with no congestion probable for a long term of years, wood fuel in abundance within reasonable reach in that portion of the country which could be thus served more economically than with other fuel; little or no economy in prospect in the use of local timber supply for building purposes, and the natural conditions as to natural surface water supply quite ideal,—to conserve and increase forest products at public expense solely for the benefit of the people of the future, and under such conditions that the benefits would in the remote time be as likely to go to those outside the taxing jurisdiction as to those within it, would seem to be, at best, a great stretch of the police power.[79]

Here, Marshall reasoned, protecting streamflow was not a major problem, so this rationale for forest protection was less compelling. He concluded that forest conservation in Wisconsin (and presumably in Minnesota and Michigan) merely for the benefit of those shadowy future generations was constitutionally dubious.

Marshall's dicta must be read as a fairly strong criticism of using the police power for conservation. However, he put enough qualifications on his conclusion to render most state forestry programs perfectly acceptable. He agreed that the state could use general tax revenues to manage its current forested lands, possibly purchasing adjacent lands if necessary to good maintenance of the state-owned land. Indeed, he wrote, "There is a wide field of legitimate activity as to policing to prevent and protect against fire loss in the wooded portions of the state, or loss from fires originating on unoccupied lands, or liable to spread with dangerous consequences to other lands."[80] The state might also receive lands granted for educational or other public purposes and manage them according to conservation principles (as long as the goal were not to create a permanent forest reserve, and so fall afoul of the "internal improvement" prohibition.) In short, even Marshall had to concede most of the case for state forest conservation.[81] That case was put on even firmer constitutional ground by the 1924 amendment, specifically authorizing the legislature to use tax revenue for forest conservation.

Reservations like Marshall's may explain why many states adopted constitutional amendments specifically authorizing legislatures to protect forests. But textual amendments can backfire. For example, in the 1923 Ohio Supreme Court case *McNab v. Board of Park Commissioners*, the plaintiffs argued that the city was *limited* by a 1912 provision in the state constitution authorizing the state government to acquire land to conserve natural resources.[82] They argued that the amendment limited the state to creating parks only for conservation and not for recreational purposes. Fortunately for the park commission, the judge disagreed. But the case illustrates that textual amendments pose a risk that the terms might be read as restricting rather than expanding the state's power.

Overall, however, these cases suggest that despite complaints from landowners and worries about state interference in economic development, the state's authority to acquire and preserve land for forest conservation was firmly established by the end of the Progressive Era, either written into state constitutions or supported by judicial interpretation of the police and eminent domain powers. The state's interest in the commodity value of forest products, the protection offered by forests to streamflow (and thus commerce), along with the aesthetic, public health, and recreational value of forests were largely endorsed by judges. Thus the conception of forests as (what we today would call) a common pool resource providing important ecosystem services was firmly woven into constitutional doctrine during this period. But these decisions also show that courts were aware that "protecting" natural resources could become indistinguishable from "developing" natural resources. As we will see, their worries about using tax revenue to fund economic enterprises that would compete with private enterprise would also trouble forest conservation at the federal level.

The federal government's authority in this field would prove to be more uncertain. The federal government had no general police power, and the boundaries of its eminent domain power were accordingly less clear. Because the federal government had only those powers delegated to it in the Constitution, one could argue that there was a more limited set of legitimate public purposes for which it could take land. Of course, the federal government already owned a great deal of land, or was able to buy land from willing sellers, and so had little need of the eminent domain power in the early decades of the republic. The first Supreme Court decision affirming the federal government's authority to take land for public purposes did not appear until 1875. *Kohl v. United States*[83] upheld the treasury secretary's authority to acquire land for a post office, holding that the government had an inherent power to take land when necessary to carry out its proper functions. That decision, however, did not settle the question of what sort of purposes the federal government could pursue with this power.

That there were some limits on the federal government's power to take land was suggested by the 1892 case *Shoemaker v. United States*.[84] In that case, the Supreme Court upheld a condemnation proceeding to acquire land to create a park in the District of Columbia. Justice Shiras, writing the majority opinion, suggested that this use of the eminent domain power would once have been considered novel. But by 1892, most cities had public parks, and the use of eminent domain for this purpose had been uniformly upheld. The property owners argued that the federal government was more limited than were state governments and that creating public parks is not among its delegated powers. But Shiras pointed out that among the powers delegated to Congress was the exclusive power to legislate for the District of Columbia. While Congress did not have general police powers, it did have the equivalent of the police power for the District. So if a state government has authority to take lands for public parks, Congress can exercise the same authority in the District. The decision thus confirms the existence of a federal eminent domain power—but it also implies that the federal government can take land only to serve one of its specifically delegated powers.

To be sure, courts gave a great deal of deference to the federal government in evaluating the uses for which it could take land, as illustrated in the 1917 case *United States v. Graham and Irvine*.[85] A Virginia district court considered a challenge to the agriculture secretary's attempt to condemn land to create a forest reserve. The Act under which the Secretary proceeded—the 1911 Weeks Act—was the subject of a significant constitutional debate in Congress, as we will see. But by 1917, the major constitutional issues had been resolved, and Judge McDowell had no difficulty in confirming that the federal government's authority to condemn land for forest conservation had "been too long and too thoroughly settled to justify discussion."[86] The judge cited no decisions on the question, relying instead on the constitutional common sense that forest conservation is a legitimate function of federal government. Achieving that consensus was not, however, as simple as *United States v. Graham and Irvine* would suggest. Unlike the battle for state forest conservation, the battle for federal forest conservation raised significant constitutional objections.

CHAPTER FIVE

Western Forest Reserves

The campaign to reserve public land for forest reserves is the most well-known story in American conservation history. It features, for example, the battle between John Muir and Gifford Pinchot over whether forests should be preserved primarily for their noneconomic benefits or as part of a strategy for rational resource development. That conflict led to the creation of the National Park Service in 1916 and, eventually, to constitutional debates over wildlife management in national forests and parks (to be explored in chapter 7). The forest campaign also features the transfer of the national forests from the General Land Office in the Department of the Interior to the Forest Service in the USDA in 1905. The Transfer Act gave Pinchot, head of the Forest Service from 1905 to 1910, the resources to pursue coordinated natural resource management, national planning, and (importantly for us) legal reform.[1] Of course, it also led to the famed Ballinger/Pinchot affair in 1909–1910, which ended in Pinchot's dismissal and Ballinger's disgrace, and presaged the split in the Republican Party that would result in Roosevelt's third party run in 1912.

These events have been explored in painstaking detail by environmental historians.[2] But their constitutional dimensions have received less attention. Like the wildlife conservation movement, the forest conservation movement faced a considerable constitutional hurdle at the federal level: The Constitution gave the federal government no explicit authority to preserve natural resources for future generations. To be sure, it did grant the federal government authority over public lands (in the Article IV, Section 3, property clause), and those public forests became the first focus of federal conservation efforts. But these efforts generated resistance from conservation opponents, which included novel constitutional arguments aimed at limiting federal authority on public lands. Moreover, the Constitution did not explicitly grant Congress authority to acquire additional lands to preserve forests in eastern states. Conservationists thus faced two separate constitutional battles, both of which came to a head in 1911.

The USDA's Forest Service, having secured control of the national forests in 1905, was a key player in both of these battles. As historian Daniel Carpenter notes, from 1900 onward, the USDA "established a reputation . . . as the principal scientific agency of American government."[3] Through its recruitment of scientists and its creation of internal networks of cooperation, the department enjoyed an organizational culture oriented toward progressive use of scientific research. It became a respected participant in the policy process, serving as an "unrivaled supplier of drafts and amendments for Congress and president."[4] But that influence extended to the courts as well. We have already seen that USDA publications played an important role in justifying federal migratory bird conservation. The Forest Service was even more central to establishing constitutional authority for federal forest conservation. Gifford Pinchot appointed to the Forest Service legal office his friend and ally George Woodruff, as well as Philip Wells, who would take over from Woodruff in 1907. Yale-trained, like-minded Progressives, Woodruff and Wells led the two campaigns to secure federal forest conservation authority on public and nonpublic lands.

The second of these campaigns, the effort to secure federal authority to acquire land to create forest reserves in eastern states, is the subject of the next chapter. This chapter focuses on the Forest Service's response to efforts by states' rights advocates to limit federal authority to establish reserves on public lands—an effort that ended with the Supreme Court's decisions in *Light v. United States* and *United States v. Grimaud* in 1911. This campaign is a particularly good illustration of the dynamic discussed in the introduction about constitutional change: Courts did pose a potential obstacle to federal forest conservation, and opponents of conservation hoped to enhance that resistance by developing new doctrinal barriers to federal authority over public lands. But the Forest Service's legal team, backed by the USDA's reputation for scientific expertise and efficiency, was able to come up with persuasive responses to their opponents' novel arguments. Legal professionals played a key role, on both sides of the conflict, in this doctrinal development. But their success depended in part on the fact that the federal interest in forest conservation was framed, from the beginning, as an interest in what we would call their ecosystems services—an interest that made the USDA's scientific expertise central to forest conservation policy.

The Campaign for National Forests

The condition of forests on public lands was a special concern of the forest conservation movement from the 1870s on. The federal government in the nineteenth century had no effective management strategy for its forests, and forest fires were a constant threat. Moreover, it was common practice for settlers and timber companies to harvest timber from public lands—a practice that was not legally authorized. Indeed, historian John Ise's review of the public lands laws concludes that before 1878, "there was no general legal and honest way of acquiring public timber lands, or the timber itself, in many parts of the United States."[5] The Free Timber Act of 1878 authorized some free use of public timber lands, and the Timber and Stone Act passed the same year authorized the sale of timber lands to private citizens. But the laws were unclear and did little to discourage trespass in public timber lands. Indeed, there was little support in Congress or the Department of the Interior for prosecuting trespassers. On the contrary, the prevailing sentiment among policy makers was in favor of selling timber lands, or at least liberalizing the free use of timber by settlers.[6] The campaign for federal forest conservation thus faced considerable challenges.

Those challenges, however, did not appear to be rooted in the Constitution. The constitutional problem noted by Franklin Hough—namely, the lack of government authority to regulate private forestry—did not seem to apply to the federal government managing its own lands. Indeed, the first successful federal forest preservation efforts did not raise any constitutional objections. Turning Yosemite over to California in 1864 under the condition that it become a state park required some policy justification, but no one questioned the federal government's authority, under Article IV, Section 3, "to dispose of and make all needful Rules and Regulations" respecting the public lands.[7] As noted in chapter 4, the 1871 Yellowstone Reservation Act faced more opposition, but opponents did not raise constitutional arguments. Beginning in 1876, several bills proposing the creation of forest reserves were introduced into Congress, but they received little attention, either positive or negative. It is worth noting, however, that the first of these, introduced by Rep. Fort of Illinois in 1876, was a bill "for the preservation of the forests of the national domain adjacent to the sources of the navigable rivers and other streams of the United States."[8] The limitation in that bill to forests at headwaters is significant, as we will see, and may have indicated a concern about the reach of federal authority.

But the congressional battles over federal forest conservation really began with the famous rider, designated Section 24, attached to the 1891 General Revision Act, authorizing the president to create forest reserves on public lands. This act was not aimed at forest conservation at all but at remedying various defects in the confusing set of laws concerning public lands. Section 24 was added at the request of Secretary of the Interior Noble and passed by the Senate in the final days of the congressional session without discussion.

The House passed it as well, with relatively little discussion.[9] However, Congressman McRae of Arkansas did raise an objection with constitutional dimensions: McRae objected to the forest reservation provision on the grounds that it did not put any limit on the president's power to create reserves in any forested land.[10] He insisted that he had no objections to forest reserves where necessary to protect watersheds but argued that, in general, lands suitable for agriculture should be open to settlement. Congressman Payson of Illinois, in defense of the provision, responded by emphasizing that the primary purpose of the provision was in fact to protect streamflow, pointing out that there are places in the Northwest where loss of forests is threatening watersheds. "The right of a private citizen to make a home upon the public domain," he argued, "ought as a matter of public policy to be subordinated to the larger and broader principle of conserving the general good by preserving the great watersheds of the Union."[11] This debate, of course, was focused on how much power to delegate to the executive branch; neither party suggested that the Constitution might put some limit on *Congress's* authority to create forest reserves. But the exchange reflected growing concern, especially in the western states, about precisely this question: How far did federal authority over public lands extend? Could the federal government simply close vast tracts of land to settlement altogether?

In the end, Section 24 was approved as written: "The President of the United States may, from time to time, set apart and reserve, in any state or territory having public land bearing forests, in any part of the public lands, wholly or in part covered with timber or undergrowth, whether of commercial value or not, as public reservations; and the President shall, by public proclamation, declare the establishment of such reservations and limits thereof." Thus it didn't put any explicit limit on the president's authority to reserve public forests. The implications of that broad grant became apparent when President Harrison promptly used his new power to create a new Yellowstone Reserve next to Yellowstone National Park, the White River Plateau Reserve in Colorado and, in total, fifteen reserves encompassing more than thirteen million acres.[12] President Cleveland also created a couple of reserves in 1893, early in his second term in office, but halted further efforts when he realized that creating forest reserves would accomplish little without also securing the authority to manage them.

Legally, the creation of forest reserves constituted a significant change in public lands policy. Unlike most other public lands, forest reserves were not to be sold to homesteaders; they were to remain under the control of the US government. But that change was not particularly meaningful in practice without a management strategy that could actually prevent people from using and abusing these national forests. The question of whether the government should retain public lands was thus part of a more complex debate about how these forested lands should be managed: how should they be used, who should benefit from them, and who should decide?

The 1891 reservations put these questions on the legislative agenda, and between 1891 and 1897, Congress considered several forest management bills. Most of the debate over these proposals focused on how timber from the forests would be sold and who could use the reserved lands for what purposes. But, increasingly, western legislators, worried about the prospect of vast areas in their states being closed to settlement and economic development, were raising a more fundamental question: What federal purposes could be pursued through forest reservations? That is, what is the federal interest in forest conservation?

Rationales for Federal Forest Conservation
As we have seen, forest advocates had several arguments for forest preservation, and at the state level, the arguments concerning health, recreation, aesthetics, and wildlife preservation were all endorsed by legislatures and courts. In the federal Congress and the executive branch, however, two arguments dominated the debate almost (but not quite) to the exclusion of all others: Forests were to be protected to preserve a sustainable supply of wood and to protect streamflow in important river systems.

Notable by its absence was the argument that forests should be preserved for national defense. This was once the most important argument for preserving forests; indeed, the very first federal timber policy was the 1799 act creating the US Naval Reserves. Throughout the nineteenth century, the secretary of the Navy was periodically (and unproblematically) authorized to buy forested land for use to build ships.[13] This was in fact the motivation behind several early laws prohibiting removing timber from the public domain. But the development of iron ships after the Civil War made this rationale obsolete, and most of the naval reserves were returned to the states during the post–Civil War period. Thus the most obvious federal interest in forests was no longer available; other federal interests would have to be identified.

President Harrison did not explain in detail his rationale for the 1891 forest reservations. His proclamations merely stated that they were reserved "for the public good."[14] But we do have explanations from several of the key advocates for these reserves. The American Forestry Association—the principal organization lobbying for reserves through the 1880s—petitioned Congress for forest reserves in 1889, citing only two reasons: to protect valuable timber for the nation's future need for wood and to protect the water supply and improve the climatic conditions, to benefit agriculture in the arid states. Bernhard Fernow, chief of the USDA Division of Forestry from 1886 to 1898, published an influential bulletin in 1891 titled "What is Forestry?" reiterating the chief goals of forestry: to produce "certain useful material" and to "sustain or possibly improve certain advantageous natural conditions." Forests could be viewed "as a crop" or "as a cover to the soil," which "bears a very important relation to other conditions of life."[15] The view of trees as a commodity is important to his case for forest management, but not more important than what we now call the "ecosystem services" view: the conception of forests as contributing to the functioning of ecological systems. Fernow underscores the point in his subsequent 1891 report: The division's management priorities, he states, are, first, to ensure a continuous forest cover of the soil on mountain slopes and crests for the purpose of preserving or equalizing waterflow in streams and preventing flooding and, second, to ensure a continuous supply of wood. He interprets the goal of the 1891 act as being to prevent waste of forest resources by forest fires and to provide for the needs of local settlers—although he acknowledges that preserving wild game and scenic landscapes is compatible with those goals.[16]

Fernow's work was supported by Edward Bowers, who began service as an inspector in the General Land Office in 1886 and collaborated closely with Fernow on forest conservation. In a paper presented in December 1890 to the American Economics Association, he focused on the commercial value of forests and their value, particularly in the arid mountainous region of the West, "as a cover to the mountains from which the water supply is drawn for the extensive irrigation that now exists on the lower lands." He also addressed the economic incentives leading to waste of forest resources. Currently, he argued, settlers have no incentive to make a home on forested lands, because those lands are largely unsuited to agriculture. So they enter the land, cut the trees, and move on quickly; they have no incentive to husband their resources since they have no intention to stay on the land. Or, as soon as they acquire title, they sell the land to lumbermen, who are wealthy enough to waste the poorer portions of the timber. In either case, the land generally ends up in the hands of large timber interests, who are paying much less than the timber is worth and who have little incentive to practice sustainable forestry. Therefore, he concludes, "no timber bearing lands, now the property of the United States, should be subject to entry under the settlement laws."[17]

A more moderate view was expressed by Lewis Groff, Commissioner of the General Land Office, in his 1890 report. The report commented on Senate Bill 1394, which proposed to allow (some) settlers in certain western states free access to timber on public lands. Groff was skeptical about the more ambitious forest reserve proposals, but he did acknowledge the need to protect public forests and emphasized the importance of one uniform national policy. The proposed bill, he believed, was objectionable because it gave special privileges to citizens in some states that were not available to citizens in other states. His view was that "the Government is not a corporation nor individual owning the public lands. It merely holds them in trust; and, like the trustee of an estate, it should permit such use of the proceeds thereof by the persons in whose interests it is acting as will enable them to subsist and maintain themselves."[18] The legal term "trustee" is important here, as we shall see; it resonates with a long-standing constitutional tradition that usually supports a more states' rights position. Here, Groff is using the concept to promote a nationalist outlook. He goes on to say he would support a general policy allowing free use of public forests for local needs but also advocates laws that preserve forests "in localities where it is necessary to insure a proper and equitable water-supply and prevent or check the inundations and floods which so frequently devastate portions of our country." He identifies mountain slopes as areas particularly in need of forest cover.[19]

In short, the leading voices on forest policy in the executive branch all supported protecting forests to ensure the long-term availability of wood and, where necessary, to protect streamflow. Those two rationales were also dominant in Congress. Recall that Congressman Fort's 1876 bill would have protected forests "adjacent to the sources of the navigable rivers and other streams of the United States." Later bills settled on a more expansive formula, as in Congressman McRae's 1893 bill providing that "no public forest reservations shall be made except to protect and improve the forest within the reservation or for the purpose of securing favorable conditions of water flow and continuous supplies of timber to the people."[20] That formulation was becoming standard in the many forest reserve bills considered in the 1890s, although not without some dissent. (Congressman Pickler, for example, objected to this language on the grounds that it would prevent the president from using the reserve power to create national parks.)[21] But what is interesting about these congressional debates is the broad consensus in favor of protecting forests at important headwaters. Even the very restrictive 1895 bill offered by Senator Teller of Colorado—a leading opponent of federal forest conservation—specified that forest reserves could be created by the president for only two purposes: to secure favorable conditions for water flow and to secure a continuous supply of timber to the people in the state or territory where the reserve was located.[22]

What is clearly missing from these arguments are the health, aesthetic, recreational, and wildlife preservation values that typically supported state forest conservation efforts. As noted earlier, those values supported the creation of the first national parks, and there were legislators who embraced them. Indeed, Congress created several national parks between 1872 and 1915, as well as passing the Antiquities Act[23] in 1906 and the National Park Service Organic Act[24] in 1916, in the service of these values. Interestingly, the creation of the national park system generated no constitutional debate at all. Historian Alfred Runte points out that proponents of national parks avoided controversy by arguing that the chosen lands had no agricultural value.[25] For example, Mt. Rainier National Park (1899) is rugged, inhospitable terrain; Crater Lake National Park (1902) is an extinct volcano; Wind Cave National Park (1903) is of course a complex of caves; Mesa Verde

National Park (1906) is in the middle of the desert. But equally important to avoiding controversy was the fact that all the parks created during this period were on public lands (and so already owned by the federal government); indeed, most were within forest reserves (and so already closed to settlement). To be sure, the limits of Congress's authority to manage public lands would eventually be questioned by opponents of forest reserves, but no one raised any concerns about using the property power to protect the scenic value of these (otherwise valueless) landscapes.

Nor did the 1906 Antiquities Act raise any constitutional concerns. The act was designed to be a very limited grant of authority falling squarely within the power granted by Article IV, Section 3. It gave the president the authority to protect objects of historic or scientific interest by reserving relatively small tracts of public land ("the limits of which in all cases shall be confined to the smallest area compatible with proper care and management of the objects to be protected"). Legislators clearly believed that national monuments would be very small and would not pose the same kind of threat to economic development that the extensive forest reserves did.[26] But the act did provide further support for the view that protecting the aesthetic, scientific, and historical value of landscapes was a legitimate goal of the federal government—at least, on its own property. That view is reflected as well in the 1916 Act to create the National Park Service. Proponents of that bill had a long fight to convince Congress that some public lands should be managed for their scenic and recreational value *only*.[27] But whether the federal government had *constitutional* authority to pursue aesthetic, recreational, and other "quality of life" values in its management of public lands wasn't at issue in that debate.

Nevertheless, aesthetic and recreational values were not used by policy makers to justify the creation of forest reserves. Instead, proponents of the reserves continued to rely primarily on the role of forests in protecting watersheds. As we will see, the streamflow argument would be central to the campaign to secure federal authority to create forest reserves in eastern states for specific doctrinal reasons. But it would also form an important background to the Forest Service's efforts to secure management authority on public lands, since it made the Forest Service's scientific expertise critical to achieving the purposes of the reserves. Before turning to those efforts, however, we need to understand the emerging constitutional case against forest reserves.

Constitutional Complaints

In the 1890s, opponents were not raising constitutional objections to the new forest reserve policy. Indeed, even the infamous "Washington's Birthday Reserves" did not spark constitutional complaints. These reserves were the result of President Cleveland's decision to act on the recommendations of a National Forest Commission report, which advised the creation of thirteen new reserves encompassing twenty-one million acres. Cleveland had postponed creating forest reserves in the hopes of working out a plan for managing them. In the absence of such legislation, he decided to proclaim these new reservations on February 22, 1897—just before he left office. This action set off a storm of controversy throughout the West. The controversy received considerable coverage in the press, and the arguments for and against federal forest conservation were widely debated. But these debates did not yet have a constitutional dimension.

In response to westerners' furor over the new reserves, Congress finally enacted the first major federal forest management policy in 1897.[28] This act settled on McRae's original language delimiting the president's power to create reserves: "No national forest shall be established, except to improve and protect the forest within the boundaries, or for the purpose of securing favorable conditions of water flows, and to furnish a continuous supply of timber for the use and necessities of citizens of the United States."[29] It also explicitly provided that land more valuable for agriculture or mining could not be reserved. More importantly for outraged westerners, the law suspended the president's February 22 order for nine months, opened the new reserves to mining, and allowed the secretary of the Interior to give free timber to settlers. But it also authorized the secretary to sell timber from public lands and to make rules and regulations for protecting them (albeit without authorizing funds to carry out that mission).[30]

In practice, this act did more to confirm than to constrain the president's power to create reserves. Indeed, all thirteen of President Cleveland's reserves arguably satisfied the conditions of that Act. The National Forest Commission report helpfully explained the rationale for each of the reserves it recommended to the president: Streamflow protection was either the sole or one important rationale for creating the San Jacinto, Stanislaus, Uinta, Mt. Rainier, Washington, Bitter Root, Lewis and Clark, Flathead, Black Hills, Teton, and Big Horn forest reserves. Several of these were also important for serving the local demand for wood, although none of them (in the authors' view) had commercially valuable timber. Only the

Olympic and Priest River reserves had no value for streamflow; they were designated solely because of the high commercial value of their timber resources. The report also noted, as additional reasons for protection, that Mt. Rainier and Flathead had sublime scenery, and Teton had some value as a game preserve.[31] But clearly the Forest Commission considered those secondary values, not strong enough in themselves to justify reserving that land.

There was little need to resort to those secondary values in any case, since the 1897 Act was quite expansive. Scientists tended to define "forest" broadly, including grasslands and shrub forests that contributed to flood regulation and soil conservation, even if their use for timber production was questionable. President Cleveland's forest reserves accordingly included much land that was not obviously forested. Not surprisingly, then, the 1897 Act did little to mollify the West. Westerners were not uniformly opposed to federal forest conservation, of course. The forest conservation movement had made progress in several western states. As mentioned in the previous chapter, western states began to create forest conservation policies in the 1890s—efforts that were undermined when the federal government put much of their forested land into reserves. Still, farmers and western cities typically supported state or federal forest reserves aimed at protecting watersheds. A wide variety of interests opposed federal reserves, however. Ranchers and miners worried about losing their open access to public lands, and many ordinary settlers worried about losing access to fuel, building supplies, and water rights in federal forests.[32] These specific economic concerns drove the public debate. But as that debate developed, opponents of forest conservation gradually began to frame their objections in constitutional terms.

They had a challenging job. Federal forest conservation rested on a pretty strong constitutional foundation. Conservationists could cite the Article IV, Section 3 property clause, along with congressional statutes like the 1891 and 1897 acts, a series of Supreme Court decisions confirming that the president could reserve lands for public purposes, and a constitutional tradition that public lands should benefit the nation as a whole rather than particular sections or regions. These textual and doctrinal authorities combined to create a presumption that federal government had broad authority to manage public lands to serve the national interest. Opponents of the reserves therefore had to create constitutional arguments limiting that authority—and they were no less creative than the wildlife advocates in doing so. Indeed, over the next several years they would develop constitutional arguments against specific exercises of federal management authority. But their chief constitutional argument against the reserves themselves rested on the fundamental constitutional value of equality: Because federal government had no holdings in eastern states when they formed the union, western states should also be able to enter the union with control of all their land so that they would be on an "equal footing" with the eastern states. Federal forest reserves threatened that principle; reserving forest lands meant that western states would enter the union with much of their territory remaining under federal control. Thus opponents of federal forest reserves began to call for cession of public lands to the states as a matter of constitutional right.

Equal Footing Doctrine and Public Lands

Despite the Property Clause, federal authority over public lands was never an uncontroversial constitutional principle. Against this clear textual grant of authority stood an important constitutional tradition originating in the principle, first declared in the Northwest Ordinance, that new states "shall be admitted . . . into the Congress of the United States, on an equal footing with the original States in all respects whatever, and shall be at liberty to form a permanent constitution and State government."[33] Paul Conable provides a useful summary of the context for this language. Seven of the original thirteen colonies claimed a good deal of western land. The other six colonies were concerned that their lack of western lands placed them at a disadvantage. Thus, in 1780, the Confederation Congress worked out a deal: the states with western lands ceded them to the federal government, on the condition that they be formed into states with "the same rights of sovereignty, freedom, and independence, as the other States."[34] The equal footing language adopted in the Northwest Ordinance was repeated in the original cessions of land from the states to the federal government.

Subsequently, the federal government acquired about 1.84 billion more acres on the American continent, mostly by treaty: the Louisiana Territory by purchase in 1803, Florida by treaty in 1819, Texas by annexation in 1845, the Oregon Territory by treaty in 1846, about 330 million acres in the Mexican War of 1848, the Gadsden Purchase lands in 1853, and Alaska in 1867.[35] These lands were the focus of considerable debate. They were originally to be sold in order to pay the national debt, but that debt was nearly extinguished by 1829. This left the federal government with (in the words of historian David Currie) "a giant reservoir of potential congressional influence on domestic policy in the capacious fields otherwise reserved to the several states."[36] In other words, the vast public domain threatened the balance between federal and state power, which in turn threatened the balance among different states and regions.

Accordingly, during the nineteenth century, the federal government adopted a consistent policy of disposing of the public domain to private citizens and ceding limited amounts to the states. For example, the Homestead Act of 1862 famously promised 160 acres to settlers who promised to live there for five years (at a nominal fee of $26). This period also saw the beginning of land grants to railroad companies to encourage rail construction.[37] But the policy of privatizing public land didn't quell the fears of states' rights advocates. On the contrary, every time Congress granted public lands to the states—usually to pursue "internal improvements" or economic development—it provoked sectional conflict and raised concerns about government's involvement in the economy.[38] Thus calls for ceding the whole public domain to the states were actually a long-standing theme in nineteenth-century debate.

As early as 1828, Governor Edwards of Illinois complained that the new states (like Illinois) could not be equal to the old states as long as the federal government retained public lands within those states. Under his view, the federal government should not retain any authority over public lands once a state was admitted to the Union.[39] This issue came up with every new statehood negotiation, each of which included some agreement concerning which public lands would be ceded to the state. Alabama, Indiana, Louisiana, and Missouri all asked for (but did not get) complete cession of public lands within their borders, using the language of equal footing.[40] As historian John Leshy has explained, eastern state representatives resisted these calls, arguing that since the lands had been secured by the whole nation's blood and treasure, the whole nation should benefit from them. The western state representatives, however, argued that they needed the land to grow and prosper and enter the union on an "equal footing" with the older states.[41]

Most policy makers granted that both sides of the debate had reasonable concerns and endorsed the principle that old and new states should have the same governing powers. But the equal footing doctrine, in its extreme form, would mean that the federal government had *no constitutional authority* to retain control of any public lands once the state was organized.

That principle had little doctrinal support; the federal government had frequently withdrawn public lands from settlement with the intent of retaining federal control, and the Supreme Court endorsed the practice in 1868.[42] To be fair, however, those withdrawals had concerned very small plots of land, to be reserved for military bases or other federal buildings. The scale of the forest reserves was unprecedented, and one could argue that withdrawing vast areas of lands from state control was different in kind than reserving a few post offices, military bases, and lighthouses. That, at any rate, is what some conservation opponents would claim.

They did have some case law to build on. The leading case on equal footing doctrine is the 1845 *Pollard v. Hagan*.[43] Plaintiffs in this case claimed ownership of land in Mobile Bay, Alabama, by virtue of a grant from the federal government. The lands in question were under water at high tide, and defendants insisted that the federal government never owned that land—that the state retained ownership of lands under navigable waters. Justice McKinley agreed. Like much of the public domain, this portion of Alabama was ceded from Georgia to the United States. Under McKinley's reading of that agreement: "When Alabama was admitted into the union, on an equal footing with the original states, she succeeded to all the rights of sovereignty, jurisdiction, and eminent domain which Georgia possessed at the date of the cession, except so far as this right was diminished by the public lands remaining in the possession and under the control of the United States."[44] The plaintiff had claimed that the United States in fact acquired this territory, including ownership of the navigable waters, from the 1819 treaty with Spain, but the judge concluded that the 1819 treaty didn't actually concern the Alabama territory at all. Thus the only question was how to interpret the original cession from Georgia. The court concluded that since states normally retain ownership of land under navigable waters (even though the federal government does acquire a navigation servitude, under the Commerce Clause), Alabama also retained ownership of that land.

The Court did endorse the "federal trusteeship" theory: the principle that the federal government held the ceded lands in trust to create new states.[45] States' rights proponents argued that once the territory becomes a state, the federal government has accomplished the purpose of the trust, and so its trusteeship over all public lands in the state should end.[46] But the court rejected that implication; it noted that the United States and Alabama agreed during the statehood negotiations that the federal government would retain control of some public lands in the state, and that agreement was constitutionally valid. The Article IV property clause authorized "the passage of all laws necessary to secure the rights of the United States to the public lands, and to provide for their sale, and to protect them from taxation."[47] The case therefore merely holds that the land under navigable waters was not among the public lands included in the agreement.

Most subsequent cases drawing on the equal footing doctrine simply confirm that new states have the same police power as old states.[48] Nevertheless, the language of state sovereignty in these cases provides some support for the states' rights position. Nor should this surprise us. As constitutional theorist Mark Graber points out, on contentious issues, American constitutional traditions do not typically speak with one voice. "When political controversies have long excited a constitutional community, the central legal claims of all prominent participants will be well grounded in . . . constitutional logics."[49] Compromises over these issues provide both parties with precedents and principles they can draw on when the issue erupts again. The equal footing doctrine gained new life when controversy over the forest reserves arose in the early years of the twentieth century (as it would again in the 1980s and periodically since then).

Historian Michael McCarthy, documenting western popular resistance to federal reserves from 1891 to 1907, notes that many of the opponents "believed—or said they believed—that the state had a kind of moral right to control any land contained within it." But in fact, it took several years before opponents of conservation began applying the equal footing doctrine to forest reserves. With the exception of an investigation in 1901–1902 of Congress's authority to regulate wildlife in forest reserves within states (a subject that we will return to in chapter 7), constitutional arguments were not prominent in congressional debate about forest reserves until, suddenly, the equal footing doctrine appears in a 1906 debate about an obscure bill (S. 1661) about school lands. The bill concerned forest reserves in Idaho. A long-standing element of public lands policy was that when a state is admitted to the Union, certain sections of the public lands within its borders are designated for use to support public schools. In Idaho, some of the sections in question lay within forest reserves, so the Governor had exchanged them for other plots—a fairly common practice.[50] But Senator Heyburn of Idaho objected (apparently believing that the state had gotten an unfair deal in the exchange). The aim of his bill was to prohibit school lands from being included in forest reserves without compensation.

However, he framed the issue as a constitutional one: The bill was necessary for Congress to "take hold of the question of the creation of the forest reserves and the control and management of them under the authority the Constitution of the United States vested in us to control the public lands." Heyburn's primary constitutional complaint was that the 1891 Act had given the executive authority that ought, under the Property Clause, to be vested in Congress. But he also drew attention to the second half of that clause, which seemed to be aimed at protecting states' rights: "The Congress shall have Power to dispose of and make all needful Rules and Regulations respecting the Territory or other Property belonging to the United States; and *nothing in this Constitution shall be so construed as to Prejudice any Claims of the United States, or of any particular State.*"[51] It was Senator Fulton, however, who raised the equal footing doctrine explicitly with this question to Heyburn:

> Having in mind our theory of government, (whether it be stated expressly in the Constitution or not, it is certainly a part of our constitutional law), that new States when admitted into the Union shall come in on an equal footing in all respects whatsoever with the original States, is not that theory violated when the Government withdraws permanently a large portion of the lands included within the boundary of the new State and holds it not for benefit of the citizens of that State, but without their consent, . . . the benefit of the whole country?[52]

Senator Heyburn did not take up this invitation to offer a constitutional analysis of equal footing doctrine as applied to forest reserves. He responded to the question by making a very general reference to pre–Civil War debates about public lands and then returned to his principal argument: that Congress rather than the executive branch should be in charge of negotiating what happens to the school lands.

Further development of the equal footing argument was prompted by the 1906 grazing permit controversy. The idea of requiring a permit to graze in national forests had been debated for several years, but several officials in the executive branch doubted the secretary of the Interior had the authority to require one. This was a key issue on which the more conservative lawyers in the Department of the Interior had prevailed, until the national forests were transferred to the USDA in 1905 and Woodruff and Wells took up the problem. They proved to be far more creative and entrepreneurial than the Interior legal corps. Woodruff tackled the permit question by soliciting an opinion by the US attorney general on the subject, which confirmed that the 1897 act authorizing the secretary of the Interior to regulate the forest reserves did include the power to create a fee-based permit system.[53] Accordingly, the agriculture secretary (who was now in charge of the reserves) issued regulations in 1906 requiring that stockmen using the national forests secure grazing permits.

This change in policy generated considerable resistance, and foes of forest conservation (in the words of Philip Wells) "opened a vigorous fight on the Service in the press, in Congress, and in the court."[54] They took the fight to the 1907 Denver Public Lands Convention, which became a watershed event in the conservation movement. The Convention was organized to be a forum for the expression of western sentiment on Roosevelt's forest policy and Gifford Pinchot's management of the Forest Service. But the program committee (under the chairmanship of anti-conservationist Senator Teller) framed the agenda as an investigation not of federal forest policy but of federal constitutional authority over public lands.

The program committee issued a memorial that outlined their constitutional theory: The public lands were originally acquired from the first thirteen colonies on the condition that "the territory so ceded shall be [laid] out and formed in states . . . and that the states so formed shall be Republican states and admitted members of the Federal Union, having the same rights of sovereignty, freedom and independence as the other states."[55] According to the committee, the object of all parties to this "contract" was "to convert the lands into money to pay the debts and to erect new states over the territory thus ceded." Thus "whenever the United States had fully executed this trust, the power of the United States over these lands was to cease." Therefore, the federal government can retain possession of these lands perpetually "only for certain purposes necessary to government and by consent of the states." The committee goes on to cite *Pollard v. Hagan*, claiming that "the United States have no constitutional capacity to exercise municipal jurisdiction, sovereignty or eminent domain within the limits of a state or elsewhere, except in the cases in which it is expressly granted."[56]

The committee pointed out that many new states "have already completed their contract with the government and have acquired the entire control over the territory within their borders by the settlement of the public lands." That is, although the federal government did retain control of public lands within many states when they were formed, that control was to be temporary, until the land was transferred to settlers. This new policy of perpetual ownership of public lands, according to the committee, was "dangerously near the assumption of municipal sovereignty." Moreover, "Congress has had but little to do with this change in policy, and it seems to have resulted largely through a delegation of authority to the executive branch of the government to 'make rules and regulations' in regard to the areas withdrawn." The memorial goes on to identify several objectionable actions by the Forest Service, as well as the fact that the states can't tax federal lands. But its general point is that "the Western states, being admitted with all the rights of the older states, have always considered the right to settle these public lands with citizens one of the privileges of statehood." It therefore proposed that the convention consider the following questions:

1. Has the United States government the constitutional right to hold the public lands within the borders of a new state in perpetual ownership and under municipal sovereignty without the consent of the state?

2. When the new states were admitted with all rights and privileges of the older states, did not the agreement include the right to acquire the public lands for its citizens under the laws of the United States?

3. The withdrawal of large tracts of public lands in the West, having been urged upon the ground of public necessity, does such a public necessity exist in fact as would warrant the large withdrawals already made?

4. Has the United States constitutional capacity to engage in merchandising timber and coal in competition with citizens of the state, and if so, is there any limit to that capacity?

5. If the United States has the power under the constitution to embark on an extensive and monopolistic scale in the development and merchandising of the resources of the public lands, would such action be in the interest of the progress and development of the states?

6. Would the power proposed to be conferred by Congress upon the Department of Agriculture, to "regulate and control gazing upon unappropriated and unreserved lands of the United States," retard the settlement and gradual absorption of the public lands into private ownership as contemplated by the constitution?

7. Has the government of the United States the constitutional power to interfere with public or private enterprise in the construction of irrigation works and the utilization of the waters of the streams [within] the state for irrigation or other purposes, or to deny such projects a right of way over public lands?[57]

In short, for the program committee, the question of federal forest policy had become the question of federal constitutional authority over public lands.

That question did not dominate the proceedings, however. The opening address by Secretary of the Interior Ballinger (representing the administration's pro-conservation policy) did not address the constitutional questions at all. Senator Teller followed him, but he simply asked, "What are our rights here?" and answered, "The Supreme Court of the United States has declared in the most emphatic manner that the natural wealth of this state belongs not to the general government but to us, to our people. The Supreme Court of the United States has declared that the waters of this state belong to the state."[58] But he had little else to contribute to the constitutional argument.

However, the first speaker on the second day, T. J. Walsh, did focus on the legal issue—but not in support of equal footing doctrine. Walsh's point was to criticize the president's withdrawing from settlement the public coal lands, an action he had taken to prompt Congress to create a leasing program for those lands. Walsh (perhaps recognizing the weakness of the equal footing argument) began by acknowledging that "since the earliest years of our national existence" the president had reserved portions of the public domain for some particular purpose, and the Supreme Court had affirmed this power.[59] But he went on to suggest that "the power thus lodged in the President and sanctioned, as it is, by long usage and judicial approval, is not without limit."[60] Specifically, the land must be reserved "for a specific lawful purpose" or public use (again citing several decisions). Moreover, that purpose must be authorized by Congress.[61] He goes on to argue that public lands policy has generally been opposed to leasing; the goal has always been to create freeholders, not tenants. But he also admitted that the federal government has leased public lands from time to time. In sum, this attack on the withdrawal of the coal lands tended to confirm the validity of forest reserves.

Robert Bonynge's address was more on point. He declared:

I plant myself, gentlemen, upon this proposition, which I think is supported by the constitution of the United States and the legislation that has been adopted from the beginning of our government to the present time, that it is not in accord with the constitution, nor is it in accord with our history or the history of our legislation, for the national government to retain permanent control and permanent ownership of large tracts of land in the separate and independent states.[62]

He insisted that he was a "nationalist" but rejected Roosevelt's inherent power theory, that "whenever it can be shown that the national government can discharge a function perhaps better than the states can do it, per force, the national government has the power to enter upon that project." The federal government can exercise only the powers delegated to it by the Constitution. He thus turned to Article IV of the Constitution and pointed out that Section 3 of that article has two parts. The second paragraph does give Congress authority to make rules and regulations for the public lands, but it follows "a sub-division which provides for the creation of new states out of the western territory."[63] Those sections together "placed in the Federal Constitution the guarantee and the pledge that the policy of disposing of the public lands for the purpose of creating new states, for carrying out that object and purpose for which those lands were ceded to the National Government, should be pursued by the Government."[64]

However, even Bonynge acknowledged that Congress could authorize the president to create forest reserves as long as the ultimate goal of the policy was to promote settlement of the state, and he even confessed that the 1897 reservations were, technically, legal (if not wise).[65] In sum, none of the speakers was able to mount a persuasive case that the federal government lacked legal authority to create the forest reserves. They did embrace the principle, stated in *Pollard* and confirmed in the Supreme Court decision *Kansas v. Colorado* (decided that year), that states retain ownership of the waters of the states. But the convention ended up resolving merely that the public lands were "a trust to be disposed of in all cases to actual settlers for the cultivation and the making of homes" and that "forest reservations should be created only where they do not infringe this policy."[66] Since the purpose of federal forest reserves was to preserve water and timber resources for settlers, conservation proponents could easily argue that the reserves met that condition. Moreover, the convention acknowledged "the necessity, where forest reservations are created, of the government's making all such reasonable regulations as may be necessary to the preservation of the same and preventing conflicts in connection therewith." They asked only that national policy aim that "valuable resources shall be kept from the monopolistic control of corporations or others, to the end that they shall be owned by, distributed among, and at reasonable rates, enjoyed by the whole people."[67]

Equal footing doctrine had no more success at the 1908 Conference of Governors on the Conservation of Natural Resources. Constitutional issues were a prominent theme at the conference; indeed, President Roosevelt likely organized this unprecedented gathering of state-level actors in deference to the federal structure of the nation. He hoped to rally their support for conservation proposals that would dramatically centralize power over natural resources (notably, creating a multipurpose water planning agency). And the tone of the conference was indeed largely supportive of a strong role for federal government in natural resource management. Only one governor, Frank Gooding of Idaho, brought up equal footing doctrine. Criticizing federal control of national forests, he insisted that "Idaho is asking for the same spirit of the Constitution that has been given to all the states east of the Rockies."[68] But most of the governors argued that the states lacked the capacity to manage large-scale natural resources. North Dakota Governor Burke responded directly to Gooding: "Great fear has been expressed that in the conservation of our natural resource the Nation might encroach on the rights of the States, and yet there are some delegates who want to give to the States the control of the National Forests. In my judgement there is no necessity for any conflict between the State and the Nation." On the contrary, federal government has a right to manage its own property, and as it does so, "there is no chance for a conflict between the State and Nation." But should Congress give the State authority to manage forest reserves, "there would at once arise many opportunities for conflict."[69] No one else asked for public lands to be returned to the states.

Thus like the Denver Public Land Convention, most state governors were reluctant to embrace equal footing doctrine. Senator Teller, however, remained an enthusiastic proponent, and he would soon have the chance to try out the theory on the Supreme Court.

Light v. United States
Resistance to the new grazing permit program persisted through 1909 and 1910, led by activists like Elias M. Ammons in Colorado, who called it

an "arbitrary discretionary power [resulting] in tyrannical abuses."[70] The Forest Service officers viewed Ammons as a crank, but Forest Service Grazing Inspector Will Barnes reported that the call to give public lands to the states had spread throughout the southwest (and he noted darkly that the idea was so popular he expected the proponents to win—"and of course you know what that means: . . . Political management").[71] This resistance resulted in the Forest Service taking legal action against stockmen who were grazing their cattle or sheep in the reserves without a permit, and the resulting cases allowed the foes of federal forest conservation to raise a variety of constitutional objections to federal conservation authority. In 1911, two test cases were decided on the same day by the US Supreme Court, both victories for the Forest Service: *United States v. Grimaud*[72] and *Light v. United States.*[73] As Philip Wells notes in his reminiscences, *Light v. United States* was the more significant of the two because defendant Fred Light attacked the constitutionality of the forest reserves as a whole, drawing principally on equal footing doctrine.

Fred Light was a good candidate for this test case. He headed the Roaring Fork and Eagle River Stockgrowers' Association in Colorado and led a movement to boycott the permit fee among stockmen grazing cattle in the Holy Cross forest reserve.[74] In 1908, the Forest Service asked the US Circuit Court for an injunction against Light, prohibiting him from grazing his cattle in the reserve. Light offered several arguments in the circuit court against the injunction. In addition to insisting that the president had no constitutional authority to create the reserves, he also claimed that the cattle had wandered into the reserve on their own and that it was up to the Forest Service to fence them out (as required by Colorado law). The Forest Service, however, had reason to be confident; it had just won a very similar case, *United States v. Shannon,*[75] in the Ninth Circuit. Shannon, a Montana stockman, had made the same arguments against the Forest Service's authority to prohibit grazing in the reserves. Judge Gilbert rejected them:

> It is clear that the state of Montana had no dominion over the public lands lying within its borders, and no power to enact legislation directly or indirectly affecting the same. It could not give to the people of that state the right to pasture cattle upon the public domain, or in any way to use the same. Its own laws in regard to fencing and pasturing cattle at large must be held to apply only to land subject to its own dominion.[76]

Light's suit met the same fate in the Eighth Circuit Court. He appealed, and the Supreme Court heard the case in February 1911.

Fred Light had an impressive legal team. He was represented in the circuit court by Ethelbert Ward, who was also one of the speakers at the Denver Public Lands convention and a gifted litigator. In the Supreme Court, he was represented by James H. Teller, brother to Henry Teller (who was also on the brief) and future chief justice of the Colorado Supreme Court. The brief for Light focused on two questions: the narrower question of whether the state fencing law applied to the forest reserves and the broader question of whether the federal government had the constitutional capacity "permanently to devote large tracts of public land within the boundaries of a state to purposes other than governmental."[77] The brief argued that the government holds public lands not as a sovereign but as a proprietor, and therefore is subject to Colorado's law requiring landowners to fence their land. To hold otherwise would deprive the state of police power over a large area of its territory. This would in turn deny to the state that equality with other states to which it is entitled (citing *Pollard*, *Ward v. Race Horse*, other equal footing cases, and *Kansas v. Colorado*).

On the second question, the brief attacked the notion that forest conservation is a legitimate purpose of federal government. It began with the principle that the federal government holds public land in trust for the people, to be disposed of to promote the settlement and prosperity *of the states in which they are situated.* The people of the nation as a whole benefit from public lands only indirectly, through the growth and prosperity of each state. And according to the appellant, the forest reserves do not benefit the state; they constitute an abandonment of these lands, checking the settlement and economic development.[78] The brief also rejected the state incapacity argument, insisting that even if forest reserves are desirable, the fact that the federal government is in a better position to create them than the states does not give the federal government power to do so. A grant of power is required. The brief explained,

When the Constitution was adopted, the energies of the country were largely devoted to clearing the land of trees, and no one then supposed that the time would come when the preservation of great forests would be regarded as necessary. . . . Consequently, it is useless for us to look for a grant of power which may be supposed intentionally to include the authority [to preserve forests].[79]

The federal government's response to these arguments was offered by Ernest Knaebel. His brief first suggested that Light did not have standing to complain about infringement on the state's sovereignty, being merely a private citizen. He argued also that the state fence law applied only to private parties, not to the United States, and in any case the state law did not protect cattle owners who deliberately drove their cattle to trespass.

Turning to the constitutionality of forest reserves, Knaebel insisted that public lands are held in trust for the people of the whole United States, not particular states.[80] He further offered precedents, such as *United States v. Gratiot*,[81] rejecting the theory that federal government could not own public lands within states (a theory not actually argued by appellant). More to the point, he insisted, "To say that tenure by a State of all the lands, or any particular proportion or quantity of the lands, comprising its territory is essential to its full sovereignty would be, of course, absurd."[82] He pointed out that the convention creating the state of Colorado specified that public lands would remain under the ownership and control of the federal government. But even without that agreement, he contended that the Property Clause gave Congress power "without limitation" to govern public lands. Finally, he insisted that forest conservation is natural, reasonable, and beneficent to the people of the entire country and among the instrumentalities of federal government, just like lighthouses and military bases.

The Court delivered a unanimous opinion in favor of the United States. That outcome, we should note, was not entirely predictable, given recent changes on the court. Between 1909 and 1911, through death and retirement, four positions on the court opened up: those of Justices Peckham, Brewer, Fuller, and Moody. President Taft elevated Justice Edward White to Chief Justice to replace Fuller, and appointed Justices Lamar, Van Devanter, Lurton, and Hughes. They joined Holmes, Day, McKenna, and John Marshall Harlan. But it was far from clear what implications these appointments would have for conservation policy. For example, Justice Van Devanter, from Wyoming, did serve as assistant attorney general for the Department of the Interior from 1896 to 1900, which might have made him sympathetic to forest conservation. But he also represented Wyoming in *Ward v. Race Horse*, so he was intimately familiar with equal footing doctrine. Justice Lamar, on the other hand, was a close friend of Woodrow Wilson and generally supportive of expanding administrative authority, and he wrote the opinions in both *Light* and *Grimaud*.

Lamar's opinion in *Light* is brief. First, he notes that *United States v.*

Grimaud, just decided, disposed of the question about whether Congress could delegate rulemaking authority to the Forest Service (a question raised in the petition on appeal but not briefed). Importantly, he also accepted the United States' version of the facts, assuming that Light had willfully allowed his cattle to graze on the reserve, which state law did not allow. This made it unnecessary for the court to address the vexed question of whether the state's fencing law applied on public lands. On equal footing doctrine, Lamar was concise but decisive: "It is contended . . . that Congress cannot constitutionally withdraw large bodies of land from settlement without the consent of the State where it is located."[83] He dismissed this theory simply by citing cases holding that Congress is authorized to dispose of public lands. Citing the Property Clause, he noted that "the full scope of this paragraph has never been definitely settled. Primarily, at least, it is a grant of power to the United States of control over its property."[84] His authority for that proposition is *Kansas v. Colorado,* the same case that Teller and Barnett were hoping would put some limits on Congress's power over public lands. But Lamar made it clear that the Supreme Court would not provide any support for that project:

> All the public lands of the nation are held in trust for the people of the whole country. . . . And it is not for the courts to say how that trust shall be administered. That is for Congress to determine. The courts cannot compel it to set aside the lands for settlement; or to suffer them to be used for agricultural or grazing purposes; nor interfere when, in the exercise of its discretion, Congress establishes a forest reserve for what it decides to be national and public purposes.[85]

At the very least, the United States has all the rights of an individual proprietor of land, and those rights are sufficient to allow it to reserve lands from settlement and to create a permit system for grazing.

Brief as it is, the *Light* opinion decisively rejected the equal footing challenge to federal forest conservation policy and confirmed Congress's broad authority to decide what counts as a "national and public purpose" under the Property Clause.

United States v. Grimaud

To further underscore its support for the Forest Service, the Supreme Court decided *United States v. Grimaud* the same day. The constitutional issue in *Grimaud* was narrower than the issue in *Light* but also more contentious:

whether the Forest Service had authority to bring criminal charges against Grimaud for grazing his sheep in the Sierra Forest Reserve without a permit. The regulation in question was the same as in *Light* and *Shannon*, but in those cases the Forest Service had sought an injunction, a civil remedy. Criminal charges raised a different constitutional problem. There was a long-standing rule that federal criminal law must have a statutory basis; that is, there are no common law federal crimes.[86] But Congress had not criminalized grazing in the forest reserves without a permit. Instead, the 1897 Act delegated to the Interior secretary the authority to create regulations, the violation of which could be prosecuted as crimes. That procedure, according to several lower federal courts, ran afoul of the nondelegation doctrine.

Legal scholar Logan Sawyer offers an excellent overview of *Grimaud's* legal significance; I can do no better than to summarize his analysis. He explains that the nondelegation doctrine was one of the constitutional doctrines developed by courts in response to the growth of the administrative state: "The emergence of the administrative state as a serious institutional competitor to courts, legislatures, and political parties cast questions about the propriety and limits of administrative government in a new light, and lawyers, judges, and legal academics began debating how the growing authority of the administrative state fit with the restrictions of the Constitution."[87] The nondelegation doctrine was supposed to preserve the separation of powers by preventing the legislature from delegating to the executive branch its law-making power. As Justice John Marshall put it in the leading case of *Wayman v. Southard*, the legislature can delegate some rulemaking power. But "the line has not been exactly drawn which separates those important subjects, which must be entirely regulated by the legislature itself, from those of less interest, in which a general provision may be made, and power given to those who are to act under such a general provision to fill up the details."[88]

Drawing that line continued to bedevil courts. As Sawyer argues, up until *Grimaud*, the standard view was that administrative agencies could perform tasks that looked "administrative," like setting standards, finding facts, or "filling up the details." But making general policy, and especially criminalizing conduct, was categorized as "legislative." Thus the Forest Division could create a permit system—which looked like standard administration—but it could not make its violation a crime. This reasoning was confirmed by a California district court in 1900 in *United States v. Blasingame*,[89] striking down a criminal charge brought against Blasingame for grazing his sheep in forest reserves. The opinion, by Judge Wellborn, was brief and almost barren of doctrinal analysis, but it was widely publicized (especially by the Wool Growers Association in San Francisco) and cited thereafter by trespassing grazers, much to the frustration of the Interior's forest rangers.[90]

Wary of the nondelegation doctrine, the lawyers of the Department of the Interior tended to seek injunctions rather than criminal penalties against those violating the grazing rules. This strategy was upheld against a nondelegation charge by the Ninth Circuit in the 1903 case of *Dastervignes v. United States*.[91] The judge did not explain his reasoning in detail, but the decision was not appealed or challenged in subsequent cases.[92] Unfortunately, however, injunctions were ineffective. As Commissioner Pimple complained to the secretary of the Interior in 1903, "proceedings by injunction are not effective because the damage is done before the injunction can be obtained." He cited as an example a case in which proceedings against five sheep owners were begun on May 25 and an injunction issued on July 31, the trespassers having been in the forest reserve for three months. He wanted the power to arrest trespassers on the spot and bring them to court and even drafted a bill in the hopes that Congress would explicitly make trespass in the forest reserves a crime.[93] But no such law was passed, and efforts to bring criminal charges against violators failed.

Sawyer attributes the failure to poor legal representation.[94] He notes that James Whitten, the chief legal officer of the General Land Office, tended to interpret the Interior secretary's authority quite narrowly. The lawyers in the Department of Justice were more aggressive, and an 1898 opinion by Solicitor General John Richards argued that the act of 1897 did allow the secretary of the Interior to prosecute those who violated its forest regulations.[95] However, they were unable to persuade the courts. The Department of the Interior lost every criminal case it brought from 1900 to 1904 on nondelegation grounds.[96] Moreover, at this point, Congress had not yet given federal appellate courts jurisdiction to hear government appeals in criminal cases. So the Department of the Interior was powerless to appeal these losses to a higher court. (This situation was changed by the Criminal Appeals Act of 1907). In 1904, the Arizona Supreme Court (relying on *Dastervignes*) did give the Interior lawyers a victory.[97] Nevertheless, the Department of the Interior wasn't inclined to continue criminal prosecutions in the face of judicial resistance.

In 1905, however, management of the national forests was transferred to the USDA, and Congress explicitly authorized Forest Service officers to arrest trespassers and take them into custody. Supported by this statute, Pinchot took on the delegation doctrine by marshaling favorable precedents, asking the secretary of agriculture to request an official opinion from the attorney general on the issue, and instructing his staff to start arresting trespassers and bringing them directly to the nearest US commissioner for a hearing.[98] He then put his legal team of George Woodruff and Philip Wells to work on the constitutional problem. As Sawyer recounts, they attacked the nondelegation doctrine on two fronts: They leaned heavily on Congress's right to protect its property (thus characterizing the rules as an exercise of property rights rather than legislative power), and they insisted that creating the grazing rules did not in itself create a federal crime. Rather, Congress defined the crime by attaching a criminal sanction to violation of the rules. That is, they argued that the act of 1897 made it a crime to use the forest reserves without the consent of the secretary of agriculture. "The Secretary's regulations did not define that crime, they simply told the public how to get the Secretary's consent."[99]

This argument persuaded several courts.[100] Thus, in 1909, Philip Wells urged the Department of Justice to appeal the lower court's dismissal of charges against Grimaud, which rested on the delegation doctrine.[101] The Supreme Court took the appeal and heard arguments in October 1909. Unfortunately, the court was reduced to eight by Justice Peckham's recent death, and they were unable to muster a majority opinion. The 4–4 judgment left the lower court's decision standing. However, the case was scheduled for rehearing, and the court—with its four new Justices—heard arguments in March 1911.

Grimaud's lawyer rested his case entirely on the nondelegation doctrine. The United States' brief followed the strategy developed by Woodruff and Wells, arguing that trespassing on public lands without permission is already a crime; the government, as a property owner, may prohibit trespass. The Forest Service regulations merely provide a procedure for gaining that permission.

Justice Lamar began his opinion for the court by pointing out, "From the various acts relating to the establishment and management of forest reservations it appears that they were intended 'to improve and protect the forest and to secure favorable conditions of water flows.'"[102] He noted that "to pasture sheep and cattle on the reservation, at will and without restraint, might interfere seriously with the accomplishment of the purposes for which they were established. But a limited and regulated use for pasturage might not be inconsistent with the object sought to be attained by the statute. The determination of such questions, however, was a matter of administrative detail."[103] To underscore the point, Lamar emphasized that the permitting system is not to be viewed as implementing a general policy but rather as allowing local forest officials to engage in land management, making case-by-case judgments based on relevant ecological factors: "What might be harmless in one forest might be harmful to another. What might be injurious at one stage of timber growth, or at one season of the year, might not be so at another."[104] Indeed, Lamar showed a firm grasp of the ecological situation faced by the Forest Service: "In the nature of things it was impracticable for Congress to provide general regulations for these various and varying details of management. *Each reservation had its peculiar and special features*; and in authorizing the secretary of agriculture to meet these local conditions Congress was merely conferring administrative functions upon an agent, and not delegating to him legislative power."[105] This ecological conception of forests was thus critical to supporting Lamar's conclusion that making rules for the forest is an administrative and not a legislative task.

Lamar went on to cite several cases drawing a similar line between legislative and administrative functions. But the key part of the argument runs as follows:

> It is true that there is no act of Congress which, in express terms, declares that it shall be unlawful to graze sheep on a forest reserve. But the statutes, from which we have quoted, declare, that the privilege of using reserves for "all proper and lawful purposes" is subject to the proviso that the person so using them shall comply "with the rules and regulations covering such forest reservation." The same act makes it an offense to violate those regulations, that is, to use them otherwise than in accordance with the rules established by the Secretary. Thus the implied license under which the United States had suffered its public domain to be used as a pasture for sheep and cattle . . . was curtailed and qualified by Congress, to the extent that such privilege should not be exercised in contravention of the rules and regulations.[106]

He thus adopted the Forest Service's central argument: "If, after the passage of the act and the promulgation of the rule, the defendants drove and grazed their sheep upon the reserve, in violation of the regulations, they were making an unlawful use of the Government's property. In doing so they thereby made themselves liable to the penalty imposed by Congress."[107]

Sawyer notes that *Grimaud* had important implications for administrative law, marking the beginning of the modern view that there is no categorical difference between legislative power to make laws and executive power to make rules, merely a difference in the degree of discretion held by legislatures and agencies. That view would be adopted in 1928 in *J. W. Hampton v. United States*, in which the Supreme Court articulated the modern doctrine that Congress may delegate rulemaking power to agencies as long as it lays down an "intelligible principle" to guide such discretion.[108] He argues as well that there is no new legal development after 1905 that explains the government's success in *Grimaud*; it was merely the quality, persistence, and creativity of the Forest Service legal team that resulted in this doctrinal transformation.[109] We may add to that list the scientific reputation of the USDA, to which the court was consistently willing to defer on matters related to conservation, as well as the conception of forests as unique and complex ecosystems requiring scientific authority to manage.

Grimaud and *Light* were widely interpreted as settling the question of the constitutionality of the forest reserves on public land. Sawyer notes that the number of criminal prosecutions for grazing trespass rose from eight in 1911 to forty-nine in 1912, and in 1912 the department reported that overgrazing had ceased to be a problem.[110] Equal footing doctrine, while not quite laid to rest, would no longer figure prominently in debates over the reserves. Even Fred Light would acquire a grazing permit.[111] The decisions were not quite as sweeping a victory as the Forest Service might have liked, however. Justice Lamar in *Light* carefully reserved the question of how far state law would govern in the reserves, and from the states' point of view, that was a key question. It was well-established that states could not tax federal property.[112] But would state criminal, water, and game laws apply? Or would the Forest Service end up establishing its own independent enclaves within western states, with its own wildlife and water management strategies? We will turn to those questions in chapter 7.

The *Grimaud* and *Light* decisions also left open another pressing constitutional problem: Could federal government extend forest conservation beyond the public lands? What authority did the federal government have to protect forests in the eastern states, for example? The Property Clause was of limited value here, since it said nothing about the federal government's power to acquire land, much less regulate private landowners. To extend federal authority beyond the western public lands, conservationists would have to develop new arguments under the Commerce Clause—arguments in which ecological science, and the ecosystem services conception of forests, would be central.

CHAPTER SIX

Eastern Forest Reserves

While western states were complaining about the federal forest program, several eastern states were beginning to agitate for their own federal reserves. Since the federal government did not own much land in eastern states, creating federal reserves in the East raised new constitutional difficulties: While the Property Clause allowed the federal government to reserve its own forested public lands from settlement, under what authority could the federal government *acquire* land to preserve forests? To modern constitutional sensibilities, it might seem unproblematic for the government to buy land. But there was intense constitutional debate throughout the nineteenth and early twentieth centuries over the purposes for which federal tax money could be spent, and as we have seen, forest preservation was not obviously a federal function. Justifying this use of federal dollars would entangle the forest conservation movement with the movement to expand federal authority to construct large-scale irrigation projects in the West, which posed similar constitutional problems. We will therefore address both debates in this chapter.

On the face of it, irrigation projects would seem to have little do with the goals of conservation. Despite the fact that proponents liked to call their efforts "water conservation," irrigation looks more like economic development than reserving natural resources from exploitation. But Gifford Pinchot famously insisted that "conservation stands for development" of natural resources, for the use of the present as well as future generations.[1] Indeed, we know from chapter 4 that the more sophisticated forest reserve programs could look like a government-funded economic enterprise,

much like a government-run irrigation project. And the frequent characterization of forest reserves as a kind of natural reservoir also supported the
link between forest reserves and man-made reservoirs. Thus the forest conservation and irrigation movements would join forces in the 1890s, seeking
to develop a common constitutional foundation for creating forest reserves
in the East and irrigation projects in the West. They failed; the two federal
policies would ultimately proceed under separate constitutional authorities. But their failure is significant for constitutional development. The
irrigation movement could have argued for expanding federal authority
under the Commerce Clause to allow large-scale federal projects aimed at
economic development—an argument that would have supported both
forest reserves and irrigation projects. But the leaders of the irrigation
movement in Congress ultimately decided to rely on the property power
instead. As we will see, that decision left the forest conservationists with a
narrow reading of the commerce power as the basis for eastern reserves—a
reading that made the hydrological connection between forests and rivers
central to their case for federal forest conservation authority.

Eventually, forest conservation proponents would promote a broader
interpretation of the spending power to support the creation of forest reserves, and the courts would accept that reading. By the New Deal era,
constitutional limits on spending for conservation were largely overcome.
Even the National Park Service was eventually authorized to buy land to
expand the national park system for purely recreational purposes. But by
the time these doctrinal shifts occurred, the ecosystems services view of
forests—the conception of forests as providing ecological services integral
to the national economy—was firmly established as constitutional common sense.

Eastern Forest Reserves

The first organized effort to establish federal forest reserves in the East focused on the southern Appalachian Mountains and the White Mountains in
New Hampshire. The Appalachian National Park Association, Appalachian
Mountain Club, American Forestry Association, and American Association
for the Advancement of Science all petitioned Congress in 1899 for a forest
reserve in North Carolina, Tennessee, and adjacent states, to reverse the
damage the timber industry had wreaked on these eastern forests.[2] What
the petitioners envisioned, in fact, was a park—a great forest park on the

model of New York's Adirondack Park. Thus to the general public, advocates offered the usual set of arguments for creating parks, including their ecological, scenic, and commercial value. After all, the federal government had bought several small sites to create military parks (at Gettysburg and Antietam, for example).[3] It's possible—likely, even—that the courts would have affirmed federal power to buy land to serve the aesthetic and recreational values served by national parks.

The Supreme Court had in fact taken a very deferential view of the federal government's power to acquire land, even land within the borders of states, throughout the nineteenth century. Much of the land within state borders that the federal government acquired during this period was purchased under the authority of Article I, Section 8, Clause 17 of the Constitution, the Enclave or Cession Clause. This clause grants Congress the power to "exercise [exclusive jurisdiction] over all Places purchased by the Consent of the Legislature of the State in which the Same shall be, for the Erection of Forts, Magazines, Arsenals, dock-Yards, and other needful Buildings."[4] It has been interpreted as justifying federal acquisition of land for just about any purpose Congress sees fit. As the court stated in the 1885 decision *Van Brocklin v. Tennessee*: "The United States, at the discretion of Congress, may acquire and hold real property in any State, whenever such property is needed for the use of the government in the execution of any of its powers, whether for arsenals, fortifications, light-houses, custom-houses, court-houses, barracks or hospitals, or for any other of the many public purposes for which such property is used."[5] The qualifying phrase "in the execution of any of its powers" might be read as limiting this authority, but the concluding phrase "for any other of the many public purposes for which such property is used" suggests that Congress had broad discretion to make that judgment.

But conservation advocates might have been uneasy about relying on the Enclave Clause. The statement in *Van Brocklin* was mere dicta. The federal government's authority to acquire the land wasn't actually challenged in that case; the petitioners were questioning the state's power to tax land owned by the federal government. Indeed, most of the nineteenth-century cases concerning the Enclave Clause focused on whether the federal or state government had jurisdiction over the land in question, not whether the federal government had the power to acquire the land in the first place. These questions of jurisdiction under the Enclave Clause are relevant to the conflicts over federal management authority in the forest preserves, as we will see in chapter 7. But the Enclave Clause was not cited by either side in the debates that were about to erupt over whether the federal government could acquire land for conservation purposes.

As *Van Brocklin* suggests, it was not judicial resistance sparking those debates. As of the mid-1890s, the court showed no interest in putting any limits on federal land acquisition. For example, it held in 1896 *United States v. Gettysburg Railway Co.* that creating a military park was a "public purpose" for which the eminent domain power could be used, extending the war power to anything that might "enhance [a citizen's] love and respect for those institutions for which . . . heroic sacrifices were made."[6] But the fight over the Appalachian and White Mountain proposals wasn't waged in court; it was waged in Congress and the executive branch—and key actors in those arenas had more restrictive views about the legitimate purposes for which federal tax dollars could be used. A military park at Gettysburg had at least a tenuous link to the war power; a recreational resort in the mountains had less obvious connection to any federal purpose. Advocates accordingly petitioned Congress not for a park but for a forest reserve, and they confined their arguments to the two familiar rationales for forest conservation: to protect the commodity value of the hardwood forest and to protect its function in regulating streamflow.

Bills to protect the Appalachian and White Mountain forests were introduced regularly between 1901 and 1908, but the first bill to receive sustained attention in Congress was introduced by North Carolina Senator Pritchard in 1902. His speech was carefully constructed to address what he clearly anticipated would be the chief argument against the bill: Nothing in the Constitution authorizes the federal government to protect forests that don't lie on federal lands. Pritchard addressed the question squarely. He framed the bill as a response to the increased flooding, irregular streamflow, and soil erosion suffered by downstream states as a result of the deforestation of the steep mountains in North Carolina and Tennessee: "It is the well-settled policy of the Government to appropriate money whenever it becomes necessary to do so in order to facilitate commerce and transportation in those states along the coast, as well as those through which our large rivers flow. . . . Any expenditure which facilitates transportation and encourages the development of commerce is legitimate and proper."[7] He pointed out that the federal government spends "immense sums" on dredging harbors, so it is "right and proper and much less expensive, as a precautionary measure, to appropriate money to preserve the forests" to prevent soil erosion—particularly in states that were not geographically located so as to benefit from harbor development.[8] He also cited the value of ensuring a regular streamflow for hydropower plants being established downstream of the mountains. He summed up the rationale concisely: "The primary object of the proposed forest reserve is to perpetuate the forest on the steep mountain slopes of this Southern Appalachian region in such a way as to prevent or minimize the floods on the streams rising in this mountain region and to perpetuate their value as a source of power for the development of manufacturing interests."[9] He acknowledged that the mountains have value as a pleasure and health resort, but that was not his reason for supporting the measure. Finally, he concluded that federal government must take on this project because private actors lack the incentives to engage in long-term forest preservation, and upstream states lack the incentives to protect forests in order to benefit downstream states. The efforts of New York and Pennsylvania to protect their forests, he noted, were aimed at protecting rivers that lie entirely within their borders. Federal action is necessary to protect interstate rivers.

Pritchard's speech lays out the main argument that conservation proponents would continue to press in Congress: that forest conservation is an exercise of Congress's authority, under the Commerce Clause, to improve navigable waters in order to promote economic development. The state incapacity argument is particularly noteworthy, because if the only goal of the policy were to protect wood supplies for future generations, then states could do so themselves under their police power. The rationale for federal intervention rests entirely on the ecological theory that forests in Tennessee and North Carolina are protecting *water* resources that benefit farmers and businesses in Georgia and other downstream states.

Resting forest conservation on Congress's authority to aid economic activity downstream was not as uncontroversial as Pritchard implied, however. The Commerce Clause undoubtedly gave the federal government the authority to *regulate* commerce, including commerce on navigable waterways.[10] But whether and how far it could *promote* commercial activity by spending money was far from settled. To understand the problem faced by the proponents of the eastern forest reserves, we will have to take a fairly extensive detour into this constitutional debate over the federal spending power, particularly as it applied to water resources.

Water Reclamation

Federal authority to protect and develop water resources was a major theme in the nineteenth-century debate over federal funding of "internal improvements" to promote commerce. As discussed in the introduction, Southern Democrats favored a narrow reading of the Article I, Section 8 spending clause (giving Congress authority to "To lay and collect Taxes, Duties, Imposts and Excises, to pay the Debts and provide for the common Defence and general Welfare of the United States"), arguing that Congress could spend federal revenue only for those objects specifically enumerated in the rest of Section 8. Building roads, canals, and other improvements, they contended, was not a federal function. That argument reemerged during the post–Civil War debate about water reclamation.

The campaign for federal water reclamation and irrigation in the arid West began in the 1870s but picked up momentum when John Wesley Powell, the director of the US Geological Survey, received authorization from Congress to survey the arid lands of the West in 1888. Western leaders were well aware that settling these lands would require investment in irrigation, and one of the main themes in western politics was the debate over whether irrigation projects should be funded by private companies, state government, federal government, or some combination of the three. Powell had some creative ideas about the governance of western watersheds, but he endorsed the prevailing view that federal constitutional authority over water did not extend to constructing irrigation projects. Importantly, that view was shared by the nation's premier water development agency, the Army Corps of Engineers.[11]

The Army Corps of Engineers (ACE) had been responsible for federal programs to develop water resources since 1824. After the Supreme Court decision in *Gibbons v. Ogden*, Congress authorized the ACE to take on projects aimed at improving the navigability of rivers, which initially meant clearing obstacles and straightening and deepening channels. After the Civil War, however, the ACE started to pursue more ambitious projects, including building canals, locks, and dams to facilitate river commerce. It also (beginning in 1879) gradually entered into flood control through levee construction. Nevertheless, the ACE's official position was that its primary mission was navigation, and other goals of water resource development were secondary.[12] Water storage and irrigation would be a significant expansion of its power, and the ACE did not support such an expansion.

In the 1880s, federal irrigation projects didn't seem necessary; state and private parties were investing enough in irrigation projects to satisfy westerners. But the economic downturn in 1893 renewed calls for federal intervention. At this point, California lawyer George Maxwell and Frederick Newell, a hydraulic engineer with the US Geological Survey, emerged as national leaders of the movement for a federal irrigation program. They organized the National Irrigation Association and won support for federal action from the National Board of Trade and the National Association of Manufacturers, among others.[13] The irrigation movement in Congress was led by several westerners, including Wyoming Senators Francis Warren and Joseph Carey and Nevada Senator Francis Newlands.

Their first successful bill, the 1894 Carey Act, generated considerable debate but raised no significant constitutional issues. The Act provided that the federal government could cede to states with arid lands one million acres of public land for water reclamation. The state could either irrigate the land itself or contract with private companies. They would not receive the patents to the tracts until they were irrigated and occupied by settlers. This policy was modeled (with some improvements) on the 1850 Swamp Land Act, which ceded swamplands to states so that they could drain and develop them.[14] While the Swamp Land Act had led to considerable fraud, no one questioned its constitutionality. The debates over the Carey Act, to the extent they touched on constitutional issues at all, merely reinforced the constitutional common sense that federal government cannot spend general tax revenues on irrigation but may dispose of public lands for this purpose.[15]

The Carey Act was a failure. Most of the irrigation companies that sought land under its provisions failed—primarily because of the general economic malaise of the 1890s but also because the Department of the Interior was inefficient at processing land claims. But support for a federal irrigation program kept growing. In particular, Senator Warren kept the cause alive in Congress by seeking small appropriations to conduct a survey of potential reservoir sites in Wyoming and Colorado. In 1896, he succeeded in winning support for this survey by amending a bill appropriating funding to improve rivers and harbors, arguing that reservoirs at the Missouri headwaters would promote commerce. That amendment generated some debate, but constitutional concerns were not raised. Instead, a few senators objected that irrigation wasn't germane to river and harbor development, which was the subject of the bill. Warren agreed to drop the word "irrigation" in the amendment and received the funding.[16]

Unfortunately for Warren, the survey, carried out by ACE engineer Hiram Chittenden, concluded that storage reservoirs would not significantly contribute to flood control or navigability on the Missouri River. But Chittenden did identify several sites in Wyoming and Colorado that would be suitable for reservoirs to aid in irrigation.[17] Warren thus returned to Congress in 1899 and again proposed an amendment to the rivers and harbors appropriation bill to fund construction of three reservoirs in Wyoming. This proposal did generate a long debate in both the House and the Senate over the constitutional authority of federal government to spend tax revenues on irrigation projects.

The amendment's supporters in the House relied heavily on the commerce power. The federal navigation servitude was broad, supporting virtually any project that could claim to improve the navigability of rivers. In fact, a case before the Supreme Court while the debate was taking place promised to confirm this broad reading of the navigation servitude. In November 1898, the court heard arguments in *United States v. Rio Grande Dam and Irrigation Company*[18] concerning whether the United States could enjoin construction of a dam across the Rio Grande in the New Mexico Territory (part of a private irrigation project) to protect the navigability of the river. In May 1899, about three months after the congressional debate on Warren's amendment, the court would rule that it could do so under the federal power to protect navigable waters. The significance of the decision is that the Rio Grande was not in fact navigable in New Mexico; it became navigable much further downstream. But the court held that the federal navigation servitude allowed Congress to prohibit "any obstruction to the navigable capacity, *and anything, wherever done or however done, within the limits of the jurisdiction of the United States* which tends to destroy the navigable capacity of one of the navigable waters of the United States."[19] In other words, federal power over water resources extended to any land with an important hydrological connection to navigable waters. The implications for forest conservation would soon be clear, but the case also demonstrates that the commerce power could be an expansive source of authority for the storage reservoirs that were central to irrigation projects.

For example, Congressman Carter's argument in favor of Warren's proposal began by reminding the House that they had approved a reservoir at the headwaters of the Mississippi River (Lake Itasca), which was justified as an attempt to reduce flooding and improve navigation by regulating streamflow downriver. He argued that a similar rationale could support constructing reservoirs at the headwaters of streams in arid regions—and if those reservoirs could also provide water for irrigation, that should be constitutionally permissible.[20] That was as far as the constitutional debate went in the House, but a more elaborate exploration of this argument took place in the Senate.

Wisconsin Senator Spooner, a noted expert in constitutional law, objected that regardless of the language about navigation in the amendment, the "real object of the proposed expenditure is to secure the construction of reservoirs in the States for irrigation purposes," which the federal government had no constitutional authority to engage in. When asked why the federal government could improve rivers and harbors, he responded that those works aimed at "facilitating the *transportation* of commerce, not creating a subject of commerce."[21] That distinction may sound like quibbling, but it had strong support in constitutional doctrine. The courts typically held that an item manufactured within a state did not become subject to the federal interstate commerce power until it entered the "stream of commerce" by being introduced into the interstate transportation system. Thus "commerce" could be distinguished from manufacturing and agriculture by involving the transportation of goods.[22]

Nevertheless, "commerce" could be interpreted more broadly. After all, Justice Marshall in *Gibbons* famously defined commerce as "the commercial intercourse between . . . parts of nations, in all its branches."[23] The amendment's supporters thus sought to undermine Spooner's distinction. Senator Allen asked whether improving rivers and harbors and building canals did not "aid commerce." Spooner agreed they did. And railroads (which Congress had also funded)? Spooner conceded that point as well. Allen then brought up levees, which protected farmlands from flooding. Spooner argued that the main purpose of levees was to keep the Mississippi River, "which is a great national highway," within certain limits. The benefit to the farmland is only incidental. That, of course, must have sounded absurd even to Spooner, who knew full well that the rationale for the levees was to protect and promote agriculture in the floodplain.

But Senator Clark had the most effective argument. He pointed out that Spooner "did not object to the provision by this Government to conserve water . . . by taking 1,000,000 or 1,500,000 acres from the public domain and out of the control of the States and out of settlement for the very purposes which he says this can not accomplish." Clark was referring to the Big Horn Forest Reserve, which was located near the proposed sites of these reservoirs. Spooner insisted that he had objected to the forest reserve—but had to concede that he objected only to the method by which they were created (by executive order). He could not deny that he supported federal authority to create forest reserves to conserve water at the headwaters of streams; indeed, that position had been endorsed by virtually everyone, including the strongest foes of federal conservation. At that point, Spooner insisted somewhat weakly that reserving forests was different from building reservoirs, but he did not attempt to defend the distinction.[24]

This exchange is significant for two reasons: First, it illustrates the erosion of the traditional limits on federal spending. Once Congress authorized the construction of levees to protect farmland on the floodplain, it was hard to argue that other public works projects to aid agriculture were beyond federal power. Second, it highlighted a key connection between water reclamation and forest reserves: The forest reserves were promoted as naturally occurring reservoirs. That analogy would have important constitutional implications, but those implications weren't developed during this interchange.

However, a different approach was suggested toward the end of the debate by Ohio Senator Foraker. He noted that "nearly all the arid land which is to receive the benefit of irrigation is public land belonging to the United States Government. Clearly the Government has the inherent power to improve its own property."[25] (Indeed, the Supreme Court in the *Rio Grande* case would confirm "the right of the United States, as the owner of lands bordering on a stream, to the continued flow of its waters; so far at least as may be necessary for the beneficial uses of the government property.")[26] On that ground, he could support the proposal. This argument received little attention in the debate, but, as we will see, in the next few years it would move to center stage.

In the end, Warren was unable to win enough support from eastern representatives, and the amendment was defeated. But the debate revealed that any further proposals for federal irrigation projects would encounter constitutional objections, and irrigation supporters had to be ready to meet them.

The Newlands Reclamation Act

Initially, reclamation advocates seemed likely to follow Senator Clark's reasoning, supporting federal irrigation authority by linking it to forest conservation. The two movements had often been at odds with one another, but they joined forces in the 1890s.[27] George Maxwell and Frank Newell promoted the alliance as a way of broadening the support in Congress for both forest reserves and irrigation projects.[28] The political logic of the alliance was straightforward: Western representatives would support eastern forest reserves if eastern representatives supported western irrigation projects. The scientific logic behind the alliance was the forest-streamflow connection: Leaders of both movements argued that forest preservation was critical to preserve the streamflow on which irrigation depended. But the constitutional logic was important as well: The irrigation proponents argued that if the federal government could create forest reserves to conserve water, why not also create man-made reservoirs? Theodore Roosevelt's First Annual Message to Congress follows that logic:

> The forests are natural reservoirs. By restraining the streams in flood and replenishing them in drought they make possible the use of waters otherwise wasted. They prevent the soil from washing, and so protect the storage reservoirs from filling up with silt. Forest conservation is therefore an essential condition of water conservation.
>
> The forests alone cannot, however, fully regulate and conserve the waters of the arid region. Great storage works are necessary to equalize the flow of streams and to save the flood waters.

Defending federal action, Roosevelt argued:

> Their construction has been conclusively shown to be an undertaking too vast for private effort. Nor can it be best accomplished by the individual States acting alone. Far-reaching interstate problems are involved; and the resources of single States would often be inadequate. It is properly a national function, at least in some of its features. It is as right for the National Government to make the streams and rivers of the arid region useful by engineering works for water storage as to make useful the rivers and harbors of the humid region by engineering works of another kind.

Importantly, by "useful" he meant "useful for agriculture." In arid lands, "the object of the Government is to dispose of the land to settlers who will build homes upon it. To accomplish this object water must be brought within their reach."[29] With his usual confidence, Roosevelt assumed the constitutional problems wouldn't pose a major barrier to such a program.

Nor did they. Both parties in their 1900 platforms endorsed a federal irrigation program, and Congress took the matter up in 1901–1902. By this point, reclamation proponents had worked out their constitutional case. But despite Roosevelt's address, the commerce power was strikingly absent from it. The reclamation advocates had apparently decided to abandon their forest conservation allies.[30] The best support for eastern forest reserves would have been congressional endorsement of either a broad reading of the spending power as extending to any subject conducive to the "general welfare," or a broad reading of the commerce power as including the power to promote commerce. But the reclamation proponents adopted neither theory.

Instead, the Newlands Reclamation Act rested almost entirely on the Property Clause. As historian Donald Pisani notes, this decision reflected Senator Newlands's desire to shift reclamation authority away from the Army Corps of Engineers and the river and harbor appropriations process. Newlands proposed that money from public lands sales be placed into a fund, controlled by the secretary of the Interior, to be used to build storage reservoirs on public lands. The water from the reservoirs would be available to irrigate those lands. The irrigated land would be sold to settlers, and the money would go back into the fund to support more irrigation projects. The proposal thus had nothing to do with controlling navigable streams; it was presented as a proposal for improving the value of public lands.

This proposal neatly sidestepped the constitutional objections plaguing earlier federal reclamation proposals. As explained in the various congressional reports on the bill, a key difference between this and earlier proposals was that this bill proposed to use not general tax revenue but money from the sale of public lands. Wyoming Congressman Frank Mondell— normally a strong advocate of states' rights—was a leading supporter of the proposal and offered the most extensive constitutional defense of it. He agreed that the Democratic Party had always insisted that general tax revenue can be spent only for purposes explicitly delegated to the federal government in the Constitution. However, he insisted that Democrats had always acknowledged that use of *other* revenues, including revenues from public lands, is limited only by the requirement that it be spent for the "general welfare." Representative Underwood in the House debate elaborated, listing the various purposes for which public land and revenues from their sale had been spent, including bounties for soldiers and sailors, expenses connected to managing the public lands, construction of canals, highways, and levees, paying for state educational institutions, and funding of railroads.[31] Mondell further opined that Congress's authority under the Property Clause is plenary. It may dispose of the public lands in any way it sees fit.[32] A few other supporters did bring up the rationale that Congress may promote commerce by developing water resources, but that argument received very little attention. The proposal was clearly designed to rest firmly on the property power.

From the reclamation movement's point of view, this constitutional argument was quite successful, and the bill's opponents had considerable difficulty countering it. Congressman Ray (New York) authored the main constitutional argument against the proposal, contained in the Minority Report to the House Report on Reclamation of Arid Lands (and repeated frequently in the congressional debate). He argued, first, that irrigation had no connection to interstate commerce—a point that the proponents did not bother to refute. Second, he contended that the Property Clause gave Congress the authority only to "dispose" of public lands, not to improve them.[33] Third, he insisted that spending money on irrigation did not serve the "general welfare." On the contrary, making public lands more valuable for agriculture would diminish the value of existing farms.

Ray undoubtedly knew that these arguments were not likely to prevail in the face of the considerable judicial authority that the property power is, in fact, plenary. So he pointed also to two other provisions of the act. Section 7 authorized the secretary of the Interior to use the power of eminent domain when necessary for construction projects, and Section 8 provided that the projects must respect state water law. Ray pointed out (correctly) that some projects would require the newly created Reclamation Bureau to acquire water rights, and the secretary might use the eminent domain power to do so. This use of eminent domain, he insisted, would be unconstitutional because irrigation does not constitute a "public purpose" for federal government.

Mondell impatiently dismissed this last objection in the House debate. While he was inclined to agree that the federal government couldn't use eminent domain to acquire water rights where state law didn't allow it, he pointed out that some states did allow this use, and in any case, he did not anticipate that condemnation would be necessary for most projects.[34] After all, the federal government owned 60 to 92 percent of land in arid regions and would therefore own the water rights attached to that land.[35]

Despite resistance from some eastern representatives, the Newlands Act passed in March 1902, and the Supreme Court endorsed the theory under which it was passed in the 1907 *Kansas v. Colorado*[36] decision. This case concerned a dispute between Kansas and Colorado over water rights in the Arkansas River. Colorado had adopted a "prior appropriation" rule for water rights, whereby individual rights to water were acquired by appropriating the water and putting it to beneficial use. Large-scale irrigation projects in Colorado appropriated a significant amount of water in the river system, which deprived Kansans' of the water they wanted for their own irrigation projects. Kansas therefore sued Colorado, claiming that (under the older common law "riparian rule") they had a right to reasonable use of the water flowing through their property; upstream users couldn't interfere with that use.

Because the case was between two states, the parties could go directly to the Supreme Court for a hearing.[37] The Court was thus faced with the question of which rule to use in dividing water in an interstate stream between the two states. Colorado argued for complete state sovereignty over all the water within its borders, insisting that it had no obligation to downstream users; Kansas argued that the more traditional riparian rule should hold between states. But the Reclamation Service, which petitioned to intervene in the case, favored neither approach. Acquiring the necessary water rights for federal irrigation projects was proving to be as complicated as Congressman Ray had predicted, since every state had different laws concerning water rights. So the Reclamation Service wanted a ruling from the Supreme Court that the federal government had a right to the water in interstate rivers that superceded the claims of the states.[38]

The solicitor general supported his assertion of federal ownership of waters in interstate streams with two theories: First, he drew on Roosevelt's "inherent sovereignty" argument, insisting that Congress must have the authority to resolve interstate conflicts over natural resources and therefore should have sovereignty over interstate water. That argument, unsurprisingly, was tersely rejected by Justice Brewer. Second, and more plausibly, the solicitor general argued that the interstate commerce power supported federal water rights. He reasoned that water in interstate streams is an article of interstate commerce, and federal control of this water was necessary to regulate this commerce. Unfortunately for the Reclamation Service, though, it proved to be too late to resurrect the commerce power argument. Justice Brewer followed Congress's logic in passing the Newlands Act, holding that reclamation was *not* an exercise of the commerce power. According to Brewer, federal reclamation projects rested on the federal government's power under the Property Clause to manage public lands. But states, he held, retained the authority to determine water rights within their borders.[39] (He concluded, interestingly, by asserting *the court's* authority to divide the water between the two states, concluding that Colorado's use of the water had not yet damaged Kansas sufficiently to warrant intervention. We will discuss this exercise of power by the Supreme Court in chapter 9.)

As we have seen, *Kansas v. Colorado* would be cited frequently by proponents of the equal footing doctrine, because it did confirm state authority over water rights, constituting one of the rare defeats in the Supreme Court for federal conservation proponents (if we can call irrigation projects "conservation"). But it also confirmed the plenary nature of the property power, which ultimately supported western forest conservation. Nevertheless, the decision shows that the debate over the Newlands Act did not work a dramatic shift in constitutional doctrine—certainly not the shift that forest conservationists were hoping for. Reclamation proponents backed away from their most radical argument: that the commerce power allowed federal government to develop water resources to aid agriculture and other economic activities directly. As it turned out, later attempts by Newell, Pinchot, and others to expand federal authority to develop water resources for purposes other than navigation would continue to run into constitutional objections—not from the courts but from legislators and, critically, President Taft. It's hard to evaluate a counterfactual, of course, but these objections might have been weakened if the reclamation proponents had secured a consensus in Congress in 1902 on expanding either the spending power or the commerce power to encompass irrigation projects.[40]

However, the debate over the Reclamation Act did reveal growing support for more expansive interpretations of federal authority in economic development. It also confirmed Congress's broad powers under the Property Clause over public lands and underscored once again the enduring consensus that Congress had authority under the Commerce Clause to create reservoirs to manage flooding on navigable streams. It is against this background that Senator Pritchard, in April 1902, proposed that the federal government appropriate money to create forest reserves in Appalachia and the White Mountains.

Appalachian-White Mountain Debate

The movement for federal forest reserves in eastern states gained ground between 1901 and 1906, but constitutional doubts continued to plague advocates. Accordingly, in 1906, Representative Lever of South Carolina sought the help of the US Forest Service legal team of Woodruff and Wells in developing a bill authorizing forest acquisition that would pass constitutional muster. Wells's account of their legal strategy illustrates the constitutional territory created by the reclamation debate.

Wells wrote that he believed Lever's forest reserve proposal was defective because it did not aim at the only constitutional rationale for acquiring lands for forest conservation: to protect the navigability of streams. Thus he "placed the new bill squarely on the navigation improvement basis" by confining the area to be purchased to the watersheds of navigable streams and declaring in the title that its purpose was the maintenance and improvement of navigability.[41] This bill and a companion bill on the White Mountain reserve were introduced to the House, and Speaker Cannon (generally a foe of forest conservation) referred them to the House Judiciary Committee for an evaluation of their constitutionality. That strategy, if intended to kill the bills, backfired. Over some dissent, the committee report (issued in January 1908) confirmed that Congress did have the authority to protect navigable streams through forest conservation.

The committee's analysis began with the rule established in *McCulloch v. Maryland* interpreting Congress's power: "Let the end be legitimate, let it be within the scope of the Constitution, and all the means which are appropriate, which are plainly adequate to the end, which are not prohibited, but consistent with the letter and spirit of the Constitution, are constitutional."[42] The committee then considered the purpose of the bill, which was not, they concluded, to own forests. Rather, the committee aimed to "conserv[e] and regulat[e] water supply and flow of . . . streams in the interests of agriculture, water power, and navigation." It noted that only one of these purposes needed to be constitutional for the measure to be legitimate.[43] Importantly, the committee declined to consider whether the theory that protecting forests aided streamflow was correct. It concluded that one purpose of the bills (if not the only purpose) was to control the watersheds of navigable rivers.[44] The question, then, was whether Congress can acquire lands and establish forest reserves to improve the navigability of navigable rivers.

That question was answered by a line of Supreme Court opinions confirming Congress's power under the Commerce Clause to regulate navigable waters. Moreover, citing *United States v. Rio Grande Dam and Irrigation Company*, it noted that this power extends beyond the navigable part of the river.[45] And if Congress can legislate against obstructions that interfere with navigation, "why has not Congress an equal power to legislate in the same way to *increase* the 'navigable capacity' of such streams?"[46] In the committee's view, if Congress could prevent the construction of a dam to ensure streamflow, it could also prevent the destruction of a forest for the same reason.

The committee also addressed *Kansas v. Colorado*. While that decision denied the power of the federal government to control the water within a state for the purposes of reclamation, it also supported its power to do so for the purposes of navigability.[47] The committee proceeded to consider whether the federal government can acquire land within a state, citing *Kohl v. United States*[48] and other cases confirming that it can.[49] It also, interestingly, opined that federally owned land should be subject to state law, except that the state cannot tax the federal government nor interfere with the purposes for which the federal government acquired the land.[50] That issue would loom large in later debates over federal forest policy. But the opinion emphatically supported the Appalachian and White Mountain bills.

Dissenting from the committee's opinion was Representative Jenkins, the chair of the committee. He authored a minority report arguing strenuously that the proposed forest reserves were not within Congress's commerce power. His argument, although not as well-constructed as the majority opinion, was straightforward: He agreed that Congress may do whatever is necessary to promote navigation but argued that acquiring these forests is not necessary, nor is navigation the true object of the bills. In making this argument, he forwarded a narrow construction of congressional power, rejecting the broad reading in *McCulloch v. Maryland.* Instead, he echoed a long tradition (not endorsed by the courts but enjoying considerable support from Democratic strict constructionists) limiting Congress to only those means *absolutely essential* to accomplishing its goals. Reminding his readers that the state owns the soil under and adjacent to navigable streams (citing *Martin v. Waddell*,[51] *Pollard v. Hagan*,[52] and

Kansas v. Colorado), he insisted that the connection between forests and streamflow is not sufficiently proven to justify what is basically a land grab to expand the federal forest program.[53]

Jenkin's dissent notwithstanding, the committee's opinion was taken as authoritative in the subsequent long and heated debate over eastern forest reserves, which occupied Congress from 1908 to 1911. In July 1909, Representative John Weeks introduced the bill that would eventually become the Weeks Act. Following the committee's reasoning, the bill authorized states to cooperate with one another and with the federal government to protect watersheds of navigable streams and authorized the federal government to acquire land at the headwaters of navigable streams for this purpose. Opponents, rather than attacking the committee's constitutional reasoning directly, followed Jenkin's line and argued that protecting streamflow was not the purpose of the measure at all. For example, Representative Smith complained that the language concerning navigation was added late in the campaign as a mere subterfuge for what was really an attempt by the Forest Service to enter fully into commercial timber production, a view echoed by Senator Teller.[54] They also suggested that the bill was supported by investors in hydropower, implying that promoting hydropower was also not a valid purpose under the Commerce Clause. That point received less attention, however, perhaps because the fact that hydropower developers were concerned about forest conservation supported the theory that forests do in fact affect streamflow.

Questioning that theory was opponents' other line of attack. It was during this debate that opponents of forest conservation mounted the first sustained attacked on the scientific theory underpinning the forest-streamflow connection. Historian Gordon Dodds recounts this erosion of scientific consensus—or perhaps, to put it more accurately, the development of a more nuanced view of the effects of forests on streamflow.[55] Leading the attack was Lieutenant Colonel Hiram Chittenden of the Army Corps of Engineers (ACE) (the same Chittenden who had conducted Warren's reservoir survey in 1898). Chittenden, who had served in the ACE since 1884 and had considerable experience with river management, published in 1908 a critique of the streamflow theory.[56] His basic argument is hard to dispute: He acknowledged that forests can affect streamflow but insisted that the effect depends on many variables and that empirical evidence on the matter is wanting. More specifically, he agreed that forests could retain run-off during normal rainfall events, but he questioned their efficacy under more extreme flooding or drought conditions. Further, because forests prevent snow from drifting and because an even blanket of snow melts more quickly, forests might end up reducing streamflow from melting snow. He also rejected the belief that forests substantially increased rainfall (and on that point, most scientists by 1908 agreed). Finally, and more controversially, he argued that logging forests doesn't contribute to soil erosion; rather, roadbuilding and agriculture is responsible for increased erosion in the Appalachian and White Mountains.[57]

Chittenden's empirical evidence, however—the same as that used by proponents of the streamflow theory—was quite limited. Even more interestingly, the paper did not oppose federal forest conservation. On the contrary, Chittenden recognized that the streamflow theory was integral to the constitutional status of the Appalachian/White Mountain proposal, but he considered the constitutional debate to be a waste of time. Brushing aside fine constitutional distinctions, he asked what is the difference between building reservoirs for irrigation purposes and building them to provide hydropower? If Congress can create parks and reserves on public lands, why shouldn't it be able to buy land to do the same? He in fact suggested that "every State in the Union would ratify an amendment giving to Congress the power to legislate for the conservation and development of the natural resources of the country."[58]

Despite this endorsement, Chittenden's paper, along with a handful of studies questioning the streamflow theory by other ACE scientists, the head of the US Weather Bureau, and independent scientists, was heavily relied upon by congressional opponents of the forest reserve measure.[59] But they were fighting a losing battle. The proposal had broad public support, and the states in question wanted federal forests. And the law itself seemed fairly limited, authorizing acquisition of land only at the headwaters of navigable streams—lands that would have to be certified by the US Geological Survey as contributing to streamflow protection.

Of course, the law only *seemed* limited. The forest conservation movement may have been saddled with a crabbed reading of the commerce power, but even under that reading, its ecological understanding of forests had the potential to expand federal power greatly—as its opponents understood. Even in 1902, Senator Spooner was complaining about the potential scope of this "monumental" project of "controlling rainfall." Senator Bailey agreed: "I think there will be no end to the policy which it will inaugurate. The Government will buy land that has trees to preserve the forest, and next it will buy land that has no trees in order to make a forest."[60] Representative Parker in 1910 argued that under this logic, the government could condemn an entire watershed or acquire all the land in a state to convert to forest.[61] Indeed, as we've seen, Edward Corwin would exploit the forest-streamflow connection in his 1916 defense of the Weeks-McLean Act, linking migratory birds to healthy forests that are essential to protecting streamflow in navigable waters. With the passage of the Weeks Act in 1911, Congress endorsed an ecological conceptualization of the land and water as complex, interdependent systems. Under this view, federal authority to promote the navigability of rivers could lead to federal regulation of, well, just about anything.

Anyone familiar with the usual story about the Lochner era might expect the federal courts to put some limits on this expansive regulatory power. But they did not. Indeed, the courts had little opportunity to rule on the constitutionality of the Weeks Act; the only case I could discover that addressed it was the 1917 decision *United States v. Graham and Irvine.*[62] Graham and Irvine objected to the federal government condemning their land for inclusion in a national forest, arguing that the Weeks Act didn't authorize condemnation and that the federal government had no constitutional authority to acquire land by condemnation anyway. The judge disagreed. An 1888 Act conferred general condemnation authority on the secretary of treasury, and the constitutional question "has been too long and too thoroughly settled to justify discussion."[63]

The Expansion of Federal Spending Authority

The Weeks Act was a victory for the Forest Service, but the rationale under which it passed was still limited. It did not justify acquiring land for the creation of new national parks or protecting wildlife. To be sure, the director of the National Park Service, Stephen Mather, would exercise considerable ingenuity in finding other ways to acquire land, such as carving parks out of existing forest reserves, persuading private parties or state governments to acquire land and donate it to the federal government, and arranging for private landholders to exchange their holdings within parks for other public lands.[64] Wildlife preserves were similarly carved out of public lands in most cases. The National Bison Range is an odd exception: In 1908, in the midst of the debate over the Appalachian and White Mountain debate, Congress authorized—without opposition—appropriations to buy land that had been in the Flathead Indian Reservation in order to create the bison refuge.[65] But further money to buy land for wildlife preservation was not forthcoming.

Congressional resistance to buying land for conservation eroded during the 1920s, however, and the courts supported this change in policy with a more expansive interpretation of the spending power. A critical support for this expansive interpretation was the ecological conception of forests that had been developed in the course of the debates over the eastern forest reserves and federal wildlife policy. Indeed, a key legal foundation for the expansion of federal conservation spending was ratification of the Migratory Bird Treaty in 1916. Under its aegis, Congress passed the Upper Mississippi Wildlife and Fish Refuge Act[66] in 1924 and the Migratory Bird Conservation Act in 1929. The first allowed the Bureau of Biological Survey to acquire land in Illinois and Minnesota for bird refuges; the second extended that power to the rest of the country.[67] The impact of the treaty combined with ecological science on the federal spending power is illustrated in the 1928 federal appellate court decision *United States v. 2,271.29 Acres*, upholding the 1924 Act.[68]

The Wisconsin legislature had originally consented to Congress acquiring 2,271 acres along the Mississippi River for a wildlife refuge but now argued that this acquisition was unconstitutional under either the US Constitution or the Wisconsin Constitution. In rejecting the federal constitutional argument, the court noted that the federal law implemented the Migratory Bird Treaty, and the power to do so was affirmed by *Missouri v. Holland*.[69] The court noted, however, that the federal government probably did not have the authority to establish refuges for other kinds of game, citing *United States v. Shauver*[70] and *United States v. McCullagh*.[71] But, importantly, it concluded that the federal government could regulate other kinds of wildlife in a bird refuge as far as necessary to maintain the refuge as a haven for migratory birds:

> Congress apparently recognized the fact that, as a necessary and natural result of establishing such a refuge, nonmigratory birds, game generally, and, in so far as the lands were overflowed, fish, would resort thereto and breed therein, so that incidentally the area would become a refuge for many kinds of game. Their increase in the area might or might not become inimical to the welfare of migratory birds. On the other hand, the presence of some varieties of other game and fish, and the conservation of aquatic plants, etc., will undoubtedly be of great value to the

area as a refuge for migratory fowl. So it seems quite essential that, as an incident to the maintenance of the refuge for migratory birds, those in charge have some power of regulation over the number and kinds of other game present, and also, in order that the migratory birds may be secure in their refuge, that hunters and fishermen be at times excluded.[72]

Thus the ecological relationships among migratory birds and other organisms—the ecological conception of nature endorsed by *Missouri v. Holland*—supported federal acquisition of land in any habitat favored by migratory birds and the extension of federal authority over other wildlife.

This case is also interesting for the court's interpretation of the impact of the federal government's expanding acquisition authority on state sovereignty. The state argued that the land in question included land under navigable waters (referring to land along the Mississippi River that periodically flooded), which it held in trust for the people of the state and could not alienate, under the public trust doctrine. The court thought that the land in question was not under navigable waters. But even if it was, the court insisted that under *Missouri v. Holland*, the state could alienate the land for the purpose of bird conservation, because "there can exist in the state of Wisconsin no trust or obligation to its people requiring it to refuse consent that the national government carry out the latter's constitutional powers."[73] Since the state could certainly establish such a refuge itself, it can also consent to the federal government doing so. As the court put it, "the [state] Legislature may subordinate the rights of hunting, fishing, swimming, and navigation to the greater public need of better hunting, fishing, and navigation."[74] Thus in contrast to the public trust decisions asserting exclusive state authority over wildlife, the court here adopted a cooperative vision of federal and state power in this area. Under this view, the state could, as it were, delegate its conservation authority to the federal government. After all, both state and federal government had the same interest: protecting wildlife habitat in order to protect wildlife.

This expansion of federal spending on wildlife conservation was accompanied by a similar expansion of federal spending on forest reserves. In fact, in 1924, Congress virtually abandoned the navigable stream limitation on federal authority to create forest reserves. As historian Gordon Dodds points out, by the 1920s, the streamflow theory was no longer orthodoxy, and even the Forest Service was turning to other rationales for forest preservation.[75] Dodds attributes this decreased emphasis on the streamflow theory to the breakdown of scientific consensus, but it is better explained by the fact that the streamflow theory was no longer needed as a rationale for the reserves. (As we will see in the next chapter, the Forest Service was perfectly willing and able to proceed in the face of scientific controversy.) Instead, forest advocates focused on the alternative approach to justifying buying land for forest reserves: They pressed for a new, broader reading of the spending power.

The 1924 Clarke-McNary Act[76] extended the Forest Service's authority to acquire forests to land in the watershed of navigable streams that may be necessary for regulating the flow of navigable streams or which is *suitable for the production of timber.* In other words, it authorizes the federal government to acquire forested land that does not contribute to navigability—and its passage generated almost no constitutional debate. It was preceded by months of hearings on a variety of issues, however, and at one of those hearings, George Woodruff (now attorney general of Pennsylvania) offered a new theory concerning Congress's power to acquire land for forest conservation. He began with the first paragraph of Article I, Section 8: "The Congress shall have Power To lay and collect Taxes, Duties, Imposts and Excises, to pay the Debts and provide for the common Defence and general Welfare of the United States." We will recall that Philip Wells and the Judiciary Committee had followed a tradition of reading this clause to allow federal spending only for purposes expressly delegated to federal government. But Woodruff noted that many constitutional authorities— including President Monroe (reconsidering his veto of the Cumberland Road), along with familiar nationalists like Alexander Hamilton and Supreme Court justice Joseph Story—took the more expansive view of that clause, concluding that it authorized Congress to spend money on anything that would contribute to the "general welfare." Woodruff combined that clause with the Article IV property clause, which allowed the federal government to "dispose of" its property, *including its tax revenues,* in any way it liked. Together, he argued, these clauses indicate that government may raise money and spend it for the general welfare, without limitation.[77]

The argument was persuasive to the bill's authors, and Congress showed little interest in the constitutional question. When Representative McLaughlin tentatively raised the Constitution in debate, Representative Clarke assured him that the solicitor of the Forest Service had declared the act constitutional, and that ended the discussion.[78] In 1936, the Supreme Court endorsed Woodruff's view that the government can spend money for any purpose not explicitly prohibited,[79] and a 1939 decision by a federal district court followed his logic to uphold federal spending on forest conservation.

This 1939 decision is worth reviewing, since it brings together several of the constitutional transformations we have been discussing and demonstrates how they work together to support the Conservation Constitution. *In re United States*[80] arose when the federal government sought to condemn land in New York as part of a USDA wildlife management program involving reforestation. The federal government was proceeding under the authority of the National Industrial Recovery Act,[81] which allowed the secretary of agriculture to carry out conservation programs and to use eminent domain to do so. New York objected to this use of eminent domain and the federal spending power.

The court agreed with New York that the federal government's authority to take property was limited to "public purposes," and the spending power was similarly limited to "the general welfare." But it concluded that preserving forests, even on a small scale, is a national interest:

> It is clear that forestation, prevention of soil erosion and flood control have come to be recognized in the mind of Congress as public necessities if we are to conserve our natural resources. Little question could be raised regarding the authority of the state to fulfill any of these programs. Likewise there can be no doubt that forestation, and flood control on even minor streams, and control of soil erosion even over a comparatively small area affect an interest which is "national and general as contradistinguished from local or special." The nature of the program for wildlife-reforestation projects indicates an activity involving a scope much more extensive than a single state.[82]

The nature of the wildlife-reforestation program, the court noted, necessarily involved more than one state, since it involved migratory animals. It quoted *Missouri v. Holland* for the principle that "here a national interest of very nearly the first magnitude is involved. It can be protected only by national action in concert with that of another power. The subject matter is only transitorily within the State and has no permanent habitat therein."[83] It went on to assert:

> The time for thinking that our natural resources are inexhaustible has passed. Today we realize that they are not, and recent years have shown

realization of this in large appropriations by the Federal and State governments in aid of re-forestation; flood control; and prevention of soil erosion. There can be no doubt that projects looking to flood control, re-forestation and prevention of soil erosion may in and of themselves affect that "general welfare." As to the establishment of game refuges there can be little doubt under any circumstance. It is quite possible that these projects for re-forestation and conservation and flood control may seem to affect only streams and lands within the particular state; that they are local only. But that seldom so results. Further, the projects are not to be considered separately but as part of the entire program contemplated by the acts. These activities may well be and are in aid of the "general welfare" and hence in the "public interest," irrespective of the demands of the economic interests of the country.[84]

The court thus refused to separate the conservation of forests and soil from wildlife conservation; they were all interdependent elements of a comprehensive effort to protect natural ecosystems for the many ecosystem services they provided. The final clause of the quoted passage is particularly interesting, since it suggests that the national interest in conservation may not even be economic and may even be opposed to its economic interests. The federal interest in protecting forests is so patent that "there can be no doubt" that it is a valid subject of the spending power.

Of course, this reasoning remains rooted in the ecosystem service conception of forests and wildlife. It provides less support for the idea that there is a federal interest in the aesthetic and recreational values protected by national parks. Nevertheless, the virtual abandonment of limits on the federal spending power benefited the national park system as well. The National Park Service was finally given limited authority to buy sites with historic value in 1935,[85] and other New Deal programs authorized acquisition of several new park sites. True, the NPS had to wait until the creation of the Land and Water Conservation Fund in 1964 for general acquisition authority.[86] But after the New Deal, constitutional limits on federal spending for conservation were no longer an issue.

Still, it's important to note that these constitutional debates over forest reserves all focused on government control of the federal government's own land or acquisition of land. They didn't directly address whether the federal government could regulate what a private landowner can do. The logic underlying the Weeks Act would suggest that Congress could regulate private forest management, at least where it affected navigable waters. But a small constitutional battle in the years leading up to the Clarke-McNary Act indicates that using Congress's regulatory power to impose regulations on the timber industry was not taken for granted. William Greeley, chief of the Forest Service from 1920 to 1928, explains that Gifford Pinchot, eager to impose federal regulation on the timber industry, worked with several lawyers to find "constitutional grounds on which the federal government might exercise this police power." They considered a prohibition on shipping in interstate commerce those forest products that were not cut in conformity with USDA rules. That was the strategy used by Congress to discourage child labor—but this child labor policy was struck down in 1918 by the Supreme Court.[87] Pinchot's group therefore abandoned that strategy, concluding that imposing a federal tax might be more effective. But Pinchot's efforts to expand federal authority in this direction were ultimately defeated not by constitutional issues but by growing support among key actors (including Greeley and McNary) for a more cooperative approach to forest regulation.[88] Instead of imposing regulations directly on private landowners, the Clarke-McNary Act authorized the federal government to provide funds to states and private forest owners to support cooperative fire protection and reforestation efforts. They left private forest regulation to the states.

Ashwander v. T.V.A.

In sum, by the 1930s, constitutional doctrine had evolved to incorporate an ecological conception of forests. That constitutional "common sense" in turn supported the expansion of the federal property, commerce, and spending powers to encompass forest conservation. In light of these doctrinal developments, the famous 1936 decision, *Ashwander v. T.V.A.*,[89] looks less anomalous than it is usually considered. On the contrary, this decision upholding the Tennessee Valley Authority (TVA)—an ambitious attempt to unify land and water resource management and economic development in one federal agency—rested on long-standing precedents supporting federal authority over natural resource conservation. Faced with a challenge to the hydroelectric dam that was a centerpiece of the project, the federal government pointed to the commerce power (improving navigation on the Tennessee River) and the property power, along with the always-useful war power. The Court—the same court that struck down the Agricultural Adjustment Act,[90] the Bituminous Coal Act,[91] and several other New Deal measures—had no difficulty finding the TVA well within Congress's delegated powers. Key precedents included *Gibbons v. Ogden*[92] and a series of decisions upholding an expansive reading of the Property Clause (including *Light v. United States*[93] and *Kansas v. Colorado*).[94] The key difference between the TVA and most other New Deal interventions in the economy is that the TVA had natural resource conservation as a central goal.[95]

To its critics, of course, the TVA illustrated that their fears about the federal government's expanding authority over natural resources were well-founded. In 1910, George Knapp had warned the public that under the mantle of conservation, the federal government threatened to become "a gigantic feudal landlord, ruling over unwilling tenants by the agency of irresponsible bureaus."[96] In *Ashwander*, the court seemed to support just such a "feudal" agency, with very little regard to its impact on state authority. But how serious was that impact? How did federal ownership of large-scale forest reserves affect state sovereignty? The next chapter focuses on that question: What is the relationship between state and federal authority on public lands held for conservation purposes?

CHAPTER SEVEN

Managing Federal Lands

In 1901, President Roosevelt proposed the creation of game reserves in federal forests. The proposal raised a thorny issue: Can the federal government restrict hunting on public lands that lie within state boundaries? Congressman Lacey, just having secured passage of the Lacey Act, was acutely aware of the sensitivity of states' rights advocates on the issue of hunting, so he asked US Attorney General Philander Knox for a legal opinion.[1] While federal authority to regulate hunting in the territories seemed clear, Lacey wrote, many of the proposed reserves lay within the boundaries of states. Did the federal government have any authority beyond that of an ordinary landowner over this property? How exactly did the Constitution navigate "this borderland of State and national authority"?

That question would prove to be one of the most persistently troublesome constitutional issues raised by conservation policy. Conservationists, in the course of their legal campaigns, had succeeded in establishing that both state and federal government had a legitimate interest in conserving natural resources. But that shared authority leads to the central challenge of federalism, the problem of imperium in imperio: How can two sovereigns govern the same physical territory? The creation of forest reserves and national parks expanded the federal footprint within state borders, even as state governments were creating more extensive natural resource management regimes themselves. Conflicts were inevitable, as were demands for judicial resolution of them.

There were many points of conflict over fencing, trespass, and other land use issues, most of which made their way to the courts. But the most extensive constitutional debate focused on the management of wildlife in federal forests that lay within the borders of states. This issue brought federal policies into potential conflict with state game laws. The constitutional dimensions of this conflict were explored primarily by executive and legislative branch actors, until the issue finally made its way to the Supreme Court in *Hunt v. United States*[2] in 1928. Throughout this period, the courts typically endorsed an expansive reading of federal power to protect public lands, even if the means chosen to do so conflicted with state policy. Importantly, however, this judicial support consisted less in doctrinal innovation than in a tendency to accept federal scientific authority over the claims of the states' scientists. Once the courts accepted the protection of complex ecosystems as a legitimate end of government, conflicts between state and federal government over means inevitably came down to which government had the best scientists. And, as Daniel Carpenter argued, that question strongly favored federal agencies with reputations for competence-based legitimacy—agencies like the Forest Service.[3]

The Wildlife Refuge Debate

From 1902 until 1929, wildlife advocates campaigned for a statute authorizing the president (or secretary of the Interior or of agriculture) to create wildlife refuges on public lands. The campaign had numerous successes. As mentioned in chapter 3, Theodore Roosevelt created fifty-one bird refuges on public lands via executive order, and that power was implicitly affirmed by the 1906 Act to protect game birds in these refuges.[4] Hunting was banned in Yellowstone in 1894,[5] and thereafter hunting would not normally be allowed in national parks. The National Park Service Organic Act[6] affirmed that the purpose of the parks included "conserving wildlife," and no objections (constitutional or otherwise) were raised to this policy in congressional debate.

But restricting hunting and fishing in federal forest reserves was more controversial. In 1902, the first national game refuge bill was proposed, and although it passed the Senate and received a favorable report in the House, it wasn't passed. Subsequently, numerous bills were introduced, but only a handful of refuges were established, such as the Wichita Mountains Game Refuge (1905); the Grand Canyon National Game Refuge (1906); the National Bison Range (1908); and the Pecos National Game Refuge (1912). No general federal refuge law was passed until the 1929 Migratory Bird Conservation Act, authorizing the Department of the Interior to acquire land within state borders for bird refuges. Unlike the creation of the national parks, efforts to create game refuges sparked a long-running constitutional debate focused on the source and extent of federal authority over public lands within states.

The debate began in 1902, with a provision of a bill proposing to transfer control of the federal forest reserves from the Department of the Interior to the USDA (a transfer that would eventually be accomplished in 1905). The 1902 bill also provided that the secretary could set aside portions of the forest reserves as game refuges, with the consent of the governor in which the forest was located. This was the proposal that prompted Congressman Lacey's letter, as well as a similar inquiry from Gifford Pinchot, to US Attorney General Knox.

Knox's 1902 Opinion

In his letter to Knox, Lacey explained his understanding that with regard to forest reserves in the Territories, Congress could accept or modify territorial laws concerning trespass, setting fires, and other normal management matters. But with regard to forest reserves in the states, he asked, since these were withdrawn from entry to serve a "national purpose," "would the powers of regulation and control be greater than those which may be exercised in the preservation and management of ordinary public lands?" In particular, he wondered whether Congress had the power to legislate directly to protect game or was limited to enforcing state game laws.[7] Gifford Pinchot's letter focused more narrowly on whether the secretary of the Interior had been given authority by Congress to ban hunting in the reserves.[8]

Pinchot's question was dealt with fairly easily. As discussed in chapter 5, Congress in 1897 had provided that the secretary of the Interior "may make such rules and regulations and establish such service as will insure the objects of such reservations, namely, to regulate their occupancy and use and to preserve the forests thereon from destruction." It also, however, provided that "the State wherein any such reservation is situated shall not, by reason, of the establishment thereof, lose its jurisdiction, nor the inhabitants thereof their rights and privileges as citizens, or be absolved from their duties as citizens of the State."[9] The statute does not specifically refer to authority over wildlife. Knox interpreted these sentences to mean that Congress had not granted the Secretary authority to change "the settled policy and practice of the Government," which currently allowed hunting.[10] The natural implication of this opinion might be that Congress could, if it chose, prohibit hunting in forest reserves, even if those reserves lay within the borders of states. But Knox's lengthy reply to Lacey's inquiry recognized the complexity of the issue.

Part of the complexity stems from the fact that there are many ways that the federal government can come into control of land. Some federal land, for example, is acquired under the Enclave Clause. As mentioned in chapter 6, under Article I, Section 8, Clause 17, the federal government had the power to exercise "exclusive Legislation" over "all Places purchased by the Consent of the Legislature of the State in which the Same shall be, for the Erection of Forts, Magazines, Arsenals, dock-Yards, and other needful Buildings." There was little controversy that this clause allowed Congress to govern federal enclaves without regard to any conflicting state laws. But Knox set aside the Enclave Clause as a source of authority over the forest reserves. He didn't elaborate on his reasoning, but it was probably because the forests were not "purchased by the Consent" of the state; they were simply reserved from entry. The reserves differed from national parks in this respect; states typically ceded jurisdiction of the parks to the federal government by statute. As we will see, Congressman Frank Mondell would contend that this is why the power of Congress to ban hunting in national parks was never a constitutional issue.

Forest reserves, however, were carved out of federal lands without state consent, so the Enclave Clause did not apply. Knox therefore based his analysis on the Property Clause. Congress's authority to regulate reserves located in the Territories, he began, undoubtedly derived from Congress's power to make all needful rules and regulations "respecting the territory or other property of the United States."[11] The question, then, is whether the framers intended this power to end when a territory becomes a state. The answer, he reasoned, rests on the meaning of "territory" in the clause. Citing the 1840 Supreme Court decision *United States v. Gratiot*,[12] he argued that this word denotes not organized territories (the political units) but simply any land belonging to the United States. And because there is nothing in the clause limiting that power, it does not end simply because the territory in which the land is located has become a state. He bolstered his reading of the clause by asserting that the ratifying states would never have agreed to give up to rival states authority over the vast territories— territories "which had been wrested from Great Britain by the blood and treasure of the people of all the States."[13]

Knox reasoned further that Congress, holding this territory in trust for the benefit of the whole nation, cannot sacrifice any power that it needs to manage that territory. In other words, we should not interpret the various acts creating new states as ceding the federal government's essential authority over federal lands. He concludes, then, that the federal government must have a legislative power deriving from the Property Clause that extends beyond the normal property rights of an ordinary proprietor. For example, while an ordinary private landowner can prevent people from trespassing by claiming the protection of state trespass laws, the federal government not only can use state trespass laws but also can enact its own trespass laws governing entry on federal lands.

That point, Knox recognized, required some further explanation, because there was a Supreme Court decision that seemed to hold otherwise: the 1885 decision *Fort Leavenworth Railroad Co. v. Lowe*.[14] Fort Leavenworth was (and is) a federal military post in Kansas. Fort Leavenworth Railroad owned property (easements, tracks, etc.) within the post, and the state wanted to impose a tax on that property. The railroad claimed that the federal government had exclusive jurisdiction over the military post, so the state tax power could not reach any property located within its borders. The Court disagreed. The federal government did not purchase the fort from the state under the Enclave Clause procedures; it acquired the land long before Kansas became a state. However, the state did formally cede jurisdiction over Fort Leavenworth to the United States in 1875—but the act of cession explicitly reserved the power to tax the railroad. In short, because the state had not ceded complete jurisdiction to the federal government, it retained the power to tax the railroad. That was the narrow holding in the case, but Justice Field went on to review the general rule concerning federal lands within state borders:

> Where . . . lands are acquired in any other way by the United States within the limits of a State than by purchase with her consent, they will hold the lands subject to this qualification: that if upon them forts, arsenals, or other public buildings are erected for the uses of the general government, such buildings, with their appurtenances, as instrumentalities for the execution of its powers, will be free from any such interference and jurisdiction of the State as would destroy or impair their effective use for the purposes designed. . . . But, when not used as such instrumentalities, the legislative power of the State over the places acquired will be as full and complete as over any other places within her limits.[15]

Knox found this characterization of state authority over public lands "as full and complete as over any other places within her limits" somewhat puzzling, since it was "opposed to the uniform practice of the Government from the beginning" and also inconsistent with later decisions by the court. However, he noted that the court in this case was considering a narrow question: whether the state, in ceding jurisdiction to the federal government, could retain the power to tax the railroad. The Court merely confirmed that the state could reserve that power; it was not presented with any question concerning the extent of federal authority in Fort Leavenworth. In short, he was inclined to dismiss Field's broad language as dicta.

The 1897 case *Camfield v. United States*[16] was, for Knox, a more useful guide. This case arose out of an ingenious attempt by Camfield to secure control of twenty thousand acres of public land. Camfield's scheme took advantage of the federal government's practice of dividing public lands into square parcels, numbering them, and then giving to railroads the odd-numbered lots to sell to settlers. Camfield acquired from a railroad all the odd-numbered plots in two townships, so he owned a vast checkerboard of parcels. He then built a fence entirely on his own land, but enclosing all the even-numbered lots as well. The US District Attorney brought suit to compel Camfield to remove the fence, making use of an 1885 federal law that prohibited enclosures that obstructed access to public lands. Camfield claimed that the federal government lacked power to enact the law, but Justice Brown disagreed.

Brown began by noting that the common law recognized that a fence on one's own land might constitute a nuisance to an adjoining landowner. He went on to state:

> While we do not undertake to say that Congress has the unlimited power to legislate against nuisances within a State, which it would have within a Territory, we do not think the admission of a Territory as a State deprives it of the power of legislating for the protection of the public lands, though it may thereby involve the exercise of what is ordinarily known as the police power, so long as such power is directed solely to its own protection.[17]

This reasoning, Knox pointed out, was consistent with earlier decisions[18] supporting Congress's power to pass laws governing use of public lands.

That power undoubtedly extended to banning hunting on federal land. After all, a private landowner may prohibit anyone from hunting on his own land.[19] His position, then, was that Congress can assert the ordinary rights of a proprietor by means of a general statute. Importantly, he did not consider whether Congress could *allow* hunting on public lands in violation of state game laws. But Lacey was not concerned with that more difficult question; his only interest was in confirming Congress's power to protect wild animals from being hunted in forest reserves, not in protecting forest reserves from wild animals.

Doctrinal Background

Knox's analysis is consistent with a long line of judicial decisions confirming the federal government's power to manage its property without regard to state law. Those decisions are worth looking at in more depth, to understand the constitutional concerns raised by the practice of treating federal government as a special sort of property owner within a state. *United States v. Gratiot*, for example, highlights a key issue. In this case, the federal government had leased to defendants a lead mine in the Indiana Territory. After the territory was organized into the state of Illinois, the federal government sued defendants for payment on the lease. Defendants argued that the lease wasn't valid because the federal government had only the power to sell, not to lease, public lands. To rule otherwise, they contended, would be to allow the federal government to establish a widespread system of tenantry. Their attorney explained their logic thus:

> Formerly the lead mines in the now state of Missouri were leased. This was while a territorial government existed there: when Missouri became a state, opposition was made to the system, and to the practice under it. They were successfully resisted, and the whole system was driven out of the state of Missouri. In that state there is no longer a body of tenantry, holding under leases from the United States.
>
> The practice of leasing the lead mines then went into the territory of the United States above Missouri: into the territory of Illinois. It was resisted there, but ineffectually; this resistance cannot be sustained in a territory with equal force as it can be in a state. Illinois has become a state; and she will no longer allow this use of the public lands within her boundaries.[20]

In other words, their argument rested on the claim that a state should be able to protect its citizens from the creation of an oppressive, feudal property system perpetrated by the federal government.

Justice Thompson rejected that argument, however, insisting that "Congress has the same power over [the lead mine] as over any other property belonging to the United States; and this power is vested in Congress without limitation. . . . The disposal must be left to the discretion of Congress."[21] He rejected the states' rights argument by pointing out that the statute authorizing leasing of the mine was passed before Illinois became a state: "She cannot now complain of any disposition or regulation of the lead mines previously made by Congress."[22]

Subsequent judicial decisions largely affirmed Thompson's broad view of Congress's authority over federal lands within a state. Knox relied on *Jourdan v. Barrett*[23] and *Gibson v. Chouteau*,[24] for example, which both held that a state's statute of limitations barring actions to eject trespassers could not be raised as a defense against an action by the federal government to eject trespassers on public lands. As Justice Field reasoned in *Gibson*, "It is matter of common knowledge that statutes of limitation do not run against the State. . . . As legislation of a State can only apply to persons and things over which the State has jurisdiction, the United States are also necessarily excluded from the operation of such statutes."[25] In other words, the federal government is not like an ordinary property owner (who would be subject to the statute of limitations). It is a co-sovereign and under the property power has "the absolute right to prescribe the times, the conditions, and the mode of transferring this property, or any part of it, and to designate the persons to whom the transfer shall be made." The state cannot "interfere with this right or embarrass its exercise."[26] The same logic supported the 1885 decision *Van Brocklin v. Tennessee*,[27] which held that the state cannot tax land owned by federal government, even if it is acquired outside of Enclave Clause procedures.

Those decisions tended to establish federal lands as special territory largely exempt from state authority. But such a rule could not be absolute, as the judges well knew. After all, what if the federal government hasn't enacted any laws—criminal, tort, even family law—in place of the state laws displaced by federal ownership? The prospect of creating a lawless enclave within the borders of states is probably what motivated Justice Field to affirm some state authority over Fort Leavenworth in the *Fort Leavenworth Railroad Co. v. Lowe*, discussed above. *Chicago Rock Island & Pacific Railway Company v. McGlinn*[28] (also decided in 1885) followed the same logic. McGlinn's cow was struck by a train traveling through Fort Leavenworth. A Kansas statute required the railroad company to compensate the cow's owner in this situation, but the railroad argued that since the accident took place within the federal reservation, the state law should not apply. Justice Field disagreed, because "whenever political jurisdiction and legislative power over any territory are transferred from one nation or sovereign to another, the municipal laws of the country, that is, laws which are intended for the protection of private rights, continue in force until abrogated or changed by the new government or sovereign."[29] Since the Kansas law did not conflict with the law of the United States in any respect, it remained in force unless or until the federal government changed it.[30] Importantly, however, that rule did not prevent the federal government from sharing jurisdiction over crimes committed on federal land, as demonstrated in the 1892 case *Benson v. United States*.[31] This decision held that the federal district court could exercise jurisdiction over a murder committed in Fort Leavenworth, even though the crime was committed on farmland and not on land actually used for military purposes. The defendant's lawyer insisted that under *Fort Leavenworth* and *McGlinn*, the federal government had no jurisdiction over farmland, but Justice Brewer rejected that claim simply by stating that "in matters of that kind the courts follow the action of the political department of the government. The entire tract had been legally reserved for military purposes."[32] It's hard to reconcile this conclusion with *Fort Leavenworth* and *McGlinn*; the decision reflects the court's flexible, pragmatic approach to these questions of shared jurisdiction.

In sum, by the end of the nineteenth century, precedent supported the view that under the property power, the federal government had the power to sell, lease, and otherwise establish rules concerning the disposal of public lands within state borders, as well as the power to govern those living on that land, as far as necessary to achieve federal purposes. However, state law remained in effect on public lands, as long as it did not interfere with federal purposes. Indeed, state "municipal law" would remain in effect even after the state formally ceded jurisdiction to the federal government, unless it interfered with the federal use of the land or the federal government changed those laws. This line of doctrine should allow the federal government to ban hunting on public land if necessary to achieve federal purposes, as Knox concluded. But it hardly speaks with a single voice: The decisions provide plenty of support for the view that states should retain some authority to regulate the use of federal lands within their borders, especially those lands acquired outside of Enclave Clause procedures.

Development of the Hunting Debate

The debate over hunting in federal forests fueled the development of constitutional arguments restricting federal management authority over public lands. Congressman Lacey, of course, embraced Knox's analysis, introducing his opinion into the *Congressional Record* in the debate over the 1902 proposal to allow game refuges in forest reserves and referring to it repeatedly in congressional hearings, committee reports, and debates over the issue over the next several years.[33] But this broad claim of federal authority prompted opponents to develop alternative constitutional theories. Wyoming Congressman Frank Mondell took the lead in developing a response to Knox's argument. In 1903, he authored a response to a report by the House Committee on Public Lands on a proposal authorizing the president to create wildlife refuges in forest reserves. Mondell's somewhat intemperate argument calls the bill "radical" and even "stark raving mad."[34] The bill would allow the president to close off vast expanses of state land to hunting, an affront to states' rights and a shock to westerners who had "proudly imagined they had been admitted to the Union with the same privileges, powers, and prerogatives granted and reserved by the people of the other States of the Union."[35] That language suggests that Mondell was thinking about equal footing doctrine, but over the next several years he developed a more narrow critique of Knox's analysis, focusing on state authority over wildlife. His case against federal game refuges rested primarily on two decisions Knox had neglected to consider: *Geer v. Connecticut*[36] and *Ward v. Race Horse.*[37]

Mondell's legal analysis shows up in various congressional reports and debates over the next several years,[38] but the best articulation of his full position is in the 1916 hearing before a subcommittee of the House Committee on Agriculture concerning the Hornaday proposal discussed in chapter 3.[39] The bill proposed to authorize the secretary of agriculture to establish game refuges in federal forest reserves, with the consent of the governor of the state in which the forest was located. In this hearing, Mondell went up against R. W. Williams from the office of solicitor of the USDA and a leading authority on game law.[40] The resulting debate offered an in-depth exploration of the constitutional question.

Mondell argued that Congress had no authority to regulate hunting on forest reserves within states. Agriculture Secretary Carl Hayden had relied on Knox's 1902 opinion in endorsing the bill, so Mondell focused on refuting that argument: First, Knox's opinion rests on the federal government's power to protect its property. Mondell did not deny that power, but wildlife, he contended, is not federal property. Under *Geer v. Connecticut*, the states own wildlife. To be sure, the federal government can protect its lands, trees, and waters, so "the Government would have a perfect right to fence its lands against wild animals."[41] But it has no property interest in wild game. States are the only government with authority to preserve wildlife.

Under that authority, he continued, states can regulate hunting even on public lands. To support that proposition he relied on the 1896 Supreme Court decision *Ward v. Race Horse*, supporting state game laws over federal treaty rights on public lands. Indeed, his legal argument rests almost entirely on his broad reading of that case, so it is worth revisiting it. As discussed in chapters Three and Five, in *Ward v. Race Horse*, the state of Wyoming prosecuted Race Horse, a member of the Bannock Indian tribe, for hunting on public land (outside of the boundaries of the Bannock reservation) in violation of state law. Race Horse argued in defense that his tribe's 1869 treaty with the United States granted members of his tribe the right to hunt on unoccupied lands beyond the borders of the reservation. The Supreme Court nevertheless upheld the conviction. Justice White's opinion reasoned:

> The power of all the States to regulate the killing of game within their borders will not be gainsaid, yet, if the treaty applies to the unoccupied land of the United States in the State of Wyoming, that State would be bereft of such power, since every isolated piece of land belonging to the United States as a private owner, so long as it continued to be unoccupied land, would be exempt in this regard from the authority of the State. Wyoming, then, will have been admitted into the Union, not as an equal member, but as one shorn of a legislative power vested in all the other States of the Union, a power resulting from the fact of statehood and incident to its plenary existence.[42]

This decision was consistent with White's hostile view of Indian treaty rights, but also with his support for state wildlife authority (as reflected in *Geer*, decided the previous year). Its cavalier treatment of treaty rights met with a good deal of criticism, however, and its authority was undermined by later decisions—in particular, the 1905 Supreme Court decision *United States v. Winans*,[43] upholding the Yakima tribe's right to fish in the

Columbia River in violation of state game laws. But, as we have seen, courts, legislators, and litigants continued to cite *Ward* as a leading case on equal footing doctrine.[44] Frank Mondell had represented Wyoming in Congress while *Ward* was making its way through the courts and had supported Wyoming's position by introducing a bill to terminate the Bannock tribe's hunting rights (or at least require them to conform to state game laws).[45] But here he was using *Ward* not to challenge treaty rights but to support the view that the federal government could not regulate hunting within the borders of a state at all. To do so would be to impair state sovereignty.

R. W. Williams responded to Mondell's reasoning with Knox's argument, which he said was the basis of the long-standing position of the Interior and Agriculture Departments on federal authority over wildlife on public lands: Just as a private landowner can bar hunting on his own land, the federal government can bar hunting on federally owned land. In response to Mondell's reliance on *Geer*, Williams reminded the committee members that the Supreme Court was currently considering *United States v. Shauver*,[46] in which the federal government argued that the federal government rather than states owned migratory wildlife.[47] However, he didn't rely on that argument; on the contrary, he agreed with Mondell that "states have authority over the protection of game."[48] He rested his argument for the refuge bill on the federal government's title to land, not to wildlife.

As for *Ward v. Race Horse*, Williams was asked to explain his position on that case but unfortunately was interrupted before he could respond in detail.[49] However, he did point out that the bill in question merely prohibited hunting on federal land when the state would allow it. If allowed to respond in full, he probably would have reminded his audience that *Ward* concerned a federal treaty *allowing* hunting when the state *prohibited* it—a question not raised (yet) by the game refuge proposal. In addition, he referred to *Light v. United States*,[50] which confirmed that the federal government had at least the rights of an ordinary proprietor over public lands, as well as the more recent *United States v. Midwest Oil*.[51] This 1915 decision upheld an executive order temporarily withdrawing some oil-rich public lands from entry. Justice Lamar's opinion for the court relied on *Camfield* and *Light* for the proposition that "Congress not only has a legislative power over the public domain, but it also exercises the powers of the proprietor therein" and that Congress had acquiesced in this exercise of executive power.[52] Mondell's weak response to this point demonstrates the impact of *United States v. Grimaud*[53] and *Light* on the anti-conservationist position. All he offered in support of his restrictive view of federal power was that the federal government's right to protect its property could not extend to the right "to punish in its sovereign capacity acts which do not harm its property."[54]

But it wasn't only judicial precedents that had weakened Mondell's position. Williams also bolstered his case by pointing out that Congress had already established several game refuges on public lands—and Mondell himself had acquiesced in that practice. Williams cited in particular the Wichita and Grand Canyon Game Refuges, the 1906 Act protecting birds in federal bird refuges, and the practice of banning hunting in national parks. Mondell was better prepared for this argument, however. He responded, first, that all of the national parks had ceded exclusive jurisdiction to the federal government; such was not the case with forest reserves.[55] Second, hunting was banned in the Grand Canyon in anticipation that it would soon become a national park. As for the Wichita refuge, it was a special case: It was located in "Indian land," and the Indians were a "lawless, outrageous set" that the state was unable to govern.[56] He also addressed the bird refuges created through executive order, which was obviously a sore point. He insisted that his acquiescence to the 1906 bird protection act was premised on the promise (of Congressman Lacey) that it would *not* be read as authorizing the president to create any more refuges by executive order.[57]

But in the end, Mondell conceded most of the conservationists' position. In his final statement, he even declared, "I am not insisting that the Federal Government has no right to keep hunters off its land" (which, of course, is exactly what he was insisting in his opening statement). His final position was that the federal government could not criminalize the taking of game on public lands; it could impose only civil penalties for trespass.[58] But of course once he admitted that the federal government could impose civil penalties, it would be hard to avoid the conclusion that it could impose criminal sanctions for violating those regulations. That, after all, was the holding in *United States v. Grimaud.*

The only other constitutional theory offered in this debate came from William Temple Hornaday, the chief supporter of the bill. Hornaday argued that Congress's power to create wildlife refuges derived from the power to spend money for the general welfare.[59] Williams, however, had carefully rejected the spending power as a source of authority, no doubt aware of the prevailing view of the limits of this power (as discussed in chapter 6).

This hearing reflects the state of legal opinion on federal wildlife authority on public land within states in 1916. Two key points about the congressional debate should be noted: First, Williams focused exclusively on justifying a federal ban on hunting when state law would allow it, rather than affirming a broader right to either allow or ban hunting regardless of state law. As we will see, this second proposition would also arise and require constitutional defense—a defense that the Knox argument did not easily provide. The second point, however, is that Mondell's argument conceded a much broader federal property power than Williams was asking for. Mondell explicitly confirmed the federal government's power to protect its property from trespass and even from damage done by wild animals. He anticipated that protecting property from damage by animals would consist merely of fencing them out, but the Forest Service would eventually claim authority to use more lethal strategies for controlling game.

Mondell's concessions reflect that fact that he was fighting an uphill battle against a growing body of Supreme Court precedents confirming broad federal authority to manage public lands. We have already discussed *United States v. Grimaud, Light v. United States*, and *United States v. Midwest Oil*, which upheld the authority of the federal government to manage public lands under the property power. That judicial trend continued in 1917 in *Utah Power and Light v. United States*.[60] This suit was brought by the United States against three companies that had built and were operating hydroelectric dams in forest reservations. The defendants argued that state law determined their rights on public lands that lay within the borders of state, and the various states in question had authorized their use of the land. Moreover, the lands were vacant and not being used for any particular purpose by the federal government, so their dams did not interfere with federal purposes.

Justice Van Devanter rejected these arguments. Under the Property Clause, Congress could and did enact legislation governing entry into and use of the forest reserves: "True, for many purposes a State has civil and criminal jurisdiction over lands within its limits belonging to the United States, but this jurisdiction does not extend to any matter that is not consistent with full power in the United States to protect its lands, to control their use and to prescribe in what manner others may acquire rights in them."[61] Citing *Jourdan, Gibson, Camfield,* and *Light,* he continued that "inclusion within a State of lands of the United States does not take from Congress the power to control their occupancy and use, to protect them from trespass and injury and to prescribe the conditions upon which others may obtain rights in them, even though this may involve the exercise in some measure of what commonly is known as the police power."[62] The defendants' chief mistake was that the federal government *had* enacted rules and regulations governing the use of the forest reserves. This was not a situation in which states were exercising their police power over public lands in the absence of federal legislation. As in *Benson,* the court deferred to the federal government's judgment about what constituted a valid federal purpose and use of federal land.

Despite this judicial support for federal authority, however, the conflict between state and federal governments over wildlife in federal reserves would not diminish. On the contrary, it became more heated during the 1920s, as the federal government began pursuing a more aggressive deer management strategy that came into direct conflict with state policies.

Hunt v. United States

The 1920s are usually considered an era of conservative reaction against Progressive reforms, along with the return of a conservative jurisprudence in the courts. But as we have already seen with regard to forest policy, national conservation activity continued apace during this period and constitutional objections to spending on federal conservation programs diminished considerably. Nevertheless, wildlife management remained a point of conflict, as in the wake of *Missouri v. Holland*[63] and the Migratory Bird Treaty Act, both state and federal activity in this arena expanded.

Chapter 2 discussed the expansion of state regulation of fish and game, with the creation of new fish and game commissions and more enforcement mechanisms. At the federal level, too, wildlife regulation was growing more institutionalized, particularly after *Missouri v. Holland* affirmed federal authority over migratory birds. Authority for managing wildlife was divided primarily between the USDA's Forest Service (in national forests) and the Interior's new National Park Service (in national parks). The Bureau of Biological Survey provided expert advice to both agencies. This period was notorious for conflict between the management philosophies of the Forest Service (which favored multiple uses of forests) and the NPS (which sought to maintain "natural" conditions and restrict resource extraction in parks).[64] But federal conservation efforts also fueled conflict between federal and state governments.

Federal/state conflict was probably inevitable, given the expansion of federal authority to acquire land for conservation purposes. In addition to the creation of new national parks, the 1924 Upper Mississippi Wildlife and Fish Refuge Act[65] authorized the Bureau of Biological Survey to acquire land in the upper Mississippi River basin for a wildlife refuge. This expansion continued into the 1930s: The 1929 Migratory Bird Conservation Act[66] gave the secretary of the Interior general authority to acquire land for wildlife refuges, and in 1934 three acts completed federal wildlife conservation policy. The first explicitly granted the president authority to establish game sanctuaries in national forests; the Duck Stamp Act taxed duck hunters to create a fund for waterfowl refuges, thus providing a steady source of revenue for federal conservation programs; and the third act aimed at improving coordination among federal agencies in protecting wildlife habitat.[67] All of these programs expanded the federal government's geographic footprint, not just in the West (where most public lands were located) but in many eastern states. Clarifying who had authority over wildlife in these federal reserves would be an important focus of constitutional debate during this period.

Much of the conflict over wildlife management policy focused on maintaining populations of desirable game animals. The Forest Service, lacking explicit legal authority to create regulations protecting wildlife in national forests, had developed a policy of cooperating with states in the management of game. Under a typical cooperative agreement, some of the forest service officers would become deputy game wardens under state law, allowing them to enforce both state game and federal forest regulations. Some states went so far as to create state game refuges within federal forests or even to cede full authority over wildlife in federal forests to the Forest Service. (North Carolina, for example, ceded authority of game management in the Pisgah National Forest to the Forest Service, which led to *Chalk v. United States*,[68] discussed below). The Forest Service also attempted to influence state game laws either through direct discussion with state game wardens or by influencing state game protective associations.[69] But achieving a coordinated strategy for each forest could be quite challenging, since state officers were subject to different political pressures than were Forest Service officers.

Conflict also evolved over the question of whether to manage predators.

In the 1920s, governmental programs of lethal predator control—which were popular with farmers, ranchers, and hunters—came under attack from the newly created American Society of Mammalogists.[70] Wildlife managers caught in the conflict hoped that a more scientific approach to wildlife management would help to resolve such policy debates among federal agencies and between state and federal actors. Ecology was evolving as an academic field, with theoretical and methodological advances leading to more systematic studies of ecological relations being published in the 1920s (including Charles Elton's seminal work, *Animal Ecology*, in 1927). Much progress was made during the 1920s in formulating questions that were central to wildlife management, such as how many animals the land could support and what the relative impacts of food availability, disease, and predators were on population growth. But answering those questions proved quite difficult. Even conducting accurate counts of elusive animals such as deer was (and remains) a fundamental challenge for wildlife experts.[71] Nevertheless, as this growing body of experts came to dominate government wildlife agencies, conservation policy debates often became debates about different scientific theories, and ecological science increasingly structured discourse about the means and ends of wildlife management. Ecological science also proved to be an important support for federal wildlife authority in the courts, as we see in the most important Supreme Court case on conservation policy during this period, *Hunt v. United States*.

Hunt grew out of the famous effort to control the deer population in the Grand Canyon Game Preserve. Created by Theodore Roosevelt in 1906, the preserve encompassed the Kaibab National Forest (covering the Kaibab Plateau on the north rim of the canyon) and part of what would become (in 1919) the Grand Canyon National Park—all of which lay within the borders of Arizona, which became a state in 1912. The Kaibab Plateau had been used for livestock grazing and timber production, but by the early 1920s these uses had diminished.[72] To the growing constituency for national parks, the chief value of the Kaibab lay in the recreational value of its pine forest and wildlife. The deer management problem arose out of concerns in the early 1920s that the deer population was exceeding the Kaibab's "carrying capacity." "Carrying capacity" was itself a relatively new idea in ecology, borrowed from range science. In the Kaibab, it meant that the grazing deer seemed to be impairing the pine forest's ability to regenerate. Forest Service personnel concluded that the problem lay in the Plateau's geographic situation. The Kaibab Plateau starts in sagebrush desert just north of Arizona and runs south, rising to nine thousand feet above sea level (becoming forested as it gains elevation) before dropping abruptly into the Grand Canyon. It is bounded on three sides by sheer cliffs, making it nearly impossible for deer to migrate onto or off of it. Unfortunately, the federal government's own predator-control program had reduced the number of mountain lions, wolves, and other "natural checks" on the Kaibab deer population. Thus the forest seemed to be at risk of being destroyed by its growing population of deer.[73] Managing this relatively isolated forest and its deer proved to be an important learning experience for the Forest Service and for the field of ecology. But the management challenges were not purely ecological.

The Kaibab National Forest is under the authority of the Forest Service, which has responsibility for most of the game preserve as well. But part of the preserve lay within the borders of the Grand Canyon National Park. So the Park Service shared responsibility for the deer herd. The state of Arizona, of course, also claimed authority over all the wildlife within its borders. And the scientists at the Bureau of Biological Survey, which was supposed to serve both the Forest Service and the National Park Service, were involved in the management question as well. During the 1920s, these groups came into conflict over whether to reduce the Kaibab deer herd by allowing deer hunting on the plateau. The Forest Service and Biological Survey, worried by evidence of heavy browsing by the deer on the trees and shrubs, favored allowing either commercial hunting or at least sending government employees out to cull the herd. Secretary of the Interior Hubert Work and National Park Service director Stephen Mather, on the other hand, were concerned that allowing hunting in the game preserve would undermine their efforts to protect wildlife in the Grand Canyon National Park and set a precedent that might lead to opening national parks to recreational hunting.[74] Arizona's Governor Hunt also opposed the hunt, because he considered the large herds of deer on the peninsula to be an important tourist attraction.[75]

Without support from the state of Arizona, the Forest Service's authority to open the reserve to hunting was in question. That question drove a good deal of interaction between the field officers and their supervisors back in Washington, DC, as well as assorted lawyers working for the Service. That discussion is worth exploring in detail, because it illustrates how constitutional doctrine influences agency decision-making, as well as the role agency personnel can play in generating and forwarding legal arguments.

In 1923, the chief of the Biological Survey, Edward Nelson, asked R. W. Williams—now serving as the solicitor of the Forest Service—for an opinion. Importantly, his question was not the one addressed by Knox's opinion and the 1916 congressional hearing: The issue was not whether the federal government could *prohibit* hunting in national forests when state law *allowed* it but whether the federal government could *allow* hunting on its own land when state law *prohibited* it.

The answer, according to Williams, was no.[76] The primary problem, for Williams, was the Lacey Act. Whatever constitutional powers the federal government might have over the deer in the Kaibab, hunting the deer would involve doing something with the deer carcasses—most likely selling them or shipping them out of Arizona. But the federal Lacey Act prohibited selling or shipping out of state any wildlife taken in contravention to state law. Nelson, in a memorandum on the subject, noted that getting permission from the state officials for a deer hunt was politically necessary in any case. On that point, Williams had assured him that if the state agreed, the Lacey Act wouldn't prohibit exporting surplus deer.[77]

This opinion was sufficient to discourage Nelson's plan for commercial hunting, at least temporarily. Instead, Agriculture Secretary Henry C. Wallace convened an investigating committee in 1924 to study the problem of deer control on the Kaibab peninsula. Members of the committee included prominent conservationists John Burnham (chair), Heyward Cutting, and T. Gilbert Pearson, as well as T. W. Tomlinson of the American National Livestock Breeders Association. But the committee's report relied heavily on the experts in the Forest Service and Biological Survey, and unsurprisingly they came to the conclusion that the deer population in the Kaibab required "scientific management," which meant culling the population. The committee members were well aware of the uncertainty about the size of the deer population; estimates ranged from twenty to fifty thousand. Their report compromised on what they decided was a conservative figure of twenty-five thousand. But they also concluded that because the "natural checks" such as predatory animals had been reduced, the deer population was likely to keep increasing. Thus they proposed that to protect the forest, half of the estimated 25,000 deer should be removed as soon as possible, either by trapping and relocating them or by hunting.[78]

The report did not settle the management debate. Stephen Mather publicly disputed it in an issue of *Outdoor America*, whose editor supported Mather's anti-hunting position, as did Arizona Governor Hunt.[79] Meanwhile, assistant forester Will Barnes was pressing his superiors to initiate a lawsuit to test the legal question. Barnes had no legal training, but that didn't stop him from arguing strenuously that the 1906 Act creating the game preserve gave the secretary of agriculture absolute authority over game animals in the preserve. But (he wrote in a letter to the District Forester R. H. Rutledge), "I found myself. . . . in the minority, opposed by the Solicitor's office and by about everybody else connected with the whole affair."[80]

Nevertheless, Forest Service officials decided to reconsider the legality of holding a public deer hunt. In September 1924, after reviewing a draft of the Burnham report, assistant forester E. A. Sherman and Forest Service grazing inspector Chris Rachford again consulted with R. W. Williams. We have no record of Williams's reply, but either with or without his blessing, the Forest Service opened the plateau to hunting for eight days in November 1924.[81]

This hunt prompted swift action by the state of Arizona. Because the hunt was not in accordance with Arizona game laws, Governor Hunt promptly ordered that the hunters be arrested. Will Barnes wrote to Rutledge arguing in favor of letting the matter go to court as a "friendly test case" and even wrote to the *Phoenix Republican* laying out his theory that the secretary of agriculture had complete authority over the deer. However, a telegram from Chief Forester William Greeley to Rutledge cautioned that the solicitor's office was still doubtful about winning the case if the matter went to court.[82] The Forest Service accordingly backed down, temporarily, and stopped issuing hunting licenses.

Over the next several months (and in the wake of a disastrous attempt to trap and relocate the deer), the Forest Service tried to resolve the conflict. They did manage to secure an agreement with Arizona's game warden to allow the federal employees to conduct a hunt when needed, but Governor Hunt remain opposed and scuttled the agreement. In October 1925, Agriculture Secretary William Jardine authorized the Forest Service to open the peninsula to deer hunting despite the state's opposition. Again, hunters licensed by the Forest Service were threatened with arrest by the state game warden. At this point, the US District Attorney John B. Wright, Assistant District Attorney George Hill, and Manley Thompson from the

Forest Service law office met to discuss the issue and decided to petition the US district court for an injunction to prevent the state from enforcing its game laws in the Kaibab National Forest.[83]

The case was heard by the District Court of Arizona, which issued its decision for the United States in May 1927. Arizona appealed the decision, and the Supreme Court heard the case in October 1928, ultimately upholding the lower court's decision. What is striking about both opinions, however, is that they are remarkably barren of doctrinal analysis. The federal government's brief in the district court invited the court to reject the "fiction" of state ownership of wildlife.[84] But the court declined that invitation. It was the scientific data and theories provided by the Forest Service that guided the judge's decision.

The Forest Service's case relied in large part on the 1924 report, with supporting statements from several witnesses testifying to the degraded condition of the forest and the thin, apparently starving deer. Arizona also presented affidavits from witnesses who had found the forest and deer to be in good condition.[85] But Judge Ross's opinion accepted the Forest Service's account:

> The case shows that the number of deer upon [the peninsula] increased from the comparatively small number of about 3,000 or 4,000 to about 30,000 in 1925, according to an estimate of the United States Forest Service, and to such an extent that in years of scant rainfall the feed upon the preserve was so insufficient that large numbers of them died from starvation, and others sustained life only by eating many of the young trees growing upon the lands, and in many instances the twigs and young growth of the old trees, to the serious damage of the property of the complainant.[86]

The judge did not explain exactly what he meant by "damage." The typical case supporting the right of landowners to protect their property usually concerned crops, domestic animals, or trees with commercial value.[87] But in this case, the Forest Service was trying to protect vegetation that wasn't likely to be logged or grazed by cattle, and it was doing so primarily for the benefit of the deer herd itself. It seemed to be going beyond conventional economic understandings of "damage."

Indeed, the federal government's brief emphasized the Forest Service's management goal of protecting both the deer herd and the forest by "maintaining a balance" between deer and forest—a distinctively ecological idea.[88] Judge Ross accepted that goal, citing Forest Service estimates that 10,000 more deer had died since November 1924, due to insufficient forage, so that only 10 percent of the fawns born in 1924 survived. Importantly, he also accepted the Forest Service's evidence that "the deer confine themselves to the government's reservation (with the possible exception of a few stragglers from time to time), and move from place to place in herds." Briefly dismissing Arizona's entire argument concerning state ownership of wildlife, Ross continued,

> Whether they be the personal property of the United States, as contended by the complainant, or the property of the state of Arizona, for the benefit of its people, as claimed by the defendants, we do not find it necessary to decide, for in either event we think there can be no doubt of the right of the government of the United States to do whatever is necessary for it to do upon its own property to protect it from the depredations complained of, including the killing or removal of whatever number of the deer as many be necessary, without any regard to the game laws of the state of Arizona.[89]

Arizona had apparently conceded the Forest Service's right to kill any particular deer found damaging any particular tree. Ross extended that right by reasoning that "to limit such right to those particular instances would, in our opinion, be a violation of plain common sense, as the fact is shown beyond dispute that the deer move from place to place upon the property in large herds." Citing the Property Clause, he continued that as owner of the land, "the government is legally and justly entitled to protect the entire property of every kind and character, and by means and methods of its own selection exercised through its own agents."[90] In short, the judge entirely embraced the Forest Service's view that protecting the government's property means protecting the forest ecosystem—its regenerative capacity—by maintaining the deer herd at a suitable size.

The decision is strikingly deferential to the Forest Service's expertise, for the facts cited by the judge were not nearly as settled as the opinion suggests.[91] On the contrary, the Kaibab deer problem had become a subject of widespread debate among ecologists. As historian Christian Young explains in his account of the Kaibab deer controversy, throughout this period officials from the Park Service, the Biological Survey, and the Forest Service (including Aldo Leopold) were engaged in a lively discussion with outside experts such as Charles Adams of the American Society of Mammalogists and British ecologist Charles Elton about the factors influencing the deer population. There was little consensus among these experts even on the size of the deer population, much less the factors affecting it and its impact on the forest. Even some Forest Service scientists questioned the population estimates in the 1924 report.[92] The court's analysis gives no hint of these scientific uncertainties.

The decision was not a complete victory for the Forest Service, however. Ross did qualify that the Forest Service's authority did not "include the licensing of hunters to transport deer killed on the reserve to places outside the same in violation of the game laws of Arizona."[93] This qualification posed some difficulty for the Forest Service, since they hoped to bring in hunters from out of state.[94] Will Barnes, with the support of regional law officer Manley Thompson, accordingly pressed Forest Chief Greeley to appeal the decision.[95] But the solicitor general advised that it would be unwise to appeal. Taking a cautiously conservative position, he wrote that the United States had "no greater power over wild game than any other proprietor," meaning that the Forest Service could remove animals that were damaging its property but no more.[96] We see here and throughout this case how legal doctrine matters: Government law officers like R. W. Williams exercised a veto over agency actions, as well as discouraging agency officials from resorting to the courts or appealing decisions. But that power does have its limits. In this case, Arizona decided to appeal the decision, which finally gave Barnes his longed-for test case before the Supreme Court.

The appeal to the Supreme Court followed the same pattern as the litigation in the lower court. The United States' brief (authored by Solicitor General William Mitchell, R. W. Williams, and attorney Robert Reeder) again argued that the federal government had not only the rights of an ordinary landowner but a broader legislative authority to regulate and protect the public domain.[97] It cited in support *Camfield, Utah Power and Light, McKelvey v. United States*[98] (a 1922 decision upholding the conviction of cattle ranchers who obstructed the use of the public range by a group of sheep ranchers) and the 1927 decision *United States v. Alford*[99] (upholding an indictment for lighting a fire near, not on, the public domain). This power allowed the Forest Service not only to kill deer but also to license hunters to take the game out of state (contrary to the district court's conclusion).[100]

Arizona's primary argument[101] was that the state owned the deer. It cited in support the long list of decisions supporting state ownership of wildlife decided before *Missouri v. Holland,* including *Geer v. Connecticut, United States v. Shauver, United States v. McCullagh,*[102] and *Ward v. Race Horse.* It also cited the Lacey Act for the proposition that even if the federal government could kill the deer, it couldn't transport the carcasses out of state in violation of state law.[103] In response to the Forest Service's chief argument, it insisted that the state could prohibit ordinary proprietors from hunting on their own land, offering a misleading quote from *Light v. United States* suggesting that the federal government had *only* the rights of an ordinary proprietor on public lands. (*Light* in fact held that the federal government had *at least* the rights of an ordinary proprietor.)[104]

But Arizona's most creative argument was that, although property owners may kill destructive animals even in violation of state game laws, the owner must show that, at the time of the killing, the particular animals killed were injuring or about to injure the property. The state cited no authorities for that proposition, but it did have some support in case law. For example, *State v. Burk,* a 1921 case out of Washington, suggested that a homeowner could shoot wild animals that were destroying his crops, but the judge noted that "it seems that such killing is justified only when the animal is actually doing injury."[105] However, that statement is mere dicta, since the elk in question in *Burk* were actually running through his cornfield when they were shot. The general rule is that the property owner must reasonably believe that the animal will do damage.

Was the Forest Service's belief reasonable? Arizona thought not. For example, the brief pointed to evidence showing that only a portion of the reserve was being affected by the deer. Such evidence could not justify the "wholesale slaughter of any and all deer" in the reserve.[106] The state also reminded the court that much of the Forest Service's evidence was contradicted by the state's witnesses. In particular, it argued that deer could easily migrate off the peninsula in a northerly direction, feeding on the sagebrush in that part of the reserve. Blaming the poor condition of the deer in 1924 on a drought, the brief concluded that active management of the deer is unnecessary. After all, "deer lived in said reserve long before white men ever saw this country and during all of the time since then nature has kindly taken care of them and will continue to do so, if permitted to take its course."[107] Of course, this appeal to the balance of nature doesn't take into consideration the effect of reducing predators in the forest. But it does point out the very real uncertainties inherent in the ecosystemic conception of the Kaibab forest.

Unfortunately for Arizona, the Supreme Court declined the state's invitation to examine the "reasonableness" of the Forest Service's position.[108] Instead, it affirmed the lower court's decision that the hunt was a valid exercise of the federal power to protect public lands under the Property Clause. Justice Sutherland's short opinion, like the lower court's, is largely free of doctrinal analysis. In concluding that "the power of the United States to . . . protect its lands and property does not admit of doubt," he did not even address *Geer* or *Ward v. Race Horse*.[109] Instead, he followed the federal government's brief in citing *Camfield, Utah Power and Light, McKelvey* and *Alford* for the proposition that the federal government had the power to protect its lands, notwithstanding state law.

Of course, the state had conceded that the federal government could kill the deer if they were actually damaging the forest. Thus the courts' central disagreement with Arizona was less about doctrine but about what sort of evidence was needed to show damage to the federal property. The Supreme Court echoed the trial court's conclusion that "the deer have greatly injured the lands in the reserves by over-browsing upon and killing valuable young trees, shrubs, bushes and forage plants" and that "thousands of deer have died because of insufficient forage."[110]

In short, the court's decision was important not because it exempted the federal government from state game laws; it did not clearly do that. Although its reliance on *Camfield* and *Utah Power and Light* suggest that the court endorsed a broad reading of the property power, the decision could be read as holding merely that the federal government has the power of an ordinary proprietor to protect its property. More significant is the judiciary's deferential approach to the Forest Service's use of scientific evidence and overall conception of the forest as a complex ecosystem needing protection. Both the lower court and the Supreme Court accepted the Forest Service's view, grounded in ecological science, of what counted as damage, how that damage was to be ascertained, what caused the damage, and the best way to reduce that damage—even though these were all issues that were still hotly contested by ecologists in and outside of the federal government.

As historian James Foster shows, that trust in the Forest Service was widely shared. After the decision was announced, Arizona's game warden D. E. Pettis attempted to drum up support among other state game wardens for federal legislation prohibiting hunting in the Grand Canyon. But he had little luck, because many of the wardens trusted the Forest Service more than they trusted the government of Arizona. Indeed, in 1929, with a new governor in place, Arizona itself decided to support the Forest Service's hunting policy.[111]

After *Hunt*

Surprisingly, perhaps, the *Hunt* decision didn't settle the question of the Forest Service's authority to manage hunting and fishing in federal forests. On the contrary, the Forest Service continued to seek cooperative agreements with state game managers whenever possible. Forest Service solicitor Seth Thomas noted in a 1933 memo that "the reason for the Department's not asserting full control over fish and game within the National Forests is that some of its former law officers felt that it did not have such authority in view of an old opinion of Nov. 29, 1901, rendered by Attorney General Knox."[112] As explained at the beginning of this chapter, Knox had concluded that while Congress had the constitutional authority to regulate hunting in federal forests, it had not authorized the Forest Service to do so. Thomas reviewed Knox's opinion in light of subsequent Supreme Court decisions and concluded that his original assumption that Congress hadn't authorized the Forest Service to ban hunting was in fact incorrect. Treating the regulation of hunting as integral to protecting the forest from harm, he concluded that "the Secretary of Agriculture has the same authority to regulate hunting that he has to regulate grazing on the National Forests." Moreover, "any regulations which he may issue with respect to hunting and fishing would supersede state laws with respect to the National Forests."[113]

However, that opinion quickly became irrelevant because in 1934 Congress, finally, granted the president authority to establish wildlife sanctuaries in any national forest (with the consent of the state in which it lay). This Act also authorized the agriculture secretary to establish "all needful rules and regulations" for the administration of the sanctuaries. But it included the following language: "including regulations not in contravention of State laws for hunting . . . predatory animals . . . and other species destructive to livestock or wild life or agriculture."[114] This language was interpreted by Thomas as prohibiting the Forest Service from enacting game regulations that conflicted with state law.[115]

This 1934 law did little to resolve the continuing uncertainty concerning authority over wildlife in national forests. On the contrary, the Agriculture

Secretary Henry A. Wallace promptly issued regulations concerning hunting and fishing in national forests and authorizing regional foresters to issue permits. Although Wallace stated that these regulations were intended only for forests that did not have cooperative agreements with states, many state game commissioners objected, viewing them as an attempt to displace state game laws.[116] And once again, the conflict ended up in court in *Chalk v. United States*, a 1940 federal appellate court decision concerning deer management in the Pisgah National Forest.

North Carolina and the Forest Service had a cooperative agreement that gave the Forest Service primary responsibility for managing game in the forest, but that cooperation broke down in 1939. The issue in the case was precisely the same as in *Hunt*: The Forest Service wanted to hold a deer hunt[117] to reduce the herd in order to protect the forest, and North Carolina objected. However, the legal context for this decision was different, because the federal government had acquired the Pisgah National Forest under the 1911 Weeks Act rather than through reservation. Moreover, in 1915 North Carolina (which at that time had no game laws) ceded jurisdiction over game animals to the United States by statute. In 1916, Congress amended the Weeks Act to grant the secretary of agriculture the authority to create rules and regulations concerning hunting in forests acquired under that act. Congressional debate made it clear that this amendment was intended to authorize the Forest Service to manage wildlife in the Pisgah National Forest.[118]

North Carolina's legal position was accordingly quite weak, and it lost in both the trial court and the appellate court. The appellate court opinion by Judge Northcott cited *Hunt* for the proposition that "the power of the United States to thus protect its lands and property does not admit of doubt . . . the game laws or any other statute of the state to the contrary notwithstanding."[119] As in *Hunt*, the court accepted the Forest Service's evidence that the deer were causing damage and that the herd could be effectively reduced by hunting and trapping.[120] And as in *Hunt*, the court did not discuss what was to count as damage to these forest lands. Damage, it seems, is anything that interferes with the Forest Service's ecologically informed management goals. North Carolina appealed the decision, but the Supreme Court declined to review it.[121]

On the other hand, North Carolina's position had support in Congress. Even while the appeal was in process, the House Select Committee on Wildlife Conservation was holding hearings on the subject of state and federal authority over wildlife conservation.[122] The first witness, Seth Gordon, was executive director of Pennsylvania's game commission, and he immediately raised the constitutional question (citing *Geer v. Connecticut*) and both the Kaibab and the Pisgah conflicts.[123] Several other witnesses echoed his call for the Forest Service to rescind its hunting and fishing regulations, and some even called for federal forests to be given back to the states. Such political pressure ultimately led the USDA to replace the 1934 regulations with a new policy, somewhat more favorable to state authority but still retaining control of fish and game management in forests without cooperative agreements.[124]

In short, the extent of federal authority over wildlife in federal forests remained, and remains, a contested issue.[125] Regardless of what the courts may say, the sharing of wildlife authority between state and federal government is probably inevitable as long as they share authority over the wildlife's habitat. Indeed, this shared authority looks very much like part of Bruce Ackerman's "matrix of institutional relationships and fundamental values that are usually taken as the constitutional baseline in normal political life."[126] The cooperative relationship persists as both an ecologically and politically necessary practice, supported by Congress and executive branch agencies, in spite of what federal officials believe to be their plenary power over public lands. In terms of the "constitution of judges," however, the doctrinal trend is clear. The *Hunt* decision was another in an impressive series of Supreme Court victories for the federal government's control over public lands, extending back to the *Grimaud* and *Light* decisions.

In sum, the *Hunt* case presented the court with the question of what the federal government could do in pursuit of conservation. Its answer was that under the property power, the federal government could do anything that its scientists could support. State authority had to give way to the federal interest in protecting public land—even as, under the influence of ecological science, the concepts of "protection" and "land" grew ever more complex. But *Hunt* concerned a conflict between state and federal government only. It did not answer the even more troubling question: How far can state or federal government intrude on private rights in pursuit of environmental goals?

CHAPTER EIGHT

State and Local Pollution Control

The Progressives' environmental agenda did not end with forests and wild-life. They also aimed to make industrial cities more habitable—a complex undertaking involving not only restrictions on harmful emissions and solid waste but also land use regulations and municipal infrastructure projects, ranging from sewer systems to garbage collection agencies.[1] These policies, like other Progressive environmental management efforts, faced constitutional challenges. The state's interest in controlling pollution to protect public health was well-established, but dealing with urban pollution involved the government more deeply in restricting private property rights. Thus the growing body of local land use regulations generated constitutional debate and often ended up in court.

Constitutional objections to pollution control measures focused primarily on the due process clause of the federal (or, in some cases, state) Constitution, contending that the regulations infringed liberty or property rights without an adequate reason. Similar arguments often defeated labor regulations in the lawsuits that gave the so-called Lochner era its reputation for judicial conservatism. But while judges were suspicious of labor regulations, they largely confirmed municipalities' pollution control measures. As those measures became more ambitious, cities gradually won the authority to manage urban landscapes to serve human health and well-being. This area of doctrine does not feature as prominently the dynamic, systemic conception of nature supporting government authority over natural resources. But we do see courts gradually learning to see urban landscapes, like forests, as complex systems that require proactive management to support human health and well-being.

Pollution Politics

Rapidly industrializing cities in the late nineteenth century provided a wealth of hazards to residents' health and quality of life. Historian Robert Gottlieb provides a concise list of challenges: "water quality, sewage and sanitation, solid and hazardous waste generation and disposal, ventilation and air emissions, occupational and public health."[2] Urban groups, including business leaders, middle-class reformers, the growing cadre of university-trained social and natural scientists, physicians, and labor activists organized around these urban pollution issues. These coalitions began forming in the mid-nineteenth century but coalesced into an identifiable movement that formed part of the Progressive coalition between the 1880s and the 1920s.[3]

The urban reform movement was complex both in composition and in the array of issues it addressed. One important strand of reform united the emerging professions of public health experts and sanitation engineers. Led primarily by physicians, the public health movement began in the 1850s and gathered steam after the Civil War.[4] By the late nineteenth century, public health had become a routine government service, reflected in the proliferation of municipal and state health boards after the Civil War. The American Public Health Association formed in 1872, becoming the leading national advocate for public health policy.[5] At the same time, sanitary engineering was developing as a field of expertise, supported by the establishment of the American Society for Civil Engineers in 1852. Civil engineering began with the canal and railroad building projects of the early nineteenth century, but the profession added municipal infrastructure to its agenda after the Civil War.[6] Along with public health professionals, engineers offered advice, staffed city agencies, and led the effort to find technological solutions to urban problems.

The chief urban problem, according to both groups, was disease. Cholera, smallpox, yellow fever, malaria, and typhoid periodically ravaged American cities throughout the nineteenth century. Chronic diseases like dysentery also took a steady toll.[7] And under the prevailing scientific view, these diseases were best addressed through pollution control. From roughly 1860 to 1900, public health professionals and sanitary engineers were united by the "filth" theory of disease, holding that contagious diseases are caused by unhealthy miasmas emanating from the earth and water.[8] Under this theory, removing waste and protecting the purity of water and air were public health measures—a traditional function of state and local government in the United States since the founding era. Cities routinely removed public nuisances, enacted quarantine laws to deal with the outbreak of contagious diseases, hired street cleaners, improved drainage, and took other steps to address suspected sources of disease.[9] In fact, New York enacted a comprehensive health law as early as 1796, creating a New York City Health Office and giving the city broad authority to protect public health through inspections, quarantines, and eliminating suspected sources of disease such as privies, cesspools, and slaughterhouses. Other cities followed suit, and by the end of the nineteenth century, most major cities had departments of public health with authority to impose regulations on businesses and private residences to manage waste.[10]

After 1900, however, the public health movement shifted its attention away from environmental reform as medical science abandoned the "filth" theory of disease. Breakthroughs in biology and chemistry during the nineteenth century identified the role of pathogens, or germs, in causing illness. By the 1880s, scientists had identified the pathogens responsible for several major diseases, along with their transmission mechanisms. As historian Martin Melosi recounts, germ theory led public health officials increasingly to focus on inoculation and vaccines as their chief weapons in their war on contagious disease.[11] Thus public health departments gradually abandoned their environmental health mission, leaving sanitation to city engineers.

But the engineers did continue to improve the urban environment. During the late nineteenth and early twentieth centuries, cities made major improvements in their water systems. Indeed, Melosi reports that by 1880, about one-third of urban residents had not only running water but also water closets. This development dramatically increased the amount of wastewater that cities had to manage, so during the last two decades of the nineteenth century, cities laid thousands of miles of sewer lines.[12] In addition to managing wastewater, cities gave attention to street-cleaning, to better systems for collecting residential and commercial garbage, and to separating the more noxious land uses from residential districts. While much of the progress in these areas was technological (such as new water and air filtration devices), most of the new technologies were accompanied by new policies, ranging from land use regulations and mandated technologies to restrictions on individual behavior, all of which were justified in large part as contributing to public health.

But public health was not the only rationale for these policies. The City

Beautiful movement emerged in the 1890s to advocate for greater attention to the aesthetics of the urban landscape. Their proposals ranged from creating parks, installing outdoor art, and regulating architectural styles to reducing noise, organizing the public to combat littering, improving waste collection, and taking measures against air pollution.[13] Reformers aimed to improve public health, but they also appealed to aesthetic values and argued that civic "cleanliness" would increase property values.[14] As Melosi astutely notes, "Fusing visual appeal of City Beautiful with the more traditional health argument broadened the impact of sanitary reform in the public sphere without fundamentally changing its purpose or goals."[15] It also would help these policies survive judicial scrutiny, as we will see.

Another strand in the urban reform movement, of course, was the campaign for industrial health and safety, led by reformers such as Jane Addams. Addams's model of civic organizing around urban "settlements" like Hull House in Chicago offered her supporters a way to address a wide variety of urban ills, including municipal sanitation.[16] But of course much of her work focused on industrial health and safety. Addams and her supporters led a long battle for workers' rights that culminated in the creation of the federal Workers' Health Bureau, the primary advocate for industrial health during the 1920s. In terms of policy, the occupational health and safety initiative won many battles at the state level but faltered in the 1920s, as trade unions decided to focus more narrowly on wages and hours. This campaign to reform industrial practice and working conditions is part of the larger story of Progressive labor policy in the courts, represented by decisions like *Lochner v. New York*[17] and *Muller v. Oregon*[18] (about a maximum hours statute promoted as a measure to protect workers' health). That story is ably told by others, and I won't address it here.[19]

As for industrial (as opposed to municipal or residential) pollution, reformers did address industrial *air* pollution. We will discuss this smoke abatement campaign in more detail below. Industrial *water* pollution, however, received less attention during this period. Reformers targeted water pollution from the new municipal sewer systems, and by 1905, forty-four states had statutes restricting the discharge of untreated sewage into streams (although only a few included enforcement provisions).[20] This focus on sewage was one result of the new germ theory of disease, which identified pathogens in human waste as a major threat to public health. But industrial pollution did not become a major focus of reform until the 1920s. As legal historian William Andreen reports, Pennsylvania and Ohio took the lead in the 1920s in developing classification systems to identify water bodies that should be protected from industrial pollution. Connecticut, too, created a state water pollution control commission, independent of the state health department, and authorized it to protect fish and recreation.[21] But these efforts were very limited, resulting in protection for only a few streams. As for the country's great interstate waters, major constitutional difficulties impeded efforts to protect those sinks from industrial waste, as we will see in the next chapter. This chapter will focus on the civic dimension of pollution politics: the campaign to create cleaner, healthier, more attractive urban habitats.

That campaign resulted in considerable technological innovation. Civil engineers gave us indoor running water, paved streets, landfills and incinerators, water filtration systems, waste management systems, and reliable heat and power. But these features of modern life required institutional and policy innovation as well. Cities created health boards and sanitation departments, developed land use regulations, and imposed new restrictions on private actors in their efforts to protect public health and improve the quality of urban life. These measures expanded government power, so they required constitutional justification. But to understand how courts treated the constitutional questions posed by these new laws and ordinances, we must begin with the nineteenth-century legal framework for addressing pollution: the law of nuisance.

Nuisance Law and the Police Power

Traditionally, cities regulated health and safety hazards through the law of nuisance.[22] Nuisance is a common law tort, a harm imposed by one actor on another, usually involving some disturbance to the quiet enjoyment of one's property. Throughout the nineteenth century, courts heard nuisance cases in which private individuals sued their neighbors (for damages or, sometimes, an injunction) for interfering with their property rights by creating noxious odors, unsafe conditions, or polluted water. Governments, too, could bring nuisance actions and could also prospectively declare (by ordinance or statute) whole categories of behavior to be "public nuisances," constituting a general danger to the community. Nuisance could encompass anything from obstruction of a public right-of-way and fire hazards to selling unsafe food and drugs and morals legislation (against prostitution, gambling dens, etc.) Ultimately, however, it was up to the court to decide whether the action complained of was actually a danger—and here the court had substantial discretion.

That discretion is important, because the law of nuisance was generally taken to define the state's police power, its inherent power to protect the health and welfare of the public. That is, the state could regulate anything that was considered to be a common law nuisance. Because judges had discretion over what counted as a nuisance—what was a reasonable or unreasonable restriction on private behavior—they had considerable discretion in evaluating whether regulations enacted by local governments lay within the police power.[23]

In general, pollution control, as a public health measure, was squarely within the realm of the police power. Justice Marshall in *Gibbons v. Ogden* was merely repeating conventional wisdom when he identified "health laws of every description" as part of the "immense mass of legislation" over which states retained control when they created the Union.[24] As long as judges were persuaded by the "filth" theory of disease, measures aimed at cleaning up the urban environment were fairly easy to justify. This theory supported traditional public health measures such as quarantines, health inspection of ships entering ports, and removal of suspected sources of disease. Courts generally approved these measures, regardless of their (quite severe) impact on personal liberty and property.[25]

But the cities' new, more comprehensive and proactive approaches to regulating the urban environment went beyond traditional public health measures. After the turn of the century, cities not only expanded their pollution-control systems but also began enacting regulations aimed at aesthetic goals, such as increasing green space, regulating building styles, and adopting comprehensive zoning codes that dictated the character of every neighborhood in the city. As we will see, courts treated aesthetic regulations with more suspicion. Eventually, however, judges accepted the expansion of the police power to encompass not just public health but the overall quality of life provided by the city—not by redefining that power but by adopting the more complex understandings of urban life and its ills proposed by reformers.

Public Health and Pollution Control

The government's power to protect public health is the foundation for virtually all pollution control policies in the United States. To be sure, pollution can affect ecological functioning in ways that impair agricultural productivity and recreational interests in the natural environment. But throughout the Progressive era and well into the twenty-first century, public health has been the dominant objective of pollution control policy. That focus has much to do with constitutional law: Public health provides firm constitutional grounds for state and local government regulation.

Consider, for example, the experience of New York City, a leader in public health in the late nineteenth century. The state created the New York Metropolitan Board of Health in 1866, a regional agency with the power to remove dangers to public health, to open hospitals and dispensaries, and to respond to disease outbreaks with quarantines and other regulations.[26] While not entirely novel, the creation of a regional agency to carry out tasks previously assigned to cities created conflicts that ended up in court. The agency's attempts to regulate land use—the regulations with the most direct impact on the business community—generated the most resistance. The board ran into legal difficulty almost immediately, when it attempted to shut down a street market in New York City. The city treasurer (who collected rents on the stalls) challenged the board's authority to prohibit the market. The city argued that street markets are not nuisances per se and that the evidence showed this market was orderly and well-conducted. The Board lost this initial skirmish. Judge Ingraham of the New York Supreme Court agreed that the board had been delegated the authority to regulate markets "so far as relates to the cleanliness, ventilation and drainage thereof, and to the prevention of the sale, or offering for sale, of improper articles therein."[27] But the board wanted to remove the stalls altogether, and the judge did not see any evidence that the mere presence of the stalls on the street constituted a danger to public health. He conceded, however, that "I consider the powers of a board of health to be very extensive, and in some respects without control."[28] He merely insisted that the board confine its efforts to nuisances that were more clearly related to public health.

However, the board won another lawsuit the same year, this time before the New York Court of Common Pleas. In this case, a group of butchers challenged the Health Board's regulations restricting the driving of cattle in the city streets and setting up butchering operations in street stalls without a permit from the board. Regulation of businesses concerned with animals, and particularly the slaughtering of animals, would prove to be a major source of litigation for cities and health boards.[29] Slaughterhouses were commonly considered to be potential, or even per se, nuisances.[30] The butchers, however, argued that these regulations violated the due process clause of the New York Constitution. (The Fourteenth Amendment, prohibiting states from restricting liberty without due process, would not be ratified until July 1868.) They also argued that the power to impose the regulations was legislative in character and could not be delegated. The judge firmly rejected these arguments, seeing nothing unusual in the powers exercised by the board. On the contrary,

> All that is declared by the act is, that the board may remove or abate a public nuisance, which is merely declaring that it may do what, by the law, a private person may do. It was an established rule of the common law, long before the bill of rights was enacted, that a public nuisance might be removed, taken away or abated, by any person aggrieved thereby, if in so doing he did not disturb the public peace.[31]

The judge considered the power delegated to the board well within the discretionary powers typically enjoyed by cities in protecting public health.[32]

The next legal challenge came in 1867, again by a butcher protesting a prohibition on slaughterhouses in New York City south of Forty-Second Street, or anywhere in Brooklyn, without a permit. The judge once again looked to the common law of nuisance: He held that the state authorized the board to prohibit only actions that would be considered a nuisance under the common law, and slaughtering animals was not necessarily a nuisance. He pointed to the evidence that "the premises are well sewered, and the business of slaughtering is conducted there by the plaintiff with the greatest care and cleanliness that it is capable of."[33] (Note that this is not actually a constitutional argument; rather, the decision rested on the judge's construction of the statute that created the board.)

This confusion was finally resolved in 1868 by the New York Court of Appeals. In *Metropolitan Board of Health v. Heister*, butchers once again challenged both the restriction on driving cattle through city streets and an order shutting down two slaughterhouses. The court upheld all the regulations and rejected a broad set of challenges to the board, including a due process claim:

> No one has been deprived of his property or of his liberty by the proceedings in question. The commissioners have provided that cattle shall

not be driven upon certain streets except at certain hours of the day. They have also provided that the business of slaughtering cattle shall not be carried on in the city of New York south of a designated line. These regulations take away no man's property. If Mr. Heister owns cattle, his ownership is not interfered with. He may sell, exchange and traffic in the same manner as any other person owning cattle may do. If he owns a slaughter-house, his property remains intact. He may sell it, mortgage it, devise it or give it away, and may use it just as any other man or all other men in the State combined may do.[34]

This decision largely settled the matter of the Metropolitan Health Board's constitutionality. But it was not the end of litigation by butchers against slaughterhouse restrictions. These slaughterhouse cases are worth examining in some detail, to illustrate the relationship between common law nuisance and the police power as well as the courts' supportive attitude toward public health measures.

The Slaughterhouse Cases

Between 1865 and 1920, at least seventeen reported decisions (including the two from New York) entertained constitutional claims against slaughterhouse ordinances. (See table 8.1).

The most famous of these is the 1873 US Supreme Court decision known as the *Slaughterhouse Cases*.[35] This case consolidated three challenges to Louisiana's law removing New Orleans slaughterhouses from the shores of the Mississippi River. The law prohibited the slaughtering of animals anywhere in the city except at locations operated by Crescent City Stock Landing and Slaughterhouse Co., thus creating a (regulated) monopoly. The butchers in the city brought suit under the newly enacted Fourteenth Amendment, arguing that Louisiana's statute impaired their right to exercise their trade in violation of either the privileges and immunities clause, the due process clause, or the equal protection clause of the amendment. They also, creatively but implausibly, argued that the law violated the Thirteenth Amendment's prohibition on involuntary servitude.

This case became famous because it was the Supreme Court's first opportunity to interpret these new constitutional provisions. But the butchers' arguments (except for the Thirteenth Amendment claim) were not novel. Like New York butchers, they argued that the regulation took a valuable right, essentially a property right in their business, without a good

Table 8.1: Cases challenging the constitutionality of slaughterhouse restrictions, 1865–1920.[1]

Case	Disposition
1. *Schuster v. Metropolitan Board of Health*, 49 Barb. 450 (N.Y.App.Div. 1867).	Ordinance struck down
2. *New York Metropolitan Board of Health v. Heister*, 37 N.Y. 661 (1869)	Ordinance upheld
3. *Chicago v. Rumpff*, 45 Ill. 90 (1867)	Ordinance struck down
4. *State ex rel. Belden v. Fagan*, 22 La.Ann. 545 (1870)	Ordinance upheld
5. *Slaughterhouse Cases*, 83 U.S. 36 (1873)	Ordinance upheld
6. *Taylor v. State*, 35 Wis. 298 (1874)	Ordinance upheld
7. *Tugman v. Chicago*, 78 Ill. 405 (1875)	Ordinance struck down
8. *Ex Parte Heilbron*, 65 Cal. 609 (1884)	Ordinance upheld
9. *Vilavasa v. Barthet*, 39 La.Ann. 247 (1887)	Ordinance upheld
10. *Darcantel v. People's Slaughterhouse & Refrigerating Co.*, 44 La.Ann. 632 (1892)	Ordinance upheld
11. *Spokane v. Robison*, 6 Wash. 547 (1893)	Ordinance upheld
12. *Rund v. Fowler*, 142 Ind. 214 (1895) (overruled by Elkhart v. Lipschitz)	Ordinance upheld
13. *Portland v. Meyer*, 32 Ore. 368 (1898)	Ordinance upheld
14. *Crowley v. West*, 25 La.Ann. 526 (1900)	Ordinance struck down
15. *Elkhart v. Lispchitz*, 164 Ind. 671 (1905)	Ordinance struck down
16. *Kuchler v. Weaver*, 1909 Ok. 55 (1909)	Ordinance upheld
17. *Board of Health v. Schwarz*, 84 N.J.L. 500 (1913)	Ordinance upheld

1. I compiled this list by searching the NexisUni database using the search terms "slaughterhouse" and "constitution!"

reason. Nor was the decision novel: The Supreme Court, like the New York court, rejected the constitutional arguments. Justice Miller wrote, "The regulation of the place and manner of conducting the slaughtering of animals, and the business of butchering within a city, and the inspection of the animals to be killed for meat, and of the meat afterwards, are among the most necessary and frequent exercises of [the police] power."[36] He also denied that operating a slaughterhouse was among the privileges protected by the privileges and immunities clause. To define those privileges, he referred to *Corfield v. Coryell*,[37] which had interpreted the Article IV privileges and immunities clause as protecting a fairly limited set of rights pertaining to the federal government. To be sure, that clause also pertained to "protection by the government, with the right to acquire and possess property of every kind, and to pursue and obtain happiness and safety, *subject, nevertheless, to such restraints as the government may prescribe for the general good of the whole.*"[38] That is, it did not restrict the state's police power to protect the public good; it merely required that the state not discriminate among its citizens. As for the equal protection clause and the Thirteenth Amendment, he concluded that these provisions aimed to protect freedmen. In sum, Miller was unwilling to grant that such a routine exercise of state authority as a regulation of slaughterhouses was affected by any of the new amendments. Although three justices dissented, they objected only to the provision of the law that gave one company the exclusive right to operate a slaughterhouse, not to the general attempt to regulate slaughterhouses in the interests of public health.[39]

One might expect that a Supreme Court decision would have put an end to constitutional challenges to slaughterhouse regulations, but it did not. Due process arguments kept showing up in challenges to regulations on businesses concerning animals, but I found only one case decided after the *Slaughterhouse Cases* in which an explicit due process argument prevailed. In *Bates v. District of Columbia*, decided in 1874, the DC Circuit Court of Appeals struck down a health board regulation prohibiting manufacturers from using animal products in the district. The board was created by an act of Congress, and its regulation was challenged by a soapmaker who used prohibited animal products. The soapmaker argued that the regulation destroyed his property rights in his business, thus taking his property without due process in violation of the Fifth Amendment's due process clause. Surprisingly, the judge agreed: "*Where rights are secured by the existing law, there is no power in any branch of the Government to take them away;* but where they are held contrary to the existing law, or a forfeiture by its violation, then they may be taken from him, not by an act of the legislature, but in the due administration of law before the judicial tribunals of the State."[40] That is, the judge reasoned that the government could bring a nuisance action, and if the court decided that *this particular* soapmaker was creating a nuisance, the business could be closed down. But the government could not declare that all use of animal products was a nuisance—particularly since Bates's family had been making soap and candles on this land for more than forty-six years, and his neighbors had ample notice of this fact when they moved into the neighborhood. Notably, the judge didn't mention the *Slaughterhouse Cases*, and he impatiently dismissed an opinion by the federal Department of Justice that had supported the regulation.[41] In his view, this regulation was fundamentally unfair to Bates and therefore inconsistent with due process.

Bates, however, does not appear to have been cited by any subsequent court. In contrast, the precedents supporting public health measures against constitutional challenges continued to be cited favorably for several decades. Of the seventeen slaughterhouse cases involving constitutional claims, the courts upheld the restriction under the police power in twelve (see table 8.1). We have already considered the *Schuster* decision, which was overruled by *Heister*. In two other cases, the court held that the regulation exceeded the city's charter, not the constitutional limits on the state's police power.[42] The remaining two victories for butchers come out of Chicago: In *Chicago v. Rumpff*,[43] the Illinois Supreme Court struck down a Chicago ordinance giving one company a monopoly on the slaughterhouse business. The court considered this ordinance unreasonably to privilege one company. Similarly, in *Tugman v. Chicago*,[44] the court struck down an ordinance that prohibited new slaughterhouses from opening but allowed existing ones to operate. In both cases, the court objected to the unfairness of favoring one set of butchers over the others; in neither case did the court question the city's general authority to regulate slaughterhouses to protect public health.

The slaughterhouse cases demonstrate the deference that courts gave to cities and health boards, particularly where the state legislature explicitly granted the local entity power to regulate such businesses. Indeed, even the business owners who challenged these regulations typically did not dispute the government's authority to prohibit nuisances; they simply wanted an individualized judgment concerning whether their business was a health hazard (which a traditional nuisance action would provide). But courts were largely willing to allow cities and health boards to create prospective regulations prohibiting entire categories of business instead of requiring them to proceed on a case-by-case basis.[45]

Waste Management and the Police Power

In addition to land use regulations, two other kinds of municipal pollution policy generated constitutional complaints: awarding exclusive contracts to waste collection companies and mandating that residences hook up to sewer lines (and remove privy vaults, cesspools, and the like). The first kind of complaint is illustrated by *River Rendering Co. v. Behr*.[46] The city of St. Louis had granted the River Rendering Co. the exclusive privilege to remove dead animals from the city, and Behr complained that the ordinance prevented him from selling his animal carcasses, which were valuable articles of commerce. The court agreed. It reasoned that the death of the animal didn't terminate the owner's property rights, "and while he may be required to make such use or disposition of the carcass as will prevent a nuisance, stench or other inconvenience to the neighborhood, the municipal authorities cannot arbitrarily deprive him of his property by giving it to another."[47] This decision was eventually overruled by *Valley Spring Hog Ranch Co. v. Plagman*[48] in 1920, but at least a few other courts did find such exclusive contracts constitutionally suspect.[49] The issue received extended discussion in a 1905 decision from the Maine Supreme Court, *State v. Robb*. Robb challenged an ordinance requiring that citizens put their waste out for collection by the municipal sanitation department. Robb wanted to continue his practice of collecting refuse from various businesses to feed his hens and pigs and argued that this new regulation constituted a restraint of trade, created a monopoly, and constituted an unwarrantable interference with the rights of the refuse owners. The court rejected these arguments. Judge Savage acknowledged that a couple of decisions (including *River Rendering*) held otherwise, but the weight of authority supported the proposition that

a city in the exercise of the police power granted to it by the state may, by reasonable ordinance, regulate the collection and disposal of substances within the city, which are of such a condition and of such a character as to be nuisances per se, and deleterious to the public health or comfort, or which are liable to become nuisances and noxious and deleterious, unless immediate care is taken to prevent their becoming so.[50]

He reserved judgment on whether the city could prevent a private individual from retaining such waste for his own purposes. The US Supreme Court, however, did consider that question in *California Reduction Co. v. Sanitary Reduction Works*, decided the same year. The Court noted the challenges of developing an effective municipal waste program and concluded that it must defer to the judgment of the Board of Supervisors. In any case:

the destruction of garbage and house refuse, under the authority of the municipal authorities, proceeding upon reasonable grounds, and at a place designated by law, as a means for the protection of the public health, cannot be properly regarded, within the meaning of the Constitution, as a taking of private property for public use, without compensation, simply because such garbage and house refuse may have had, at the time of its destruction, some element of value for certain purposes.[51]

As for policies requiring homeowners to remove cesspools and privy vaults and to hook up to the city's sewer system, courts generally supported these policies against constitutional claims. There was an early decision, *Gregory v. New York*, in which the Metropolitan Board of Heath hired a contractor to remove the waste from all privies and sinks in New York City. The city objected to paying for this work, and the court held that the board had exceeded its powers: It had to declare formally that the privies and sinks were a nuisance before having them removed.[52] But a long line of decisions upheld cities' and boards' authority to remove privies and cesspools, order sewer hook-ups, and even impose assessments to pay for sewer lines.[53] The new sewer systems would create another kind of constitutional conflict over interstate water pollution, which we will investigate in the next chapter. But the courts did not pose an obstacle to these new waste management regimes.

Of course, slaughterhouses, waste and offal, and privies were all familiar problems to nineteenth-century judges. It is perhaps unsurprising that they found the police power adequate to support even fairly intrusive regulations to combat these well-known sources of disease. But state and local public health authority proved to be a solid foundation for more novel pollution control measures as well, as we can see in the campaign to reduce urban smoke.

Air Pollution

Smoke from coal-burning residences, factories, and trains was a major focus of the urban environmental reform movement. The smoke abatement movement began in 1867, when St. Louis enacted the first municipal anti-smoke ordinance, requiring tall smokestacks to disperse industrial smoke. Other cities followed suit with ordinances against using bituminous coal (which is smokier than anthracite) or simply declaring dense smoke to be a nuisance.[54] Reformers also pursued technological innovation. For example, the International Association for Prevention of Smoke—the first nationwide professional organization devoted to air quality—sought pollution control through advances in boiler technology.[55] As historian David Stradling describes, the Progressives' efforts to reduce smoke were multifaceted, aiming at transformation of the nation's energy system through policy, engineering advances, and new business practices. Smoke ordinances were a major tool in this transformation, and by 1912, nearly all American cities had a smoke abatement policy.[56]

One of the most common ways to regulate smoke was simply by declaring dense smoke to be a per se public nuisance, allowing the city to bring a lawsuit against anyone producing excessive smoke. The threat of heavy fines was meant to motivate the producer of the smoke either to find some way to reduce it (thus forcing technological innovation) or to simply shut down the facility. The strategy didn't always work, of course. As historian Noga Morag-Levine documents, cities often found it difficult to prove that the smoke was dense and persistent enough to constitute a nuisance. However, the development of the Ringelmann chart, a tool for describing the density of smoke plumes, eased this evidentiary problem. After the chart became widely available in the United States in 1897, cities increasingly used nuisance lawsuits to control the major emitters (usually factories and railroads).

Morag-Levine and Stradling both argue that constitutional issues plagued these early smoke ordinances, but I think they overstate the constitutional problems. To be sure, facility owners did often raise constitutional (among other) objections as defenses. Most commonly, they complained that the ordinance either exceeded the power delegated to the city in its charter or was simply an unreasonable regulation of liberty and property in violation of due process. Occasionally these challenges prevailed. Morag-Levine and Stradling cite in particular the 1897 decision from the Missouri Supreme Court, *St. Louis v. Heitzeberg Packing & Provision Co.*, which struck down St. Louis's 1893 ordinance declaring dense smoke to be a nuisance.[57] The court in *Heitzeberg* concluded that while the city did have the power to abate any smoke that constituted a nuisance in fact, it could not declare dense smoke in general to be a nuisance per se—at least, not without enabling legislation from the state legislature permitting it to make such judgments. A few states reached the same conclusion about municipal charter powers, and this rule proved to be an obstacle for reformers, who had to persuade the state legislature to pass such enabling legislation.[58] It should be noted, however, that the *Heitzeberg* decision went against a substantial body of precedent supporting a city's discretion to declare per se nuisances.[59] In any case, as a constitutional matter, the decision doesn't question the power of the state to ban smoke or to enable cities to do so.

Overall, I found thirty cases decided between 1880 and 1920 in which a state or municipal smoke ordinance was challenged. (See table 8.2).

In six of those decisions, the municipal ordinance was struck down as exceeding the city's charter. In three additional cases, the court held that a city smoke ordinance, while valid, could not be enforced against a railroad operating under a state charter unless the city could prove that the railroad was negligent. In all other cases, the smoke ordinance was sustained against constitutional challenges. This judicial support is striking given the rudimentary state of the scientific case for health effects of smoke. As both Stradling and Morag-Levine argue, there was little medical research to support smoke abatement policy until, in 1906, the American Medical Association published studies by German scientist Louis Ascher demonstrating some of the health impacts of smoke. Further studies bolstered the public health case for smoke ordinances.[60] But the judicial decisions don't reference these studies; on the contrary, the courts in the smoke ordinance cases typically took for granted that smoke is a nuisance, showing no interest in engaging with the scientific debate.

The same deference guided the US Supreme Court in the only smoke ordinance case to reach it. In 1915, the court upheld Des Moines's smoke ordinance, easily dismissing the appellant's constitutional arguments:

So far as the Federal Constitution is concerned, we have no doubt the State may by itself or through authorized municipalities declare the emission of dense smoke in cities or populous neighborhoods a nuisance and subject to restraint as such. . . . Nor is there any valid Federal constitutional objection in the fact that the regulation may require the discontinuance of the use of property or subject the occupant to large expense in complying with the terms of the law or ordinance.[61]

Morag-Levine notes, however, that in considering whether the ordinance fell within the authority delegated by the state to the city, the court held that "this grant of authority would seem to be sufficient to authorize the passage of an ordinance of a reasonable nature, such as we believe the one now under consideration to be. . . . That such rules and regulations are valid, *subject as they are to final consideration in the courts, to determine whether they are reasonably adapted to accomplish the purpose of a statute,* has been frequently held."[62] Morag-Levine concludes that this language about judicial review of the reasonableness of the ordinance reflects the court's growing tendency to second-guess the reasonableness of measures

Table 8.1: Cases challenging the validity of smoke ordinances, 1880–1920.[1]

Case	Disposition
1. *Harmon v. Chicago*, 110 Ill. 400 (1884)	Ordinance upheld
2. *St. Paul v. Gilfillan*, 36 Minn. 298 (1886)	Ordinance exceeds charter
3. *People v. Lewis*, 86 Mich. 273 (1891)	Ordinance upheld
4. *Marshall Field & Co. v. Chicago*, 44 Ill. App. 410 (1892)	Ordinance upheld
5. *State ex rel. McCue v. Sheriff of Ramsey County*, 48 Minn. 236 (1892)	Ordinance exceeds charter
6. *Cincinnati v. Miller*, 1893 Ohio Misc. LEXIS 244 (1893)	Ordinance upheld
7. *Sigler v. Cleveland*, 4 Ohio Dec. 161 (1896)	Ordinance exceeds charter
8. *St. Louis v. Heitzeberg Packing & Provision Co.*, 141 Mo. 375 (1897)	Ordinance exceeds charter
9. *Cleveland v. Malm*, 7 Ohio Dec. 1214 (1898)	Ordinance exceeds charter
10. *Brooklyn v. Nassau E.R. Co.*, 44 A.D. 462 (1899)	Ordinance upheld
11. *Moses v. United States*, 16 App. D.C. 428 (1900)	Ordinance upheld
12. *State v. Tower*, 185 Mo. 75 (1904)	Ordinance upheld
13. *St. Paul v. Haugbro*, 93 Minn. 59 (1904)	Ordinance upheld
14. *Glucose Refining Co. v. Chicago*, 138 F. 209 (N.D. Ill. 1905)	Ordinance upheld
15. *Palmer v. District of Columbia*, 26 App. D.C. 31 (1905)	Ordinance upheld
16. *Bowers v. Indianapolis*, 169 Ind. 105 (1907)	Ordinance upheld
17. *Burkhardt v. Cincinnati*, 18 Ohio Dec. 450 (1907)	Ordinance exceeds charter
18. *Cincinnati v. Burkhardt*, 1908 Ohio Misc. LEXIS 132 (1908)	Ordinance upheld
19. *Atlantic City v. France*, 75 N.J.L. 910 (1908)	Ordinance upheld
20. *Rochester v. Macauley-Fien Milling Co.*, 199 N.Y. 207 (1910)	Ordinance upheld
21. *Pennsylvania v. Standard Ice Co.*, 59 Pgh. L.J. 101 (1911)	Ordinance exceeds charter
22. *State v. Chicago*, Milwaukee & St. Paul Railway Co., 114 Minn. 122 (1911)	Ordinance upheld
23. *Chicago v. Dunham Towing and Wrecking*, 161 Ill. App. 307 (1911	Ordinance upheld
24. *Chicago v. Dunham Towing and Wrecking*, 175 Ill. App. 549 (1912)	Ordinance upheld
25. *Erie R.R. Co. v. Jersey City*, 83 N.J.L. 92 (1912)	Ordinance valid but derogates charter rights
26. *People v. New York Edison*, 159 A.D. 786 (N.Y. 1913)	Ordinance upheld
27. *Pennsylvania R. Co. v. Jersey City*, 84 N.J.L. 716 (1913)	Ordinance valid but derogates charter rights
28. *People v. New York C. & H. R.R. Co.*, 159 S.D.D. 359 (N.Y. App. 1913)	Ordinance valid but derogates charter rights
29. *Northwestern Laundry v. Des Moines*, 239 U.S. 486 (1915)	Ordinance upheld
30. *Dickow v. Cincinnati*, 31 Ohio Dec. 266 (1920)	Ordinance upheld

1. I compiled this list by searching NexisUni, and I found additional cases in Eugene McQuillin, "Abatement of the Smoke Nuisance in Large Cities," *Central Law Journal* 46 (1898): 147–153; Eugene McQuillin, "Abatement of Nuisance in Large Cities by Legislative Declaration That Discharge of Dense Smoke is a Nuisance Per Se," *Central Law Journal* 60 (1905): 343–349; and Noga Morag-Levine, *Chasing the Wind* (Princeton: Princeton University Press, 2003).

enacted under the police power.[63] She refers also to a 1905 article by a contemporary legal commentator, Eugene McQuillin, underscoring the fact that smoke abatement ordinances must be reasonable.[64] Indeed, we see the same language of reasonableness in the cases discussed above, particularly those concerning exclusive waste collection contracts. Those cases resonate with the line of cases using the doctrine of substantive due process to strike down state laws regulating industry and protecting workers, such as the regulation of bakeries at issue in *Lochner v. New York*. However, the court's language about the reasonableness of the ordinance in the *Northwestern Laundry* case (as in most of the waste collection cases) was aimed at interpreting how much power was delegated to the city under the statute—not whether the state had authority to declare smoke to be a nuisance per se. And McQuillin's point was that the state's police power *clearly* encompassed this power to abate smoke nuisances, so that all that was left to decide was whether the specific municipal ordinance was not discriminatory. That is, he was emphasizing the familiar rule that such ordinances may not arbitrarily favor one group of emitters over another. Far from limiting cities' power, that rule means that cities would do best to draft broad ordinances that encompass all potential emitters.[65]

In short, while smoke ordinances were subject to the same constitutional objections that could be levied at any municipal regulation, courts—without any investigation of the scientific basis for public health claims—overwhelmingly concluded that smoke was a legitimate subject of state and municipal regulation. This is not to deny that the threat of litigation on constitutional and other legal grounds shaped the policies pursued by reformers. But defending state and local government's power to address air pollution did not require any novel constitutional arguments or doctrinal innovation. As Stradling notes, by 1915, many urban residents had come to assume that municipal governments had not only the authority but also the obligation to improve air quality.[66]

The same deference was not forthcoming, however, when cities pursued goals less firmly rooted in their public health authority, as we see in the decisions concerning zoning and similar urban planning tools.

Urban Planning

After 1900, cities increasingly enacted building codes, zoning ordinances, and other land use regulations that went beyond traditional nuisance abatement. Pressured by urban reformers and middle-class homeowners, cities adopted building height restrictions, regulated billboards, mandated set-backs, and created comprehensive zoning schemes that protected entire neighborhoods from industrial uses. In 1901, New York, again a leader in urban reform, enacted the Tenement House Act to improve the construction of apartment complexes and followed up with additional building standards.[67] These regulations were supported by reports that emphasized the threat that poor housing posed to public safety and health. But reform didn't stop with individual building standards. The City Beautiful movement celebrated, among other things, green space and fresh air, and sought to achieve these goals with a new legal device: zoning. Zoning was a way of imposing a set of standards—concerning building use, building design, lot size, setbacks, and so on—on whole neighborhoods. At its most extreme, the city might zone entire categories of land uses out of an area.

In 1916, New York City (encouraged by a state enabling statute) adopted the nation's first comprehensive zoning resolution. The plan divided the city into zones and specified the type of land uses (e.g., residential, commercial, industrial) allowed in each zone. The ordinance aimed to reduce congestion in some districts, protect residential buildings in others, and generally impose a vision on what had been a chaotic process of development.[68] This approach to urban development spread rapidly. By the 1920s, city planners could draw on a newly published "Zoning Primer," a model zoning ordinance, and a model city planning statute—all the products of the federal Department of Commerce (under Commerce Secretary Herbert Hoover).[69] Historian Wayne Batchis reports that by 1926, 564 cities had zoning ordinances.[70] But despite its popularity, this new set of land use controls generated a substantial body of litigation.

The history of urban planning in the courts has received much more attention from legal historians than have the other environmental policies we've investigated. Scholarly debate typically focuses on the impact of zoning, which has been celebrated for making urban landscapes more livable but also criticized for enabling racial segregation, sprawl, and lack of affordable housing.[71] I don't intend to engage that debate here; my purpose is more limited. I argue that in this area of law, as in the others we've investigated, reformers offered a variety of different ends that local land use controls could achieve, ranging from beautification to stabilizing property values to civic pride. But in court, they focused on the goal that had doctrinal support: protecting the health and safety of the community.[72]

They did not have an easy fight. In contrast to the other policies we've reviewed, judicial treatment of local land use regulations tends to support the conventional Lochner-Era story. Many state courts, as well as some Supreme Court justices, worried that these regulations unreasonably interfered with private property rights, and they were often struck down. To be sure, there were so many cases between 1890 and 1930 addressing so many different kinds of local land use controls that judges and litigants alike had difficulty identifying any clear trends.[73] The US Supreme Court usually viewed local land use regulation favorably, but it heard relatively few cases. Most of the litigation took place in state courts, and state judiciaries varied quite a lot in their treatment of municipal land use regulation.

One principle received at least lip service throughout this period, from even the most supportive courts: Regulations that have a credible relationship to public health or safety lie within the police power, but regulations that focus on mere aesthetics—landscape or building design features—do not. The case's outcome often depended on whether the court could be persuaded that a given restriction addressed a real menace to the public health. If it seemed to express either personal animosity toward the property holder or the fleeting tastes of the current majority, it was constitutionally suspect. Accordingly, proponents of zoning focused their legal arguments on demonstrating how zoning contributed to public health and safety. Legal historian Eric Claeys has collected a wealth of examples of planning experts discussing the constitutional rationale for zoning. One will suffice here, Frederick Law Olmsted's 1910 Address to the Second National Conference on City Planning:

> The principle upon which are based all building codes, tenement-house laws, and other such interferences with the exercise of free individual discretion on the part of land-owners, is that no one may be permitted so to build or otherwise conduct himself upon his own property as to cause unreasonable danger or annoyance to other people. At what point danger or annoyance becomes unreasonable is a matter of gradually shifting public opinion interpreted by the courts.[74]

Olmsted and others hoped to influence this "shifting public opinion," and in some states, they had considerable success. Massachusetts courts, for example, were generally a friendly forum for land use regulations. The Massachusetts line of decisions begins in 1899 with *Attorney General v. Williams*.[75] The attorney general sought to prevent Williams from violating a newly enacted building height law restricting buildings around the public park in Boston's Copley Square. The statute provided for compensation to the owners affected by the law, so Williams challenged it not as a police regulation but as effecting an unconstitutional taking of his property without a proper "public purpose." As we have seen in previous chapters, the "public purpose" requirement in takings doctrine was easy to meet, and by 1899 it was well-established that parks satisfied it. Here, the court not only declared that the improvement of the park was a valid public purpose but also opined that the measure could be justified under the police power (thus not requiring compensation). According to Judge Knowlton, "regulations in regard to the height and mode of construction of buildings in cities are often made by legislative enactments in the exercise of the police power, for the safety, comfort, and convenience of the people and for the benefit of property owners generally. The right to make such regulations is too well established to be questioned."[76]

That last point is debatable. Knowlton relied for support on *Waterton v. Mayo*[77] and *Sawyer v. Davis*.[78] But the *Waterton* case upheld a prohibition on slaughterhouses; it had nothing to do with building height. *Sawyer* upheld a restriction on the height of wooden buildings, but the court did not explain its reasoning. (The restriction was likely aimed at reducing the fire risk.) Moreover, a second case in 1905, *Commonwealth v. Boston Advertising Co.*,[79] cast *Williams* in doubt. Striking down a prohibition on billboards around a public park, the court reasoned that the restriction was not a legitimate exercise of the police power because it had no clear relationship to health or safety:

> We think . . . that the well being of the ordinary person who uses a public park or parkway never can be so far affected by the visibility of signs, posters or advertisements placed on other ground as to injure his health. No doubt their presence there may hide from him fine views, or may turn into a disagreeable *ensemble* what otherwise would be a pleasing outlook, or the sign or poster or advertisement may be itself ugly, or, if not so, may be displeasing because of incongruity. At most the presence of signs, posters and advertisements upon lands or buildings near a public park or parkway is an offence against good taste, and in that way alone detracts from the pleasure only of the frequenters of such places.[80]

But the 1907 decision in *Welch v. Swasey*[81] provided a clear victory for the reformers. Once again, a landowner challenged a Boston building height ordinance. The court, again in an opinion authored by Judge Knowlton, concluded that the statute was within the police power because "the erection of very high buildings in cities, especially upon narrow streets, may be carried so far as materially to exclude sunshine, light and air, and thus to affect the public health. It may also increase the danger to persons and property from fire, and be a subject for legislation on that ground."[82] In other words, the regulation had some relationship (albeit tenuous) to public health and safety. This decision was affirmed by the U.S. Supreme Court in 1909, in an opinion closely following Knowlton's reasoning, and was widely cited thereafter.[83]

The Massachusetts judiciary also supported more comprehensive zoning schemes. In 1920, the Massachusetts legislature passed a statute authorizing cities to create zoning plans, on the theory that such plans would "promote the health, safety, convenience and welfare of the inhabitants," "lessen the danger from fire," "improve and beautify the city or town," "harmonize with its natural development," and "assist the carrying out of any schemes for municipal improvement."[84] The Massachusetts Supreme Court issued an advisory opinion approving of the statute and upheld it against constitutional attack in *Building Inspector v. Stoklosa*.[85] By this point, the court was willing to assume that such regulations served a legitimate purpose. Even the most controversial zoning restrictions—those creating residential districts composed entirely of single-family houses—were acceptable in Massachusetts. The court in *Brett v. Building Commissioner*[86] explained that this restriction lessened the risk of fire: "It seems to us manifest that, other circumstances being the same, there is less danger of a building becoming ignited if occupied by one family than if occupied by two or more families. Any increase in the number of persons or of stoves or lights under a single roof increases the risk of fire."[87] Furthermore:

> It may be a reasonable view that the health and general physical and mental welfare of society would be promoted by each family dwelling in a house by itself. Increase in fresh air, freedom for the play of children and of movement for adults, the opportunity to cultivate a bit of land, and the reduction in the spread of contagious diseases may be thought to be advanced by a general custom that each family live in a house standing by itself with its own curtilage.[88]

This reasoning is hardly ironclad; one could presumably achieve the same result by regulating building standards for apartment complexes. But note that the court's thinking about the urban landscape of risk is becoming considerably more complex. The court's support for zoning rested on the judge's ability to think like an urban planner, considering how fire, disease, exercise, and air quality relate to the type of buildings in a neighborhood, their uses, and their location.

Other states were less uniformly supportive of zoning. For example, in the 1915 decision *Calvo v. New Orleans*,[89] the Louisiana Supreme Court struck down a regulation establishing Carrollton Avenue in New Orleans as a residential area. The court concluded that the city's charter authorized it only to abate nuisances; this regulation, it concluded, was not aimed at any nuisance but was based on aesthetic considerations alone.[90] But in 1918, the Louisiana legislature authorized cities to create zoning plans, and in 1921 the citizens of Louisiana included a zoning provision in their constitution. Accordingly, in *State ex rel. Civello v. New Orleans*,[91] the court reconsidered, concluding that its earlier decisions were incorrect. Residential districts, it reasoned, might serve to reduce the costs of policing and wear and tear on roads, and any business is liable to become a nuisance in a quiet residential area.[92] Interestingly, the court also suggested that aesthetics could be a valid reason for zoning: "The beauty of a fashionable residence neighborhood in a city is for the comfort and happiness of the residents, and it sustains in a general way the value of property in the neighborhood."[93]

The Minnesota judiciary, too, changed its mind about zoning. In the 1916 decision *State ex rel. Lachtman v. Houghton*,[94] the state supreme court struck down an ordinance prohibiting businesses in a residential area, concluding that the regulation exceeded the police power.[95] However, in 1920, the same court upheld the city of Houghton's use of eminent domain to create a residential district.[96] The new measure proposed to compensate landowners whose property values were lowered by the regulation. The court reasoned that the measure had a valid public purpose, in that it created a residential district that protected property values as well as preventing "extortion":

> The occurrences have been common in our large cities of unscrupulous and designing persons securing lots in desirable residential districts, and then passing the word that an apartment or other objectionable structure is to be erected thereon. In order to protect themselves against heavy loss and bitter annoyance the adjacent owners, or parties interested in property in the neighborhood, are forced to buy the lots so held at exorbitant price.[97]

More generally, the court thought that such restrictions "enhance the appearance and value of the home, foster . . . civic pride and . . . tend . . . to produce a better type of citizen."[98] Finally, in *Beery v. Houghton*,[99] the court admitted that zoning was becoming common, and "the police power, . . . quickly responsive, in the interest of common welfare, to changing conditions, authorizes various restrictions upon the use of private property as social and economic changes come."[100] The court was sensitive to the argument that such restrictions might increase inequality—a common criticism of exclusionary zoning. But it noted that a broad police power can also be used to regulate businesses to the advantage of people living in poorer, mixed-use neighborhoods.[101]

New Jersey, in contrast, was consistently hostile to zoning, despite a state law enacted in 1920 that authorized cities to regulate land use to protect public health, safety, and general welfare. South Orange's restriction of a neighborhood to single-family residences was struck down in 1922 as exceeding the authority granted by this statute.[102] The same year, *Schaite v. Senior* upheld a restriction on service stations and garages.[103] But in *Ignaciumas v. Risley*, the court struck down a prohibition on businesses in residential communities, and a series of decisions striking down restrictions on apartment buildings and businesses in residential areas followed.[104]

In the 1925 decision *Wulfsohn v. Burden*,[105] the New York Court of Appeals reviewed the constitutional status of zoning laws, concluding that "courts on the whole have been consistently and sensibly progressive in adjusting the use of land in thickly populated districts to the necessities and conditions created by congested and complex conditions by upholding as a constitutional exercise of the police power zoning ordinances passed under State authority to regulate the use of land in urban districts."[106] Approving a ban on apartment buildings in neighborhoods zoned for single-family housing, Judge Hiscock pointed out that residential neighborhoods once relied on restrictive covenants to maintain their character, but it was now common practice to achieve that result by ordinance.[107] He had little difficulty upholding the restriction, noting that apartment buildings might overtax the water and sewer system, as well as the fire department. The presence of children in the neighborhood was relevant as well, since protecting their safety may require additional measures.

In sum, by 1925, there was a consensus that land use restrictions related to safety and health are within the police power and that building height restrictions, some billboard regulations, and restrictions on noxious trades would normally pass constitutional muster. Courts were increasingly hearing, and being persuaded by, the arguments of urban planners that zoning was required to manage the complex urban landscape of risk. The two principal issues dividing courts were whether aesthetic considerations alone could justify restrictions on private property use and whether cities could create residential districts consisting solely of single-family residences. In 1926, the US Supreme Court decision *Euclid v. Ambler Realty*[108] answered the second question in the affirmative, at least as far as the federal Constitution is concerned.

Euclid v. Ambler Realty

Euclid, a small suburb of Cleveland, adopted a zoning plan in 1922. Ambler Realty owned some vacant land along Euclid Avenue that it had hoped to sell for commercial development, but the zoning plan prohibited commercial uses on that tract. Ambler Realty accordingly challenged the ordinance as violating the due process or equal protection clause of the Fourteenth Amendment (as well as similar provisions in the Ohio Constitution). The district court struck down the ordinance, unconvinced that the zoning scheme had a substantial relationship to public health or safety.[109] But the Supreme Court granted review and upheld it in a 5–4 decision, with the conservative Justice Sutherland joining the Progressives to provide the fifth vote.

As legal scholar Joseph Gordon Hylton points out, the decision was consistent with the Supreme Court precedents. Even the more conservative Fuller and White courts "routinely upheld the legitimacy of local land use controls."[110] The court did strike down a land use regulation in the 1912 decision *Eubank v. Richards*.[111] The regulation directed the city to create a setback regulation if two-thirds of the property owners on a street request it. The Court considered the delegation of this authority to private citizens to be constitutionally suspect, since it allowed the citizens to enact restrictions based purely on their tastes. However, the court went the other direction a few years later in *Thomas Cusack Co. v. Chicago*,[112] upholding a regulation prohibiting billboards unless a majority of property owners in the area approved. The only other notable Supreme Court decisions striking down land use regulations involved racial discrimination.[113]

Nevertheless, the 6–3 decision in *Euclid* shows that some of the justices were growing concerned that zoning regulations posed a potential threat to property rights, as several state judiciaries had held. Ambler Realty, after all, had reasonably expected commercial development to proceed along Euclid Avenue. Its lawyer argued that the restriction "in effect erects a dam to hold back the flood of industrial development and thus to preserve a rural character in portions of the Village which, under the operation of natural economic laws, would be devoted most profitably to industrial undertakings." It thus interferes with the market to the detriment of landowners' perfectly reasonable expectations.[114] Justice Sutherland, however, was not persuaded that municipalities were powerless to determine the flow of this river of economic activity.

Although zoning laws were of relatively recent origin, he wrote, "with the great increase and concentration of population, problems have developed, and constantly are developing, which require, and will continue to require, additional restrictions in respect of the use and occupation of private lands in urban communities."[115] He thus echoed Holmes's language in *Missouri v. Holland*: "While the meaning of constitutional guaranties never varies, the scope of their application must expand or contract to meet the new and different conditions which are constantly coming within the field of their operation. In a changing world, it is impossible that it should be otherwise."[116]

Turning to the substantive issue—the creation of purely residential districts—he noted that many courts had upheld such restrictions, and he referred also to "commissions and experts" whose investigations "have been set forth in comprehensive reports."[117] One of those experts was urban planning authority Alfred Bettman, who submitted an amicus brief emphasizing the connection between zoning and traditional nuisance law. Dismissing the notion that zoning aimed at "aesthetic" goals, Bettman insisted that zoning is merely an extension of the traditional nuisance authority: It reduces the likelihood that incompatible uses will end up near each other, thus protecting the health and safety of the community without having to resort to nuisance litigation.[118]

Sutherland's opinion echoed Bettman's brief. Excluding industrial uses through zoning:

> will make it easier to provide fire apparatus suitable for the character and intensity of the development in each section; . . . it will increase the safety and security of home life; greatly tend to prevent street accidents, especially to children, by reducing the traffic and resulting confusion in residential sections; decrease noise and other conditions which produce

or intensify nervous disorders; preserve a more favorable environment in which to rear children, etc.[119]

These are the same arguments that were being accepted by the state courts, showing that zoning contributes to public health and safety. Rejecting Ambler Realty's metaphor of the city as a river of economic activity running along its natural channel, Sutherland instead embraced the planner's vision of the city as a complex landscape of risk requiring careful management.

Not everyone on the court was convinced by that vision, of course; Justices Van Devanter, McReynolds, and Butler dissented but wrote no opinions. And *Euclid* was a narrow decision. It did not, for example, address whether aesthetics alone could support land use restrictions. Nor did it mean that the Supreme Court would be entirely deferential to local government. Two years later, in *Nectow v. Cambridge*,[120] it struck down a zoning ordinance as it applied to a landowner who was in the process of selling his land to an industrial developer when the ordinance, designating the land as residential, was adopted. The trial court had asked a special master to investigate whether the ordinance as applied to this lot was necessary to promote the health and safety of the public, and the special master concluded that it was not. The lower court nevertheless upheld the restriction. The Supreme Court, in an opinion by Justice Sutherland again, reversed. Sutherland affirmed that zoning was generally permissible under *Euclid*, but he concluded that in this case, applying the restriction to this landowner violated due process. Joseph Gordon Hylton argues, I think correctly, that the key point in *Nectow* was the special master's report.[121] The Court might normally defer to the city's judgment about what the community needs, but it was hard to ignore a report from a fact-finding agent of the judicial branch. *Nectow*, in any case, did not represent a retreat from *Euclid*; it proved to be the court's final word on zoning for several decades. Zoning is now well-established as within the constitutional authority of state and local government.

Pennsylvania Coal Company v. Mahon

Before concluding this discussion, however, we must consider the 1922 decision *Pennsylvania Coal Company v. Mahon*, which is also, like *Euclid*, the subject of a substantial scholarly literature.[122] *Mahon* was one of the only two Progressive Era Supreme Court decisions that, from today's perspective, look like a loss for environmental reform.[123] But the case did not in fact involve an antipollution or urban planning regulation. It was a test case to determine the constitutionality of Pennsylvania's Kohler Act, a regulation on coal mining. Mahon had bought his house from the Pennsylvania Coal Company, which reserved the subsurface rights—including the right to subsurface support, which Pennsylvania law treated as a distinct property right—so that it could continue to mine anthracite coal beneath the house. Mahon had also waived any damages that might result from the removal of subsurface support. But the Kohler Act, passed in 1921, prohibited mining anthracite coal in any way that might cause subsidence under someone's house. Mahon sought an injunction against Pennsylvania Coal Company to prevent it from removing subsurface support, and the company argued in response that the act took its property without compensation. The Pennsylvania Supreme Court held that the act was a valid exercise of the police power, but Justice Holmes, writing the majority opinion for the US Supreme Court, disagreed. Holmes argued that the act took the subsurface support rights without an adequate reason and without compensation. Justice Brandeis wrote a dissent.

The decision is relevant to environmental policy because environmental regulations, too, may reduce the value of someone's property. And it continues to receive considerable scholarly attention because it serves as the leading case in a line of doctrine known as "regulatory takings." In contemporary constitutional law, a plaintiff might challenge an environmental regulation by claiming that the regulation takes his or her property without compensation in violation of the Fifth Amendment's takings clause. In 1922, however, that strategy wasn't available, because the courts had not yet decided whether the takings clause applied to the states.[124] Pennsylvania Coal challenged the regulation as violating substantive due process, imposing an unreasonable economic burden on the company without adequate justification.

Justice Holmes agreed. He recognized that "government hardly could go on if to some extent values incident to property could not be diminished without paying for every such change in the general law" and that property is generally "enjoyed under an implied limitation and must yield to the police power." Nevertheless, "obviously the implied limitation must have its limits, or the contract and due process clauses are gone. One fact for consideration in determining such limits is the extent of the diminution. When it reaches a certain magnitude, in most if not in all cases there must be an exercise of eminent domain and compensation to sustain the act."[125] The "implied limitation" Holmes is referring to is the state's power to prohibit public nuisances. If the state goes beyond that limit to achieve some other goal and in the process greatly reduces the value of the property in question, it must compensate the property owner. (As we have seen, cities and states did often compensate property owners when a new regulation diminished the value of their property, as in the regulations at stake in *Attorney General v. Williams* and *Twin City Co. v. Houghton.*)

So the key question in *Pennsylvania Coal* was whether this statute in fact aimed at prohibiting a public nuisance. The statute was ostensibly aimed at preventing subsidence; there had been a few high-profile cases in which a house or whole row of houses collapsed into sinkholes caused by careless mining.[126] Although a sinkhole certainly could constitute a nuisance, Holmes insisted that the statute did not aim to address a *public* nuisance. It was aimed at preventing damage to private property only. Moreover, the statute had little relation to public safety, since the coal company gave notice of its intent to mine coal in ample time for the property owners to take precautions. The right to subsurface support had been negotiated between the parties, and Holmes saw no justification for the state to interfere with this private contract.

Brandeis, in contrast, accepted the state's argument (and the state supreme court's conclusion) that subsidence could pose a danger to the public and so could be regulated as a public nuisance. He pointed out that the statute did not protect private residences only but also public streets and buildings. And "it seems, likewise, clear that mere notice of intention to mine would not in this connection secure the public safety."[127] Brandeis also rejected Holmes's claim that the property taken by the regulation was the subsurface "right to support." As he saw it, the property in question was the entire parcel of land, and the regulation merely restricted one use of the land rather than destroying its value altogether.

Scholars continue to debate the wisdom of the decision. William Fischel's excellent study of the case points out that the problem of subsidence had actually been resolved fairly successfully before the Kohler Act was passed through a voluntary agreement by the coal companies. (The major cases of subsidence after this agreement was reached were caused by one coal company whose actions were illegal even under existing law.)[128] For today's legal scholars, however, the *Pennsylvania Coal* decision is notable for Holmes's understanding of property rights. Throughout his career,

Holmes forwarded the view that property rights were not stable, enduring principles derived from natural law; they were created by state law and thus historically contingent and dynamic. (We may recall in this respect his casual rejection, in *Missouri v. Holland*, of the long-standing principle that wildlife was common property of citizens of the state.) Under Holmes's view, *every* new regulation changes one's property rights. So in evaluating the constitutionality of a regulation, the court should ask, how extreme a change does the new regulation effect? Is it fair to the property owner to change the rules in this way? As Richard Brauneis succinctly puts it, Holmes "decided that the 'property' the Constitution protected was the set of advantages that an owner could count on the state to enforce as existing positive law."[129] This conceptualization focuses constitutional inquiry on the property owner's reasonable expectations.

Holmes's approach would prove to be a useful framework for thinking about environmental regulation, but that framework would not be taken up and developed by the courts until the 1980s. In the 1920s and 1930s, *Pennsylvania Coal* had little impact on environmental reform efforts. Most environmental regulations during this era were justified as addressing public nuisances, so the "diminution of value" analysis didn't apply. The lower court in *Euclid* did cite the decision as suggesting that the Supreme Court was taking a more restrictive view of the police power, and it was also cited in a 1926 Sixth Circuit decision, striking down an Ohio zoning ordinance restricting gravel mining.[130] But both of those decisions came before the Supreme Court decided *Euclid*. Holmes's opinion in *Euclid* didn't mention *Pennsylvania Coal* at all.

In sum, Progressive Era constitutional doctrine largely accommodated new antipollution and urban planning policies—not through dramatic changes in doctrine but through new understandings about urban environments. The police power continued to support measures aimed at protecting community welfare; what changed was judicial understanding of the threats to public health and safety in complex urban environments and a growing appreciation of planning as a way to address those threats. Indeed, this line of cases suggests a gradual blurring of the line between urban and natural landscapes, as courts increasingly conceptualize both as riskscapes requiring active management by professionals to promote human health and well-being. At the least it suggests strong judicial support for municipal pollution control.

That judicial support might have extended to federal pollution control policy as well, but we can't be sure. Despite considerable pressure, Congress failed to address pollution in any substantial way, so the courts had little opportunity to consider whether Congress's power extended so far. But as the next chapter demonstrates, they did attempt to support state efforts to address interstate pollution.

CHAPTER NINE

Federalizing Pollution Control

State and local pollution control has its limits, and environmental reformers discovered those limits in their attempts to control pollution that crossed state lines. One response to interstate pollution was a campaign for federal pollution control legislation. But efforts to expand congressional authority to combat pollution largely failed, leaving this area almost entirely to state and local government.

Unfortunately, state governments had little capacity to deal with interstate pollution issues—despite the best efforts of the Supreme Court to enhance that capacity. Indeed, this area of constitutional doctrine witnessed the most dramatic transformation we have yet seen, with the Supreme Court inventing a new area of federal common law and extending its jurisdiction to a new class of cases: interstate nuisance suits. Even so, without help from Congress, controlling interstate pollution proved to be largely beyond states' capacity. But the court's doctrinal innovation and experience with this issue presaged the future expansion of federal pollution control authority.

The Campaign for Federal Water Pollution Policy

As we have seen throughout this study, water is the area over which both state and federal constitutional authority is the broadest, and water pollution was the chief focus of the campaign for federal pollution policy. Water pollution was a rapidly growing concern in the early twentieth century, thanks to the improvement in urban water systems. Those systems typically removed human waste from cities by dumping it in a nearby river. As a result, typhoid, which initially declined as municipal sewer systems improved, made a dramatic comeback in downstream cities.[1] Industrial water pollution, too, was attracting attention. By 1905, most states had some regulations concerning stream pollution. But state regulation, of course, couldn't reach out-of-state sources of water pollution.

One might think that federal government would clearly have jurisdiction over the protection of interstate waters, by virtue of the Commerce Clause. But while the commerce power extended to protecting the quantity of water in interstate rivers,[2] federal jurisdiction over water *quality* wasn't clear. The chief problem was the ambiguity of *Gibbons v. Ogden.* *Gibbons* affirmed federal jurisdiction over navigable waters for the purpose of commerce, but Justice Marshall also wrote that "health laws of every description" were part of the "immense mass of legislation" over which states retained control when they created the Union.[3] That division of authority over water seemed to leave pollution control to the states.

To be sure, the federal navigation servitude did extend to some kinds of water pollution, as demonstrated by the 1899 Rivers and Harbors Act.[4] This act prohibited the dumping of refuse in navigable waters without permission from the secretary of war and passed without constitutional objection. But the law was directed primarily at refuse that could pose an obstacle to navigation, and it exempted sewage disposal and street runoff. As explained in chapter 6, the Army Corps of Engineers was responsible for developing navigable waters, and it was reluctant to expand its mandate even into irrigation, much less water pollution.

To disrupt this constitutional consensus, pollution policy advocates had to persuade lawmakers, courts, and agency officials that there was a legitimate federal interest in regulating pollution. The most promising candidate was public health. There was a sustained effort from the 1870s on to expand federal public health authority, and the rise of bacteriology in the late nineteenth century reinforced the link between water pollution and disease. Accordingly, advocates for federal water pollution policy allied themselves with the campaign for federal public health policy. This strategy did yield some victories, but ultimately the reform campaign fell far short of overcoming congressional resistance to regulating industrial emissions.

Federal Power to Protect Public Health

The federal government has been involved in public health since the founding era. As legal scholar Arjun Jaikumar explains, Congress, relying on the war and commerce powers, enacted a federal quarantine law in 1796—but it merely authorized federal officials to assist state and local governments in administering quarantines.[5] Congress rejected a broader bill that would have given the president authority to declare and enforce quarantines of foreign commercial goods on the grounds that it would interfere with the state power to protect public health.[6] President John Adams did sign another bill in 1799[7] slightly strengthening the act, and Congress created the Marine Hospital Service (MHS), whose mission was to ensure that sailors had access to hospitals when they were in port. The MHS either contracted with or built hospitals in port cities.[8] But that was the extent of the federal government's public health policy until after the Civil War.

The first halting efforts at expanding federal health policy began in 1873, when public health advocate Christopher Cox urged Congress to establish a new federal agency, modeled on the Bureaus of Agriculture and Education.[9] In a report directed at lawmakers, Cox proposed an agency whose mandate would be carefully circumscribed to protect states' rights. Its mission would be primarily scientific, gathering useful information about health threats and supporting local quarantine efforts, rather than imposing regulations. However, he insisted that the federal government did have the power to act when a contagious disease threatened the country as a whole.[10] Cox's proposal was presented to Congress by Senator James Patterson, but neither it nor subsequent bills were passed until 1878. In that year, a yellow fever outbreak along the lower Mississippi River finally provided the impetus for the National Quarantine Act.[11] This statute authorized the MHS to impose quarantines on vessels in American ports to stop the spread of contagious diseases. In deference to states' rights, however, the statute also provided that such regulations could not conflict with state sanitary or quarantine laws. And it failed to provide the MHS with funds to carry this mission—an omission that signals its lack of congressional support.[12] One year later, advocates succeeded in persuading Congress to create a new agency, the National Health Board, to administer the quarantine act. But the board was authorized for only four years, and in 1883 opponents (citing states' rights) were able to block reenactment of the statute.[13] The National Board during this time did formulate rules for maritime quarantines, as well as quarantines for inland waterways and railroads, thus staying close to the federal government's traditional authority over interstate commerce.[14] But it lost both funding and authority and was formally disbanded in 1893.

Historian John Duffy attributes the failure of the National Health Board to the fact that states viewed their own quarantine systems as valuable sources of revenue and patronage.[15] On the other hand, epidemics frequently strained states' capacity, leading to periodic calls from states themselves for federal support. The MHS, with a growing reputation in biomedical research, was the chief beneficiary of these calls. In the 1890s, Congress granted the director of the MHS more general authority to prevent the spread of contagious diseases. An additional federal act in 1893 required state and local quarantine facilities to meet federal standards (as established by the MHS) and also allowed states to surrender their quarantine facilities to the federal government if they wished.[16]

These federal initiatives could be justified as exercises of the federal government's war power, supplemented by its authority over interstate and international commerce. Even so, they continued to run into objections from states' rights advocates. Representative Rayner, introducing the 1893 bill, had to defend federal authority to states' rights advocate Representative Crain from Texas:

> You have a right to declare war by the Constitution, but you have no right according to [Crain's] construction of the Constitution, to defend against an enemy who can desolate your seaboard and convert your prosperous cities into a withering wilderness. . . . You can provide for the common defense, but you cannot defend against an enemy that is more subtle than any enemy that ever appeared in human form. I believe that under the Constitution the Government has the absolute right to provide for the protection of the public health: and, so far as I am concerned, I am utterly opposed to leaving this to the conflicting powers of forty-four different States.[17]

We will see disease and pollution described as an "invasion" again, in interstate nuisance actions; it becomes a common trope in justifying federal action in this area. But despite Rayner's broad vision, federal public health policy was still largely confined to managing quarantines in seaports.

Still, legislative interest in federal health policy persisted, and at least some wildlife advocates thought it a good idea to join that campaign. The District of Columbia Game and Fish Protective Association, for example, sent a memorandum to Congress in 1900 in support of a bill to address pollution in interstate rivers. The memo suggested that in addition to public health, such a measure would help preserve the "finny denizens of these waters." In other words, protecting wildlife could be a legitimate secondary objective of federal public health policy. And, since fish can also be a food source, protecting their habitat also had a connection to public health.[18] But that bill, like the other stream pollution proposals considered by Congress in the early years of the twentieth century, went nowhere.

The campaign for a national public health agency, however, remained very much alive, and early in Theodore Roosevelt's administration it received support from researchers at the US Geological Survey (USGS). The USGS had been asked to investigate the nation's water supply (as part of the campaign to develop water resources in the arid West). In the course of carrying out that directive, the Service also researched pollution affecting surface water. In 1902, USGS hydrographer M.O. Leighton gave a speech to the American Public Health Association (APHA) calling for the group to attend to water pollution caused by manufacturing wastes. The APHA proved receptive and immediately set up a committee to investigate the issue.[19] Although the initiative petered out, Leighton continued to discuss with the APHA the USGS investigations of industrial waste. The Geological Survey produced thirteen reports on water pollution between 1902 and 1925, addressing both sewage and industrial waste. And, as we will see below, it provided expert testimony in *Missouri v. Illinois*,[20] one of the major interstate nuisance cases. But this research on water pollution didn't receive as much attention (or funding) as the biomedical research being pursued by the MHS.[21]

Nevertheless, the problem of pollution in interstate streams continued to be raised in congressional hearings and reports on public health—as would the constitutional objections to federal pollution control. For example, in 1909 the House Commerce Committee held hearings on a proposal to expand the powers of the MHS to research epidemics. The bill, like most of these proposals, included a provision supporting research on water pollution. An impatient Dr. Reed from Cincinnati, speaking on behalf of the American Medical Association, wanted to amend the bill to allow the MHS not only to research but also to "formulate and enforce necessary regulations for the protection of all streams and waterways within the jurisdiction of the United States government." A startled Representative Stevens pointed out that states' rights advocates already thought the bill went too far. Dr. Reed insisted that the division of jurisdiction between state and federal government was a mere detail that could be worked out, but Stevens responded, "No, they are matters of fundamental principles. They affect constitutional issues." This proposal, he objected, would require the federal government to "revolutioniz[e] the sewerage systems of . . . states [along interstate rivers.]" Yes, Reed responded. That is exactly what he wanted.[22]

Reed had no plausible constitutional argument for such an expansion of federal authority beyond the stark fact that the entire Ohio River watershed was experiencing a typhoid epidemic, and no state seemed capable of addressing it. A more legally sophisticated argument came from George Otis Smith, director of the USGS, who wrote to the same committee in 1910 in support of expanding federal public health authority. Smith pointed out that the only way a downstream state could address pollution from an upstream state was by bringing a nuisance action in federal court. He indicated that Missouri had tried that (in *Missouri v. Illinois*, discussed below). But the proceeding was very expensive, and Missouri lost. "This issue," he suggested, "is so wide and so intimately related to the whole country that it becomes a national matter in fact if not in law."[23] But Congress, of course, is bound by law, and it would need a better argument for federal involvement in public health beyond the judicially disfavored "state failure" and "inherent power" theories.[24]

Representative George Shiras III set out to create such an argument. Shiras was a member of the Committee of One Hundred on National Health, a civic group created in 1906, and he volunteered to investigate the constitutional issue for that group.[25] In the 1910 hearing, he offered to the House committee the result of that investigation, a brief setting out the following argument: The federal government, Shiras maintained, has an inherent police power. This power is the basis of its regulation of interstate and foreign commerce. That is, the federal government can regulate interstate and foreign commerce to achieve the ends of the police power: the health, safety, and welfare of the community. This, he contended, is the basis of existing federal inspection and quarantine laws.

That much was not particularly controversial, since the federal government was in fact regulating commerce to protect the public from health and safety threats posed by such commerce. Shiras's more problematic claim was that Congress may regulate any interstate intercourse (not merely commercial intercourse), wherever necessary to protect public health. To support that argument, he pointed to the fact that the Supreme Court has jurisdiction over any dispute between states. If the court has jurisdiction over, say, conflicts over water pollution, then Congress must also have authority to regulate that subject: "The right to settle such controversies includes the right to regulate the subject-matter of a controversy either by a judicial process or legislative enactment."[26]

We'll investigate the court's reasoning on this question of federal court jurisdiction over interstate pollution below. Here, I will merely note that Shiras's reasoning—that Congress's power and federal court jurisdiction must be conterminous—threatened to expand Congress's power considerably. Shiras would in fact have Congress "stay the spread of contagious diseases from foreign shores or from State to State" as well as

> control the various means of transmission, whether they be the infected waters of interstate streams, the interstate movement of diseased persons and domestic animals, the transportation of adulterated foods and impure drugs, or the maintenance of harmful conditions within a State which are provocative of communicable diseases, or of any other element of danger to the health and physical safety of persons residing beyond the borders of the offending State.[27]

Congress did already regulate goods in interstate commerce, including plants and animals. But extending that power to interstate pollution and "harmful conditions within a State which are provocative of communicable disease" was going much farther than any court had yet to approve.

Shiras's argument doesn't seem to have persuaded the House committee. Nevertheless, as George Otis Smith had pointed out in his letter, even a more limited federal agency with explicit authority to research public health issues would be useful. It could provide reliable evidence in interstate lawsuits and perhaps help states create plans for managing interstate rivers. Even the constitutionally cautious President Taft had no objection to a federal public health agency limited to enforcing federal quarantines and conducting research.[28] And that is what Congress eventually created.

In 1912, Congress finally acknowledged in law that the MHS had become a national public health agency. Renamed the Public Health Service (PHS), the agency continued to implement the quarantine law, but it was further authorized to "study and investigate the diseases of man and conditions influencing the propagation and spread thereof, *including sanitation and sewage and the pollution either directly or indirectly of the navigable streams and lakes of the United States*, and it may from time to time issue information in the form of publications for the use of the public."[29] As historian Richard Andrews notes, with this act, the Public Health Service became the first federal agency with a mandate to investigate environmental health.[30] And, like federal authority over forest conservation, this pollution authority was based on, and limited by, the federal navigation servitude.

The PHS, being principally a scientific rather than a regulatory agency, did not face challenges to its constitutionality, and it did use its environmental health authority.[31] For example, it conducted a three-year study of the Ohio River, established testing stations at some industrial facilities to gather data, and developed bacteria-based water quality standards. Those standards remained voluntary, however.[32]

The Oil Pollution Act of 1924

The one piece of pollution control policy that Congress did manage to pass during this period was the Oil Pollution Act of 1924.[33] Advocates for federal water pollution policy had been campaigning for several years, and from 1921 to 1924, numerous bills were introduced to prohibit industrial pollution. Although advocates were concerned about a variety of industrial wastes, oil pollution was the most worrisome. Representatives from coastal states, from New York to Texas, considered oil contamination of beaches and harbors to be a problem requiring some federal action. The debates and hearings over these measures attracted considerable attention, and representatives from industry lined up to oppose it. Constitutional issues were not prominent in the debate, but they were raised periodically, and the dominant views suggest that states' rights advocates had made quite a lot of progress in undermining the notion that the navigation servitude gave Congress authority over water pollution.

To be sure, there were ambitious bills under consideration in 1921 through 1924 that proposed protecting both coastal and inland navigable waters, addressing ships and industrial plants, and targeting a variety of polluting substances. (All the bills exempted municipal sewage.) But even the narrower bills raised constitutional objections. For example, in a hearing on an oil pollution bill, John Tierney of the Manufacturing Chemists Association asked whether Congress had the authority to regulate *inland* waters at all.[34] Of course, the Rivers and Harbors Act of 1899 had prohibited refuse in navigable waters for several decades; indeed, some congressmen thought that the 1899 statute already covered oil pollution.[35] But as we know, states' rights advocates had developed some new arguments since

1899, questioning how far federal authority over water actually extended. Several Supreme Court decisions (such as the perennial favorite of states' rights advocates, *Kansas v. Colorado*[36]) were interpreted as holding that states owned the water in navigable rivers; federal government merely had the power to protect navigation, not the water itself (nor, under *Geer v. Connecticut*,[37] the fish in the water).

Representative Bland of Virginia, a supporter of the proposed Oil Pollution Act, sought to clarify the question with a theory he would repeat frequently in congressional hearings. Bland insisted that Congress's authority to regulate oil pollution does *not* stem from authority over the water in navigable streams. Under such precedents as *Manchester v. Massachusetts*,[38] *Geer v. Connecticut*, and *The Abbey Dodge*,[39] states have authority over fisheries in inland (and possibly also coastal) waters, so they have sole authority to protect those fisheries from pollution. Federal authority, in Bland's view, stems from Congress's power over the *instrumentalities* of interstate commerce. Bland characterized that power as narrowly focused on commercial intercourse only, but he insisted that it did extend to prohibiting any pollution that poses a danger to navigation. The principal rationale for prohibiting oil, he argued, was that it created a fire hazard to ships.[40] Bland thus concluded that Congress could regulate both ships and industrial facilities on shore that were discharging oil into harbors used for interstate commerce. Under his theory, however, Congress had no authority to prohibit any kind of pollution that didn't pose a hazard to navigation.

Bland's narrow view of the commerce power went largely unchallenged in the hearings. This is not to say that the rest of Congress agreed with him, of course. Representative Rosenbloom, from West Virginia, sponsored another bill in 1924 that proposed to give the War Department authority to regulate pollution on inland navigable rivers, and he justified it under the property power. He argued that the federal government owned many dams along these rivers, and certain kinds of pollution could damage them.[41] That ingenious argument was not put to the test, however. Attempts to address inland water pollution went nowhere, and the Oil Pollution Act itself was narrowly drawn: It prohibited dumping oil into coastal and tidal waters, but applied to ships only, not to industrial facilities on shore. Not surprisingly, the act met no constitutional problems in court.[42] In fact, in 1936, the Ninth Circuit held that the 1899 Rivers and Harbors Act was broad enough to cover oil that was released into Lake Union in Seattle (a lake not covered by the 1924 Act, being neither coastal nor affected by tides).[43] Since the 1899 Act applied to all navigable waters in the United States, the careful attempt to limit the Oil Pollution Act to coastal waters proved both unnecessary and unavailing.

In sum, the limited nature of the Oil Pollution Act reflected not judicial resistance to federal pollution policy—there is little evidence of that—but congressional reluctance to enter into this fraught field. But to say that federal government was not involved in pollution control during this period from 1900 to the New Deal is misleading. Federal *courts* were very much involved, not merely by reviewing state and local regulations but by providing a forum and developing rules to govern disputes over interstate pollution.

The Supreme Court and Interstate Conflict

In the absence of congressional action, states were left to deal with pollution on their own. But much of the pollution that states were grappling with was entering through interstate rivers, and managing interstate rivers had always been a challenging problem for the states. The framers of the 1789 Constitution were well aware of that problem. Indeed, resolving interstate conflicts was one of the main arguments in favor of strengthening the federal government, and the proposed Constitution offered two ways to do so: Article I, Section 10 provided that "No State shall, without the Consent of Congress . . . enter into any Agreement or Compact with another State." The negative phrasing notwithstanding, this compact clause has always been taken to provide an avenue for states to resolve disputes by forming compacts. As we will discuss in the next chapter, one of the major Progressive Era contributions to environmental management was the development of interstate compacts to manage interstate waters.[44] But interstate compacts did not initially look promising; interstate pollution was a source of considerable friction between states. Some mechanism was needed to resolve these disputes, and the federal courts provided such a mechanism.

Article III of the Constitution expressly provides that the Supreme Court has jurisdiction over disputes in which a state is a party and allows such cases to originate in the Supreme Court.[45] The Supreme Court was intended to be the primary forum for resolving disputes between states over their boundaries, and there had been many such cases during the nineteenth century. But the court had also been appealed to to resolve other kinds of disputes between states, including disputes over rivers.

The first case to use this strategy to address interstate water pollution was *Missouri v. Illinois*, begun in 1901 and finally decided in 1906. The case grew out of an audacious plan by the city of Chicago to solve its sewage disposal problem by reversing the course of the Chicago River.[46] Chicago had been depositing its sewage into the Chicago River, which emptied into Lake Michigan, the source of Chicago's drinking water. As the city grew, it became increasingly difficult to draw clean water from the lake. The plan aimed to protect the lake by reversing the course of the Chicago River so that the city's sewage flowed from Lake Michigan into the Des Plaines River, and from there into the Illinois River and, eventually, the Mississippi River. The Sanitation District Board (created by the state legislature to direct this project) oversaw the seven-year, $33 million project.

Even before it opened in January 1900, the canal was causing conflict with Illinois's neighbors. Michigan and Wisconsin officials worried that it would decrease the water levels in Lake Michigan, but officials in Missouri had a more serious concern: that sewage from Chicago would pollute the drinking water of cities along the Mississippi River. The Missouri governor asked the federal government for help, but Secretary of War Elihu Root and the US attorney general both declined to act.[47] The attorney general actually recommended that the state seek relief through the courts. So Missouri's attorney general filed suit in the Supreme Court, asking it to issue an injunction preventing the city from discharging sewage into the canal.

The lawsuit would take many years to resolve, and Missouri ultimately lost. But in the course of deciding the case, the court began to create a new body of law, a federal common law of interstate nuisance. In a series of decisions from 1901 to 1907, the Supreme Court announced that it would entertain disputes between states over pollution and other natural resource management problems—even where Congress had no authority to act. It thus extended federal court jurisdiction into an entirely new area of law without any support or guidance from Congress or the executive branch.

Doctrinal Background: The *Wheeling Bridge* Case

To appreciate what was at stake in this act of judicial lawmaking, it's useful to begin with the 1851 Supreme Court case *Pennsylvania v. Wheeling and Belmont Bridge Co.*[48] This case concerned a bridge built by the company at the direction of the Virginia legislature, spanning the Ohio River at Wheeling (which was still part of Virginia in 1851). Virginia had been trying for years to persuade Congress to fund this bridge, but each time, representatives from Pennsylvania defeated the proposal. When Virginia finally decided to fund the bridge itself, Pennsylvania's attorney general sought a court order to have the bridge removed or modified. Pennsylvania's complaint was that the bridge was a nuisance because it was not high enough for steamboats to pass under it—which posed a major problem for the substantial steamboat trade at the (state-owned) port of Pittsburgh. Pennsylvania argued that the bridge affected the state's revenues from the port of Pittsburgh, and the impediment to river traffic also affected state-owned railroads running from Pittsburgh to other towns. The state was therefore suing to protect its revenue.

Pennsylvania filed suit in the Supreme Court, invoking its original jurisdiction. The majority opinion in favor of Pennsylvania was written by Justice McLean, but Chief Justice Taney's dissent explains the problem it raises most clearly: Pennsylvania, he insisted, was claiming that the bridge is a public nuisance. But to be a public nuisance, the bridge must violate some law that the Supreme Court has authority to administer. There is no such law.

Taney and McLean agreed on one point: If this were a private nuisance lawsuit by an ordinary Pennsylvania citizen, it could have been filed in the federal circuit court in Virginia.[49] That court (as directed by the Judiciary Act of 1789[50]) would apply Virginia law, and according to Taney, the bridge was perfectly legal under Virginia law; the Virginia legislature actually authorized it. (McLean was less certain about that point, since the statute authorizing it also said that the bridge could be removed if it proved to be a nuisance.) Taney and McLean also agreed that Congress *could* pass a law making the bridge illegal, under the commerce power. Again, Taney argued, Congress had not done so. There was no third alternative; there is no "federal common law," or body of judge-made law, to which Pennsylvania could appeal.

This final point requires explanation, because judges in the United States do in fact make law quite frequently. The United States inherited the English common law tradition, whereby courts decide disputes by deriving legal rules from previous judicial decisions. There was not in fact much statutory law in the early years of the American republic. Each state merely passed a statute adopting the common law (except Louisiana, which adopted the French civil law). So each state has its own version of the common law, which is applied in that state's courts. But Congress had never adopted the common law as a body of law to be applied in federal courts. It couldn't do so, because Congress's power is limited to those objects specified in Article I, Section 8. The common law addresses a wide range of issues, most of which are beyond Congress's authority. If Congress wanted to make law, it must do so by statute, and it must stick to the subjects under its delegated authority.

The nonexistence of federal common law was a well-accepted principle, at least until 1842. In that year, Justice Story announced in *Swift v. Tyson*[51] that in commercial cases concerning issues not addressed by a state statute, the federal courts were not restricted to applying the common law of the state. They could develop their own commercial common law. (That decision would ultimately be overturned by *Erie R.R. v. Tompkins*[52] in 1938.) But *Swift* did not necessarily lead to a federal common law of *nuisance*. First, Story's decision was limited to commercial transactions, not "to rights and titles to things having a permanent locality . . . and other matters immovable and intraterritorial in their nature and character."[53] His logic rested heavily on the existence of a national business community whose practices transcended any state. Nuisance law, in contrast, is very much a matter of local usage and custom. Second, public nuisance was generally considered a branch of criminal law, and one of the major themes in the debate over federal common law was that prosecuting people for common law crimes—crimes that were not set down in any statute—would extend federal power in a particularly dangerous way.[54]

This extension of federal power was what concerned Taney in the *Wheeling Bridge* decision. If there was no congressional statute prohibiting the bridge, and Virginia law allowed it, then the court had no grounds for calling the bridge a nuisance, unless it created its own principle. As Taney wrote:

> I cannot perceive how the mere grant of power to the legislative department of the government to regulate commerce, can give to the judicial branch the power to declare what shall, and what shall not, be regarded as an unlawful obstruction; how high a bridge must be above the stream, and how far a wharf may be extended into the water, when we have no regulation of Congress to guide us. In taking jurisdiction, as the law now stands, we must exercise a broad and undefinable discretion, without any certain and safe rule to guide us. And such a discretion, when men of science differ, when we are to consider the amount and

value of trade, and the number of travellers on and across the stream, the interests of communities and States sometimes supposed to be conflicting, and the proper height and form of steamboat chimneys, such a discretion appears to me much more appropriately to belong to the Legislature than to the Judiciary.[55]

Taney's concern was that if the decision was not judicial in nature—if deciding the case required the court to make policy in matters where even "men of science" disagree rather than merely apply a legal rule—then the court shouldn't have taken jurisdiction in the first place. This case, he concluded, wasn't "justiciable."

Of course, the issue wasn't as clear as Taney suggested. He acknowledged that the court *did* decide boundary disputes between states without any guidance from Congress. Congress, he noted, was not authorized to legislate concerning the boundaries of states (at least, the states existing when the Constitution was adopted). But he considered those disputes to be governed by international law, the body of judge-made law developed to govern relations between different nations.[56] In this case, however, international law didn't apply; the states were not independent sovereigns with respect to interstate rivers. They were subject to Congress's authority to protect interstate navigation, and Congress clearly did have the power to prohibit the bridge. It had simply decided not to act. And "if Congress have not thought proper . . . to exercise this power, and public mischief has arisen, . . . it does not follow that the judicial power of the United States may step in and supply what the legislative authority has omitted to perform."[57]

McLean's majority opinion seemed to acknowledge the force of Taney's argument. He agreed that there is no federal common law of nuisance. But he insisted, first, that Pennsylvania was not bringing an action to abate a *public* nuisance. He treated this as a *private* nuisance suit by Pennsylvania to defend its own property rights, just like any private citizen can. This would be a tort action, not a criminal action. As for the question of which law to apply, McLean accepted Pennsylvania's argument that Congress had in fact provided the court with guidance. It had consented to the compact between Virginia and Kentucky, which stated that "the use and navigation of the River Ohio . . . shall be free and common to the citizens of the United States."[58] Taney objected that this language simply meant that citizens of other states may use the river on the same terms as did citizens of

Virginia. But the majority was satisfied that the compact, along with other regulations of steamboats on navigable rivers, provided a sufficient legislative basis for saying that the bridge was not consistent with federal law.[59]

To resolve the case, the court fashioned a complex order requiring the company to either remove or modify the bridge to permit steamboat traffic. Congress, however, was unhappy with this result. It promptly passed a statute declaring the bridge to be lawful, and in a later decision, the court followed Congress's lead and dissolved its injunction.[60] So the case, while never formally overruled, was treated with great suspicion by later courts. After all, the acts admitting states to the union typically did include language about navigable rivers remaining free and common to U.S. citizens, but states routinely built bridges over navigable waters just the same. The *Wheeling Bridge* decision invited a potentially daunting host of lawsuits by downstream states to remove bridges, dams, and other water projects. The Court therefore erected its own barrier to these lawsuits. In subsequent cases, it held that one must show that Congress had *explicitly* prohibited the project in question in order to win an injunction against it. The Court's position as of the 1888 decision *Willamette Iron Bridge Co. v. Hatch* was that "the power of Congress to pass laws for the regulation of the navigation of public rivers, and to prevent any and all obstructions therein, is not questioned. But until it does pass some such law, there is no common law of the United States which prohibits obstructions and nuisances in navigable rivers."[61]

Of course, the situation was different by 1900, because Congress *had* passed a law that could provide a basis for public nuisance actions concerning interstate rivers. The 1899 Rivers and Harbors Act included (in addition to the prohibition on dumping refuse) a section prohibiting the building of any obstruction in navigable waters that was not authorized by Congress. This amendment was in fact passed in response to the *Willamette Iron Bridge* decision.[62] But the 1899 Act prohibited only material or structures that impeded navigation. It did not address, for example, pollution by bacteria. So a state seeking to address water pollution from an upstream state in federal court still faced the problem raised by Taney: How should the Supreme Court decide such disputes?

The Problem of State Standing

Nor was this the only barrier to states seeking to address interstate pollution in the Supreme Court. Equally problematic was the question of under what circumstances a state may invoke the court's original jurisdiction.

This issue is illustrated in the 1900 Supreme Court decision *Louisiana v. Texas*.[63] The state of Louisiana asked the Supreme Court to enjoin an embargo imposed by the Texas health officer, prohibiting all commerce between New Orleans and Texas. The embargo was enacted in response to an outbreak of yellow fever in New Orleans, but Louisiana contended that this was just an excuse; the real reason for the embargo was to benefit Texas businesses at the expense of Louisiana businesses. Louisiana thus claimed to be acting on behalf of the businesses of New Orleans. Texas argued that the Supreme Court should not take jurisdiction of the case, because there was no real dispute between the two states. Louisiana, it claimed, was not the true party in the case; the business interests in New Orleans were the actual parties claiming injury.

Justice Fuller wrote the opinion dismissing the suit for lack of jurisdiction. Texas's argument needed careful consideration, because it raised the possibility that the lawsuit was an attempt to evade the Eleventh Amendment, which prohibited federal courts from hearing "any suit . . . commenced or prosecuted against one of the United States by citizens of another State." The Eleventh Amendment aimed to give states immunity from being sued by private citizens in federal courts without their consent. Therefore, to take advantage of the Supreme Court's original jurisdiction, a state must show that it is not acting for private citizens and that something of its own is at stake.[64] A state's property interests generally constituted adequate grounds for jurisdiction. (This was Pennsylvania's interest in the *Wheeling Bridge* case, specifically, the revenues from the port.) However, a state's interest in enforcing its laws was generally not a proper ground for federal jurisdiction. Several decisions had prohibited states from using the federal courts to enforce a criminal law.[65] Similarly, after the Civil War, the court had refused to entertain a lawsuit by Georgia asking the court to enjoin the secretary of war from enforcing a federal law that essentially dissolved Georgia's government to replace it with a new one. That case, the court held, was a political dispute—a dispute over the state's sovereignty—that didn't lend itself to judicial resolution.[66] In short, there were some kinds of state interests that couldn't be effectively defended in a courtroom. But the court had never denied that there might be other, nonpecuniary, interests that a state *could* defend in federal court.

Fuller, in deciding that Louisiana did have standing, relied heavily on *In re Debs*. In this 1895 case, the US attorney general sought an injunction to prevent a railway union from going on strike, arguing that the federal government had an interest in protecting interstate commerce. That case, while not precisely on point, raised a similar question: Can the federal government act to protect the business interests of private citizens? The Court allowed the suit in *Debs* to go forward, reasoning,

> Whenever the wrongs complained of are such as affect the public at large, and are in respect of matters which by the Constitution are intrusted [*sic*] to the care of the Nation, and concerning which the Nation owes the duty to all the citizens of securing to them their common rights, then the mere fact that the Government has no pecuniary interest in the controversy is not sufficient to exclude it from the courts or prevent it from taking measures therein to fully discharge those constitutional duties.[67]

Fuller used this language to explain Louisiana's interest in this case: "The State of Louisiana presents herself in the attitude of parens patriae, trustee, guardian or representative of all her citizens." That is, the state was taking action because the matter affected its citizens at large. Fuller seemed willing to accept that logic—but he nevertheless denied jurisdiction on the grounds that Louisiana did not actually have a dispute with *the state* of Texas. The state, in authorizing its health officer to enact a quarantine, was acting properly. Louisiana's dispute was with the health officer, which it accused of abusing his authority. And "the remedy for that would clearly lie with the state authorities."[68]

In short, the decision seemed to confirm that a state could have standing to vindicate the rights of its citizens in the Supreme Court. But it did not provide much guidance in determining how many citizens or which rights must be at stake. After all, the Eleventh Amendment must mark *some* limit to a state's power to act for its citizens. And the decision also highlighted the difficulty of determining whom to sue: States can act only through their officers, so when does a state official's action constitute an action by the state? Given these complexities, it would take some creative legal argument to persuade the Supreme Court to entertain a case concerning pollution in interstate rivers.

Missouri v. Illinois

Missouri's argument before the Supreme Court was developed by the state's attorney general Edward Crow. As explained in a *Chicago Tribune* article, he saw this as a straightforward nuisance case: "The State has a direct inter-est in the matter, first, because the health of the citizens of the great City of St. Louis is directly menaced; second, because thousands of our citizens outside of St. Louis live on the bank of this largest of inland rivers, and are forced to use its waters." Coming to the legal point, he offered that "injury to the purity or quality of the water in a flowing stream, to the detriment of riparian owners, constitutes a nuisance as much as a permanent obstruc-tion." Missouri clearly owns the waters of the river up to its midpoint, and "it is within the power of the State of Missouri to protect these waters from pollution, in order to preserve the health of our citizens."[69]

In retrospect, this looks like a pretty good argument, but it would require the Supreme Court to extend its original jurisdiction in a new direction. The actual bill of complaint anticipated judicial skepticism: It insisted, first, that this was not an attempt to enforce Missouri's criminal laws; it was merely a civil suit seeking an injunction to protect its property—namely, the state's property rights in the water and soil in the Mississippi. The complaint also alleged that sewage from Chicago would render worthless all the waterworks systems built by cities along the Mississippi River. Water pollution would deprive the state of Missouri and its inhabitants of their right to use the water for domestic, manufacturing, and agricultural pur-poses—injuring not only the health of Missouri citizens but also the busi-ness interests of the state. It thus asserted, in addition to citizens' health, state interests very similar to those accepted by the court in *Wheeling Bridge* and *Louisiana v. Texas.*[70]

Illinois's attorney general (Edwin Akin), along with lawyers represent-ing the Sanitation District, asked the court to dismiss the bill for lack of jurisdiction, citing the many exceptions to the Supreme Court's original jurisdiction over controversies in which a state is a party. They relied in par-ticular on the argument that public nuisance actions were "quasi-criminal" in nature, and Missouri was not allowed to enforce a criminal law beyond its borders.[71] The brief argued further that Missouri was acting on behalf of its citizens rather than defending its own interests, denying that the state's property rights were at risk or that there was any direct conflict between the two states.[72]

The decision on this preliminary issue of jurisdiction was written by Justice George Shiras, Jr. (father of George Shiras III), and it supported Missouri's position. Shiras acknowledged the force of Illinois's argument: There were many conflicting precedents concerning what sort of conflict constitutes a "controversy between two states." But after a long review of these cases, he came at last to *Louisiana v. Texas*. Shiras quoted Fuller at length, and in particular the language from *In re Debs*, concluding that the state of Louisiana in that case presented herself "in the attitude of parens patriae, trustee, guardian or representative of all her citizens."[73] Shiras concluded:

> It is true that no question of boundary is involved, *nor of direct property rights belonging to the complainant State*. But it must surely be conceded that, if the health and comfort of the inhabitants of a State are threatened, the State is the proper party to represent and defend them. If Missouri were an independent and sovereign State all must admit that she could seek a remedy by negotiation, and, that failing, by force. Diplomatic powers and the right to make war having been surrendered to the general government, it was to be expected that upon the latter would be devolved the duty of providing a remedy and that remedy, we think, is found in the constitutional provisions we are considering.[74]

Thus Missouri does have a sufficient stake in this issue in its role as representative or trustee—parens patriae—of its citizens. Interestingly (given the attention devoted to this question in the briefs), he did not explain why he rejected Illinois's argument that the suit was an attempt to enforce a criminal law. Finally, he concluded that the state of Illinois and the Sanitary District were proper parties to the suit. The Sanitary District was created by and executing the authority given to it by the state legislature, so it is proper to say that the action complained of is the action of the state.[75]

This decision, along with *Louisiana v. Texas*, established what has come to be termed parens patriae standing, or the right of a state to sue on behalf of the health and welfare of its citizens. This was one critical element in creating a federal common law addressing interstate pollution. But the decision did not address the other key issue: What legal rule would the court use to resolve the case?

Before addressing that question, the court reviewed the evidence. As was common practice in cases originating in the Supreme Court, the court appointed a commissioner to gather exhibits and hear testimony. That process took years, involving many hours of expert testimony and even scientific experimentation. Legal scholar Robert Percival's account of the case notes that "more than 350 witnesses testified and more than 100 exhibits were presented before Commissioner Bright, producing a record that consumed 13,160 typewritten pages."[76] This massive report was presented to the court in May 1905, which issued its final decision, refusing the injunction, in February 1906.

The decision was a loss for Missouri, but it was still a victory for proponents of pollution control. Justice Holmes's decision for the court focused on the troublesome question left unaddressed by Shiras: What law should he draw on to decide the dispute?[77] He acknowledged the problem with adjudicating matters that are beyond Congress's power to regulate: "The result of a declaration of rights by this court would be the establishment of a rule which would be irrevocable by any power except that of this court to reverse its own decision, an amendment of the Constitution, or possibly an agreement between the States sanctioned by the legislature of the United States."[78] Nevertheless, some matters evidently do warrant such intervention. Warning that the court should not do so unless the case is "of serious magnitude, clearly and fully proved, and the principle to be applied . . . one which the court is prepared deliberately to maintain against all considerations on the other side," he went on to consider the principle to be applied in this case.

One might expect that he would begin with Illinois law, since the action complained of took place in Illinois. That was the approach that Taney thought proper in *Wheeling Bridge*. But Holmes instead began with Missouri's laws, which "offers a standard to which defendant has the right to appeal."[79] Unfortunately for Missouri, he noted that Missouri did allow cities to release untreated sewage into the river. Moreover, the evidence did not clearly show that Chicago sewage was increasing the risk of typhoid. Although he assumed the "prevailing scientific explanation of typhoid fever to be correct," the data concerning its prevalence along the Mississippi was disputed.[80] Illinois argued that water from Lake Michigan now flowing into the Illinois River, by increasing the total volume of water in the river, improved water quality (and there was some expert testimony to support that view). In contrast to the judicial deference to federal Forest Service agents in *Hunt v. United States*,[81] here the court did not defer to either side. The burden of proof was on Missouri, and its evidence was not compelling enough to justify an injunction. In dismissing Missouri's bill, however, Holmes agreed that new evidence could justify an injunction in the future.

Developing a Common Law of Interstate Nuisance

The *Missouri v. Illinois* decision, notably, was unanimous, and it was not anomalous. It was one of several decisions opening the Supreme Court to state lawsuits over natural resources. Holmes's opinion cited another recent case, the 1902 decision in *Kansas v. Colorado*, which followed similar logic. This was the same dispute over water rights in the Colorado River that yielded the 1907 decision discussed in chapter 6. The 1902 decision was just a preliminary skirmish, but it was significant because the court relied on Shiras's opinion in *Missouri v. Illinois* to hold that it could exercise jurisdiction. Justice Fuller wrote the majority opinion, announcing that the court had "no special difficulty" in finding that this conflict over the apportionment of water rights constituted a justiciable controversy between states. Kansas had some property rights at stake, but Fuller was also willing to accept its right to assert parens patriae standing on behalf of its citizens. And he was unworried about the question of which legal rule to apply: "Sitting, as it were, as an international, as well as a domestic tribunal, we apply Federal law, state law, and international law, as the exigencies of the particular case may demand."[82] This decision, also, generated no dissents, and as we know, the court followed it up in 1907 by deciding the substantive issue.

The 1907 *Kansas v. Colorado* opinion, although not addressing interstate nuisance, is an important entry in this line of decisions. Much of the difficulty of apportioning water rights between Kansas and Colorado stemmed from the fact that the two states treated water rights differently. Kansas recognized the common law rule that riparian owners are entitled to a continual flow of water, while in Colorado, those who appropriate water first are entitled to its use. Justice Brewer addressed this problem by noting, "It does not follow, however, that because Congress cannot determine the rule which shall control between the two States or because neither State can enforce its own policy upon the other, that the controversy ceases to be one of a justiciable nature, or that there is no power which can take cognizance of the controversy and determine the relative rights of the two States."[83] That is, the Supreme Court could apportion rights in interstate streams *even though Congress could not*. This point is important to the development of interstate nuisance law, because it was still doubtful whether Congress's commerce power extended to pollution in interstate rivers. Casting aside any concerns about the expansion of federal power or the inability of Congress to correct the Supreme Court's decisions, Brewer explicitly rejected the claim that "there is no common law of the United States as distinguished from the common law of the several States."[84] Citing *Swift v. Tyson*, he concluded that the court can also develop equitable principles that have the force of law in deciding disputes between states.[85] As we know, Brewer went on to decide that Colorado's use of the water was reasonable and not unduly harmful to Kansas residents. This decision, too, was unanimous. White and McKenna concurred but wrote no opinion.

Moreover, on the same day that the court issued this decision, it also issued its opinion in *Georgia v. Tennessee Copper Co.*,[86] the other foundational interstate nuisance case. This case involved air pollution, a subject even more remote from the federal commerce power than water pollution. There was nothing comparable to the federal navigation servitude to justify federal regulation of air pollution. Nevertheless, at the urging of Georgia's attorney general, the Supreme Court waded confidently into this area as well.

Georgia v. Tennessee Copper Company

Tennessee Copper Company operated a smelter in the southeast corner of Tennessee, which produced a considerable amount of sulfurous smoke that spread over the border into Georgia.[87] Residents in Georgia had sued in Tennessee courts to enjoin emissions from the smelter, but the Tennessee Supreme Court declined to issue an injunction, although it did award plaintiffs damages. The residents finally appealed to Georgia's state government to do something about the situation. Georgia's governor, Joseph Terrell, was a former attorney general who had argued before the US Supreme Court, and he took up the cause with alacrity.[88] First, he prompted the legislature to appoint a commission, including the state chemist and geologist, to investigate the smoke problem. The commission's 1903 report concluded that not only was the smoke a nuisance, but it was also damaging valuable timber and potentially harming agriculture. The report emphasized in particular the threat of deforestation, drawing on the familiar theory about the role of forests in protecting watersheds.[89] On the basis of this report, the governor sent a letter to Tennessee's governor, asking him to take action. The Tennessee governor declined, insisting that he had no authority to order the smelter to stop operating and suggesting that Georgia seek relief from the courts. Accordingly, in January 1904, Georgia's attorney general, John Hart, filed suit against Tennessee Copper

Co. in the Supreme Court, invoking the court's original jurisdiction. The lawsuit would not go forward immediately; it led to efforts to negotiate a resolution, and the company agreed to modify some of its practices. But these efforts didn't reduce the smoke, so in 1905 Georgia renewed the lawsuit, asking the court for an injunction to halt the emissions (and prevent new furnaces from coming online).

Although this lawsuit was against a private party rather than a state, Georgia faced the same challenges to the court's jurisdiction that Missouri had faced. The company's lawyers argued that Georgia was not a proper party to the suit because it did not have sufficient pecuniary interest at stake. Georgia's brief, drawing on the 1903 report along with research by the US Forest Service,[90] alleged that the smoke damaged agricultural lands and thereby lessened the state's tax revenue, as well as leading to deforestation with resulting impacts on its streams. Tennessee Copper's lawyers insisted that the effect of the smoke on tax revenues was negligible, and there was no significant damage to any stream.[91]

Thus far, the jurisdictional argument sounds much like the *Wheeling Bridge* case. But Attorney General Hart, relying on Justice Shiras's opinion in *Missouri v. Illinois*, argued also that the smoke threatened the state's interest in protecting the health of the citizens. Using the language of invasion, he argued,

> The Constitution of the United States guarantees protection to the State of Georgia against any invasion whatever, whether such invasion be by force of arms or other means, by another State or its citizens, or by a foreign government. It is sufficient that the means be hostile or harmful and be such that Georgia cannot prevent or protect herself against without the use of force upon foreign territory. . . . The acts complained of . . . result in laying the territory of the State in waste more surely and completely than could be accomplished by any invading army bent upon its destruction.[92]

The complaint also underscored the fact that he was claiming the smoke was a *public* nuisance, and private citizens typically did not have the right to abate a public nuisance. The state was essentially bringing this suit in the Supreme Court to enforce its laws and to protect the state's sovereignty.

Of course, Georgia's insistence that this was a suit to enforce its public nuisance laws seems to invite the objection that states may not use federal courts to enforce criminal statutes.[93] But Attorney General Hart apparently thought the 1902 *Missouri v. Illinois* decision obviated the problem. The defendant's reply brief didn't address that argument either but instead focused on whether the smoke had damaged any *public* right or interest. It argued that the smoke affected only a handful of private citizens who could easily sue the company in Tennessee courts; the state's own property wasn't affected.[94] Both sides assumed that the basic issue of whether states could use the Supreme Court to abate interstate nuisances had been answered, and the main question now was what sort of injuries would give the state standing to invoke this jurisdiction.

Justice Holmes, writing the court's opinion, confirmed that assumption. In a brief (eight-paragraph) opinion, he first addressed Georgia's standing to bring suit. His handling of this issue is noteworthy: He agreed with Tennessee Copper that "the very elements that would be relied upon in a suit between fellow-citizens as a ground for equitable relief are wanting here. The State owns very little of the territory alleged to be affected, and the damage to it capable of estimate in money, possibly, at least, is small."[95] But Georgia alleged that "a wholesale destruction of forests, orchards and crops is going on."[96] And as a "quasi-sovereign":

> The State has an interest independent of and behind the titles of its citizens, in all the earth and air within its domain. It has the last word as to whether its mountains shall be stripped of their forests and its inhabitants shall breathe pure air. It might have to pay individuals before it could utter that word, but with it remains the final power. The alleged damage to the State as a private owner is merely a makeweight.[97]

This language resonates with the passage Holmes would write thirteen years later, in *Missouri v. Holland*, that protecting wildlife was a "national interest of very nearly the first magnitude" and that the national government was not required to "sit by while a food supply is cut off and the protectors of our forests and our crops are destroyed."[98] Georgia, too, was not required to sit by in the face of environmental damage. In fact, Holmes thought that the state had a clearer right to an injunction than would a private citizen. For "it is not lightly to be required to give up quasi-sovereign rights for pay; and, apart from the difficulty of valuing such rights in money, if that be its choice it may insist that an infraction of them shall be stopped."[99] On the contrary,

It is a fair and reasonable demand on the part of a sovereign that the air over its territory should not be polluted on a great scale by sulphurous acid gas, that the forests on its mountains, be they better or worse, and whatever domestic destruction they have suffered, should not be further destroyed or threatened by the act of persons beyond its control, that the crops and orchards on its hills should not be endangered from the same source.[100]

In short, Holmes recognized a distinctive state interest in environmental integrity—an interest that is conceptually distinct from property rights and that may in fact be impossible to value in monetary terms. It is striking that he did not even highlight the risk to public health posed by the smoke. He awarded Georgia an injunction simply on the evidence that the smoke was enough to "threaten damage on so considerable a scale to the forests and vegetable life, if not to health, within the plaintiff State as to make out a case within the requirements of *Missouri v. Illinois.*"[101]

There were no dissents to this sweeping decision. Justice Harlan, however, did file a concurring opinion. He objected to Holmes's implication that the state was subject to different rules than a private citizen would be. He wrote, "When the Constitution gave this court original jurisdiction in cases 'in which a State shall be a party,' it was not intended, I think, to authorize the court to apply in its behalf, any principle or rule of equity that would not be applied, under the same facts, in suits wholly between private parties."[102] Beyond this language, neither Harlan nor Holmes discussed the source of the law it was applying.

In sum, *Missouri v. Illinois* and *Georgia v. Tennessee Copper Co.* established that a state may bring suit to vindicate its "quasi-sovereign" interest in environmental integrity and that the court will decide these cases in accordance with its own federal common law principles. It is worth noting that this emergence of a federal common law of interstate nuisance was not the result of any campaign by leaders in the antipollution movement. The critical actors in this story are state attorneys general and Supreme Court justices. Indeed, one of the lawyers for Tennessee Copper complained that the court decided the case "upon a ground which never occurred to anybody on either side of the case."[103] However, as historian Duncan Maysilles notes in his study of the *Georgia v. Tennessee Copper* case, one of Georgia's attorneys, Ligon Johnson, was also a forest conservation advocate, and he helped to gather the Forest Service research that supported the state's argument.[104] Maysilles suggests that this research may account for Georgia's victory, in contrast to Missouri's loss. But Missouri's loss notwithstanding, parens patriae standing would grow to be an important foundation for environmental reform.[105] Moreover, the idea that states are trustees of the natural environment also affected other areas of constitutional doctrine, including the court's treatment of the police power.

Consider, for example, the 1908 Supreme Court decision *Hudson County Water Co. v. McCarter*.[106] This case arose from New Jersey's 1905 statute prohibiting water companies from transporting the state's water out of the state. Hudson County Water Company, appealing an adverse decision in the New Jersey court, argued that the statute exceeded the state's police power by interfering with obligations of contracts and interstate commerce and by taking property without due process. The state claimed that the company's withdrawal of water from its rivers impaired its rights as a downstream riparian owner, but also that it had an interest as a representative of the public in preserving the waters of the state—citing *Kansas v. Colorado* and *Georgia v. Tennessee Copper Co.*

The New Jersey courts rested their decision for the state on the common law principles restricting riparian owners from diverting an unreasonable amount of water to the prejudice of the state's residual property interest in the water. But Justice Holmes, who wrote the Supreme Court's opinion, preferred to put the decision "upon a broader ground than that which was emphasized below, since in our opinion it is independent of the more or less attenuated residuum of title that the State may be said to possess." Citing *Kansas v. Colorado* and *Georgia v. Tennessee Copper Co.*, he continued that the state "as *quasi*-sovereign and representative of the interests of the public has a standing in court to protect the atmosphere, the water and the forests within its territory, irrespective of the assent or dissent of the private owners of the land most immediately concerned."[107] That after all was the basis of *Geer v. Connecticut*,[108] which to Holmes seemed a greater imposition on property rights. Indeed, Holmes held, "few public interests are more obvious, indisputable and independent of particular theory than the interest of the public of a State to maintain the rivers that are wholly within it substantially undiminished, except by such drafts upon them as the guardian of the public welfare may permit for the purpose of turning them to a more perfect use."[109] In remarkably broad language, Holmes declined even to investigate the state's rationale for the statute:

The constitutional power of the State to insist that its natural advantages shall remain unimpaired by its citizens is not dependent upon any nice estimate of the extent of present use or speculation as to future needs. The legal conception of the necessary is apt to be confined to somewhat rudimentary wants, and there are benefits from a great river that might escape a lawyer's view. *But the State is not required to submit even to an aesthetic analysis. Any analysis may be inadequate.* It finds itself in possession of what all admit to be a great public good, and what it has it may keep *and give no one a reason for its will.*[110]

This reading of the police power proved to be too broad for later courts. During the Progressive Era, the court rejected similar attempts to prevent natural gas from being transported out of state.[111] The principle that groundwater was not an article of commerce would ultimately be rejected by the Supreme Court in the 1982 case *Sporhase v. Nebraska.*[112] Still, the opinion demonstrates an enduring judicial consensus that states have a very strong interest in managing natural resources. Whether the Supreme Court was the best forum to defend that interest, however, was far from clear, as Georgia learned in its decades-long battle to enforce the court's decision.

Judicial Management of Interstate Nuisance

The Supreme Court decision in *Georgia v. Tennessee Copper Co.* was not the end of the smoke problem for Georgia. The state—not eager to lose the jobs that Tennessee Copper brought to the region—decided not to enforce the injunction immediately. Rather, with the threat of the injunction in the background, Georgia continued to negotiate with the company until, in 1915, it agreed to a set of conditions acceptable to it. However, the state continued to wrestle with a smaller company, Ducktown Sulphur, Copper, and Iron Co., which also contributed to the smoke problem. Although Georgia did win an injunction against Ducktown Sulphur, it proved difficult to enforce.[113] The Supreme Court appointed Dr. John McGill, a chemist, to inspect the Ducktown facility, and he made a report suggesting that the injunction be modified to allow more emissions. By this point, the United States had entered World War I, and demand for copper increased dramatically. In 1918, the secretary of the Navy asked the Georgia legislature to relax the injunction, and that, combined with continued lobbying from both Tennessee Copper and Ducktown, led the Georgia legislature to reduce its demands. The injunction against Ducktown remained in place for several years, however. It was finally dissolved in 1938, when Tennessee Copper acquired the company.[114]

In light of this history, was *Georgia v. Tennessee Copper Co.* a success? It did help to bring the parties to the table and gave Georgia a valuable bargaining chip. But the story hardly makes a compelling case for pollution regulation by the judiciary. As Robert Percival concludes, there are serious drawbacks to interstate nuisance actions, including "the length and complexity of the litigation that must be undertaken to pursue them, and the court's difficulties in formulating and enforcing remedial orders against government entities."[115] These problems became apparent as more states took advantage of parens patriae doctrine.

Between 1908 and 1930, several states brought disputes over natural resources to the Supreme Court. Their success was mixed. Missouri and Kansas, as we know, asserted parens patriae standing to challenge the federal Migratory Bird Treaty Act in *Missouri v. Holland* but lost the case. New York also attempted to use the Supreme Court to protect its waters. In a case very similar to *Missouri v. Illinois*, New York in 1908 petitioned the Supreme Court to issue an injunction preventing the state of New Jersey and the Passaic Sewerage Commission from discharging sewage into New York Harbor.[116] The lawsuit led to years of negotiation. Testimony was taken between 1911 and 1913, but the case was not argued until 1918. By that time, the court thought the record needed to be updated. Additional testimony was taken, and the case was argued again in 1921. Finally, the court issued its decision, holding that the evidence was not sufficient to support an injunction. Indeed, Justice Clarke's opinion for the court sounds very much like Holmes's decision for Illinois fifteen years earlier. Although he had no difficulty holding that New York had parens patriae standing, he cited *Missouri v. Illinois* for the proposition that "the threatened invasion of rights must be of serious magnitude and it must be established by clear and convincing evidence."[117] The expert witnesses disagreed on several vital questions, and science of sanitation was evolving rapidly. Clarke in fact suggested that the court was starting to regret getting involved in this sort of litigation:

> We cannot withhold the suggestion, inspired by the consideration of this case, that the grave problem of sewage disposal presented by the large and growing populations living on the shores of New York Bay is

one more likely to be wisely solved by cooperative study and by conference and mutual concession on the part of representatives of the States so vitally interested in it than by proceedings in any court however constituted.[118]

But the lawsuits kept coming. In 1922, the Supreme Court decided *Wyoming v. Colorado*, another lengthy suit over water rights in the Laramie River originally brought in 1911.[119] The case was argued three times over its eleven-year history, and Justice Van Devanter's majority opinion consists mostly of a lengthy review of the evidence concerning the average volume of water in the stream. His order divided the water between the two states, with Wyoming receiving the lion's share based on its prior appropriation—much to the dismay of many downstream states, as we will see in the next chapter.[120]

Three cases decided in 1923 raised further questions about the wisdom of allowing these parens patriae suits. In *Massachusetts v. Mellon*, Massachusetts sought to enjoin enforcement of the federal Maternity Act, which made grants to states to improve maternal health, on the grounds that it exceeded Congress's spending power.[121] Justice Sutherland denied the state standing, refusing to concede that "a State, as parens patriae, may institute judicial proceedings to protect citizens of the United States from the operation of the statutes thereof."[122] In his view, the United States is the only government entitled to represent citizens of the United States as parens patriae.

Just a few days later, the court decided two consolidated cases, *Pennsylvania v. West Virginia* and *Ohio v. West Virginia*, which also raised questions about parens patriae standing.[123] Pennsylvania and Ohio sued West Virginia to enjoin enforcement of the state's statute requiring suppliers of natural gas to meet the needs of customers within the state before exporting the gas out of state. The natural gas suppliers were organized as public utilities and supervised by the state's Public Service Commission, which was given authority to administer the policy. Pennsylvania and Ohio argued that the statute unconstitutionally interfered with interstate commerce. West Virginia defended the constitutionality of the statute but also argued that Pennsylvania and Ohio lacked standing to represent their citizens. This case was argued five times between 1921 and 1923, until the court finally enjoined enforcement of the statute. But Holmes, McReynolds, and Brandeis all dissented.

Justice Van Devanter wrote the court's opinion, finding easily that the states had parens patriae standing, citing the usual string of cases beginning with *Missouri v. Illinois*.[124] The majority of his opinion was devoted to arguing that the statute interfered with interstate commerce. Justice Holmes agreed that the court had jurisdiction but, following the logic of his *Hudson County Water Co.* decision, argued that the state may give a preference to its citizens in the use of the state's natural resources.[125] Both McReynolds and Brandeis, however, had doubts about allowing the court to take jurisdiction, and their arguments highlight some of the problematic dimensions of parens patriae cases. First, the litigation was, in their view, premature. The lawsuit was filed before the policy had gone into effect, so it was impossible to say how it would affect anyone's interests. As Brandeis pointed out, the policy was administered by the Public Service Commission, and it wasn't clear how they would exercise their discretion. Parens patriae cases seemed to invite this sort of litigation, aimed at challenging a general policy on principle rather than waiting to see how it works in practice.

But Brandeis and McReynolds also thought that there was no obvious state interest here. McReynolds argued that it was similar to *Louisiana v. Texas*, which he read as holding that "the vindication of the freedom of interstate commerce is not committed to any State as parens patriae."[126] Brandeis argued more specifically that the state was not necessarily a good representative of its citizens in this case. The real interested parties in West Virginia, after all, were the natural gas companies: "It is the rights of these twelve corporations, if of anyone, which would be invaded by enforcing the statute."[127] He would prefer to see those companies bring suit against West Virginia if they felt the statute infringed their rights. And those companies were not the only interested parties who weren't represented in court. In speculating on how the court might fashion an adequate remedy, Brandeis noted that the state exported gas also to Indiana, Maryland, and Kentucky, none of whom were involved in the lawsuit. He reasoned:

> The Court should, in no event, go further than to compel West Virginia to share its production equitably with other States now dependent upon it for a part of their gas supply. But in order to determine what is equitable, (that is, what part of the West Virginia production that State might require its public service corporations to retain and what part they should be free to export to other States) it would obviously be necessary to marshal the resources and the demands, or needs, of the

six States, and to consider, in respect to each, both the conduct of the business therein and the circumstances attending its development. The factors necessary to be considered in determining what division of the West Virginia production would be fair, the conditions under which the determination would have to be made, and the character of the questions to be decided are such that this Court would be obliged to refuse to undertake the task.[128]

In sum, this parens patriae lawsuit looked less like vindicating individual rights—the core of the court's function—and more like crafting policy, which (as Taney warned) the court is not very well-designed to do.

The final case, *North Dakota v. Minnesota*, was a more typical nuisance case, but it still ended up on the Supreme Court's docket three times.[129] North Dakota complained that Minnesota's attempts to straighten the Mustinka River—a project involving creating cut-off ditches—led to an increase in the volume of water entering the Bois de Sioux River, causing flooding and considerable damage to North Dakota farmers. North Dakota accordingly asked the Supreme Court to award damages and to issue an injunction preventing Minnesota from using the cut-off ditches. The Court heard arguments in 1921 and 1923, ultimately denying North Dakota relief. Chief Justice Taft wrote the court's opinion.

On the jurisdiction question, Taft noted that North Dakota could not maintain a suit for damages, reminding them of the Eleventh Amendment.[130] North Dakota did have standing to seek an injunction, but its evidence was not clear and convincing. As usual, the states had produced conflicting expert testimony; indeed, even North Dakota's experts seemed to disagree about the effect of the drainage ditches on flooding. Although Taft did an impressive job of summarizing the evidence, he complained, "It is difficult for a court to decide issues of fact upon which experts equal in number and standing differ flatly and when their conclusions rest on estimates upon the correctness of which the court, without technical knowledge, can not undertake to pass."[131] In the end, he gave more weight to Minnesota's scientists, who seemed more careful in their use of data, and dismissed the bill.[132]

In sum, the Supreme Court's desire to resolve interstate conflicts over natural resources may have exceeded its capacity.[133] Not surprisingly, the threat of litigation became a standard argument for resolving interstate disputes some other way—either through congressional action or interstate compacts. But as long as key congressional and executive branch actors were committed to the view that states have the primary authority to protect public health, the court seemed committed to supporting their efforts to do so. After all, the complexity of these lawsuits did not stem from the complexity or novelty of the basic rights being forwarded: clean water, clean air, a safe place to live. It stemmed from the growing complexity of our shared understanding of the socioecological systems that provide these goods.

The courts continued to wrestle with that complexity. The federal common law of interstate nuisance survived the Supreme Court's decision, in *Erie R.R. v. Tompkins*, to abandon federal commercial common law. The Court would eventually retreat from hearing state-initiated interstate nuisance cases in the 1970s, as Congress finally created a more comprehensive federal pollution control regime (a regime justified in large part as an alternative to these interminable lawsuits). But interstate nuisance remains a part of our constitutional tradition and continues to be offered as a potential vehicle for addressing new environmental threats like climate change.[134] And parens patriae standing has only continued to evolve, becoming an important foundation for state-initiated public interest litigation and a key element of the contemporary green state.[135]

CHAPTER TEN

The Conservation Movement's Constitutional Legacy

In the introduction to this book, I highlighted the Mt. Vernon Compact, the 1785 meeting called by George Washington to reach an agreement on fishing, navigation, and commerce on the Potomac River and other tributaries of the Chesapeake Bay. It seems fitting to end with another famous interstate river agreement: the 1922 Colorado River Compact. The compact was not a conservation measure. On the contrary, it was part of an economic development plan that included the distribution of water rights in the Colorado River between upper and lower basin states (the compact itself), the construction of the massive hydroelectric complex that would eventually be named the Hoover Dam, and a new irrigation canal from the Colorado River to California's Imperial Valley. This project constituted a dramatic and enduring assertion of federal authority over economic development in the arid West. And it was negotiated under the leadership of the quintessential small-government advocate, Herbert Hoover.

This is what I meant when I said in the introduction that managing the natural environment has become a major impetus for state building. The Colorado River Project was made possible, in large part, by the expansion of state and federal constitutional authority for conservation from 1870 on. The federal navigation servitude, the property power, the treaty power, and interstate common law all worked to support it. Opponents struggled to raise constitutional objections, but they were unable to counter the growing power—and the growing legitimacy—of the emerging green state.

The Colorado River Project

The story of the Colorado River Compact illustrates how far environmental management had evolved by the 1920s. In 1785, five commissioners from Maryland and Virginia could meet for a week at Mt. Vernon and produce an agreement that would be quickly ratified and implemented by their respective legislatures. The Colorado River Compact, in contrast, involved years of negotiation, conflict among powerful and well-organized interest groups, wide-ranging public debate, critical involvement by federal officials, congressional lobbying, and international negotiation—all of it propelled forward by the constant threat of litigation. It resulted not in a stable agreement but in a framework for ongoing negotiations, litigation, and conflict. This is what modern environmental management looks like. In the Colorado River Compact, we see the birth of the modern green state.

The story is told in great detail by historian Norris Hundley in his seminal work *Water and the West*.[1] Here I will offer only a brief overview. The major groups pursuing the compact include, first, the farmers in California's Imperial Valley, who depended for water on an irrigation canal that ran from the Colorado River through Mexico to the Valley. They wanted an "All-American Canal" that would be less vulnerable to Mexican politics. The second key player was the federal Reclamation Service, which wanted to build a dam on the Colorado to serve a number of purposes, including generating hydroelectric power. Importantly, however, the Reclamation Service insisted that creating a large reservoir would help manage the river's water so that all claimants would have enough for their needs. The proposed dam therefore became inextricably linked to the interstate compact, which focused on distributing water rights. The third group consisted of the seven states depending on the Colorado River, who came on board to protect their respective interests in the river's water. The compact was thus one element in a larger development plan to apportion water rights, build a canal to serve Imperial Valley, and build a federal dam on the river.

In 1922, under the guidance of Secretary of Commerce Herbert Hoover, the seven states completed the first step in this project by negotiating the Colorado River Compact. This agreement divided water rights between the upper basin states (Wyoming, Colorado, Utah) and the lower basin states (Arizona, Nevada, New Mexico, and California), with some water reserved for Mexican claimants and Native American tribes. At that point, Arizona—under the leadership of Governor Hunt—decided that the agreement promised too much water to California and too little to serve Arizona's future needs. The Arizona legislature declined to ratify the agreement, and Arizona's senators and congressional representatives led the campaign to persuade Congress to reject the compact.

Congress debated the agreement for several years and ratified it in 1928, in a bill that also authorized the "All-American Canal" and the dam in Boulder Canyon, which would provide flood control, irrigation, and hydroelectric power.[2] The Boulder Canyon Project Act dealt with Arizona's recalcitrance by ensuring that Arizona's current water rights were provided for in the agreement, which would go into effect when California and five of the other six states ratified it. Arizona promptly brought suit against California in the Supreme Court challenging the act's constitutionality.[3] But Arizona had a weak hand, for the fight against the compact and the dam played out on a constitutional landscape shaped, in large part, by the conservation movement.

Interstate Compacts

Interstate compacts were hardly new; states had been forming compacts since before the Revolution, and continued to do so during the nineteenth century. The Supreme Court not only enforced them but also held in a pair of decisions in 1893 that some such compacts do not need congressional approval to be valid. In *Virginia v. Tennessee*, concerning a boundary dispute, Justice Field pointed out that, for example, "in case of threatened invasion of cholera, plague, or other causes of sickness and death, it would be the height of absurdity to hold that the threatened States could not unite in providing means to prevent and repel the invasion of the pestilence, without obtaining the consent of Congress, which might not be at the time in session."[4] Congressional approval was required only for "any combination tending to the increase of political power in the States, which may encroach upon or interfere with the just supremacy of the United States."[5]

Legal scholars Felix Frankfurter and James Landis, reviewing congressional action approving interstate compacts, found sixteen between 1789 and 1900, most of which concerned boundaries. But the pace of interstate compact-making picked up considerably after 1900, and the subjects of these compacts expanded as well. Frankfurter and Landis report twenty-two compacts approved by Congress between 1900 and 1925, when their article was published.[6] Many of these Progressive Era compacts concerned rivers. Most of the Progressive Era river compacts focused on jurisdiction over crimes committed on interstate waters or the division of water rights, but they had the potential to do more.[7] In 1915, Oregon and Washington concluded an agreement concerning the protection of fish in the Columbia River. And, as mentioned in chapter 9, Justice Clarke opined in *New York v. New Jersey* that an interstate compact would be a better way to resolve the disputes concerning the states' respective uses of interstate waters for sewage disposal.[8]

The sudden popularity of interstate compacts owes a great deal to the Supreme Court's decisions in *Missouri v. Holland,*[9] *Georgia v. Tennessee Copper Co.,*[10] and *Kansas v. Colorado.*[11] As Norris Hundley recounts, the idea of resolving disputes over the Colorado River through an interstate compact was ridiculed when it was first proposed by Delph Carpenter in 1912.[12] Carpenter, a Colorado lawyer, was a leader in the Colorado River negotiations and also part of Colorado's legal team in the lengthy 1922 Supreme Court case *Wyoming v. Colorado*[13] (discussed in chapter 9). He argued throughout the Colorado River negotiations that a compact was preferable to litigation. Nor was he alone: Virtually everyone who advocated interstate compacts defended them as preferable to the expensive and interminable lawsuits that were filling the Supreme Court's docket.[14] But while courts did not have the political or administrative capacity to manage critical regional resources like rivers, they could create the conditions for negotiation. In the case of the Colorado River Compact, it was *Wyoming v. Colorado* that motivated many of the doubtful parties to support the compact. Recall that in *Wyoming v. Colorado*, Justice Van Devanter declined to follow the *Kansas v. Colorado* precedent in apportioning water in the Laramie River between the two states. Reasoning that both Wyoming and Colorado used prior appropriation principles to determine water rights, Van Devanter did the same, giving the larger share to Wyoming. His decision was carefully limited to the facts of this case, but many of the parties involved in the Colorado River negotiations thought that the decision raised at least some uncertainty about how the court might resolve future conflicts over water rights in the Colorado River. That uncertainty provided an important impetus to the states to negotiate their own agreement.[15]

To be sure, the possibility of litigation as an alternative to negotiation also allowed for defection: Arizona preferred to take its chances in court. But here the state faced a daunting set of precedents supporting federal management of natural resources.

The Constitutional Debate

The constitutionality of interstate compacts was so well-accepted that Arizona's representatives, in developing a constitutional argument against the Boulder Canyon Dam Act, barely mentioned the compact. Although they did complain about the compact going into effect without their ratification, they had no judicial precedents suggesting that this procedure was illegitimate. Accordingly, Arizona focused instead on the dam. The dam would span the river between Arizona and Nevada, which gave Arizona a potential states' rights argument against it.

The dam was by far the most controversial part of the plan. There were complex financial and engineering questions to be considered, especially given the scale of the proposed project—at 726 feet tall, it would be the largest concrete structure ever built and (in 1938) the tallest dam in the world. But legal and particularly constitutional issues were also salient, thanks in large part to Arizona's representatives. A nicely concise summary of the constitutional debate is found in the 1928 report of the House Committee on Irrigation and Reclamation.[16] The majority report argues that the federal government's authority to build the dam stems, first, from the Commerce Clause. The Colorado River is a navigable stream, and it is well-established that the federal government may build dams to provide flood control on navigable rivers. The flood control would also support interstate commerce by protecting railroads and highways that cross the river downstream from the proposed dam. Second, the Property Clause allows the federal government to create reservoirs to provide irrigation to improve public lands. The federal government is the biggest landowner in the Colorado River Basin, and the dam will improve and protect this property (including additional irrigation projects downstream). The report doesn't address hydroelectric generation explicitly, but proponents of the bill would argue in congressional debate that the federal government can pursue additional goals, like hydroelectricity, when it builds a dam to manage floodwaters.[17]

Arizona's Representative Douglas countered this argument with a key point: The Colorado River, he argued, is not in fact navigable. It may have once carried river traffic, but now it is too filled with silt to be used for shipping. His minority report conceded that if it were navigable, the federal government could build a dam to prevent flooding. But he insisted that the proposed dam is clearly not intended for that purpose, because it's much higher than needed to regulate floodwaters. The true purpose of the dam is clearly to produce hydroelectric power, and the commerce power does not extend to building hydroelectric plants.[18]

Douglas also objected to the compact going into effect without Arizona's ratification, but he cited no judicial decisions addressing that issue. Moving on to the property power, he seemed to concede that the federal government can build irrigation projects to improve federal lands, but again he insisted that the dam is much bigger than needed for this purpose.[19]

Congressional debate expanded on these points. Opponents emphasized the question of the river's navigability, because if it was not navigable, then the state had a much stronger claim to jurisdiction over it. Unfortunately for that argument, precedents like *United States v. Rio Grande Dam and Irrigation Company*[20] extended the federal navigation servitude into unnavigable parts of navigable rivers to protect that navigability, and one goal of the dam was to improve navigation both downstream (by removing much of the silt that had been filling the river) and upstream.[21] But beneath this doctrinal discussion was a more fundamental objection. Utah's Representative Leatherwood complained that this hydroelectric project "means the surrender to a federal bureaucracy of control over the most vital economic resource of the States in the Colorado River basin."[22] Douglas agreed that "the fundamental issue . . . is whether or not the federal government is going to undertake the burden of running an industrial enterprise." If the federal government can enter a state, ignore the state's law, take state land, and set up an enterprise without the state's consent, well, what is left of state sovereignty? This project, he argued, will end up giving the secretary of the Interior (who would be in charge of the dam) full control over the Colorado River "erect[ing] upon the ruins of the rights of States a great tyrannical socialistic bureaucracy." And that, he submitted, is the death of democracy.[23]

But as Secretary of the Interior Garfield put it in a congressional hearing, federal control is necessary because:

The jurisdiction of a single state is not broad enough to deal with all the problems that necessarily arise in the construction and development of such a project. . . . The United States alone has the power properly to safeguard the interest and rights of all those who may be affected by such a major development, and is further, the only political agency that can deal with and settle the international questions.[24]

Arizona lost the congressional debate, and it lost in the Supreme Court as well.

The lawsuit, *Arizona v. California*,[25] followed a pattern we have come to recognize from the conservation cases: Arizona asserted parens patriae standing, citing *Georgia v. Tennessee Copper Co.* and the other interstate nuisance cases, and offered the usual list of precedents from *Pollard's Lessee v. Hagan*[26] to *Kansas v. Colorado* on state ownership of water and the beds of interstate streams. California and the United States (which intervened in the case) relied primarily on the commerce power. The other states involved in the compact also submitted a brief, arguing that the compact was valid and that the act is within the property power—citing the usual list of cases from *Gibson v. Chouteau*[27] to *Light v. United States*[28] and *Utah Power and Light v. United States.*[29] The court wrote a brief opinion, deferring to the federal scientists and upholding the act.

Justice Brandeis began by rejecting Arizona's chief argument. The river, he concluded, is navigable: "We know judicially, from the evidence of history, that a large part of the Colorado River south of Black Canyon was formerly navigable, and that the main obstacles to navigation have been the accumulations of silt coming from the upper reaches of the river system, and the irregularity in the flow due to periods of low water."[30] The federal government's engineers expected the dam to improve navigability, and Brandeis deferred to their expert judgment. He declined to consider whether the stated purpose of the act was just a subterfuge for its true aim of creating a hydroelectric plant. As we have seen repeatedly in the conservation campaign, Congress may accomplish all sorts of purposes, from irrigation to forest conservation, as long as it is also, arguably, addressing navigation. As Brandeis put it, "The fact that purposes other than navigation will also be served could not invalidate the exercise of the authority conferred, even if those other purposes would not alone have justified an exercise of Congressional power."[31]

But Brandeis made it clear that the federal government's authority here rested not merely on the navigation servitude:

Since the grant of authority to build the dam and reservoir is valid as an exercise of the Constitutional power to improve navigation, we have no occasion to decide whether the authority to construct the dam and reservoir might not also have been constitutionally conferred for the specified purpose of irrigating public lands of the United States. Compare *United States v. Rio Grande Dam and Irrigation Co.*, 174 U.S. 690, 703; *United States v. Alford*, 274 U.S. 264. Or for the specified purpose of regulating the flow and preventing the floods in this interstate river. Or as a means of conserving and apportioning its waters among the States equitably entitled thereto. Or for purpose of performing international obligations. Compare *Missouri v. Holland*, 252 U.S. 416.[32]

This paragraph sets out the three pillars of federal conservation policy: the *Rio Grande* case extended the navigation servitude; *United States v. Alford*[33] extended the property power by upholding a federal prosecution for lighting a fire near (not in) a federal forest; and *Missouri v. Holland*, of course, concerned the treaty power. These pillars, Brandeis implies, could also support this huge, centralized economic development project.

As for Arizona's water rights, Brandeis recognized them but insisted that they were protected: "The continued use of the 3,500,000 acre-feet of water already appropriated in Arizona is not now threatened" by the act.[34] The court could not entertain the state's more speculative claim that compact would limit Arizona's ability to claim additional water rights in the future.

In sum, by 1930, constitutional doctrine had so evolved to make the Hoover Dam project remarkably easy to justify. Arizona had no persuasive constitutional argument against what would prove to be (in Hundley's words) "the emergence of the government in Washington as the most powerful authority over the Colorado River and, by extension, over other interstate and navigable streams as well."[35] Indeed, Representative Douglas was quite right in arguing that the act would put the most important natural resource in the arid West under the authority of a federal bureaucracy. But Secretary of the Interior Garfield was also right that "the United States alone has the power properly to safeguard the interest and rights of all those who may be affected by such a major development, and is further, the only political agency that can deal with and settle the international questions."

The Colorado River Compact and the development projects it fostered had many deficiencies. The Compact itself overestimated the amount of water in the Colorado River, it did not address water quality, and negotiations left out some rights holders altogether, such as Native Americans. It did not so much resolve conflicts as create a framework for further negotiation and debate. But in many ways, the creation of the compact shows the American green state in action: It resulted from a process that brought together high-level state officials, federal officials, and civic groups; it included stakeholder negotiations, public debate, and congressional lobbying; and all of it took place in the shadow of litigation. It demonstrates the American state's growing ability to manage natural resources to serve national goals. Critical to that ability were the doctrinal developments that I have called the Conservation Constitution.

The Conservation Constitution

My aim in this book was to explain how lawyers and judges reworked constitutional doctrine to accommodate the expansion of state power over the natural environment during the Progressive Era. More specifically, how did legal decision-makers conceptualize the natural environment, its relation to human society, and the public interests at stake to create the constitutional "common sense" that federal and state governments have authority to protect natural resources and the integrity of ecosystems in the interests of future generations? Not surprisingly, that process of constitutional change was complicated, and it left a complicated legacy. While they did not resolve all debates about the legitimacy of government regulation of the environment, they did create the framework that structures those debates and the foundation the supports our contemporary environmental protection regime.

What does that foundation look like? Most importantly, it is woven of many threads. The doctrines that contribute to state environmental authority include public trust doctrine—which, although limited by the Supreme Court as a matter of federal law, is still alive as a matter of state law.[36] In addition, the police power, the eminent domain power, public nuisance doctrine, parens patriae standing, and the compact clause all support state-level environmental protection. At the federal level, environmental authority is supported by the interstate and international commerce power, the property power, the federal eminent domain power, the treaty power, the war power, interstate nuisance doctrine, and the spending power. I have highlighted in particular the doctrines supporting government authority over water, including public trust and the federal navigation servitude. But it would be misleading to claim that any single doctrine was decisive in explaining the success of conservation policy in the courts; rather, I want to draw attention to the sheer density of doctrines that were mobilized to support conservation. This multiplicity of doctrines makes governmental environmental authority quite resilient. Retrenchment in one area would likely lead to expanded authority in another.

For example, a current constitutional debate is whether courts should expand regulatory takings doctrine to protect property owners' reasonable expectations of returns on their investment. Such an expansion might make environmental regulation more difficult—but, on the other hand, it would make the case for urban planning authority stronger: A well-considered development plan would protect investors even more effectively than would litigation over takings claims. Similarly, if the courts narrowed the federal property power to restrict the federal government's authority to protect public lands, it is likely that federal spending to protect public lands would increase. After all, the same land management goals can often be accomplished through either regulating or incentivizing private behavior.

Similarly, the federal structure of the American constitution also increases the resilience of governmental authority over natural resources. Thanks to a broad interpretation of the state police power and deference to federal agencies, *all* levels of government are empowered to manage socioecological systems to serve an expanding set of environmental values. Shared, overlapping authority for the landscape is a hallmark of the American state. Thus, if the courts concluded that federal power over interstate commerce doesn't include (for example) protecting endangered species, they would likely conclude that the state police power over wildlife does extend so far—and vice versa. Although the courts have rejected Roosevelt's "inherent power" doctrine, the principle that power to protect natural resources must lie *somewhere* in the American governmental system pervades constitutional law.

But constitutional power is not only a matter of changing doctrine. Also contributing to the resilience of the Conservation Constitution is the constitutional common law: the shift, from the nineteenth to the twentieth century, from conceptualizing nature as a collection of commodities to understanding the natural world as comprising complex, interdependent ecosystems that provide services integral to the national economy and therefore as requiring active management by government. To be sure, that ecological model means that environmental conflict will often be a matter of competing scientific authorities, and deference to government scientists is no longer to be taken for granted. Interminable legal battles over environmental science are part of the legacy of the Progressives' Conservation Constitution. Still, those battles often assume and therefore reinforce the basic premises of earth systems science. Although it is easy to raise doubts about any claim of ecologists, it's difficult to challenge the general model of nature as interconnected systems supporting human life. That model supports in turn the ecosystem services idea: judicial recognition that several legitimate governmental interests, both local and national, can be served by protecting natural landscapes. This is most prominent in the judiciary's treatment of wildlife and forests, but we see also in the pollution cases a willingness to conceptualize urban landscapes in complex ways.

These new models of natural and urban landscapes were developed by scientists pursuing their own scholarly and professional ends (although often supported by federal spending on scientific research). But they were taken up and forwarded—in legislatures, agency decision-making, and judicial forums—by legal professionals seeking to expand constitutional authority in these areas. Those legal professionals are a third source of constitutional resilience. Constitutional doctrine matters to state building because governmental actors make it matter. Constitutional principles aren't trump cards that operate automatically to define the bounds of acceptable policy, but neither are appeals to these principles mere lip service. Rather, we should see constitutional arguments in the campaign for conservation policy as attempts to influence key actors who considered it their professional responsibility to veto policy when it crossed constitutional lines. Those actors include judges but also executive and legislative branch officers who often shaped the arguments that would be made in court. My story highlights familiar figures in the conservation campaign such as John Lacey, Gifford Pinchot, Henry Teller, and Frank Mondell, but also less familiar legal professionals like Chandler Anderson, George Woodruff, Philip Wells, and R. W. Williams. For these actors, changing public policy included modifying constitutional principles. In other words, they were "playing for the rules," seeking both specific policy outcomes but also changes in the rules of the constitutional game.

Under this view, the success of the conservation movement in the courts was due to the doctrinal background—the legal rules surrounding water resources, wildlife, and public lands—and the authority of respected scientific agencies like the USDA. But it was also due to the skillful deployment of those doctrinal and scientific resources by some of the era's best lawyers. This cadre of legal professionals has grown into a formidable force in the twenty-first century, enforcing and expanding the constitutional rules supporting governmental environmental authority.

Of course, the United States also has a formidable collection of legal professionals working *against* environmental regulation. As Mark Graber has argued, constitutional traditions typically don't speak with one voice.[37]

The constitutional legacy of the Progressive Era conservation movement includes both the winning and the losing arguments—both the dominant, judicially favored federal conservation tradition and the subordinate states' rights tradition. Its heirs include the protestors of Standing Rock, insisting on federal authority to protect public lands and interstate rivers, but also the protestors at the Malheur National Wildlife Refuge, referencing equal footing doctrine and states' rights. These conflicts may focus on statutory interpretation and agency decision-making, but they are rooted in long-standing constitutional debates.[38]

These contemporary conflicts remind us also that the Progressive Era Conservation Constitution, while resilient, was not complete. The Progressives left us with important unfinished business. Most prominently, the Conservation Constitution was not fully inclusive. In 1920, women had only just won the constitutional right to vote, racial minorities still faced daunting obstacles to political participation, and the status of Native Americans and their treaty rights was shrouded in confusion. As a result, the distributive consequences of environmental regulation—the question of who gets access to natural lands and who is burdened by industrial pollution—were not adequately addressed in the Progressive Era. Those issues would be taken up more systematically in the American Indian movement in the 1970s and the environmental justice movement in the 1980s. But inclusion remains a work in progress. The battle for recognition of marginalized groups is ongoing, and contemporary environmentalists are forwarding conceptions of the political community that would expand the political community even further, to future generations and nonhuman entities. Representing these interests in environmental decision-making will likely require new thinking, new constitutional principles, and even new kinds of politics.[39]

On a related note, procedural justice was also neglected by the Progressives. Focused on building administrative agencies capable of managing our vast natural resources, they gave less attention to how those agencies would operate.[40] The need for more systematic, inclusive, and transparent administrative procedures was addressed in the 1946 Administrative Procedure Act and developed by judicial, legislative, and executive action over subsequent decades. But this, too, is an ongoing struggle. Information management is a major issue for the twenty-first-century state: How can we produce reliable scientific information and communicate it to the public so that the regulated community understands the basis of government action? More generally, the legitimacy of the administrative state itself has become a target for reformers seeking to reduce the scale of federal government. Attacks on public administration are both driven by and affect our ability collectively to manage the nation's natural resources. Defending the Conservation Constitution means defending the process values enshrined in administrative law: the value of inclusive, transparent, rational, science-based decision-making.

Third, environmental problems in the twenty-first century may require more centralized economic planning, and federal planning authority remains weak. Most Progressive Era environmental policies were regulatory and reactive, as opposed to proactive attempts to direct economic development in a sustainable direction. To be sure, the Progressives won planning authority at the local level, and municipal urban planning is now a well-accepted practice. States' police power does support some sustainable development strategies, such as renewable energy portfolio standards. And, as the story of the Hoover Dam demonstrates, increasing federal economic planning authority may be less a matter of doctrinal innovation than forging a supportive political consensus. The scale and complexity of socio-ecological systems and the ecosystem service conception of nature make a strong case for central planning. But the subordinate states' rights tradition is still very much alive, and much federal environmental management remains vulnerable to the claim that it is unacceptably "socialist." Thus federal economic planning has generally evolved by means of crises, from the Great Depression of the 1930s to the Great Recession of 2008. Improving our institutional and political tools for national economic planning might help us avoid these crises or at least navigate them better.

Finally, twenty-first-century environmental management has an important and inescapable international dimension. The most serious environmental challenges we face are global: climate change, biodiversity loss, and securing ecologically sustainable and resilient communities as the world's population approaches 10 billion. Addressing these challenges requires the state to participate in international negotiations, forge alliances, and respond to transnational environmental publics. International institutions are critical to supporting this capacity for international action. And so is moral authority: The influence of the American state depends in large part on its performance as an ecological trustee of its own natural resources. Participating in global environmental governance may look, to some, like a sacrifice of sovereignty. But the story of the Progressive Era suggests a different view: stronger, more effective international institutions can be compatible with expanding national capacity for environmental management, just as federal environmental authority has often supported state and local environmental management. There is no reason to believe environmental authority is a zero-sum game.

But there is reason to believe that our Constitution—not only the unwritten constitution but also the constitution of judges—will have to evolve further as we grapple with the environmental challenges ahead of us. As Justices Holmes and Sutherland both remind us, the Constitution of the United States "called into life a being the development of which could not have been foreseen completely by the most gifted of its begetters." Sutherland might insist that "the meaning of constitutional guaranties never varies," but even he admitted that "the scope of their application must expand or contract to meet the new and different conditions which are constantly coming within the field of their operation." And so both Holmes and Sutherland, I think, would counsel us to consider constitutional questions "in the light of our whole experience and not merely in that of what was said a hundred years ago."[41] And our experience teaches us that the better able we are to manage our natural environment in cooperation with other nations, the better able we will be to secure the general welfare and achieve the blessings of liberty promised by the American Constitution.

Notes

Chapter 1. Introduction

1. "Oregon Standoff Timeline," *Oregonian/OregonLive*, February 15, 2017, accessed April 26, 2017: http://www.oregonlive.com/portland/index.ssf/2017/02/oregon_standoff_timeline_41_da.html; "Two Convicted and Two Acquitted of Conspiracy in Oregon Occupation Trial," *Oregonian/OregonLive*, March 11, 2017, accessed April 26, 2017: http://www.oregonlive.com/oregon-standoff/2017/03/oregon_occupation_trial.html.

2. "Over 70 Arrested at Standing Rock as Dakota Access Aims to Finish Pipeline," *Guardian*, accessed September 20, 2018: https://www.theguardian.com/us-news/2017/feb/01/standing-rock-arrests-dakota-access-pipeline-construction.

3. Robyn Eckersley, *The Green State* (Cambridge, MA: MIT Press, 2004); James Meadowcraft, "Greening the State?" in *Comparative Environmental Politics*, ed. Paul Steinberg and Stacy VanDeveer (Cambridge, MA: MIT Press, 2012).

4. Norman Vig and Michael Faure, "Introduction," in *Green Giants*, ed. Vig and Faure (Cambridge, MA: MIT Press, 2004), 1.

5. Meadowcraft, "Greening the State?" 64.

6. Jack Balkin, "The Framework Model and Constitutional Interpretation," Yale Law School, Public Law Research Paper No. 545 (posted May 20, 2015), 9.

7. John Leshy, "Constitutional Conflicts on Public Lands," *University of Colorado Law Review* 75 (Fall 2004): 1101–1125.

8. Samuel Hays, *Conservation and the Gospel of Efficiency* (Pittsburgh: University of Pittsburgh Press, 1959); James Penick, *Progressive Politics and Conservation* (Chicago: University of Chicago Press, 1968).

9. Thomas Dunlap, *Saving America's Wildlife* (Princeton: Princeton University Press, 1988); Richard Judd, *The Untilled Garden* (Cambridge: Cambridge University Press, 2009). See also David Stradling, *Smokestacks and Progressives* (Baltimore, MD: Johns Hopkins University Press, 1999); Richard Judd, *Common Lands, Common People* (Cambridge, MA: Harvard University Press, 1997); John Reiger, *American Sportsmen and the Origins of Conservation* (New York: Winchester, 1975); Marge Davis, *Sportsmen United* (Mt. Juliet, TN: Bench Top, 1997).

10. Hays, *Conservation and the Gospel of Efficiency*; Penick, *Progressive Politics and Conservation*; Kurt Dorsey, *The Dawn of Conservation Diplomacy* (Seat-

tle: University of Washington Press, 1998); Sarah Phillips, *This Land, This Nation* (Cambridge: Cambridge University Press, 2007); Neil Maher, *Nature's New Deal* (Oxford: Oxford University Press, 2008); Kendrick Clements, *Hoover, Conservation, and Consumerism* (Lawrence: University Press of Kansas, 2000).

11. Frank Graham, *The Adirondack Park* (New York: Alfred A. Knopf, 1978); Martin Melosi, *Garbage in the Cities*, rev. ed. (Pittsburgh: University of Pittsburgh Press, 2005); Davis, *Sportsmen United*; Stradling, *Smokestacks and Progressives*; John Cumbler, *Reasonable Use* (Oxford: Oxford University Press, 2001).

12. Michael McCarthy, *Hour of Trial* (Norman: University of Oklahoma Press, 1977); Judd, *Common Lands, Common People*.

13. James Tober, *Who Owns the Wildlife?* (Westport, CT: Greenwood, 1981); Sally Fairfax et al., *Buying Nature* (Cambridge, MA: MIT Press, 2005); Donald Pisani, *To Reclaim a Divided West* (Albuquerque: University of New Mexico Press, 1992); Duncan Maysilles, *Ducktown Smoke* (Chapel Hill: University of North Caroline Press, 2011).

14. 198 U.S. 45.

15. Julie Novkov, *Constituting Workers, Protecting Women* (Ann Arbor: University of Michigan Press, 2001), 1–2.

16. 300 U.S. 379.

17. Novkov, *Constituting Workers, Protecting Women*, 1–11.

18. Stephen Skowronek, *Building a New American State* (Cambridge: Cambridge University Press, 1982), 46, 122, 152.

19. Skowronek, *Building a New American State*, 31.

20. Theda Skocpol tells a similar story of judicial obstruction in *Protecting Soldiers and Mothers* (Cambridge, MA: Belknap, 1992).

21. McCarthy, *Hour of Trial*, 155–199.

22. 206 U.S. 46 (1907).

23. 260 U.S. 393 (1922). The policy in question in *Mahon* was not really an environmental regulation, but the decision is now considered to have implications for local environmental management.

24. Donald Pisani does argue that *Kansas v. Colorado* was a significant loss for the cause of multipurpose river development. Pisani, *To Reclaim a Divided West*, 325.

25. *Ashwander v. T.V.A.*, 297 U.S. 288 (1936).

26. Daniel Carpenter, *The Forging of Bureaucratic Autonomy* (Princeton: Princeton University Press, 2001), 4.

27. Carpenter, *The Forging of Bureaucratic Autonomy*, 16–17.

28. Barry Cushman, "Rethinking the New Deal Court," *Virginia Law Review* 80 (1994): 201–261, 249–256.

29. Paul Pierson, *Politics in Time* (Princeton: Princeton University Press, 2004), 133–134.

30. Pierson, *Politics in Time*, 137–142.

31. Stephen Griffin, "Constitutional Change in the United States," Tulane Public Law Research Paper No. 11-03 (July 18, 2011), 3.

32. Bruce Ackerman, *We the People*, vol. 1 (Cambridge, MA: Belknap, 1991), 59.

33. *United States v. Butler*, 297 U.S. 1 (1936); *N.L.R.B. v. Jones & Laughlin Steel Corp.*, 301 U.S. 1 (1937); *United States v. Darby Lumber*, 312 U.S. 100 (1941); *Wickard v. Filburn*, 317 U.S. 111 (1942). Stephen Griffin, "Constitutional Change in the United States," 11–12.

34. Jack Balkin and Sandford Levinson argue that revolutions in constitutional doctrine occur through "partisan entrenchment": Franklin D. Roosevelt was able to appoint eight New Dealers to the Supreme Court between 1937 and 1942, which helped to entrench the New Deal constitutional order in constitutional doctrine. "The Processes of Constitutional Change: From Partisan Entrenchment to the National Surveillance State," SSRN Research Paper 120 (September 17, 2006), 120.

35. Ronald Kahn and Ken Kersch, "Introduction," in *The Supreme Court and American Political Development*, ed. Ronald Kahn and Ken Kersch (Lawrence: University Press of Kansas, 2006), 17–18.

36. Kahn and Kersch, "Introduction," 18.

37. Balkin and Levinson, "Processes of Constitutional Change," 110; Kahn and Kersch, "Introduction," 18.

38. Pamela Brandwein, *Reconstructing Reconstruction* (Durham, NC: Duke University Press, 1999); Karen Orren, *Belated Feudalism* (Cambridge: Cambridge University Press, 1991); Novkov, *Constituting Workers, Protecting Women*.

39. Peter Appel, "The Power of Congress 'Without Limitation': The Property Clause and Federal Regulation of Private Property," *Minnesota Law Review* 86 (2001): 1–130.

40. Ernst Haeckel, "Address to Jena Faculty" (1869), quoted in Frank Egerton, "History of Ecological Sciences, Part 47," in *Bulletin of the Ecological Society of America* 94 (July 2013): 222–224, 229. See also Frederic Clements, *Research Methods in Ecology* (Lincoln: University of Nebraska, 1905), xviii. On the history of ecology, see Frank Egerton, "History of Ecological Sciences, Part 59: Niches, Biomes, Ecosystems, and Systems," *Bulletin of the Ecological Society of America* 98 (October 2017): 298–337; Frank Egerton, "The History of Ecology: Achievements and Opportunities, Part One," *Journal of the History of Biology* 16 (Summer 1983): 259–310. On its influence in the United States, see Curt Meine, *Aldo Leopold: His Life and Work* (Madison: University of Wisconsin Press, 1988), 184; Christian Young, *In the Absence of Predators* (Lincoln: University of Nebraska Press, 2002), 4–5.

41. John Larson, *Internal Improvement* (Chapel Hill: University of North Carolina Press, 2001), 10–18; Adam White, "Infrastructure Policy: Lessons from American History," *New Atlantis* 35 (Spring 2012): 3–31, 7–10.

42. *Proceedings of a Conference of Governors, May 13–15, 1908* (Washington, DC: Government Printing Office, 1909), 6.

43. White, "Infrastructure Policy," 10–11.

44. 22 U.S. 1.

45. 22 U.S. 1, 189–190.

46. Charles Reid, "America's First Great Constitutional Controversy," *University of St. Thomas Law Journal* 14 (2018): 105–192.

47. James Monroe, "Message from the President of the United States with His Objections to the Bill for the Preservation and Repair of the Cumberland Road" (Washington, DC: Gales & Seaton, May 4, 1822).

48. Kent Newmyer, "John Marshall, McCulloch v. Maryland and the Southern States' Rights Tradition," *John Marshall Law Review* 33 (2000): 875–934; Douglas Irwin, "Antebellum Tariff Politics," *Journal of Law and Economics* 51 (2008): 715–741; David Currie, "The Constitution in Congress: The Public Lands, 1827–1861," *University of Chicago Law Review* 70 (2003): 783–820.

49. 60 U.S. 393 (1857).

50. Jacqueline Keeler, "Educating the Oregon Militia on The Northern Paiute's 'Trail of Tears,'" *Indian Country Today*, January 7, 2016, accessed June 12, 2018: https://newsmaven.io/indiancountrytoday/archive/educating-the-oregon-militia-on-the-northern-paiute-s-trail-of-tears-PyOQlcTWI06EPzAkqb4qKQ.

51. See, for example, Felix Cohen, *Handbook of Federal Indian Law, Rev. Ed.*, ed. Rennard Strickland (Charlottesville, VA: Michie-Bobbs-Merrill, 1982); Vine Deloria and Clifford Lytle, *The Nations Within: The Past and Future of American Indian Sovereignty* (New York: Pantheon, 1984); David Wilkins, *American Indian Sovereignty and the U.S. Supreme Court* (Austin: University of Texas Press, 1997).

52. 163 U.S. 504 (1896).

53. White authored *Geer v. Connecticut*, 161 U.S. 519 (1895) and *Ward v. Race Horse*; Van Devanter was the lead attorney for Wyoming in *Ward* and authored the opinion in *Utah Power and Light v. United States*, 243 U.S. 389 (1917).

Chapter 2. State Wildlife Conservation

1. Ann-Marie Szymanski, "Wildlife Protection and the Development of Centralized Governance in the Progressive Era," in *Statebuilding from the Margins*, ed. Carol Nackenoff and Julie Novkov (Philadelphia: University of Pennsylvania Press, 2014), 144.

2. John Reiger, *American Sportsmen and the Origins of Conservation* (New York: Winchester, 1975), 31–39; James Tober, *Who Owns the Wildlife?* (Westport, CT: Greenwood, 1981), 69–102; Kurkpatrick Dorsey, *The Dawn of Conservation Diplomacy* (Seattle: University of Washington Press, 1998), 33–40.

3. Tober, *Who Owns the Wildlife?*, 24–26; Yasuhie Kawashima and Ruth Tone,

"Environmental Policy in Early America," *Journal of Forest History* 27, no. 4 (October 1983): 168–179.

4. Szymanski, "Wildlife Protection," 146–147.

5. John Cumbler, *Reasonable Use* (Oxford: Oxford University Press, 2001), 95–96, 167.

6. U.S. Fish Commission, *Report 1871–1872* (Washington, DC: Government Printing Office, 1873).

7. William Temple Hornaday, *The Extermination of the American Bison* [1889] (Washington, DC: Smithsonian Institution Press, 2002).

8. *Waters v. People*, 23 Colo. 33 (1896).

9. 33 Cong. Rec. 4871–4872 (April 30, 1900).

10. Thomas Dunlap, *Saving America's Wildlife* (Princeton: Princeton University Press, 1988), 14–15.

11. Henry Fairfield Osborn, "Introduction," in *The Extermination of the American Bison.*

12. Richard Judd, *Common Lands, Common People* (Cambridge, MA: Harvard University Press, 1997), 79–85.

13. Tober, *Who Owns the Wildlife?*, 85–88.

14. *Stoughton v. Baker*, 4 Mass. 522 (1808); *Cmmwlth v. Ruggles*, 10 Mass. 391 (1813).

15. *Hooker v. Cummings*, 20 Johns. 90 (1822); *Corfield v. Coryell*, 6 F. Cas. 546 (E.D. Penn 1823); *Roger v. Jones*, 1 Wend. 237 (1828).

16. *Smith v. Levinus*, 8 N.Y. 472 (1835).

17. 3 Cai. R. 175 (N.Y. 1805).

18. 6 N.J.L. 1.

19. 6 N.J.L. 1, 148.

20. 6 N.J.L. 1, 150–151.

21. 41 U.S. 367.

22. 41 U.S. 367, 411.

23. For example, *Gough v. Bell*, 22 N.J.L. 441 (1850).

24. Richard Lazarus, "Changing Conceptions of Property and Sovereignty in Natural Resources," *Iowa Law Review* 71 (1986): 631–716.

25. 4 Mass. 522.

26. 4 Mass. 522, 528.

27. For example, *Comm'rs on Inland Fisheries v. Holyoke Water Power Co.*, 104 Mass. 446 (1870); *Swift v. Falmouth*, 167 Mass. 115 (1896); *Parker v. Illinois*, 111 Ill. 581 (1884).

28. Michael Blum and Lucas Ritchie, "The Pioneer Spirit and the Public Trust," *Environmental Law* 35 (Fall 2005): 673–720, 689; Tober, *Who Owns the Wildlife?*, 19.

29. Blum and Ritchie, "The Pioneer Spirit and the Public Trust," 676.

30. Tober, *Who Owns the Wildlife?*, 18.

31. "A Proposition to Gentlemen Sportsmen," *Forest and Stream* (November 25, 1880), 323.

32. Tober, *Who Owns the Wildlife?*, 58; Judd, *Common Lands, Common People*, 44.

33. Ernst Freund, *The Police Power* (Chicago: Callaghan & Co., 1904), 442.

34. 97 Ill. 320.

35. 97 Ill. 320, 333.

36. 58 Minn. 393 (1894).

37. 58 Minn. 393, 400. See also *Ex Parte Maier*, 103 Cal. 476 (1894).

38. Lazarus, "Changing Conceptions of Property," 6665–6675. See, for example, *Commonwealth v. Vincent*, 108 Mass. 441 (1871); *State v. Randolph*, 1 Mo. App. 15 (1876).

39. Dale Goble and Eric Freyfogle, *Wildlife Law: Cases and Materials* (St. Paul, MN: Foundation, 2002), 387.

40. 12 Me. 222.

41. 12 Me. 222, 229. See also *State v. Robert*, 59 N.H. 256 (1879).

42. "Trespass and Game Protection," *Forest and Stream* (May 7, 1874), 201.

43. 6 F. Cas. 546 (E.D. Penn. 1823).

44. 6 F. Cas. 546, 551.

45. 161 U.S. 519.

46. *State v. Saunders*, 19 Kan. 127 (1877) (striking down a prohibition on shipping prairie chickens into or out of the state).

47. Brief for Plaintiff in Error, *Geer v. Connecticut*, 161 U.S. 519 (1895), 5.

48. 161 U.S. 530.

49. 161 U.S. 530, 534.

50. 161 U.S. 530, 552.

51. 94 U.S. 391.

52. 94 U.S. 391, 395.

53. Judd, *Common Lands, Common People*, 42–43.

54. Judd, *Common Lands, Common People*, 128–129.

55. Defenders of the fee policy argued that New Jersey residents were required to join a hunting club and pay dues in order to hunt; the fee simply imposed the same financial burden on out-of-state residents. Neither side seemed willing to defend outright discrimination on nonresidents, in spite of favorable Supreme Court precedent. Untitled Article, *Forest and Stream*, August 28, 1879, 591; Letter, *Forest and Stream*, January 1, 1880, 951.

56. 334 U.S. 385. Later cases did draw on the Equal Protection Clause to prohibit racially discriminatory restrictions, however. See the discussion of *In re Ah Chong*, 7 F. 733 (D. Cal. 1880) in chapter 3.

57. *State v. Kemp*, 73 S.D. 458 (1950).

58. Although enforcement mechanisms remained weak, even at the local level. Szymanski, "Wildlife Protection," 148–151; Judd, *Common Lands, Common People*, 174–176.

59. 12 Me. 222, 229.

60. *Gentile v. State*, 29 Ind. 409 (1868); *Phelps v. Racey*, 60 N.Y. 10 (1875).

61. 82 U.S. 500, 506. See also *Manchester v. Massachusetts*, 139 U.S. 240 (1891).

62. 155 U.S. 461 (1894).

63. 155 U.S. 461, 535.

64. 128 U.S. 1 (1888).

65. Reiger, *American Sportsmen*, 71.

66. Elaine McIntosh, *American Food Habits in Historical Perspective* (Westport, CT: Praeger, 1995), 82; Harvey Levenstein, *Revolution at the Table* (New York: Oxford University Press, 1988), 23–24.

67. Cumbler, *Reasonable Use*, 14–16, 26; Reginald Horsman, *Feast or Famine* (Columbia: University of Missouri Press, 2008).

68. Horsman, *Feast or Famine*, 341.

69. Rudolf Clemen, *The American Livestock and Meat Industry* (New York: Ronald, 1923), 173, 211; Levenstein, *Revolution at the Table*, 21, 30–31.

70. Tober, *Who Owns the Wildlife?*, 77.

71. "The Price of Meat," *Chicago Tribune*, May 10, 1874.

72. Levenstein, *Revolution at the Table*, 27.

73. Levenstein, *Revolution at the Table*, 26.

74. 23 Colo. 33.

75. Levenstein, *Revolution at the Table*, 35.

76. See, generally, Susan Pearson, *The Rights of the Defenseless* (Chicago: University of Chicago Press, 2011); Kimberly Smith, *Governing Animals* (Oxford: Oxford University Press, 2012).

77. Cumbler, *Reasonable Use*, 95–96, 167.

78. Szymanski, "Wildlife Protection," 146–149, 151, 153–154.

79. See, e.g., *McNab v. Board of Park Commissioners*, 108 Ohio St. 497 (OH 1923).

80. 198 U.S. 45 (1905), discussed in the introduction.

81. 220 N.Y. 423.

82. Ernest Stirling, "The Return of the Beaver to the Adirondacks," *American Forestry* 19 (January 1913): 292–299; Robert Peck, "The Renaissance of the Beaver," *Forest and Stream* 111 (April 1921): 152.

83. 220 N.Y. 423, 427.

84. 220 N.Y. 423, 427.

85. 220 N.Y. 423, 428.

86. 220 N.Y. 423, 431.

87. Of course, recreation is an ecosystem service, too, but not one that the court was initially very concerned about.

Chapter 3. The Road to *Missouri v. Holland*

1. 252 U.S. 416 (1920).

2. Richard Judd, *Common Lands, Common People* (Cambridge, MA: Harvard University Press, 1997), 163–168.

3. Congress imposed a limited closed season on deep-sea mackerel fishing (beyond state territorial waters) for five years in 1887 and outlawed hunting on federally owned land in Yellowstone National Park in 1894. An Act relating to the importing and landing of mackerel caught during the spawning season, 24 Stat. 434 (1887); An Act to protect birds and animals in Yellowstone National Park, 28 Stat. 73 (1894). Neither measure encountered significant constitutional objections.

4. John Reiger, *American Sportsmen and the Origins of Conservation* (New York: Winchester Press, 1975), 119.

5. 45 *Cong. Glob.* 626 (May 13, 1872).

6. US Fish Commission, *Report 1871–1872* (Washington, DC: Government Printing Office, 1873), xxxiv–xxxv. See also US Fish Commission, *Report 1872–1873* (Washington, DC: Government Printing Office, 1874), xxxv.

7. *The Civil Rights Cases*, 109 U.S. 3 (1883).

8. 22 U.S. 1.

9. 6 F. Cas. 546 (E.D. Penn 1823).

10. 59 U.S. 71.

11. 59 U.S. 71, 75. See also *Manchester v. Massachusetts*, 139 U.S. 240 (1891).

12. "Fish Culture and Fish Law," *Forest and Stream*, March 10, 1881, 111.

13. 223 U.S. 166.

14. 223 U.S. 166, 174–175.

15. 7 F. 733 (D.Cal. 1883).

16. 94 U.S. 391 (1876).

17. 7 F. 733, 736–737.

18. Elihu Root, "The Real Questions under the Japanese Treaty and the San Francisco School Board Resolution," *American Journal of Internat'l Law* 1, no. 2: 273–286 (1907): 278.

19. See generally Mark Cioc, *The Game of Conservation* (Athens: Ohio University Press, 2009).

20. Kurkpatrick Dorsey, *The Dawn of Conservation Diplomacy* (Seattle: University of Washington Press, 1998), 58.

21. Dorsey, *The Dawn of Conservation Diplomacy*, 58.

22. Dorsey, *The Dawn of Conservation Diplomacy*, 78.

23. Dorsey, *The Dawn of Conservation Diplomacy*, 78.

24. Dorsey, *The Dawn of Conservation Diplomacy*, 89.

25. Ann-Marie Szymanski, "Wildlife Protection and the Development of Centralized Governance in the Progressive Era," in *Statebuilding from the Margins*, ed. Carol Nackenoff and Julie Novkov (Philadelphia: University of Pennsylvania Press, 2014), 142.

26. James Tober, *Who Owns the Wildlife?* (Westport, CT: Greenwood, 1981), 49; Dorsey, *Dawn of Conservation Diplomacy*, 165–176.

27. Tober, *Who Owns the Wildlife?*, 85–89.

28. 49 Cong. Rec. 1484–1485 (January 14, 1913).

29. 49 Cong. Rec. 1486.

30. 49 Cong. Rec. 4332 (February 28, 1913).

31. The Lacey Act also prohibited the importation of certain nuisance birds from other countries and authorized the secretary of agriculture to promote the preservation of wild birds—but without overriding state laws. These provisions did not raise constitutional problems.

32. Reiger, *American Sportsmen*, 119.

33. 33 Cong. Rec. 1873 (April 30, 1900) (referring to the Wilson Original Package Act, 26 Stat. 313 [1890]).

34. See *State v. Shattuck*, 104 N.W. 719 (Minn. 1905); *Silz v. Hesterberg*, 211 U.S. 31 (1908).

35. 181 F. 87 (8th Cir. 1910).

36. 103 Ark. 288 (1912).

37. Cioc, *Game of Conservation*, 67–68.

38. A good account of the constitutional arguments surrounding the migratory bird laws is found in Charles Lofgren, "*Missouri v. Holland* in Historical Perspective," *Supreme Court Review* 1975: 77–122.

39. Christopher Tiedman, *The Unwritten Constitution of the United States* (New York: G. P. Putnam's Sons, 1890), 137.

40. Lucien Alexander, "James Wilson, Patriot, and the Wilson Doctrine," *North American Review* 183, no. 603 (November 16, 1906): 971–989.

41. Theodore Roosevelt, "At the Dedication Ceremonies of the New State Capitol Building, Harrisburg, Pennsylvania, October 4, 1906," in *The Works of Theodore Roosevelt*, vol. 18, ed. Hermann Hagedorn (New York: Charles Scribner's Sons, 1925), 83.

42. Theodore Roosevelt, "First Annual Message to Congress" [1901], in *The Works of Theodore Roosevelt*, vol. 21, 121. See chapter 6 for further discussion of the context for this speech.

43. 26 Stat. 561 (1891).

44. Theodore Roosevelt, *The Rough Riders: An Autobiography* [1913], Library of America ed. (New York: Penguin, 2004), 663, 682.

45. 161 U.S. 519 (1895).

46. *Grisar v. McDowell*, 73 U.S. 363 (1868); *United States v. Payne*, 8 F. 883 (W.D. Ark. 1881).

47. 43 Cong. Rec. 2215–2216 (February 11, 1909).

48. U.S. Const. Art. I, Sec. 8.

49. Dorsey, *Dawn of Conservation Diplomacy*, 183.

50. 92 F.2d 623 (7th Cir. 1937).

51. 37 Stat. 828, 847–848 (1913).

52. 49 Cong. Rec. 4337 (February 28, 1913) (Sisson's remarks).

53. 49 Cong. Rec. 4381.

54. 47 Cong. Rec. 2564 (June 28, 1911).

55. 49 Cong. Rec. 1492 (January 14, 1913).

56. 49 Cong. Rec. 1492 (January 14, 1913).

57. L. F. Kneipp to District Forester Headley, October 29, 1913, in General Correspondence of the Forest Service 1905–1952, RG 95, Box 81 (NA-CP).

58. See, for example, letter from L. F. Kneipp to Will Barnes and reply, August 16 and 25, 1916, in General Correspondence of the Forest Service 1905–1952, RG 95, Box 80 (NA-CP), discussing how to handle Idaho's conflicting game laws.

59. Letter from A. F. Potter to Office of the Solicitor, October 24, 1913; Letter from R. W. Williams, Acting Solicitor, to the Chief Forester, October 31, 1913; in General Correspondence of the Forest Service 1905–1952, RG 95, Box 136 (NA-CP). The Forest Service did have explicit authority to arrest people for violating regulations relating to the forest.

60. Letter from Assistant Forester Will Barnes to District Forester, February 16, 1915, in General Correspondence of the Forest Service 1905–1952, RG 95, Box 78 (NA-CP).

61. Lofgren, "*Missouri v. Holland* in Historical Perspective," 80; Szymanski, "Wildlife Protection and the Development of Centralized Governance in the Progressive Era," 163–165.

62. Lofgren, "*Missouri v. Holland* in Historical Perspective," 83, 83n32.

63. Cioc, *Game of Conservation*, 69–70.

64. 214 F. 154 (E.D. Ark. 1914).

65. 214 F. 154, 155–156.

66. 206 U.S. 46.

67. 206 U.S. 46, 89.

68. Lofgren, "*Missouri v. Holland* in Historical Perspective," 85.

69. 214 F. 154, 160–161.

70. Charles Lofgren offers a good analysis of the argument in "*Missouri v. Holland* in Historical Perspective," 86–90. The government's brief for the appeal is included in the Congressional Record, 55 Cong. Rec. 4816–4818 (July 9, 1917).

71. Comment, "Treaty-Making Power as Support for Federal Legislation," *Yale Law Journal* 29, no. 4: 445–449 (February 1920), 445; Cioc, *Game of Conservation*, 70.

72. 221 F. 288 (D. Kan. 1915).

73. 221 F. 288, 292.

74. 163 U.S. 504.

75. 163 U.S. 504, 514.

76. 113 Me. 458.

77. 96 Kan. 786.

78. 113 Me. 458, 462, 464; 96 Kan. 786, 789.

79. 250 U.S. 118.

80. Memorandum by Aldo Leopold, May 5, 1916, in General Correspondence of the Forest Service 1905–1952, RG 95, Box 77 (NA-CP).

81. Letter from Graves to Redington, June 3, 1916, in General Correspondence of the Forest Service 1905–1952, RG 95, Box 77 (NA-CP).

82. 174 U.S. 690 (1899).

83. "Game Protection and the Constitution," *Michigan Law Review* 14 (June 1916): 613–625, 621.

84. Dorsey, *Dawn of Conservation Diplomacy*, 188; 49 *Cong. Rec.* 1494 (January 14, 1913).

85. Dorsey, *Dawn of Conservation Diplomacy*, 189–91.

86. 40 Stat. 755 (1918).

87. 258 F. 257 (E.D. Ark. 1919).

88. Lofgren, "*Missouri v. Holland* in Historical Perspective," 91.

89. 258 F. 257, 257.

90. Cushing, *In Droit D'Aubaine*, 8 Op. Attys. Gen. 411, 415.

91. 258 F. 257, 259.

92. 258 F. 257, 264.

93. 258 F. 775 (S.D. Texas 1919).

94. 260 F. 346 (D. Montana 1919).

95. 260 F. 346, 347–348.

96. Lofgren, "*Missouri v. Holland* in Historical Perspective," 83, 92.

97. 258 Fed. Rep. 479 (W.D. Mo. 1919).

98. 258 Fed. Rep. 479, 484.

99. Brief for Appellee, *Missouri v. Holland*, 42; Brief for Appellee, *Missouri v. Holland*, Appendix B, 74.

100. Brief for Appellee, *Missouri v. Holland*, Appendix B, 69 (citing a report by James Buckland, *The Value of Birds to Man* [Smithsonian Institute 1913]).

101. Brief for Appellee, *Missouri v. Holland*, Appendix B, 69–70.

102. Brief for Appellee, *Missouri v. Holland*, Appendix B, 71.

103. Brief for Appellee, *Missouri v. Holland,* Appendix B, 74.

104. Brief for Ass'n for the Protection of the Adirondacks, *Missouri v. Holland,* 12–18.

105. Brief for Ass'n for the Protection of the Adirondacks, *Missouri v. Holland,* 19–20 (citing *U.S. v. Grimaud,* 220 U.S. 506 (1911); *Light v. United States,* 220 U.S. 523 (1911). We will return to these cases in chapter 5.

106. 243 U.S. 389 (1917).

107. 206 U.S. 203 (1907).

108. Brief for Ass'n for the Protection of the Adirondacks, 25.

109. Brief for Ass'n for the Protection of the Adirondacks, 25.

110. Brief for Ass'n for the Protection of the Adirondacks, 47.

111. 252 U.S. 416, 433 (quoting *Andrews v. Andrews,* 188 U.S. 14, 33 [1903]).

112. 252 U.S. 416, 433 (quoting *Andrews v. Andrews,* 188 U.S. 14, 33 [1903]).

113. 252 U.S. 416, 434 (quoting *Andrews v. Andrews,* 188 U.S. 14, 33 [1903]).

114. 252 U.S. 416, 434 (quoting *Andrews v. Andrews,* 188 U.S. 14, 33 [1903]).

115. 252 U.S. 416, 434 (quoting *Andrews v. Andrews,* 188 U.S. 14, 33 [1903]).

116. 252 U.S. 416, 435 (quoting *Andrews v. Andrews,* 188 U.S. 14, 33 [1903]).

117. See Margaret McGuinness, "Symposium: Return to Missouri v. Holland: Federalism and International Law: Foreword," *Missouri Law Review* 73 (2008): 921–937. It's difficult to improve on Lofgren's masterful analysis of the opinion on this question. See Lofgren, *"Missouri v. Holland* in Historical Perspective."

118. *Hudson County Water Co. v. McCarter,* 209 U.S. 349 (1908); *Patsone v. Pennsylvania,* 232 U.S. 138 (1914).

119. Sheldon Novick, "Introduction," in *Collected Works of Justice Holmes,* vol. 1 (New York: Dover Pub. 1991), 56–57. That theory was developed in a series of decisions, including *Georgia v. Tennessee Copper Co.; Damon v. Hawaii,* 194 U.S. 154 (1904); *Kawananakoa v. Polybank,* 205 U.S. 349 (1907); and *Hudson County Water Co. v. McCarter.*

120. 441 U.S. 322.

121. Holmes did, however, emphasize that property rights could be altered only with careful attention to the citizens' vested interests acquired under the established legal regime. This was a central consideration in *Pennsylvania Coal Co. v. Mahon,* 260 U.S. 363 (1922), and was emphasized by the more recent Supreme Court decision *Lucas v. South Carolina Coastal Council,* 505 U.S. 1003 (1992).

122. *Missouri v. Illinois,* 180 U.S. 208 (1901).

123. *United Haulers Assn., Inc. v. Oneida-Herkimer Solid Waste Mgmt. Authority,* 550 U.S. 330 (2007).

Chapter 4. Forest Conservation in the States

1. Richard Judd, *Common Lands, Common People* (Cambridge, MA: Harvard University Press, 1997), 73–89.

2. Samuel Hays, *Conservation and the Gospel of Efficiency* (Pittsburgh: University of Pittsburgh Press, 1959), 27–28.

3. Thomas Cox, Robert Maxwell, Phillip Thomas, and Joseph Malone, *This Well-Wooded Land* (Lincoln: University of Nebraska Press, 1985), 170.

4. Michael Williams, "Industrial Impacts on the Forests of the United States, 1860–1920," *Journal of Forest History* 31, no. 3 (July 1987): 108–121, 108.

5. George Perkins Marsh, *Man and Nature* [1865] (Seattle: University of Washington Press, 2003), 196.

6. William Cronon, "Introduction," in *Conservation in the Progressive Era*, ed. David Stradling (Seattle: University of Washington Press, 2004), 4; Cox et al., *This Well-Wooded Land*, 180.

7. *Forests and Forestry in the American States*, ed. Ralph Widner (National Association of State Foresters 1968), 27.

8. Judd, *Common Lands, Common People*, 98.

9. Henry Klepper, "Forest Conservation in Pennsylvania," *Pennsylvania History* 48, no. 1 (1981): 41–50, 43–44; *Forests and Forestry in the American States*, 8.

10. Judd, *Common Lands, Common People*, 91–117.

11. William Irwin, *The New Niagara* (University Park, PA: Penn State University Press, 1996), 76.

12. Irwin, *The New Niagara*.

13. Frank Graham, *The Adirondack Park* (New York: Alfred A. Knopf, 1978), 45–52. See also Richard Judd on Maine's forest conservation campaign. Judd, *Common Lands, Common People*, 117.

14. "The Yosemite in Congress," *New York Times*, February 14, 1870.

15. 45 *Cong. Glob.*, 1243 (February 27, 1872).

16. 45 *Cong. Glob.*, 697 (January 30, 1872).

17. 45 *Cong. Glob.*, 697 (January 30, 1872).

18. Marsh, *Man and Nature*, 171.

19. Marsh, *Man and Nature*, 187.

20. Cox et al., *This Well-Wooded Land*, 148; Judd, *Common Lands, Common People*, 95.

21. 23 Cong. Rec. 4125 (May 10, 1892).

22. Franklin Hough, *Report upon Forestry: From the Committee Appointed to Memorialize Congress and the State Legislatures Regarding the Cultivation of Timber and the Preservation of Forests* (Washington, DC: Government Printing Office, 1878), 7–8.

23. Bureau of Land Management, Public Lands Statistics 2015, vol. 20, table 1–1 (May 2016). The federal government now owns about 28 percent of the nation's territory.

24. Hough, *Report upon Forestry*, 198.

25. Hough, *Report upon Forestry*, 12.

26. Hough, *Report upon Forestry*, 15n1.

27. New York Constitution, Art. VII (1895) (now Art. XIV).

28. Art. XVIII, Sec. 1 (1896).

29. Art. II, Sec. 36 (1912).

30. Art. XLIX, Sec. 179 (1918).

31. Art. VI, Sec. 1 (1921).

32. Art. 10, Sec. 2 (1926)

33. Art. VIII, Sec. 10 (1924).

34. *Forests and Forestry in the American States*, 56–57.

35. *Forests and Forestry in the American States*, 32, 394.

36. *Forests and Forestry in the American States*, 27–28.

37. Graham, *The Adirondack Park*, 37, 67–68.

38. Graham, *The Adirondack Park*, 70–71.

39. Graham, *The Adirondack Park*, 90.

40. Graham, *The Adirondack Park*, 85, 105.

41. New York Constitution, Art VII, Sec. 7 (1895).

42. Amy Bridges, *Democratic Beginnings* (Lawrence: University Press of Kansas, 2015), 15.

43. *New York v. Adirondack Railway Co.*, 160 N.Y. 225 (1899) (aff'd 176 U.S. 335 [1900]).

44. We will discuss judicial suspicion of aesthetic regulations in more detail in chapter 8.

45. Errol Meidinger, "The 'Public Uses' of Eminent Domain," *University of Buffalo Law Review* 11 (1980): 1–65, 20.

46. Meidinger notes a number of decisions in the 1840s and 1850s striking down statutes that authorized private parties to use eminent domain. Meidinger, "The 'Public Uses' of Eminent Domain," 24.

47. 160 N.Y. 225, 247–248.

48. The judge relied primarily on *Brooklyn Park Commissioners v. Armstrong*, 45 N.Y. 234 (1871) and *Shoemaker v. United States*, 147 U.S. 282 (1892), discussed below.

49. 176 U.S. 335, 349 (1900).

50. 220 N.Y. 423.

51. Background on this measure can be found in *Forests and Forestry in the American States*, 119–122.

52. An advisory opinion does not adjudicate a case. It is usually issued at the request of a coordinate branch of government; it has some authority but is not binding on either the entity asking for the opinion or the court issuing it.

53. The opinion is reported in *The Seventh Report of the Forest Commissioner* (Waterville: Sentinel Pub. Co., 1908), 30–35. The quote is on 31.

54. *The Seventh Report of the Forest Commissioner*, 32.

55. *The Seventh Report of the Forest Commissioner*, 33, quoting *Commonwealth v. Alger*, 61 Mass. 53 (1851).

56. *The Seventh Report of the Forest Commissioner*, 34. See chapter 8 for further discussion of "regulatory takings."

57. *The Seventh Report of the Forest Commissioner*, 35.

58. *Proceedings of the Conference of Governors*, May 13–15, 1908 (Washington, DC: Government Printing Office, 1909), 11.

59. *Forests and Forestry in the American States*, 141.

60. *Vreeland v. Forest Park Reservation Commission*, 82 N.J.Eq. 349, 351.

61. 82 N.J.Eq. 349, 351.

62. Jack Stark, "A History of the Internal Improvements Section of the Wisconsin Constitution," *Wisconsin Law Review* 1998: 829–839, 830–831.

63. 160 Wis. 21.

64. The best summary of the facts is in *In re Wausau Investment Co.*, 163 Wis. 283 (1915).

65. Art. VIII, Sec. 6. The Sanborn contract did not exceed $100,000, but Marshall concluded that all the land contracts together did violate this limit.

66. 160 Wis. 21, 75.

67. 115 Wis. 32 (1902).

68. 160 Wis. 21, 89.

69. 160 Wis. 21, 89–90.

70. 160 Wis. 21, 89–90.

71. 160 Wis. 21, 120.

72. 160 Wis. 21, 123–124

73. 160 Wis. 21, 124.

74. 160 Wis. 21, 125–126.

75. 160 Wis. 21, 125–126.

76. 160 Wis. 21, 139.

77. 160 Wis. 21, 141.

78. 160 Wis. 21, 141–142.

79. 160 Wis. 21, 141–142.

80. 160 Wis. 21, 145.

81. Moreover, because Marshall also held that the state held equitable liens on the lands in question, most of them ended up in the state's possession anyway. *In re Wausau*, 163 Wis. 283, 286.

82. 108 Ohio St. 497.

83. 91 U.S. 367.

84. 147 U.S. 282.

85. 250 F. 499 (W.D. Va.).

86. 250 F. 499, 502.

Chapter 5. Western Forest Reserves

1. Stephen Skowronek, *Building a New American State* (Cambridge: Cambridge University Press, 1982), 184.

2. Char Miller, *Gifford Pinchot and the Making of Modern Environmentalism* (Washington, DC: Island, 2001); James Penick, *Progressive Politics and Conservation* (Chicago: University of Chicago Press, 1968); Samuel Hays, *Conservation and the Gospel of Efficiency* (Pittsburgh: University of Pittsburgh Press, 1959).

3. Daniel Carpenter, *The Forging of Bureaucratic Autonomy* (Princeton: Princeton University Press, 2001), 212.

4. Carpenter, *The Forging of Bureaucratic Autonomy*, 212.

5. John Ise, *The United States Forest Policy* (New Haven: Yale University Press, 1920), 56.

6. Ise, *The United States Forest Policy*, 77.

7. Const. Art. IV, Sec. 3.

8. Ise, *The United States Forest Policy*, 45.

9. Ise, *The United States Forest Policy*, 116–117.

10. 22 *Cong. Rec.* 3613 (February 28, 1891).

11. 22 *Cong. Rec.* 3613, 3614 (February 28, 1891).

12. Ise, *The United States Forest Policy*, 120.

13. Ise, *The United States Forest Policy*, 22–23.

14. Presidential Proclamations 303, 312, 316, 319, 332, 333, 341, 342, 344, 348, 349, 350, 353, 354, 361, 362 (1891).

15. Bernhard Fernow, "What Is Forestry?" *USDA Forestry Division Bulletin* 5 (Washington, DC: Government Printing Office, 1891).

16. Bernhard Fernow, *Report of the Chief of the Division of Forestry* (1891).

17. Edward Bowers, "The Present Condition of the Forests on the Public Lands," *Publications of the American Economic Association* 6, no. 3 (May 1891): 57–74, 61, 64–65.

18. Lewis Groff, *Annual Report of the Commissioner of the General Land Office* (Washington, DC: Government Printing Office, 1890), 84–85.

19. Groff, *Annual Report of the Commissioner of the General Land Office*.

20. 25 *Cong. Rec.* 2371 (Oct 10, 1893).

21. 25 *Cong. Rec.* 2375 (Oct 10, 1893).

22. Ise, *The United States Forest Policy*, 127–128.

23. 16 U.S.C. sec. 431 et. seq.

24. 16 U.S.C. secs. 1–4.

25. Alfred Runte, *National Parks* (Lincoln: University of Nebraska Press, 1979), 49–64.

26. Runte, *National Parks*, 73.

27. Runte, *National Parks*, 97–105.

28. 16 U.S.C. secs. 473–478, 479–482, 551.

29. Forest Service Organic Administration Act, 16 U.S.C. sec. 475 (1897).

30. Ise, *The United States Forest Policy*, 141–142.

31. "Report of the National Forest Commission," in the *Report of the National Academy of Sciences for the year 1897* (Washington, DC: Government Printing Office, 1898), 18–48.

32. Michael McCarthy, *Hour of Trial* (Norman: University of Oklahoma Press, 1977), 52–61.

33. Northwest Ordinance, Art. V (1787).

34. Paul Conable, "Equal Footing, County Supremacy, and the Western Public Lands," *Environmental Law* 26 (1996): 1263–1286, 1268–1269.

35. Conable, "Equal Footing, County Supremacy, and the Western Public Lands," 1270–1271. The United States has also acquired several islands in the Pacific and the Caribbean, including Hawaii in 1898.

36. David Currie, "The Constitution in Congress: The Public Lands, 1827–1861," *University of Chicago Law Review* 70 (2003): 783–820, 817.

37. Richard Andrews, *Managing the Environment, Managing Ourselves* (New Haven: Yale University Press, 1999), 89–90.

38. Currie, "The Constitution in Congress," 812–814.

39. Paul Gates, *History of Public Land Law Development* (Washington, DC: Government Printing Office, 1968), 9; Raynor Wellington, *The Political and Sectional Influence of the Public Lands, 1828–1842* (Cambridge, MA: Riverside, 1914), 14–15.

40. Gates, *History of Public Land Law Development*, 9.

41. John Leshy, "Unraveling the Sagebrush Rebellion," *University of California-Davis Law Review* 14 (1980): 317–355, 322–323. See also Conable, "Equal Footing, County Supremacy, and the Western Public Lands" for useful background on the equal footing doctrine.

42. For example, *Grisar v. McDowell*, 73 U.S. 363 (1868).

43. 44 U.S. 212.

44. 44 U.S. 212, 223.

45. 44 U.S. 212, 222–223.

46. Similar reasoning supported Justice Taney's opinion in *Dred Scott v. Sandford* that Congress had no power to ban slavery in the territories. 60 U.S. 393 (1857), 447–448.

47. 44 U.S. 212, 224.

48. *Escanaba Co. v. Chicago*, 107 U.S. 678 (1882); *Coyle v. Oklahoma*, 221 U.S. 559 (1911).

49. Mark Graber, *Dred Scott and the Problem of Constitutional Evil* (Cambridge: Cambridge University Press, 2006), 3.

50. School lands were also a contentious issue in South Dakota, where the Forest Service was claiming management authority over these lands in the Black Hills

Forest Reserve to pursue its bark beetle eradication efforts. See letter from Gifford Pinchot to Commissioner of Schools and Public Lands dated November 10, 1906, in General Correspondence of the Forest Service 1905, RG 95, Box 3 (NA-CP).

51. 40 *Cong. Rec.* 1677 (January 29, 1906) (emphasis added).

52. 40 *Cong. Rec.* 1681 (January 29, 1906).

53. Op. Atty. Gen'l, May 31, 1905, in *Official Opinions of the Attorneys General of the United States*, vol. 25, 470–473.

54. "Philip Wells in the Forest Service Law Office," *Forest History Newsletter* 16 (April 1972): 23–29, 24.

55. "Address of the Program Committee," in *Proceedings of the Public Land Convention Held in Denver, Colorado, June 18, 19, 20, 1907*, compiled by Fred P. Johnson (Denver: Press of the Western Newspaper Union, 1907), 5.

56. "Address of the Program Committee," 6.

57. "Address of the Program Committee," 7–8.

58. Address by Sen. Teller, in "Address of the Program Committee," 47. The last point was a reference to the recently decided *Kansas v. Colorado*, 206 U.S. 46 (1907), a rare win for forces opposing federal irrigation projects but with little significance for forest conservation.

59. Address by T. J. Walsh, in "Address of the Program Committee," 59.

60. "Address of the Program Committee," 59.

61. "Address of the Program Committee," 64.

62. Address by Robert Bonynge, in "Address of the Program Committee," 78.

63. The first paragraph of Article IV, Section 3 reads "New States may be admitted by the Congress into this Union; but no new States shall be formed or erected within the Jurisdiction of any other State; nor any State be formed by the union of two or more States, or parts of States, without the Consent of the Legislatures or the States concerned as well as of the Congress."

64. "Address of the Program Committee," 79.

65. "Address of the Program Committee," 81.

66. Resolution 2, 3, in *Proceedings of the Public Land Convention Held in Denver, Colorado, June 18, 19, 20, 1907*, 9.

67. Resolution 5, in *Proceedings of the Public Land Convention Held in Denver, Colorado, June 18, 19, 20, 1907*, 9.

68. *Proceedings of a Conference of Governors in the White House, Washington D.C., May 13–15, 1908* (Washington, DC: Government Printing Office, 1909), 171.

69. *Proceedings of a Conference of Governors in the White House, Washington D.C., May 13–15*, 1908, 189.

70. "A Wrong System of Government," *Rocky Mountain News*, November 27, 1909.

71. Letter from Barnes to A. F. Potter, dated January 5, 1910, in General Correspondence of the Forest Service, 1905–1952, Box 135 (NA-CP).

72. 220 U.S. 506 (1911).

73. 220 U.S. 523 (1911).

74. McCarthy, *Hour of Trial*, 179–80.

75. 160 F. 870 (9th Cir. 1908).

76. 160 F. 870, 875.

77. Brief for appellant, *Light v. United States*, 3.

78. Interestingly, the brief also cites in support of his argument the House Committee on Judiciary, *Appalachian and White Mountain Forest Reserves Report* (January 1, 1908), discussed in chapter 6, which it reads as denying to the federal government a general power to *purchase* land for forest reserves.

79. Brief for appellant, *Light v. United States*, 33.

80. Brief for Appellee, *Light v. United States*, 25.

81. 26 F. Cas. 12 (D. Ill 1839), 13. *Gratiot* will be discussed in more detail in chapter 7.

82. Brief for Appellee, *Light v. United States*, 29.

83. 220 U.S. 523, 535–536.

84. 220 U.S. 523, 536–537.

85. 220 U.S. 523, 538.

86. We will discuss this principle further in chapter 9.

87. Logan Sawyer, "Grazing, Grimaud, and Gifford Pinchot: How the Forest Service Overcame the Classical Nondelegation Doctrine to Establish Administrative Crimes," *Journal of Law and Politics* 24 (Spring 2008): 169–208, 173–174.

88. *Wayman v. Southard*, 23 U.S. 1 (1825), 42–43.

89. 116 F. 654 (S.D. Cal.).

90. Letter from Acting Commissioner J. H. Pimple to Secretary of the Interior dated November 16, 1903, in Records Relating to Administration of Gifford Pinchot, RG 95, Box 5 (NA-CP).

91. 122 F. 30 (9th Cir.).

92. Sawyer, "Grazing, Grimaud, and Gifford Pinchot," 182.

93. Letter from Acting Commissioner J. H. Pimple to Secretary of the Interior dated November 16, 1903, in Records Relating to Administration of Gifford Pinchot, RG 95, Box 5 (NA-CP).

94. Sawyer, "Grazing, Grimaud, and Gifford Pinchot," 206–207.

95. 22 Op. of Attorney General 266.

96. 22 Op. of Attorney General 185n174. The reported cases are *United States v. Martinus*, No. 517 (D. Utah, Jan. 26, 1903) and *United States v. Blasingame. United States v. Camou* was decided on June 24, 1902, in the Northern District of California and is referenced in *United States v. Deguirro*, 152 F. 568 (N.D. Cal. 1906). Two more cases are referred to in *Annual Reports of the Department of the Interior for the Fiscal Year Ended June 30, 1903*, H.R. Doc. No. 5, at 324 (1903).

97. *Dent v. United States*, 76 P. 455 (Ariz. 1904), reh'g 71 P. 920 (Ariz. 1903).

98. Letter from Pinchot to Forest Officers and Rangers dated April 1905 and Letters between Pinchot and Charles Shinn, dated May 15 and May 29, 1905, in Records relating to Administration of Gifford Pinchot, RG 95, Box 5 (NA-CP).

99. Sawyer, "Grazing, Grimaud, and Gifford Pinchot," 193.

100. *United States v. Rizzinelli*, 182 F. 675 (D. Idaho 1910); *United States v. Domingo*, 152 F. 566 (D. Idaho 1907); *United States v. Bale*, 156 F. 687 (D.S.D. 1907).

101. 170 F. 205 (S.D. Calif. 1909), 207.

102. 220 U.S. 506, 515.

103. 220 U.S. 506, 515–516.

104. 220 U.S. 506, 515–516.

105. 220 U.S. 506, 515–516, emphasis added.

106. 220 U.S. 506, 521.

107. 220 U.S. 506, 521.

108. 276 U.S. 394, 409.

109. Sawyer, "Grazing, Grimaud, and Gifford Pinchot," 207.

110. Sawyer, "Grazing, Grimaud, and Gifford Pinchot," 200.

111. McCarthy, *Hour of Trial*, 197.

112. *McCulloch v. Maryland*, 17 U.S. 316 (1819).

Chapter 6. Eastern Forest Reserves

1. *The Fight for Conservation* (New York: Doubleday, Page, 1911), 42.

2. John Ise, *The United States Forest Policy* (New Haven, CT: Yale University Press, 1920); Richard Judd, *Common Lands, Common People* (Cambridge, MA: Harvard University Press, 1997), 91–105.

3. Sally Fairfax et al., *Buying Nature* (Cambridge, MA: MIT Press, 2005), 53.

4. Art. I, Sec. 8.

5. 117 U.S. 151 (1885), 153; see also *Chappelle v. United States*, 160 U.S. 499 (1895).

6. 160 U.S. 668, 682.

7. 35 Cong. Rec. 4710 (April 26, 1902).

8. 35 Cong. Rec. 4711 (April 26, 1902).

9. 35 Cong. Rec. 4713 (April 26, 1902).

10. *Gibbons v. Ogden*, 22 U.S. 1 (1824).

11. Samuel Hays, *Conservation and the Gospel of Efficiency* (Pittsburgh: University of Pittsburgh Press, 1959), 6–8; Donald Pisani, *To Reclaim a Divided West* (Albuquerque: University of New Mexico Press, 1992), 145.

12. Hays, *Conservation and the Gospel of Efficiency*, 8; Donald Pisani, *Water, Land, and Law in the West* (Lawrence: University Press of Kansas, 1996), 147.

13. Hays, *Conservation and the Gospel of Efficiency*, 10.

14. Paul Gates, *History of Public Land Law Development* (Washington, DC: Government Printing Office, 1968), 323.

15. For example, 26 Cong. Rec. 8432 (August 11, 1894) (remarks of Representative McRae).

16. 28 Cong. Rec. 5116–5118 (April 11, 1894); Pisani, *To Reclaim a Divided West*, 275.

17. Pisani, *To Reclaim a Divided West*, 278–279.

18. 174 U.S. 690 (1899).

19. 174 U.S. 690, 708.

20. 32 Cong. Rec. 2817 (March 3, 1899).

21. 32 Cong. Rec. 2270 (February 24, 1899) (emphasis added).

22. For example, the distinction is significant in *Kidd v. Pearson*, 128 U.S. 1 (1888).

23. 22 U.S. 189–190.

24. 32 Cong. Rec. 2269–2272 (February 24, 1899). Quotation on page 72.

25. 32 Cong. Rec. 2281 (February 24, 1899).

26. 174 U.S. 703.

27. Hays, *Conservation and the Gospel of Efficiency*, 22–26.

28. Pisani, *Water, Land, and Law in the West*, 147–148.

29. Theodore Roosevelt, "First Annual Message to Congress" [1901], in *The Works of Theodore Roosevelt*, vol. 21, ed. Hermann Hagedorn (New York: Charles Scribner's Sons, 1925), 121–122.

30. On the tension between Gifford Pinchot and Frank Newell, see Pisani, *To Reclaim a Divided West*, 334.

31. 35 Cong. Rec. 6671 (June 12, 1902).

32. 35 Cong. Rec. 6680 (June 12, 1902).

33. House Committee on Irrigation of Arid Lands, *Views of the Minority* (House Rep. 794) (March 8, 1902), 4, 7.

34. 35 Cong. Rec. 6680 (June 12, 1902).

35. 35 Cong. Rec. 6676 (June 12, 1902).

36. 206 U.S. 46.

37. Under Article III, Section 2 of the Constitution, the Supreme Court has original jurisdiction in cases in which a State is a party.

38. Pisani, *Water, Land, and Law in the West*, 40–49; James Sherow, *Watering the Valley* (Lawrence: University Press of Kansas, 1990), 108–117.

39. 206 U.S. 87–94. A federal court in 1912 would also uphold the secretary's use of eminent domain in pursuit of reclamation projects. *United States v. O'Neill*, 198 F. 677 (D. Colo. 1912).

40. Hays, *Conservation and the Gospel of Efficiency*, 119–120.

41. Philip Wells, "Philip P. Wells in the Forest Service Law Office," *Forest History* 16 (April 1972): 23–29, 28.

42. House Committee on Judiciary, *Appalachian and White Mountain Forest*

Reserves Report (January 1, 1908), 2, quoting *McCulloch v. Maryland*, 17 U.S. 316 (1819), 421.

43. *Report on Appalachian and White Mountain Forest Reserve*, 3.

44. *Report on Appalachian and White Mountain Forest Reserve*, 4.

45. *Report on Appalachian and White Mountain Forest Reserve*, 6, quoting *Rio Grande Irrigation Co.*, 174 U.S. 703.

46. *Report on Appalachian and White Mountain Forest Reserve*, 7, quoting *Rio Grande Irrigation Co.*, 174 U.S. 703.

47. *Report on Appalachian and White Mountain Forest Reserve*, 7–8, citing *Kansas*, 206 U.S. 86.

48. 91 U.S. 367 (1875).

49. *Report on Appalachian and White Mountain Forest Reserve*, 8–13.

50. *Report on Appalachian and White Mountain Forest Reserve*, 14–17.

51. 41 U.S. 367 (1842).

52. 44 U.S. 212 (1845).

53. Remarks are printed in 45 *Cong Rec.* 8997–9000 (June 24, 1910).

54. 42 Cong. Rec. 6385 (May 16, 1908); 43 Cong. Rec. 3528 (March 1, 1909); Ise, *United States Forest Policy*, 214.

55. Gordon B. Dodds, "The Stream-Flow Controversy: A Conservation Turning Point," *Journal of American History* 56 (June 1969): 59–69.

56. Hiram Chittenden, "Forests and Reservoirs in their Relation to Streamflow," *American Society of Civil Engineers Transactions* 62 (1909): 245–546, 245.

57. Chittenden, "Forests and Reservoirs in their Relation to Streamflow," 247, 251, 267, 270.

58. Chittenden, "Forests and Reservoirs in their Relation to Streamflow," 316–317.

59. Dodds, "The Stream-Flow Controversy," 64–65.

60. 35 Cong. Rec. 7286, 7287 (June 24, 1902).

61. 45 Cong. Rec. 8996–8997 (June 24, 1910).

62. 250 F. 499 (W.D. Va. 1917).

63. 250 F. 499, 502.

64. Fairfax et al., *Buying Nature*, 64, 76, 81–83.

65. Fairfax et al., *Buying Nature*, 67; 42 Cong. Rec. 5458 (April 30, 1908).

66. 16 U.S.C. secs. 721–731.

67. Fairfax et al., *Buying Nature*, 92.

68. 31 F.2d 617 (W.D. Wis.).

69. 252 U.S. 416 (1920).

70. 214 F. 154 (E.D. Ark. 1914).

71. 221 F. 288 (D. Kan. 1915).

72. 31 F.2d 617, 622.

73. 31 F.2d 617, 621.

74. 31 F.2d 617, 622.

75. Dodds, "The Stream-Flow Controversy," 66–67.

76. 43 Stat. 653 (1924).

77. Senate Select Committee on Reforestation, *Hearings pursuant to S. Res. 398 to Investigate Problems Related to Reforestation* (November 19, 1923), 1288–1292.

78. 65 Cong. Rec. 6985–6986 (April 23, 1924).

79. *United States v. Butler*, 297 U.S. 1 (1936). In 1938, the Ninth Circuit would reject a challenge to the constitutionality of Forest Service taking land not located in the headwaters of a navigable stream. *Coggeshall v. United States*, 95 F.2d 986 (9th Cir. 1938)

80. 28 F.Supp. 758 (W.D. N.Y.).

81. 40 U.S.C sec. 402.

82. 28 F.Supp. 758, 763.

83. 28 F.Supp. 758, 764.

84. 28 F.Supp. 758, 764.

85. Fairfax et al., *Buying Nature*, 118.

86. Fairfax et al., *Buying Nature*, 139.

87. *Hammer v. Dagenhart*, 274 U.S. 251 (1918). That decision would be overturned by *United States v. Darby Lumber*, 312 U.S. 100 (1941).

88. William Greeley, *Forests and Men* (Garden City, NY: Doubleday, 1951), 103–105.

89. 297 U.S. 288 (1936).

90. *United States v. Butler*.

91. *Carter v. Carter Coal Company*, 298 U.S. 238 (1936).

92. 297 U.S. 328.

93. 220 U.S. 523 (1911).

94. 297 U.S. 330–336.

95. Congress, getting the message, immediately replaced the Agricultural Adjustment Act with the Soil Conservation and Domestic Allotment Act, beginning the nation's long-standing practice of using soil conservation programs to limit agricultural production. 49 Stat. 1148 (1936).

96. Knapp, "The Other Side of Conservation," in *Conservation in the Progressive Era*, ed. David Stradling (Seattle: University of Washington Press, 2004), 36.

Chapter 7. Managing Federal Lands

1. Attorney General Knox's reply to Lacey, dated January 3, 1902, is reprinted in 35 Cong. Rec. 6517–6519 (June 9, 1902). It was reprinted also as "Correspondence in Relation to the Powers of Congress in Relation to Forest Reserves Situated in the Various States," H.Doc. 321 (January 29, 1902) (hereinafter "Powers of Congress in Relation to Forest Reserves").

2. 278 U.S. 96.

3. Daniel Carpenter, *The Forging of Bureaucratic Autonomy* (Princeton: Princeton University Press, 2001). See chapter 1 for further discussion of Carpenter's argument.

4. 34 Stat. 536 (1906).

5. An Act to Protect the Birds and Animals in Yellowstone National Park, etc., 28 Stat. 73 (1894).

6. 39 Stat. 535 (1916). Secretary of Interior Lane, in his 1918 letter to NPS Director Mather, confirmed that "hunting will not be permitted in any national park." *America's National Park System: Critical Documents*, ed. Lary Dilsaver (Lanham, MD: Rowman & Littlefield, 1994), 50.

7. Powers of Congress in Relation to Forest Reserves, 1.

8. 23 Att'y Gen Op. 589–594 (November 29, 1901).

9. 30 Stat. 11 (1897).

10. 23 Att'y Gen Op. 591.

11. He considered but rejected Justice Taney's suggestion, in *Dred Scott v. Sandford*, 60 U.S. 393 (1857), that this clause applied only to the Northwest Territory.

12. 39 U.S. 526.

13. Powers of Congress in Relation to Forest Reserves, 4.

14. 114 U.S. 525.

15. 114 U.S. 525, 539.

16. 167 U.S. 518 (1897).

17. 167 U.S. 518, 525–526 (1897).

18. For example, *Gibson v. Chouteau*, 80 U.S. 92 (1871) and *Jourdan v. Barrett*, 45 U.S. 169 (1846). Both cases rejected claims that the parties acquired a prescriptive right (under state law) to federal public lands. See discussion below.

19. Powers of Congress in Relation to Forest Reserves, 9.

20. 39 U.S. 533.

21. 39 U.S. 533, 537.

22. 39 U.S. 533, 537.

23. 45 U.S. 169 (1846).

24. 80 U.S. 92 (1871).

25. 80 U.S. 92, 99.

26. 80 U.S. 92, 99.

27. 117 U.S. 151.

28. 114 U.S. 542.

29. 114 U.S. 542, 546.

30. See also *Omaechevarri v. Idaho*, 246 U.S. 343 (1917). The police power of the State extends over the federal public domain, at least when there is no legislation by Congress on the subject.

31. 146 U.S. 325.

32. 146 U.S. 325, 331. Cf. *Palmer v. Barrett*, 162 U.S. 399 (1896). The Court allowed the state of New York to exercise jurisdiction over land that was adjacent to a naval base but being used as a city market. In that case, however, New York had expressly reserved jurisdiction if the land in question was not being used for military purposes.

33. See, for example, 35 Cong. Rec. 6510–6514 (June 9, 1902); 41 Cong. Rec. 168 (December 7, 1906); House Committee on Public Lands, *Protection of Game and Fish in Forest Reserves*, H. Rpt. 3528 (January 12, 1905).

34. House Committee on Public Lands, *Protection of Game, etc. in the Forest Reserves of the United States*, H. Rpt. 3862, 1, 3 (February 25, 1903).

35. House Committee on Public Lands, *Protection of Game, etc. in the Forest Reserves of the United States*, H. Rpt. 3862, 1 (February 25, 1903).

36. 161 U.S. 519 (1895).

37. 163 U.S. 504 (1896).

38. See, for example, House Committee on Public Lands, *Protection of Game and Fish in Forest Reserves*, H. Rpt. 3528 (January 12, 1905); House Committee on Public Lands, *Protection of Game, Etc., in the Forest Reserves in California*, H. Rpt. 4907 (June 9, 1906).

39. House Subcommittee of the Committee on Agriculture, *Hearings on Game Refuges* (June 17, 1916) (hereinafter House *Hearings on Game Refuges*).

40. In fact, Williams would serve as solicitor to the Forest Service from 1920 to 1930, and in that role he would continue to influence debate over the hunting question, as we will see.

41. House *Hearings on Game Refuges*, 8.

42. 163 U.S. 504, 514.

43. 198 U.S. 371.

44. On the continuing vitality of *Ward*, see David Wilkins, "Indian Treaty Rights: Sacred Entitlements or 'Temporary Privileges'?" *American Indian Culture and Research Journal* 20 (1996): 87–129.

45. The bill (H.R. 4444) passed the House but died in the Senate. David Wilkins, *American Indian Sovereignty and the U.S. Supreme Court* (Austin: University of Texas Press, 1997), 96.

46. On appeal from 214 F. 154 (E.D. Ark. 1914).

47. House *Hearings on Game Refuges*, 18.

48. House *Hearings on Game Refuges*, 20.

49. House *Hearings on Game Refuges*, 19, 28.

50. 220 U.S. 523 (1911).

51. 236 U.S. 459.

52. 236 U.S. 459, 474.

53. 220 U.S. 506 (1911).

54. House *Hearings on Game Refuges*, 8.

55. Williams, interestingly, raised the question of whether a state could (outside of the Enclave Clause procedures) cede authority over game. He cited a recent decision, *State v. Towessnutte*, 154 P. 805 (Wash. 1916), holding that federal treaty rights did not supercede state fishing laws. His point seemed to be that state cession was not the source of federal government's power to ban hunting in national parks. That was a weak argument, however, and he wisely did not press it. *Fort Leavenworth* and numerous other precedents clearly supported state authority to cede as much or as little jurisdiction as necessary to achieve federal ends.

56. The Wichita Mountains Wildlife Refuge was set aside from the Comanche-Kiowa-Apache Indian Reservation as a National Forest in 1901 and administered by the US Forest Service. Much of the original reservation was opened to homesteaders in 1900, in violation of the 1867 federal treaty with the tribes. That action was upheld in *Lone Wolf v. Hitchcock*, 187 U.S. 553 (1903). Assistant Attorney General Willis Van Devanter represented the federal government and Justice White wrote the opinion in the case. See Wilkins, *American Indian Sovereignty*, 105–117.

57. House *Hearings on Game Refuges*, 46–47.

58. House *Hearings on Game Refuges*, 48.

59. House *Hearings on Game Refuges*, 27.

60. 243 U.S. 389.

61. 243 U.S. 389, 404.

62. 243 U.S. 389, 404.

63. 252 U.S. 416 (1920).

64. Richard Andrews, *Managing the Environment, Managing Ourselves* (New Haven, CT: Yale University Press, 1999), 148–152.

65. 43 Stat. 650.

66. 45 Stat. 1222.

67. Game Sanctuary Act, 48 Stat. 400 (March 10, 1934); Duck Stamp Act, 48 Stat. 452 (March 16, 1934); An Act to Promote Conservation of Wild Life, Fish, and Game and Other Purposes (48 Stat. 401, March 10, 1934). The Soil Conservation Service and Civilian Conservation Corps would also be involved in wildlife conservation. Andrews, *Managing the Environment, Managing Ourselves*, 173–174; Sally Fairfax et al., *Buying Nature* (Cambridge, MA: MIT Press, 2005), 92–94.

68. 114 F.2d 207 (4th Cir. 1940).

69. For example, Alfred Kneipp, Memorandum to District Forester, February 6, 1915, in General Correspondence of the Forest Service, 1905–1952, RG 95, Box 77 (NA-CP); William Greeley, Address to the American Game Protective Association, December 9, 1924, in General Correspondence of the Forest Service, 1905–1952, RG 95, Box 141 (NA-CP). Curt Meine discussed the evolution of the Forest Service's wildlife management strategy in *Aldo Leopold: His Life and Work* (Madison: University of Wisconsin Press, 1988), 144–174.

70. Christian Young, *In the Absence of Predators* (Lincoln: University of Nebraska Press, 2002), 35.

71. Thomas Dunlap, *Saving America's Wildlife* (Princeton: Princeton University Press, 1988), 35–43; Young, *In the Absence of Predators*, 39–60, 82–96.

72. David Brown, *Bringing Back the Game* (Phoenix: Arizona Game and Fish Dept., 2012), 82–83.

73. Young, *In the Absence of Predators*, 21, 39–46; Brown, *Bringing Back the Game*, 84–88.

74. Letter from Stephen Mather to Edward Nelson, October 28, 1923; Field Assistant Horace Albright to Acting Park Service Director A. E. Demaray, October 31, 1923, in General Correspondence of the Forest Service, RG 95, Box 60 (MA-CP).

75. Young, *In the Absence of Predators*, 46–48, 96–97; Brown, *Bringing Back the Game*, 89–91.

76. E. W. Nelson, Memorandum on the Grand Canyon National Game Preserve and Methods of Utilizing its Surplus Deer (September 4, 1923) (KNF).

77. Nelson, Memorandum on the Grand Canyon National Game Preserve and Methods of Utilizing its Surplus Deer. Nelson also cited an opinion from the assistant attorney general of Minnesota on this point.

78. Young, *In the Absence of Predators*, 61–64; Brown, *Bringing Back the Game*, 91.

79. Young, *In the Absence of Predators*, 65.

80. Letter from Will Barnes to R. H. Rutledge, March 26, 1924 (KNF).

81. Young, *In the Absence of Predators*, 64–65, 70–75, 97.

82. Letter from Will Barnes to R. H. Rutledge, November 26, 1924; Forest Service Director W. Greeley to R. H. Rutledge, November 12, 1924; Letter from Will Barnes to Phoenix Republican, November 28, 1924 (KNF).

83. *United States v. Hunt*, 19 F.2d 634 (N.D. Ariz. 1927); "Hunt to Fight Men Seeking Control of Kaibab Deer," *Arizona Cattleman and Farmer*, November 24, 1925. See also James Foster, "The Deer of Kaibab," *Arizona and the West* 12 (Autumn 1970): 255–268, 259; Young, *In the Absence of Predators*, 96–98; Brown, *Bringing Back the Game*, 92–98.

84. Reply Brief of Plaintiffs, *United States v. Hunt*, 19 F.2d 634 (N.D. Ariz. 1927), 12.

85. Reply Brief of Plaintiffs, *United States v. Hunt*, 8–11.

86. 19 F.2d 634, 635.

87. Even in *Barrett v. State of New York*, 220 N.Y. 423 (1917), the property owner complained that the beavers in question impaired the commercial value of his land by destroying trees that contributed to the attractiveness of his property.

88. Reply Brief of Plaintiffs, *United States v. Hunt*, 9–10.

89. 19 F.2d 634, 640–641.

90. 19 F.2d 634, 641. The court relied on *Missouri v. Holland* for jurisdiction: "The protection of a quasi sovereign right of the state to regulate the taking of game is a sufficient jurisdictional basis, apart from any pecuniary interest it might have, for a bill by a state to enjoin enforcement of federal regulations over the subject alleged to be unconstitutional."

91. Scholars have noted that judicial review of federal agency actions during this period was generally "anemic." See, for example, Jerry Mashaw, *Creating the Administrative Constitution* (New Haven, CT: Yale University Press, 2012), 245–250. But most of the scholarship on this subject deals with agency actions that affect private rights rather than conflicts between state and federal regulatory agencies, where state sovereignty arguably weighs against deference to federal agents.

92. Young, *In the Absence of Predators*, 61–65, 82–96.

93. 19 F.2d 634, 641.

94. Young, *In the Absence of Predators*, 64.

95. Letter from Will Barnes to W. Greeley, July 5, 1927 (KNF).

96. Memorandum by Solicitor General in re *U.S. v. Hunt*, July 30, 1927 (KNF).

97. Brief for Appellees, *United States v. Hunt*, 278 U.S. 96 (1928), 13–14.

98. 260 U.S. 353.

99. 274 U.S. 264 (1927).

100. Brief for Appellees, *United States v. Hunt*, 16.

101. Arizona also insisted that an injunction was improper; the federal government should have waited until the hunters were actually arrested. Brief for Appellants, *United States v. Hunt*, 17–32.

102. 221 Fed. 288 (D. Kan. 1915).

103. Brief for Appellants, *United States v. Hunt*, 45–46.

104. Brief for Appellants, *United States v. Hunt*, 46–47.

105. 114 Wash. 370, 379, quoting 2 Cyc. 415. The court distinguished the apparently contrary holding in *Barrett v. State of New York* on the grounds that *Barrett* was a civil case, merely holding that the state wasn't liable for damages caused by the beavers in question. It didn't address whether Barrett could kill the beavers to protect his property.

106. Brief for Appellants, *United States v. Hunt*, 49.

107. Brief for Appellants, *United States v. Hunt*, 52.

108. The reasonableness of the property owner's belief is usually treated as a matter of fact, and therefore as a matter on which appellate courts would ordinarily defer to the trial court. See *State v. Ward*, 170 Iowa 185 (1915).

109. 278 U.S. 96, 100. The court did modify the injunction, requiring that the deer must be tagged before being taken out of the reserves, to show that they were killed under federal authority.

110. 278 U.S. 96, 99.

111. Foster, "The Deer of Kaibab," 262–263.

112. Seth Thomas, Memorandum regarding Federal Control of Fish and Game in National Forests, September 12, 1933 (KNF). As noted above, Knox's opinion is actually dated January 3, 1902.

113. Thomas, Memorandum regarding Federal Control of Fish and Game in National Forests.

114. Act to Establish Fish and Game Sanctuaries in National Forests, 48 Stat. 400 (March 10, 1934).

115. Addendum to Memorandum regarding Federal Control of Fish and Game in National Forests, September 12, 1933 (undated) (KNF).

116. This history is recounted in House Select Committee on the Conservation of Wildlife Resources, *Hearings before the House Select Committee on the Conservation of Wildlife Resources* (March 19, 1940), 5–9.

117. It was also removing deer and shipping them elsewhere, a practice that also angered North Carolinian hunters.

118. Weeks Act, 36 Stat. 961 (1911); Amendment, 39 Stat. 446 (1916). See 53 Cong. Rec. 10327 (July 1, 1916).

119. 114 F.2d 207, 210–211.

120. 114 F.2d 207, 210. More precisely, the appellate court declined to overturn the trial court's evaluation of the evidence on that point.

121. 312 U.S. 679 (1941).

122. House Select Committee on the Conservation of Wildlife Resources, *Hearings before the House Select Committee on the Conservation of Wildlife Resources* (March 19–20, 1940).

123. House Select Committee on the Conservation of Wildlife Resources, *Hearings before the House Select Committee on the Conservation of Wildlife Resources* (March 19–20, 1940), 1–5.

124. House Select Committee on the Conservation of Wildlife Resources, *Hearings before the House Select Committee on the Conservation of Wildlife Resources* (November 15, 16, 28, and December 9, 1941), 42–44 (remarks of H. L. Shantz, chief of the Wild Life Division of the US Forest Service).

125. See, for example, Martin Nie et al., "Fish and Wildlife Management on Federal Lands: Debunking State Supremacy," *Environmental Law* 47 (Fall 2017): 797–932.

126. Bruce Ackerman, *We the People*, vol. 1 (Cambridge, MA: Belknap, 1991), 59.

Chapter 8. State and Local Pollution Control

1. Robert Gottlieb, *Forcing the Spring* (Washington, DC: Island, 1993), 47–80; Richard Andrews, *Managing the Environment, Managing Ourselves* (New Haven, CT: Yale University Press, 1999), 109–135.

2. Gottlieb, *Forcing the Spring*, 52.

3. Gottlieb, *Forcing the Spring*, 55–56.

4. John Duffy, *The Sanitarians* (Urbana: University of Illinois Press, 1990), 20–33, 42–43, 102–103.

5. Gottlieb, *Forcing the Spring*, 56; Duffy, *The Sanitarians*, 126–127.

6. Martin Melosi, *Garbage in the Cities, Rev. Ed.* (Pittsburgh: University of Pittsburgh Press, 2005), 70–71.

7. Peter Bruton, *The National Board of Health* (University of Maryland, 1978), 6, 34–35, 50–51.

8. Bruton, *The National Board of Health*, 20–22.

9. Bruton, *The National Board of Health*, 7–12.

10. Melosi, *Garbage in the Cities*, 90–91; Duffy, *The Sanitarians*, 120–121, 138–154.

11. Duffy, *The Sanitarians*, 193; Andrews, *Managing the Environment*, 122–126.

12. Melosi, *Garbage in the Cities*, 74.

13. Melosi, *Garbage in the Cities*, 87.

14. Melosi, *Garbage in the Cities*, 93.

15. Melosi, *Garbage in the Cities*, 93.

16. Gottlieb, *Forcing the Spring*, 60.

17. 198 U.S. 45 (1905).

18. 208 U.S. 412 (1908).

19. Julie Novkov, *Constituting Workers, Protecting Women* (Ann Arbor: University of Michigan Press, 2001). I am also setting aside the movement to improve consumer product safety. This movement did result in federal legislation: The Pure Food and Drug Act and the Meat Inspection Act, both enacted in 1906. Significantly, both acts were projects supported by Harvey Washington Wiley, the head of the Bureau of Chemistry in the USDA. Wiley ended up administering the Pure Food and Drug Act, and the Meat Inspection Act was administered by the Bureau of Animal Industry in the USDA. Daniel Carpenter, *The Forging of Bureaucratic Autonomy* (Princeton: Princeton University Press, 2001), 257–270.

20. Joel Tarr, James McCurley, and Terry Yosie, "The Development and Impact of Urban Wastewater Technology," in *Pollution and Reform in American Cities, 1870–1930*, ed. Martin Melosi (Austin: University of Texas Press, 1980), 72.

21. William Andreen, "The Evolution of Water Pollution Control in the United States, Part I," *Stanford Law Review* 22 (2003): 145–201, 170–171, 182, 185 (Pennsylvania acted in 1923, Ohio and Connecticut in 1925).

22. Morton Horwitz, *The Transformation of American Law, 1780–1860* (Cambridge, MA: Harvard University Press, 1977), 74–78; William Novak, *The People's Welfare* (Chapel Hill: University of North Carolina Press, 1996).

23. On the evolution of the law of nuisance during the nineteenth century, see Horwitz, *The Transformation of American Law*, 74–78; Noga Morag-Levine, *Chasing the Wind* (Princeton: Princeton University Press, 2003), 40–47.

24. 22 U.S. 1, 203 (1824).

25. *Metcalf v. St. Louis*, 11 Mo. 102 (1847) (upholding quarantine); *People v. Corporation*, 11 Wend. 539 (N.Y. 1834) (defendants required to remove obstruction in Erie Canal as danger to public health); *Baker v. Boston*, 29 Mass. 184 (1831) (city could fill plaintiff's creek without compensation where it had become a health hazard); *Coates v. Aldermen etc. of New York*, 7 Cow. 585 (N.Y. 1827) (city's prohibition on interring dead bodies overrode church's charter right to operate cemetery); *Green v. Savannah*, 6 Ga. 1 (1849) (city may prohibit rice growing to protect public health.)

26. John Duffy, *A History of Public Health in New York City* (New York: Russell Sage, 1968), 540–570.

27. *Hoffman v. Schultz*, 31 How. Pr. 385 (N.Y. 1866), 397.

28. 31 How. Pr. 385, 397.

29. On horse stables as nuisances, see Clay McShane and Joel Tarr, *The Horse in the City* (Baltimore, MD: Johns Hopkins University Press, 2007), 120–125.

30. *Brady v. Weeks*, 3 Barb. 157 (N.Y.App.Div. 1848).

31. *Cooper v. Schultz*, 32 How. Pr. 107 (N.Y. Ct. of Common Pleas 1866), 121.

32. 32 How. Pr. 107, 125–127.

33. *Schuster v. Metropolitan Board of Health*, 49 Barb. 450 (N.Y.App.Div. 1867), 452.

34. 37 N.Y. 661 (1869), 688.

35. 83 U.S. 36.

36. 83 U.S. 36, 63.

37. 6 F.Cas. 546 (1823).

38. 6 F.Cas. 546, 551–552 (emphasis added).

39. Justices Field, Bradley, and Swayne wrote dissents. Field and Bradley explicitly confirmed the state's public health authority, and Swayne concurred in their arguments. 83 U.S. 87, 120, 128.

40. 1 MacArth. 433 (D.C. Sup. Ct., 1874) (italics in original), 447.

41. 1 MacArth. 433, 451.

42. *Crowley v. West*, 25 La.Ann. 526 (1900); *Elkhart v. Lispchitz*, 164 Ind. 671 (1905). Several states in the nineteenth century adopted "Dillon's Rule," under which cities have only the powers expressly delegated to them by the legislature or necessary to carry out their express powers. Most states now follow that rule.

43. 45 Ill. 90 (1867).

44. 78 Ill. 405 (1875).

45. See *Taunton v. Taylor*, 116 Mass. 254 (1874); *Fertilizing Co. v. Hyde Park*, 97 U.S. 659 (1878).

46. 71 Mo. 91 (1882).

47. 71 Mo. 91, 100.

48. 282 Mo. 1 (1920).

49. *In Re Lowe*, 54 Kan. 757 (1895); *Landberg v. Chicago*, 237 Ill. 122 (1908); *Stadler v. Cleveland*, 22 Ohio Dec. 783 (Ct. of Common Pleas, 1911).

50. 100 Me. 180 (1905), 193. See also *In re Zhizhuzza*, 147 Cal. 328 (1905); *Gardner v. Michigan*, 199 U.S. 325 (1905).

51. *California Reduction Co. v. Sanitary Reduction Works*, 199 U.S. 306 (1905), 323.

52. 40 N.Y. 273 (1869).

53. *Commonwealth v. Roberts*, 155 Mass. 281 (1892); *Kelley v. Mayor*, 6 Misc. 516 (N.Y. 1894); *Harrington v. Board of Aldermen*, 20 R.I. 233 (1897); *Sprigg v. Garret Park*, 89 Md. 406 (1899); *Cartwright v. Board of Health*, 39 A.D. 69 (N.Y. 1899); *Van Wagoner v. Mayor and Aldermen of Paterson*, 67 N.J.L. 455 (1902); *Tenement House Dep't v. Moeschen*, 89 A.D. 526 (N.Y. 1904); *Commonwealth v. Emmers*, 33 Pa.Super. 151 (1907); *Allman v. Mobile*, 162 Ala. 226 (1909); *Lower Merion Twp. v. Becker*, 42 Pa.Super 203 (1910); *Treasy v. Louisville*, 137 Ky. 289 (1910); *People v. Hupp*, 53 Colo. 80 (1912); *Hutchinson v. Valdosta*, 227 U.S. 303 (1913); *Attorney General ex rel. Emmons v. Grand Rapids*, 175 Mich. 503 (1913).

54. Morag-Levine, *Chasing the Wind*, 103–112; David Stradling, *Smokestacks and Progressives* (Baltimore, MD: Johns Hopkins University Press, 1999), 37–60.

55. Gottlieb, *Forcing the Spring*, 57.

56. Arnold Reitz, *Air Pollution Control Law: Compliance and Enforcement* (Environmental Law Institute 2001), 10.

57. 141 Mo. 375 (1897); Morag-Levine, *Chasing the Wind*, 113–115; Stradling, *Smokestacks and Progressives*, 64–71.

58. Morag-Levine, *Chasing the Wind*, 113, citing *Pennsylvania v. Standard Ice Co.*, 59 Pgh. L. J. 101 (1911).

59. Eugene McQuillin, "Abatement of the Smoke Nuisance in Large Cities," *Central Law Journal* 46 (1898): 147–153, 150.

60. Stradling, *Smokestacks and Progressives*, 45–52; Morag-Levine, *Chasing the Wind*, 110–111.

61. *Northwestern Laundry v. Des Moines*, 239 U.S. 486 (1915), 491–492.

62. 239 U.S. 486, 496.

63. Morag-Levine, *Chasing the Wind*, 114–115.

64. McQuillin, "Nuisance Per Se," 345. McQuillin was a leading authority on the law of municipal government and the author of *A Treatise on the Law of Municipal Corporations* (Chicago: Callaghan, 1911).

65. McQuillin, "Nuisance Per Se," 346, citing *State ex rel. McCue v. Sheriff of Ramsey County*, 48 Minn. 236 (1892), which struck down a smoke ordinance that excepted small manufacturers.

66. Stradling, *Smokestacks and Progressives*, 71.

67. Richard Chused, "Euclid's Historical Imagery," *Case Western Reserve Law Review* 51 (Summer 2001): 597–616, 601.

68. Michael Wolf, *The Zoning of America* (Lawrence: University Press of Kansas, 2008), 24–28; Raphael Fischler, "The Metropolitan Dimension of Early Zoning," *Journal of the American Planning Assoc.* 64 (Spring 1998): 170–188.

69. Chused, "Euclid's Historical Imagery," 598; Wolf, *The Zoning of America*, 29; Wayne Batchis, "Suburbanization and Constitutional Interpretation: Exclusionary Zoning and the Supreme Court Legacy of Enabling Sprawl," *Stanford Journal of Civil Rights & Civil Liberties* 8 (2012): 1–44, 8–9.

70. Batchis, "Suburbanization and Constitutional Interpretation: Exclusionary Zoning and the Supreme Court Legacy of Enabling Sprawl," 9.

71. There is a large and rich literature on *Euclid*, including Batchis, "Suburbanization and Constitutional Interpretation: Exclusionary Zoning and the Supreme Court Legacy of Enabling Sprawl"; Chused, "Euclid's Historical Imagery"; Eric Claeys, "Euclid Lives?" *Fordham Law Review* 73 (2004): 731–770; Charles Haar and Michael Wolf, "Euclid Lives," *Harvard Law Review* 115 (2002): 2158–2203; William A. Fischel, "An Economic History of Zoning and a Cure for Its Exclusionary Effects," *Urban Studies* 41 (2004): 317–340; *Zoning and the American Dream*, ed. Charles Haar and Jerold Kayden (Chicago: Planners, 1989).

72. Claeys, "Euclid Lives?" 744–751. Claeys offers a good summary of the policy arguments for zoning offered by urban planning advocates.

73. I identified well over eighty cases concerning zoning and building height restrictions (not including the *Slaughterhouse Cases*). But this doesn't cover the entire body of relevant case law. There is a whole line of doctrine concerning restrictive covenants—a clause in a deed or rental agreement restricting how the property may be used. Unlike most contract provisions, restrictive covenants are said to "run with the land," meaning that subsequent purchasers must abide by the restriction. They were therefore a private law alternative to municipal land use regulation. For a good summary of judicial treatment of restrictive covenants during this period, see Gerald Korngold, "The Emergence of Private Land Use Controls in Large-scale Subdivisions," *Case Western Reserve Law Review* 51 (2001): 617–643.

74. "Introductory Address on City Planning, in Proceedings of the Second National Conference on City Planning and Congestion of Population" (Rochester, New York, May 2, 1910), 14. For additional examples, see Claeys, "Euclid Lives?" 750–757; Mark Fenster, "A Remedy on Paper," *Yale Law Journal* 107 (1998): 1093–1123.

75. 174 Mass. 476.

76. 174 Mass. 476, 478.

77. 123 Mass. 372 (1877).

78. 136 Mass. 239 (1884).

79. 188 Mass. 348.

80. 188 Mass. 348, 351.

81. 193 Mass. 364.

82. 193 Mass. 364, 373.

83. *Welch v. Swasey*, 214 U.S. 91 (1909), 107–108.

84. *In re Opinion of the Justices*, 234 Mass. 597 (1920).

85. 250 Mass. 52 (1924). See also *Spector v. Milton*, 250 Mass. 63 (1924).

86. 250 Mass. 73 (1924).

87. 250 Mass. 73, 78.

88. 250 Mass. 73, 78.

89. 136 La. 480.

90. See also *State ex rel. Blaise v. New Orleans*, 142 La. 73 (1917).

91. 154 La. 271 (1923).

92. 154 La. 271, 282–283.

93. 154 La. 271, 284.

94. 134 Minn. 226.

95. See also *Roerig v. Minneapolis*, 136 Minn. 479 (1917).

96. *Twin City Co. v. Houghton*, 144 Minn. 1 (1920).

97. 144 Minn. 1, 19.

98. 144 Minn. 1, 20.

99. 164 Minn. 146 (1925).

100. 164 Minn. 146, 150.

101. 164 Minn. 146, 150.

102. *Handy v. South Orange*, 118 Atl. 838 (N.J. 1922).

103. 97 N.J.L. 390. See also *Max v. Saul*, 3 N.J. Misc. 265 (1925).

104. 98 N.J.L. 712 (1923); *State v. Nutley*, 99 N.J.L. 389 (1924); *Losick v. Binda*, 128 Atl. 619 (NJ 1925); *Nelson Bldg. Co. v. Binda*, 3 N.J. Misc. 420 (1925); *Ingersoll v. South Orange*, 2 N.J. Misc. 882 (1924); *Plymouth v. Bigelow*, 2 N.J. Misc. 711 (1924); *Prince v. Board of Adjustment*, 3 N.J. Misc. 547 (1925). New Jersey courts did not accept zoning until the state's constitution was amended to allow it in 1927. See *Lumund v. Board of Adjustment*, 4 N.J. 577 (1950), 585. Zoning remained controversial, however, as evidenced by the Mt. Laurel decisions: *S. Burlington County NAACP v. Mt. Laurel*, 67 N.J. 151 (1975); *S. Burlington County NAACP v. Mt. Laurel*, 92 N.J. 158 (1983); *Hills Dev. Co. v. Bernards*, 103 N.J. 1 (1986).

105. 241 N.Y. 288.

106. 241 N.Y. 288, 299.

107. 241 N.Y. 288, 299.

108. 272 U.S. 365.

109. *Ambler Realty Co. v. Euclid*, 297 F. 307 (N.D. Ohio 1924).

110. Hylton, "Prelude to Euclid," *Washington University Journal of Law and Policy* 3 (2000): 1–37, 34, citing *L'Hote v. New Orleans*, 177 U.S. 587 (1900) (restricting prostitution), *Dobbins v. City of L.A.*, 195 U.S. 223 (1904) (holding that regulation was valid but might be unconstitutional as applied); *Fischer v. St. Louis*, 194 U.S. 361 (1904); *Laurel Hill Cemetery v. San Francisco*, 216 U.S. 358 (1910).

111. 226 U.S. 137.

112. 242 U.S. 526 (1917).

113. *Yick Wo v. Hopkins*, 118 U.S. 356 (1886); *Buchanan v. Warley*, 245 U.S. 60 (1917). *Buchanan* concerned a restrictive covenant rather than a land use regulation, but the covenant would have created a racially segregated neighborhood.

114. Appellee's Brief, *Euclid v. Amber Realty.*

115. 272 U.S. 365, 386–387.

116. 272 U.S. 365, 387.

117. 272 U.S. 365, 394.

118. Garrett Power, "Advocates at Cross-Purposes," *Journal of Supreme Court History* 2 (1997): 79–87; Chused, "Euclid's Historical Imagery," 609–610; Arthur Brooks, "The Office File Box—Emanations from the Battlefield," in *Zoning and the American Dream*, ed. Charles Haar and Jerold Kayden (Chicago: Planners, 1989), 3–30.

119. 272 U.S. 365, 394. Chused offers a good analysis of the racial dimension of this argument.

120. 277 U.S. 183 (1928). But see *Miller v. Schoene*, 276 U.S. 272 (1928) (upholding order to cut down trees to prevent spread of disease); *Zahn v. Board of Public Works*, 274 U.S. 325 (1927) (upholding zoning ordinance, following *Euclid*); *Gorieb v. Fox*, 274 U.S. 603 (1927) (also upholding zoning ordinance, following *Euclid*).

121. Hylton, "Prelude to Euclid," 37.

122. 260 U.S. 363. See, for example, Robert Brauneis, "The Foundation of Our 'Regulatory Takings' Jurisprudence: The Myth and Meaning of Justice Holmes's Opinion in Pennsylvania Coal Co. v. Mahon," *Yale Law Journal* 106 (1996): 613–702; William Treanor, "Jam for Justice Holmes," *Georgetown Law Journal* 86 (1998): 813–847; Robert Brauneis, "Response: Treanor's *Mahon*," *Georgetown Law Journal* 86 (1998): 907–931; William Fischel, *Regulatory Takings* (Cambridge, MA: Harvard University Press, 1995).

123. The other was *Kansas v. Colorado*, 206 U.S. 46 (1907), in which the Supreme Court rejected the federal government's argument that it owned water in interstate rivers.

124. Brauneis, "The Foundation of Our 'Regulatory Takings' Jurisprudence," 666. As we have seen, property owners could challenge a regulation under their own state constitutions' takings clause.

125. 260 U.S. 363, 413.

126. Fischel, *Regulatory Takings*, 25–26, 31–32.

127. 260 U.S. 363, 422.

128. Fischel, *Regulatory Takings*, 29–32. Fischel also notes that the decision had little impact on coal companies. Fischel, *Regulatory Takings*, 37–42.

129. Brauneis, "The Foundation of Our 'Regulatory Takings' Jurisprudence," 701.

130. *Terrace Park v. Errett*, 12 F.2d 240 (6th Cir. 1926).

Chapter 9. Federalizing Pollution Control

1. Joel Tarr, James McCurley, and Terry Yosie, "The Development and Impact of Urban Wastewater Technology," in *Pollution and Reform in American Cities, 1870–1930*, ed. Martin Melosi (Austin: University of Texas Press, 1980), 69–70; William Andreen, "The Evolution of Water Pollution Control in the United States, Part I," *Stanford Law Review* 22 (2003): 145–201, 168.

2. *U.S. v. Rio Grande Dam and Irrigation Co.*, 174 U.S. 690 (1899).

3. 22 U.S. 1, 203 (1824); Peter Bruton, *The National Board of Health* (Unpublished dissertation, University of Maryland, 1978), 58.

4. 30 Stat. 1152, sec. 13. There was a preceding act that applied only to the waters of New York Harbor. 25 Stat. 209 (1888).

5. Act of May 27, 1 Stat. 474 (1796).

6. Arjun K. Jaikumar, "Red Flags in Federal Quarantine: The Questionable Constitutionality of Federal Quarantine after NFIB v. Sebelius," *Columbia Law Review* 114 (2014): 677–714, 686.

7. Act of Feb. 25, 1 Stat. 619 (1799).

8. John Duffy, *The Sanitarians* (Urbana: University of Illinois Press, 1990), 160–161.

9. Bruton, *The National Board of Health*, 51–52.

10. Christopher Cox, "Report Upon the Necessity for a National Sanitation Bureau," in *Public Health Reports and Papers Presented at the Meeting of the American Public Health Association in 1873*, vol. 1 (New York: Hurd & Houghton, 1875), 522–532, 528–529.

11. Act of Apr. 29, 20 Stat. 37 (1787) (preventing introduction of contagious or infectious diseases into United States). Jerrold Michael, "The National Board of Health, 1879–1883," *Public Health Reports* 126, no. 1 (2011): 123–129; Jaikumar, "Red Flags in Federal Quarantine," 689; Duffy, *The Sanitarians*, 164–167.

12. Jaikumar, "Red Flags in Federal Quarantine," 690; Michael, "The National Board of Health, 1879–1883," 126; Duffey, *The Sanitarians*, 163.

13. Michael, "The National Board of Health, 1879–1883," 127–128; Duffy, *The Sanitarians*, 166–167.

14. Duffy, *The Sanitarians*, 169.

15. Duffy, *The Sanitarians*, 162–163.

16. Act of March 27, 26 Stat. 31 (1890); Act of February 15, 27 Stat. 449, 452 (1893).

17. Remarks of Rep. Rayner, 24 Cong. Rec. 752 (January 21, 1893). See also remarks of Rep. Felton, 7 Cong. Rec. 2075–2076 (March 27, 1878).

18. Senate Committee on Public Health and National Quarantine, *Pollution of Water Supplies*, Sen. Rpt. 411 (February 19, 1900), 2.

19. Earle Phelps, "Stream Pollution by Industrial Wastes and Its Control," in *A Half Century of Public Health*, ed. Mazÿck Ravenel, 197–208 (New York: American Public Health Assoc., 1921), 202.

20. 200 U.S. 496 (1906).

21. Duffy, *The Sanitarians*, 239–240.

22. House Committee on Interstate and Foreign Commerce, *Hearings on Public Health and Marine Hospital Service*, 6–7 (January 18, 1909).

23. Letter from G. O. Smith, dated July 8, 1910, in House Committee on Interstate and Foreign Commerce, *Hearings on the Health Activities of the General Government, Part 9* (1910), 554.

24. See chapter 3 for discussion of these theories in the context of wildlife protection.

25. William Jay Schieffen, "Work of the Committee of One Hundred on National Health," *Annals of the American Academy of Political and Social Science* 37, no. 2 (1911): 77–86.

26. Remarks of George Shiras, in Senate Committee on Public Health and National Quarantine, *Hearings on Proposed Dept. of Public Health*, 44–56 (April 29, 1910). Quote is on 55.

27. Remarks of George Shiras, in Senate Committee on Public Health and National Quarantine, *Hearings on Proposed Dept. of Public Health*, 44–56 (April 29, 1910), 56.

28. Senate Committee on Public Health and National Quarantine, *Hearings on National Public Health, Part 1*, 3–4 (June 2–3, 1910).

29. 37 Stat. 309 (1912) (emphasis added).

30. Richard Andrews, *Managing the Environment, Managing Ourselves* (New Haven, CT: Yale University Press, 1999), 131.

31. A more ambitious health policy, offering to states federal grants if they complied with federal standards to reduce infant and maternal mortality, did generate a lawsuit, discussed below. *Massachusetts v. Mellon*, 262 U.S. 447 (1923) (concerning the Maternity Act, 42 Stat. 224 [1921]).

32. *Stream Pollution in the United States*, CRS Report 10–11 (January 1, 1927); Earle Phelps, "Stream Pollution by Industrial Wastes and Its Control," 204–205; Tarr, McCurley, and Yosie, "The Development and Impact of Urban Wastewater Technology," 75.

33. 43 Stat. 604.

34. House Committee on Rivers and Harbor, *Hearings on Pollution of Navigable Waters* (December 7 and 8, 1921), 155–156.

35. Statement by Hon. Briggs, in House Committee on Rivers and Harbors, *Hearings on Pollution of Navigable Waters*, 41–42 (October 25, 1921).

36. 206 U.S. 46 (1907).

37. 161 U.S. 519 (1895).

38. 139 U.S. 240 (1891).

39. 223 U.S. 166 (1912).

40. House Committee on Rivers and Harbors, *Hearings on Pollution of Naviga-*

ble Waters (Dec. 7 & 8 1921), 165. See also House Committee on Rivers and Harbors, *Hearings on Pollution of Navigable Waters* (January 23, 24, 25, 29, 30, 1924), 230–233.

41. 65 Cong. Rec. 5161–5162 (March 28, 1924). The bill is H.R. 690.

42. For example, *Hegglund v. United States*, 100 F.2d 68 (5th Cir. 1938).

43. *La Merced*, 84 F.2d 444 (9th Cir., 1936).

44. See chapter 10.

45. In the Judiciary Act of 1789, Congress gave the Supreme Court exclusive original jurisdiction in suits between two or more states. In disputes involving only one state, it shared original jurisdiction with any other court that could hear the case. *Ames v. Kansas*, 111 U.S. 449 (1884).

46. The case is described in detail in Robert Percival, "The Clean Water Act and the Demise of the Federal Common Law of Interstate Nuisance," *Alabama Law Review* 55 (2004): 717–774.

47. Percival, "The Clean Water Act and the Demise of the Federal Common Law of Interstate Nuisance," 720.

48. 54 U.S. 518.

49. That court would have "diversity" jurisdiction, which allows federal courts to hear cases between citizens of different states.

50. 1 Stat. 73, sec. 34.

51. 41 U.S. 1 (1842).

52. 304 U.S. 64 (1938).

53. 41 U.S. 1, 18.

54. *U.S. v. Worrall*, 28 F.Cas. 774 (Pa. Cir. Ct. 1798); *United States v. Hudson and Goodwin*, 11 U.S. 32 (1812).

55. 54 U.S. 518, 587.

56. 54 U.S. 518, 582.

57. 54 U.S. 518, 581.

58. 54 U.S. 518, 562.

59. McLean's reasoning is, to say the least, opaque. He also pointed to language in the Virginia law authorizing the bridge, which provided that it could be abated as a public nuisance if it impaired navigation. And he noted that the court was being asked for an equitable remedy, an injunction, and not damages. Courts traditionally have broader authority when exercising equitable jurisdiction. None of these points, however, really answer Taney's objection.

60. *Pennsylvania v. Wheeling & Belmont Bridge Co.*, 59 U.S. 421 (1856).

61. *Willamette Iron Bridge Co. v. Hatch*, 125 U.S. 1, 8. See also *South Carolina v. Georgia*, 93 U.S. 4 (1876); *Wisconsin v. Duluth*, 96 U.S. 379 (1877); *Transp. Co. v. Parkersburg*, 107 U.S. 691 (1882).

62. 21 Cong. Rec. 8604–8605 (1890).

63. 176 U.S. 1.

64. *New Hampshire v. Louisiana*, 108 U.S. 76 (1883) and *New York v. Louisiana*, 108 U.S 91 (1883), cited in *Louisiana v. Texas*, 176 U.S. 1, 16. On the historical treatment of state standing, see Anne Woolhandler and Michael Collins, "State Standing," *Virginia Law Review* 81 (1995): 387–520.

65. *Cohens v. Virginia*, 19 U.S. 264 (1821), 399; *Wisconsin v. Pelican Ins. Co.* There are various grounds for this rule, including the well-supported argument that Article III's grant of original jurisdiction to the Supreme Court in "controversies between two or more states" referred only to civil controversies, not criminal cases.

66. *Georgia v. Stanton*, 73 U.S. 50 (1868).

67. 158 U.S. 564.

68. 176 U.S. 1, 23. Louisiana also alleged that the governor had illicit motives in directing the health officer to impose the quarantine, but Fuller thought the question of officials' motives were beyond the court's power to examine.

69. "Seeks to Enjoin Canal," *Chicago Daily Tribune*, January 5, 1900, A1.

70. Brief and Argument of Complainant in Opposition to Joint Demurrer of Defendants of Bill of Complaint in *Missouri v. Illinois*, in Records of Supreme Court of the United States Original Jurisdiction Case Files, RG 267, Box 88 (NA-DC), 22–25, 26–39.

71. Defendant's Brief in Reply to Brief and Argument of Complainant in Opposition to Demurrer of Defendants to Bill of Complaint in *Missouri v. Illinois*, in Records of Supreme Court of the United States Original Jurisdiction Case Files, RG 267, Box 88 (NA-DC), 4–7. Quote is at 5.

72. Defendant's Brief in Reply to Brief and Argument of Complainant in Opposition to Demurrer of Defendants to Bill of Complaint in *Missouri v. Illinois*, 7–8; Defendant's Brief and Argument in Support of Demurrer in *Missouri v. Illinois*, in Records of Supreme Court of the United States Original Jurisdiction Case Files, RG 267, Box 88 (NA-DC), 22–24. They also argued that Missouri had waited too long to file its complaint, and so its suit should be barred by laches. Defendant's Brief in Reply to Brief and Argument of Complainant in Opposition to Demurrer of Defendants to Bill of Complaint., 8–9.

73. 180 U.S. 236 (emphasis added).

74. 180 U.S. 236, 241 (emphasis added).

75. 180 U.S. 236, 242. Shiras also rejected a claim that Missouri had not alleged fact sufficient to warrant an injunction.

76. Percival, "The Clean Water Act and the Demise of the Federal Common Law of Interstate Nuisance," 724. Those exhibits and testimony included the work of USGS scientists, mentioned above.

77. 200 U.S. 518.

78. 200 U.S. 518, 520.

79. 200 U.S. 518, 522.

80. 200 U.S. 518, 523.

81. 278 U.S. 96 (1928). See chapter 7 for discussion.

82. 185 U.S. 125, 146–147.

83. 206 U.S. 46, 95.

84. 206 U.S. 46, 96.

85. 206 U.S. 46, 98.

86. 206 U.S. 230 (1907).

87. Duncan Maysilles, *Ducktown Smoke* (Chapel Hill: University of North Carolina Press, 2011); Robert Percival "The Frictions of Federalism," University of Maryland Working Research Paper 2002–2003 (2003).

88. Maysilles, *Ducktown Smoke*, 83–84.

89. Maysilles, *Ducktown Smoke*, 87–88.

90. Maysilles, *Ducktown Smoke*, 148–155.

91. Brief and Argument of Tennessee Copper Company on Final Hearing in *Georgia v. Tennessee Copper Co.*, in Records of the Supreme Court of the United States Original Jurisdiction Case Files, RG 267, Box 394 (NA-DC), 102.

92. Summary of plaintiff's complaint in *Georgia v. Tennessee Copper Co.*; see also Maysilles, *Ducktown Smoke*, 111.

93. See Woolhandler and Collins, "State Standing," 432–434.

94. Summary of plaintiff's complaint in *Georgia v. Tennessee Copper Co.*; Brief and Argument of Tennessee Copper Company on Final Hearing in *Georgia v. Tennessee Copper Co.*, in Records of the Supreme Court of the United States Original Jurisdiction Case Files, RG 267, Box 394 (NA-DC), 82–102.

95. 206 U.S. 230, 237.

96. 206 U.S. 230, 236.

97. 206 U.S. 230, 237.

98. 252 U.S. 416, 435 (1920).

99. 206 U.S. 230, 237.

100. 206 U.S. 230, 238.

101. 206 U.S. 230, 238–239.

102. 206 U.S. 230, 239–240.

103. Maysilles, *Ducktown Smoke*, 167.

104. Maysilles, *Ducktown Smoke*, 153–154.

105. Woolhandler and Collins, "State Standing," 446–449.

106. 209 U.S. 349.

107. 209 U.S. 349, 355.

108. 161 U.S. 519 (1895).

109. 209 U.S. 349, 356.

110. 209 U.S. 349, 356–357 (emphasis added). Justice McKenna dissented without an opinion.

111. *West v. Kansas Natural Gas*, 221 U.S. 229 (1911).

112. 458 U.S. 941 (rejecting "legal fiction" that state has ownership of these resources).

113. 237 U.S. 474 (1915). Percival, "The Frictions of Federalism," 27–39; Maysilles, *Ducktown Smoke*, 170–221.

114. Percival, "The Frictions of Federalism," 39.

115. Percival, "The Clean Water Act and the Demise of the Federal Common Law of Interstate Nuisance," 774.

116. *New York v. New Jersey*, 256 U.S. 296 (1921); Percival, "The Clean Water Act and the Demise of the Federal Common Law of Interstate Nuisance," 8–11.

117. 256 U.S. 309.

118. 256 U.S. 309, 313.

119. 259 U.S. 419.

120. 260 U.S. 1 (1922).

121. 262 U.S. 447 (1923). The case was consolidated with another suit brought by a taxpayer in the DC circuit court. The Act is codified at 42 Stat. 224 (1921).

122. 262 U.S. 447, 485. Sutherland went on to dismiss the taxpayer's suit as well, holding that paying taxes was not a sufficient basis for challenging a federal law.

123. 262 U.S. 553 (1923).

124. 262 U.S. 553, 592.

125. 262 U.S. 553, 601–602.

126. 262 U.S. 553, 604.

127. 262 U.S. 553, 616.

128. 262 U.S. 553, 619.

129. 256 U.S. 220 (1921); 263 U.S. 365 (1923); 263 U.S. 583 (1924).

130. 263 U.S. 365, 374–375.

131. 263 U.S. 365, 385–386.

132. The third hearing concerned responsibility for the costs of the litigation.

133. Indeed, both Illinois and New Jersey soon ended up back in court over their water issues. *Wisconsin v. Illinois*, 278 U.S. 367 (1929); 281 U.S. 179 (1931); *New Jersey v. New York*, 280 U.S. 514 (1929); 283 U.S. 805 (1930); 283 U.S. 473 (1931); Percival, "The Clean Water Act and the Demise of the Federal Common Law of Interstate Nuisance," 6–8, 11–14.

134. For an overview of the law review literature on climate change and public nuisance, see Douglas Kysar, "What Climate Change Can Do about Tort Law," *Environmental Law* 41 (2011): 1–71, 2n3.

135. Woolhandler and Collins, "State Standing," 394.

Chapter 10. The Conservation Movement's Constitutional Legacy

1. Norris Hundley, *Water and the West* (Berkeley: University of California Press, 1975).

2. Boulder Canyon Project Act, 45 Stat. 1057 (1928).

3. *Arizona v. California*, 283 U.S. 423 (1931).

4. 148 U.S. 503, 518. See also *Wharton v. Wise*, 153 U.S. 155 (1893).

5. 148 U.S. 503, 519.

6. Felix Frankfurter and James Landis, "The Compact Clause of the Constitution: A Study in Interstate Adjustments," *Yale Law Journal* 34 (1925): 685–758.

7. Noah Hall and Benjamin Houston, "Law and Governance of the Great Lakes," *DuPaul Law Review* 63 (2014): 723–769, 730. Hall and Houston point out that Congress also approved the 1909 Boundary Water Treaty, setting out the rights of US and Canadian citizens to use surface waters that spanned the US/Canadian boundary. This treaty focused on access and navigation rather than environmental management, but it did include a prohibition on pollution—a provision included at the insistence of the Canadians. The Americans agreed only after being assured it would not be vigorously enforced.

8. 256 U.S. 296 (1921), 313.

9. 252 U.S. 416 (1920).

10. 206 U.S. 230 (1907).

11. 206 U.S. 46 (1907).

12. Hundley, *Water and the West*, 105–106.

13. 259 U.S. 419.

14. Hundley, *Water and the West*, 105, 168, 180; Delph Carpenter, "Interstate River Compacts and Their Place in Water Utilization," *Journal of the American Water Works Association* 20 (1928): 756–773, 764–765; Frankfurter and Landes, "The Compact Clause," 706–708; Revel Olson, "Legal Problems in Colorado River Development," *Annals of the American Academy of Political and Social Science* 135 (1928): 108–114, 109.

15. Olson, "Legal Problems in Colorado River Development," 109.

16. House Committee on Irrigation and Reclamation, *Report on Boulder Canyon Project* (March 15, 1928).

17. House Committee on Irrigation and Reclamation, *Report on Boulder Canyon Project*, 22–23.

18. House Committee on Irrigation and Reclamation, *Report on Boulder Canyon Project*, "Minority Views," 38.

19. House Committee on Irrigation and Reclamation, *Report on Boulder Canyon Project*, 38–40.

20. 174 U.S. 690 (1899).

21. 70 Cong. Rec. 7246–7253, 7387–7393 (April 28, 1928); 73 Cong. Rec. 9488–9510 (May 22, 1928).

22. 73 Cong. Rec. 9500 (May 22, 1928).

23. 73 Cong. Rec. 9623 (May 23, 1928).

24. 73 Cong. Rec. 9437 (May 22, 1928).

25. 283 U.S. 423 (1931).

26. 44 U.S. 212 (1845).

27. 80 U.S. 92 (1871).

28. 220 U.S. 523 (1911).

29. 243 U.S. 389 (1917).

30. 283 U.S. 423, 453.

31. 283 U.S. 423, 456.

32. 283 U.S. 423, 457–458.

33. 274 U.S. 264 (1927).

34. 283 U.S. 423, 460.

35. Hundley, *Water and the West*, 333.

36. On public trust doctrine in federal law, see *Hughes v. Oklahoma*, 441 U.S. 322 (1979). On public trust doctrine in state law, see *Pennsylvania Environmental Defense Foundation v. Commonwealth,* 161 A.3rd 911 (Penn. 2017); Richard Frank, "The Public Trust Doctrine: Assessing Its Recent Past and Charting Its Future," *University of California-Davis Law Review* 45 (2012): 665–691.

37. Mark Graber, *Dred Scott and the Problem of Constitutional Evil* (Cambridge: Cambridge University Press, 2006), 3.

38. For a good summary of contemporary constitutional issues, see Robert Percival, "Greening the Constitution: Harmonizing Constitutional and Environmental Values," *Environmental Law* 32 (2002): 809–871.

39. For an exploration of what inclusion of nonhumans might look like, see Kimberly Smith, *Governing Animals* (Oxford: Oxford University Press, 2012).

40. But see Jerry Mashaw, *Creating the Administrative Constitution* (New Haven, CT: Yale University Press, 310 (arguing that federal agencies gave more attention to developing procedural norms than is reflected in legal doctrine).

41. *Missouri v. Holland,* 252 U.S. 416 (1920), 433; *Euclid v. Amber Realty,* 272 U.S. 365 (1926), 387.

Bibliography

Archives and Databases Consulted

America's Historical Newspapers

Kaibab National Forest (KNF), Williams, AZ

National Archives (NA-CP), College Park, MD

National Archives (NA-DC), Washington, DC

NexisUni

Proquest Congressional

Table of Cases

Allman v. Mobile, 162 Ala. 226 (1909).

Ambler Realty Co. v. Euclid, 297 F. 307 (N.D. Ohio 1924).

Ames v. Kansas, 111 U.S. 449 (1884).

Andrews v. Andrews, 188 U.S. 14 (1903).

Arizona v. California, 283 U.S. 423 (1931).

Arnold v. Mundy, 6 N.J.L. 1 (1821).

Ashwander v. T.V.A., 297 U.S. 288 (1936).

Atlantic City v. France, 75 N.J.L. 910 (1908).

Attorney General ex rel. Emmons v. Grand Rapids, 175 Mich. 503 (1913).

Attorney General v. Williams, 174 Mass. 476 (1899).

Baker v. Boston, 29 Mass. 184 (1831)

Barrett v. State of New York, 220 N.Y. 423 (1917).

Bates v. District of Columbia, 1 MacArth. 433 (D.C. Sup. Ct. 1874).

Beery v. Houghton, 164 Minn. 146 (1925).

Benson v. United States, 146 U.S. 325 (1892).

Board of Health v. Schwarz, 84 N.J.L. 500 (1913).

Bowers v. Indianapolis, 169 Ind. 105 (1907).

Brady v. Weeks, 3 Barb. 157 (N.Y.App.Div. 1848).

Brett v. Building Commissioner, 250 Mass. 73 (1924).

Brooklyn Park Commissioners v. Armstrong, 45 N.Y. 234 (1871).

Brooklyn v. Nassau E.R. Co., 44 A.D. 62 (N.Y.App.Div. 1899).

Buchanan v. Warley, 245 U.S. 60 (1917).

Building Inspector v. Stoklosa, 250 Mass. 52 (1924).

Burkhardt v. Cincinnati, 18 Ohio Dec. 450 (1907).

California Reduction Co. v. Sanitary Reduction Works, 199 U.S. 306 (1905).

Calvo v. New Orleans, 136 La. 480 (1915).

Camfield v. U.S., 167 U.S. 518 (1897).

Carey v. South Dakota, 250 U.S. 118 (1919).

Carter v. Carter Coal Company, 298 U.S. 238 (1936).

Cartwright v. Board of Health, 39 A.D. 69 (N.Y. 1899).

Chalk v. United States, 114 F.2d 207 (4th Cir. 1940), cert. den. 312 U.S. 679 (1941).

Chappelle v. United States, 160 U.S. 499 (1895).

Chicago Rock Island & Pacific Railway Company v. McGlinn, 114 U.S. 542 (1885).

Chicago v. Dunham Towing and Wrecking, 161 Ill. App. 307 (1911).

Chicago v. Dunham Towing and Wrecking, 175 Ill. App. 549 (1912).

Chicago v. Rumpff, 45 Ill. 90 (1867).

Cincinnati v. Burkhardt, 1908 Ohio Misc. LEXIS 132 (1908).

Cincinnati v. Miller, 1893 Ohio Misc. LEXIS 244 (1893).

Cleveland v. Malm, 7 Ohio Dec. 1214 (1898).

Coates v. Aldermen etc. of New York, 7 Cow. 585 (N.Y. 1827).

Coggeshall v. United States, 95 F.2d 986 (9th Cir. 1938).

Cohen v. Gould, 225 N.W. 435 (Minn. 1929).

Cohens v. Virginia, 19 U.S. 264 (1821).

Commissioners on Inland Fisheries v. Holyoke Water Power Co., 104 Mass. 446 (1870).

Commonwealth v. Alger, 61 Mass. 53 (1851).

Commonwealth v. Boston Advertising Co., 188 Mass. 348 (1905).

Commonwealth v. Emmers, 33 Pa.Super. 151 (1907).

Commonwealth v. Roberts, 155 Mass. 281 (1892).

Commonwealth v. Ruggles, 10 Mass. 391 (1813).

Commonwealth v. Vincent, 108 Mass. 441 (1871).

Cooper v. Schultz, 32 How. Pr. 107 (N.Y. Ct. of Common Pleas 1866).

Corfield v. Coryell, 6 F. Cas. 546 (E.D. Penn. 1823).

Cottrill v. Myrick, 12 Me. 222 (1835).

Coyle v. Oklahoma, 221 U.S. 559 (1911).

Crowley v. West, 25 La.Ann. 526 (1900).

Damon v. Hawaii, 194 U.S. 154 (1904).

Darcantel v. People's Slaughterhouse & Refrigerating Co., 44 La.Ann. 632 (1892).

Dastervignes v. United States, 122 F. 30 (9th Cir. 1903).

Dent v. United States, 76 P. 455 (Ariz. 1904), reh'g 71 P. 920 (Ariz. 1903).

Dickow v. Cincinnati, 31 Ohio Dec. 266 (1920).

Dobbins v. City of L.A., 195 U.S. 223 (1904).

Dred Scott v. Sandford, 60 U.S. 393 (1857).

Eager v. Jonesboro, Lake City & Eastern Express Co., 103 Ark. 288 (1912).

Elkhart v. Lispchitz, 164 Ind. 671 (1905).

Erie R.R. Co. v. Jersey City, 83 N.J.L. 92 (1912).

Erie R.R. v. Tompkins, 304 U.S. 64 (1938).

Escanaba Co. v. Chicago, 107 U.S. 678 (1882).

Eubank v. Richards, 226 U.S. 137 (1912).

Euclid v. Amber Realty, 272 U.S. 365 (1926).

Ex Parte Heilbron, 65 Cal. 609 (1884).

Ex Parte Maier, 103 Cal. 476 (1894).

Fertilizing Co. v. Hyde Park, 97 U.S. 659 (1878).

Fischer v. St. Louis, 194 U.S. 361 (1904).

Fort Leavenworth Railroad Co. v. Lowe, 114 U.S. 525 (1885).

Gardner v. Michigan, 199 U.S. 325 (1905).

Geer v. Connecticut, 161 U.S. 519 (1895).

Gentile v. State, 29 Ind. 409 (1868).

Georgia v. Stanton, 73 U.S. 50 (1868).

Georgia v. Tennessee Copper Co., 206 U.S. 230 (1907); 237 U.S. 474 (1915).

Gibbons v. Ogden, 22 U.S. 1 (1824).

Gibson v. Chouteau, 80 U.S. 92 (1871).

Glucose Refining Co. v. Chicago, 138 F. 209 (N.D. Ill. 1905).

Gorieb v. Fox, 274 U.S. 603 (1927).

Gough v. Bell, 22 N.J.L. 441 (1850).

Green v. Savannah, 6 Ga. 1 (1849).

Gregory v. New York, 40 N.Y. 273 (N.Y. 1869).

Grisar v. McDowell, 73 U.S. 363 (1868).

Hammer v. Dagenhart, 274 U.S. 251 (1918).

Handy v. South Orange, 118 Atl. 838 (N.J. 1922).

Harmon v. Chicago, 110 Ill. 400 (1884).

Harrington v. Board of Aldermen, 20 R.I. 233 (1897).

Hegglund v. United States, 100 F.2d 68 (5th Cir. 1938).

Hills Dev. Co. v. Bernards, 103 N.J. 1 (1986).

Hoffman v. Schultz, 31 How. Pr. 385 (N.Y. 1866).

Holyoke v. Lyman, 82 U.S. 500 (1873).

Hooker v. Cummings, 20 Johns. 90 (N.Y. 1822).

Hudson County Water Co. v. McCarter, 209 U.S. 349 (1908).

Hughes v. Oklahoma, 441 U.S. 322 (1979).

Hunt v. United States, 278 U.S. 96 (1928).

Hutchinson v. Valdosta, 227 U.S. 303 (1913).

Ignaciumas v. Risley, 98 N.J.L. 712 (1923).

In re Ah Chong, 7 F. 733 (D. Cal. 1880).

In re Debs, 158 U.S. 564 (1895).

In Re Lowe, 54 Kan. 757 (1895).

In re Opinion of the Justices, 234 Mass. 597 (1920).

In re Rahrer, 140 U.S. 545 (1891).

In re United States, 28 F.Supp. 758 (W.D.N.Y. 1939).

In re Wausau Investment Co., 163 Wis. 283 (1915).

In re Zhizhuzza, 147 Cal. 328 (1905).

Ingersoll v. South Orange, 2 N.J. Misc. 882 (1924).

J. W. Hampton v. United States, 276 U.S. 394 (1928).

Jourdan v. Barrett, 45 U.S. 169 (1846).

Kansas v. Colorado, 185 U.S. 125 (1902); 206 U.S. 46 (1907).

Kansas v. McCullagh and Savage, 96 Kan. 786 (1915).

Kawananakoa v. Polybank, 205 U.S. 349 (1907).

Kelley v. Mayor, 6 Misc. 516 (N.Y. 1894).

Kidd v. Pearson, 128 U.S. 1 (1888).

Kohl v. United States, 91 U.S. 367 (1875).

Kuchler v. Weaver, 1909 OK 55 (1909).

La Merced, 84 F.2d 444 (9th Cir., 1936).

Landberg v. Chicago, 237 Ill. 122 (1908).

Laurel Hill Cemetery v. San Francisco, 216 U.S. 358 (1910).

L'Hote v. New Orleans, 177 U.S. 587 (1900).

Light v. United States, 220 U.S. 523 (1911).

Lochner v. New York, 198 U.S. 45 (1905).

Lone Wolf v. Hitchcock, 187 U.S. 553 (1903).

Losick v. Binda, 128 Atl. 619 (N.J. 1925).

Louisiana v. Texas, 176 U.S. 1 (1900).

Lower Merion Twp. v. Becker, 42 Pa.Super. 203 (1910).

Lucas v. South Carolina Coastal Council, 505 U.S. 1003 (1992).

Lumund v. Board of Adjustment, 4 N.J. 577 (1950).

Maine v. Sawyer, 113 Me. 458 (1915).

Manchester v. Massachusetts, 139 U.S. 240 (1891).

Marshall Field & Co. v. Chicago, 44 Ill. App. 410 (1892).

Martin v. Waddell, 41 U.S. 367 (1842).

Massachusetts v. Mellon, 262 U.S. 447 (1923).

Max v. Saul, 3 N.J. Misc. 265 (1925).

McCready v. Virginia, 94 U.S. 391 (1876).

McCulloch v. Maryland, 17 U.S. 316 (1819).

McKelvey v. United States, 260 U.S. 353 (1922).

McNab v. Board of Park Commissioners, 108 Ohio St. 497 (1923).

Metcalf v. St. Louis, 11 Mo. 102 (1847).

Miller v. Schoene, 276 U.S. 272 (1928).

Minnesota v. Rodman, 58 Minn. 393 (1894).

Missouri v. Holland, 252 U.S. 416 (1920).

Missouri v. Illinois, 180 U.S. 208 (1901); 200 U.S. 496 (1906).

Moses v. United States, 16 App. D.C. 428 (1900).

Muller v. Oregon, 208 U.S. 412 (1908).

N.L.R.B. v. Jones & Laughlin Steel Corp., 301 U.S. 1 (1937).

Nectow v. Cambridge, 277 U.S. 183 (1928).

Nelson Bldg. Co. v. Binda, 3 N.J. Misc. 420 (1925).

New Hampshire v. Louisiana, 108 U.S. 76 (1883).

New Jersey v. New York, 280 U.S. 514 (1929); 283 U.S. 805 (1930); 283 U.S. 473 (1931).

New York Metropolitan Board of Health v. Heister, 37 N.Y. 661 (1869).

New York v. Adirondack Railway Company, 160 N.Y. 225 (1899), aff'd 176 U.S. 335 (1900).

New York v. Louisiana, 108 U.S. 91 (1883).

New York v. New Jersey, 256 U.S. 296 (1921).

North Dakota v. Minnesota, 256 U.S. 220 (1921); 263 U.S. 365 (1923); 263 U.S. 583 (1924).

Northwestern Laundry v. Des Moines, 239 U.S. 486 (1915).

Omaechevarri v. Idaho, 246 U.S. 343 (1917).

Palmer v. Barrett, 162 U.S. 399 (1896).

Palmer v. District of Columbia, 26 App. D.C. 31 (1905).

Parker v. Illinois, 111 Ill. 581 (1884).

Patsone v. Pennsylvania, 232 U.S. 138 (1914).

Pennsylvania and Ohio v. West Virginia, 262 U.S. 553 (1923).

Pennsylvania Coal Company v. Mahon, 260 U.S. 363 (1922).

Pennsylvania Environmental Defense Foundation v. Commonwealth, 161 A.3rd 911 (Penn. 2017).

Pennsylvania R. Co v. Jersey City, 84 N.J.L. 716 (1913).

Pennsylvania v. Standard Ice Co., 59 Pgh. L. J. 101 (Penn. 1911).

Pennsylvania v. Wheeling and Belmont Bridge Co., 54 U.S. 518 (1851); 59 U.S. 421 (1856).

People v. Corporation, 11 Wend. 539 (N.Y. 1834).

People v. Hupp, 53 Colo. 80 (1912).

People v. Lewis, 86 Mich. 273 (1891).

People v. New York C. & H. R.R. Co., 159 S.D.D. 359 (N.Y. App. 1913).

People v. New York Edison, 159 A.D. 786 (N.Y. 1913).

Phelps v. Racey, 60 N.Y. 10 (1875).

Pierson v. Post, 3 Cai. R. 175 (N.Y. 1805).

Plumley v. Massachusetts, 155 U.S. 461 (1875).

Plymouth v. Bigelow, 2 N.J. Misc. 711 (1924).

Pollard's Lessee v. Hagan, 44 U.S. 212 (1845).

Portland v. Meyer, 32 Ore. 368 (1898).

Prince v. Board of Adjustment, 3 N.J. Misc. 547 (1925).

River Rendering Co. v. Behr, 71 Mo. 91 (1882).

Rochester v. Macauley-Fien Milling Co., 199 N.Y. 207 (1910).

Roerig v. Minneapolis, 136 Minn. 479 (1917).

Rogers v. Jones, 1 Wend. 237 (N.Y. 1828)

Rund v. Fowler, 142 Ind. 214 (1895).

Rupert v. United States, 181 F. 87 (8th Cir. 1910).

St. Louis v. Heitzeberg Packing & Provision Co., 141 Mo. 375 (1897).

St. Paul v. Gilfillan, 36 Minn. 298 (1886).

St. Paul v. Haugbro, 93 Minn. 59 (1904).

Sawyer v. Davis, 136 Mass. 239 (1884).

Schaite v. Senior, 97 N.J.L. 390 (1922).

Schuster v. Metropolitan Board of Health, 49 Barb. 450 (N.Y.App.Div. 1867).

Shoemaker v. United States, 147 U.S. 282 (1892).

Sigler v. Cleveland, 4 Ohio Dec. 161 (1896).

Silz v. Hesterberg, 211 U.S. 31 (1908).

Slaughterhouse Cases, 83 U.S. 36 (1873).

Smith v. Levinas, 8 N.Y. 472 (1835).

Smith v. Maryland, 59 U.S. 71 (1855).

S. Burlington County NAACP v. Mt. Laurel, 67 N.J. 151 (1975).

S. Burlington County NAACP v. Mt. Laurel, 92 N.J. 158 (1983).

South Carolina v. Georgia, 93 U.S. 4 (1876).

Spector v. Milton, 250 Mass. 63 (1924).

Spokane v. Robison, 6 Wash. 547 (1893).

Sporhase v. Nebraska, 458 U.S. 941 (1982).

Sprigg v. Garret Park, 89 Md. 406 (1899).

Stadler v. Cleveland, 22 Ohio Dec. 783 (Ct. of Common Pleas, 1911).

State ex rel. Belden v. Fagan, 22 La.Ann. 545 (1870).

State ex rel. Blaise v. New Orleans, 142 La. 73 (1917).

State ex rel. Civello v. New Orleans, 154 La. 271 (1923).

State ex rel. Jones v. Froehlich, 115 Wis. 32 (1902).

State ex rel. Lachtman v. Houghton, 134 Minn. 226 (1916).

State ex rel. McCue v. Sheriff of Ramsey County, 48 Minn. 236 (1892).

State ex rel. Owen v. Donald, 160 Wis. 21 (1915).

State v. Burk, 114 Wash. 370 (1921).

State v. Chicago, Milwaukee & St. Paul Railway Co., 114 Minn. 122 (1911).

State v. Kemp, 73 S.D. 458 (1950).

State v. Magner, 97 Ill. 320 (1881).

State v. Nutley, 99 N.J.L. 389 (1924).

State v. Randolph, 1 Mo. App. 15 (1876).

State v. Robb, 100 Me. 180 (1905).

State v. Robert, 59 N.H. 256 (1879).

State v. Sanders, 19 Kan. 127 (1877).

State v. Shattuck, 104 N.W. 719 (Minn. 1905).

State v. Tower, 185 Mo. 75 (1904).

State v. Towessnutte, 154 P. 805 (Wash. 1916)

State v. Ward, 170 Iowa 185 (1915).

Stoughton v. Baker, 4 Mass. 522 (1808).

Swift v. Falmouth, 167 Mass. 115 (1896).

Swift v. Tyson, 41 U.S. 1 (1842).

Taunton v. Taylor, 116 Mass. 254 (1874).

Taylor v. State, 35 Wis. 298 (1874).

Tenement House Dep't v. Moeschen, 89 A.D. 526 (N.Y. 1904).

Terrace Park v. Errett, 12 F.2d 240 (6th Cir. 1926).

The Abby Dodge, 223 U.S. 166 (1912).

The Civil Rights Cases, 109 U.S. 3 (1883).

Thomas Cusack Co. v. Chicago, 242 U.S. 526 (1917).

Toomer v. Witsell, 334 U.S. 385 (1948).

Transp. Co. v. Parkersburg, 107 U.S. 691 (1882).

Treasy v. Louisville, 137 Ky. 289 (1910).

Tugman v. Chicago, 78 Ill. 405 (1875).

Twin City Co. v. Houghton, 144 Minn. 1 (1920).

United Haulers Assn., Inc. v. Oneida-Herkimer Solid Waste Mgmt. Auth., 550 U.S. 330 (2007).

United States v. 2,271.29 Acres, 31 F.2d 617 (W.D. Wis. 1928).

United States v. Alford, 274 U.S. 264 (1927).

United States v. Bale, 156 F. 687 (D.S.D. 1907).

United States v. Blasingame, 116 F. 654 (S.D. Cal. 1900).

United States v. Butler, 297 U.S. 1 (1936).

United States v. Camou, unreported (N.D. Calif., 1902).

United States v. Cochrane, 92 F.2d 623 (7th Cir. 1937).

United States v. Darby Lumber, 312 U.S. 100 (1941).

United States v. Deguirro, 152 F. 568 (N.D. Cal. 1906).

United States v. Domingo, 152 F. 566 (D. Idaho 1907).

United States v. Gettysburg Railway Co., 160 U.S. 668 (1896).

United States v. Graham and Irvine, 250 F. 499 (W.D. Va. 1917).

United States v. Gratiot, 26 F. Cas. 12 (D. Ill 1839); 39 U.S. 526 (1840).

United States v. Grimaud, 170 F. 205 (S.D. Calif. 1909); 220 U.S. 506 (1911).

United States v. Hudson and Goodwin, 11 U.S. 32 (1812).

United States v. Hunt, 19 F.2d 634 (N.D. Az. 1927).

United States v. Martinus, No. 517 (D. Utah, Jan. 26, 1903).

United States v. McCullagh, 221 F. 288 (D. Kan. 1915).

United States v. Midwest Oil, 236 U.S. 459 (1915).

United States v. O'Neill, 198 F. 677 (D. Colo. 1912).

United States v. Payne, 8 F. 883 (W.D. Ark. 1881).

United States v. Rio Grande Dam and Irrigation Company, 174 U.S. 690 (1899).

United States v. Rizzinelli, 182 F. 675 (D. Idaho 1910).

United States v. Rockefeller, 260 F. 346 (D. Montana 1919).

United States v. Samples, 258 Fed. Rep. 479 (W.D. Mo. 1919).

United States v. Selkirk, 258 F. 775 (S.D. Texas 1919).

United States v. Shannon, 160 F. 870 (9th Cir. 1908).

United States v. Shauver, 214 F. 154 (E.D. Ark. 1914).

United States v. Thompson, 258 F. 257 (E.D. Ark. 1919).

United States v. Winans, 198 U.S. 371 (1905).

United States v. Worrall, 28 F.Cas. 774 (Pa. Cir. Ct. 1798).

Utah Power and Light v. United States, 243 U.S. 389 (1917).

Valley Spring Hog Ranch Co. v. Plagman, 282 Mo. 1 (1920).

Van Brocklin v. Tennessee, 117 U.S. 151 (1885).

Van Wagoner v. Mayor and Aldermen of Paterson, 67 N.J.L. 455 (1902).

Vilavasa v. Barthet, 39 La.Ann. 247 (1887).

Virginia v. Tennessee, 148 U.S. 503 (1893).

Vreeland v. Forest Park Reservation Commission, 82 N.J.Eq. 349 (1913).

Ward v. Race Horse, 163 U.S. 504 (1896).

Waters v. People, 23 Colo. 33 (1896).

Waterton v. Mayo, 123 Mass. 372 (1877).

Wayman v. Southard, 23 U.S. 1 (1825).

Welch v. Swasey, 193 Mass. 364 (1907), affd. 214 U.S. 91 (1909).

West Coast Hotel v. Parrish, 300 U.S. 379 (1937).

West v. Kansas Natural Gas, 221 U.S. 229 (1911).

Wharton v. Wise, 153 U.S. 155 (1893).

Wickard v. Filburn, 317 U.S. 111 (1942).

Willamette Iron Bridge Co. v. Hatch, 125 U.S. 1 (1888).

Wisconsin v. Duluth, 96 U.S. 379 (1877).

Wisconsin v. Illinois, 278 U.S. 367 (1929); 281 U.S. 179 (1931).

Wisconsin v. Pelican Insurance Co., 127 U.S. 265 (1888).

Wulfsohn v. Burden, 241 N.Y. 288 (1925).

Wyoming v. Colorado, 259 U.S. 419 (1922); 260 U.S. 1 (1922).

Yick Wo v. Hopkins, 118 U.S. 356 (1886).

Zahn v. Board of Public Works, 274 U.S. 325 (1927).

Secondary sources

Ackerman, Bruce. *We the People.* Vol. 1. Cambridge, MA: Belknap, 1991.

Alexander, Lucien. "James Wilson, Patriot, and the Wilson Doctrine." *North American Review* 183, no. 603 (November 16, 1906): 971–989.

Andreen, William. "The Evolution of Water Pollution Control in the United States, Part I." *Stanford Law Review* 22 (2003):145–201.

Andrews, Richard. *Managing the Environment, Managing Ourselves.* New Haven, CT: Yale University Press, 1999.

Appel, Peter. "The Power of Congress 'Without Limitation': The Property Clause and Federal Regulation of Private Property." *Minnesota Law Review* 86 (2001): 1–130.

Balkin, Jack, and Sandford Levinson. "The Processes of Constitutional Change: From Partisan Entrenchment to the National Surveillance State." SSRN Research Paper 120 (September 17, 2006).

———. "The Framework Model and Constitutional Interpretation." Yale Law School, Public Law Research Paper No. 545 (posted May 20, 2015).

Batchis, Wayne. "Suburbanization and Constitutional Interpretation: Exclusionary Zoning and the Supreme Court Legacy of Enabling Sprawl." *Stanford Journal of Civil Rights & Civil Liberties* 8 (2012): 1–44.

Blum, Michael, and Lucas Ritchie. "The Pioneer Spirit and the Public Trust." *Environmental Law* 35 (Fall 2005): 673–720.

Brandwein, Pamela. *Reconstructing Reconstruction.* Durham, NC: Duke University Press, 1999.

Brauneis, Robert. "Response: Treanor's *Mahon.*" *Georgetown Law Journal* 86 (1998): 907–931.

———. "The Foundation of Our 'Regulatory Takings' Jurisprudence: The Myth and Meaning of Justice Holmes's Opinion in Pennsylvania Coal Co. v. Mahon." *Yale Law Journal* 106 (1996): 613–702.

Bridges, Amy. *Democratic Beginnings.* Lawrence: University Press of Kansas, 2015.

Brooks, Arthur. "The Office File Box—Emanations from the Battlefield." In *Zoning and the American Dream,* edited by Charles Haar and Jerold Kayden. Chicago: Planners, 1989.

Brown, David. *Bringing Back the Game.* Phoenix: Arizona Game and Fish Dept., 2012.

Bruton, Peter. *The National Board of Health.* Unpublished dissertation, University of Maryland, 1978.

Carpenter, Daniel. *The Forging of Bureaucratic Autonomy.* Princeton: Princeton University Press, 2001.

Carpenter, Delph. "Interstate River Compacts and Their Place in Water Utilization." *Journal of the American Water Works Assoc.* 20 (1928): 756–773.

Chittenden, Hiram. "Forests and Reservoirs in their Relation to Streamflow." *American Society of Civil Engineers Transactions* 62 (1909): 245–546.

Chused, Richard. "Euclid's Historical Imagery." *Case Western Reserve Law Review* 51 (Summer 2001): 597–616.

Cioc, Mark. *The Game of Conservation.* Athens: Ohio University Press, 2009.

Claeys, Eric. "Euclid Lives?" *Fordham Law Review* 73 (2004): 731–770.

Clemen, Rudolf. *The American Livestock and Meat Industry.* New York: Ronald, 1923.

Clements, Kendrick. *Hoover, Conservation, and Consumerism.* Lawrence: University Press of Kansas, 2000.

Cohen, Felix. *Handbook of Federal Indian Law.* Rev. Ed. Edited by Rennard Strickland. Charlottesville, VA: Michie-Bobbs-Merrill, 1982.

Conable, Paul. "Equal Footing, County Supremacy, and the Western Public Lands." *Environmental Law* 26 (1996): 1263–1286.

Cox, Christopher. "Report Upon the Necessity for a National Sanitation Bureau." In *Public Health Reports and Papers Presented at the Meeting of the American Public Health Association in 1873.* Vol. 1. New York: Hurd & Houghton, 1875.

Cox, Thomas, Robert Maxwell, Phillip Thomas, and Joseph Malone. *This Well-Wooded Land.* Lincoln: University of Nebraska Press, 1985.

Cumbler, John. *Reasonable Use.* Oxford: Oxford University Press, 2001.

Currie, David. "The Constitution in Congress: The Public Lands, 1827–1861." *University of Chicago Law Review* 70 (2003): 783–820.

Cushman, Barry. "Rethinking the New Deal Court." *Virginia Law Review* 80 (1994): 201–261.

Davis, Marge. *Sportsmen United.* Mt. Juliet, TN: Bench Top, 1997.

Deloria, Vine, and Clifford Lytle. *The Nations Within: The Past and Future of American Indian Sovereignty.* New York: Pantheon, 1984.

Dilsaver, Lary, ed. *America's National Park System: Critical Documents.* Lanham, MD: Rowman & Littlefield, 1994.

Dodds, Gordon. "The Stream-Flow Controversy: A Conservation Turning Point." *Journal of American History* 56 (June 1969): 59–69.

Dorsey, Kurkpatrick. *The Dawn of Conservation Diplomacy.* Seattle: University of Washington Press, 1998.

Duffy, John. *A History of Public Health in New York City.* New York: Russell Sage Foundation, 1968.

———. *The Sanitarians.* Urbana: University of Illinois Press, 1990.

Dunlap, Thomas. *Saving America's Wildlife.* Princeton: Princeton University Press, 1988.

Eckersley, Robyn. *The Green State.* Cambridge, MA: MIT Press, 2004.

Egerton, Frank. "The History of Ecology, Part 1: Achievements and Opportunities." *Journal of the History of Biology* 16 (Summer 1983): 259–310.

———. "History of Ecological Sciences, Part 59: Niches, Biomes, Ecosystems, and Systems," *Bulletin of the Ecological Society of America* 98 (October 2017): 298–337.

———. "History of Ecological Sciences, Part 47: Ernst Haeckel's Ecology." *Bulletin of the Ecological Society of America* 94 (July 2013): 222–224.

Fairfax, Sally, Lauren Gwin, Mary Ann King, Leigh Raymond, and Laura A. Watt. *Buying Nature.* Cambridge, MA: MIT Press, 2005.

Fenster, Mark. "A Remedy on Paper." *Yale Law Journal* 107 (1998): 1093–1123.

Fernow, Bernhard. "What Is Forestry?" *USDA Forestry Division Bulletin* 5. Washington, DC: Government Printing Office, 1891.

Fischel, William. *Regulatory Takings.* Cambridge, MA: Harvard University Press, 1995.

———. "An Economic History of Zoning and a Cure for Its Exclusionary Effects." *Urban Studies* 41 (2004): 317–340.

Fischler, Raphael. "The Metropolitan Dimension of Early Zoning." *Journal of the American Planning Assoc.* 64 (Spring 1998): 170–188.

Foster, James. "The Deer of Kaibab." *Arizona and the West* 12 (Autumn 1970): 255–268.

Frank, Richard. "The Public Trust Doctrine: Assessing Its Recent Past and Charting Its Future." *University of California-Davis Law Review* 45 (2012): 665–691.

Frankfurter, Felix, and James Landis. "The Compact Clause of the Constitution: A Study in Interstate Adjustments." *Yale Law Journal* 34 (1925): 685–758.

Gates, Paul. *History of Public Land Law Development.* Washington, DC: Government Printing Office, 1968.

Goble, Dale, and Eric T. Freyfogle. *Wildlife Law: Cases and Materials.* St. Paul, MN: Foundation, 2002.

Gottlieb, Robert. *Forcing the Spring.* Washington, DC: Island, 1993.

Graber, Mark. *Dred Scott and the Problem of Constitutional Evil.* Cambridge: Cambridge University Press, 2006.

Graham, Frank. *The Adirondack Park.* New York: Alfred A. Knopf, 1978.

Greeley, William. *Forests and Men.* Garden City, NY: Doubleday, 1951.

Griffin, Stephen. "Constitutional Change in the U.S." Tulane Public Law Research Paper No. 11-03, July 18, 2011.

Haar, Charles, and Jerold Kayden, eds. *Zoning and the American Dream.* Chicago: Planners, 1989.

Haar, Charles, and Michael Wolf. "Euclid Lives." *Harvard Law Review* 115 (2002): 2158–2203.

Hall, Noah, and Benjamin Houston. "Law and Governance of the Great Lakes." *DuPaul Law Review* 63 (2014): 723–769.

Hays, Samuel. *Conservation and the Gospel of Efficiency.* Pittsburgh: University of Pittsburgh Press, 1959.

Hornaday, William Temple. *The Extermination of the American Bison* [1889]. Washington, DC: Smithsonian Institution Press, 2002.

Horsman, Reginald. *Feast or Famine*. Columbia: University of Missouri Press, 2008.

Horwitz, Morton. *The Transformation of American Law, 1780–1860*. Cambridge, MA: Harvard University Press, 1977.

Hough, Franklin. *Report upon Forestry: From the Committee Appointed to Memorialize Congress and the State Legislatures Regarding the Cultivation of Timber and the Preservation of Forests*. Washington, DC: Government Printing Office, 1878.

Hundley, Norris. *Water and the West*. Berkeley: University of California Press, 1975.

Hylton, Joseph Gordon. "Prelude to Euclid." *Washington University Journal of Law and Policy* 3 (2000): 1–37.

Irwin, Douglas. "Antebellum Tariff Politics." *Journal of Law and Economics* 51 (2008): 715–741.

Irwin, William. *The New Niagara*. University Park, PA: Penn State University Press, 1996.

Ise, John. *The United States Forest Policy*. New Haven, CT: Yale University Press, 1920.

Jaikumar, Arjun. "Red Flags in Federal Quarantine: The Questionable Constitutionality of Federal Quarantine After *NFIB v. Sebelius*." *Columbia Law Review* 114 (2014): 677–714.

Judd, Richard. *Common Lands, Common People*. Cambridge, MA: Harvard University Press, 1997.

———. *The Untilled Garden*. Cambridge: Cambridge University Press, 2009.

Kahn, Ronald, and Ken Kersch. "Introduction." In *The Supreme Court and American Political Development*, ed. Ronald Kahn and Ken Kersch. Lawrence: University Press of Kansas, 2006.

Kawashima, Yasuhie, and Ruth Tone. "Environmental Policy in Early America." *Journal of Forest History* 27, no. 4 (October 1983): 168–179.

Kelly, Alfred, Winfred Harbison, and Herman Belz. *The American Constitution*. 7th ed. Vol. 1. New York: W. W. Norton, 1991.

Klepper, Henry. "Forest Conservation in Pennsylvania." *Pennsylvania History* 48, no. 1 (1981): 41–50.

Korngold, Gerald. "The Emergence of Private Land Use Controls in Large-scale Subdivisions." *Case Western Reserve Law Review* 51 (2001): 617–643.

Kysar, Douglas. "What Climate Change Can Do about Tort Law." *Environmental Law* 41 (2011): 1–71.

Larson, John. *Internal Improvement*. Chapel Hill: University of North Carolina Press, 2001.

Lazarus, Richard. "Changing Conceptions of Property and Sovereignty in Natural Resources." *Iowa Law Review* 71 (1986): 631–716.

Leshy, John. "Constitutional Conflicts on Public Lands." *University of Colorado Law Review* 75 (Fall 2004): 1101–1125.

————. "Unraveling the Sagebrush Rebellion." *University of California-Davis Law Review* 14 (1980): 317–355.

Levenstein, Harvey. *Revolution at the Table*. New York: Oxford University Press, 1988.

Lofgren, Charles. "*Missouri v. Holland* in Historical Perspective." *Supreme Court Review* (1975): 77–122.

Maher, Neil. *Nature's New Deal*. Oxford: Oxford University Press, 2008.

Marsh, George Perkins. *Man and Nature* [1865]. Seattle: University of Washington Press, 2003.

Mashaw, Jerry. *Creating the Administrative Constitution*. New Haven, CT: Yale University Press, 2012.

Maysilles, Duncan. *Ducktown Smoke*. Chapel Hill: University of North Carolina Press, 2011.

McCarthy, Michael. *Hour of Trial*. Norman: University of Oklahoma Press, 1977.

McGuinness, Margaret. "Symposium: Return to Missouri v. Holland: Federalism and International Law: Foreword." *Missouri Law Review* 73 (2008): 921–937.

McIntosh, Elaine. *American Food Habits in Historical Perspective*. Westport, CT: Praeger, 1995.

McQuillin, Eugene. "Abatement of the Smoke Nuisance in Large Cities." *Central Law Journal* 46 (1898): 147–153.

McShane, Clay, and Joel Tarr. *The Horse in the City*. Baltimore, MD: Johns Hopkins University Press, 2007.

Meadowcraft, James. "Greening the State?" in *Comparative Environmental Politics*, edited by Paul Steinberg and Stacy VanDeveer. Cambridge, MA: MIT Press, 2012.

Meidinger, Errol. "The 'Public Uses' of Eminent Domain." *University of Buffalo Law Review* 11 (1980): 1–65.

Meine, Curt. *Aldo Leopold: His Life and Work*. Madison: University of Wisconsin Press, 1988.

Melosi, Martin. *Garbage in the Cities*. Rev. ed. Pittsburgh: University of Pittsburgh Press, 2005.

Michael, Jerrold. "The National Board of Health, 1879–1883." *Public Health Reports* 126, no. 1 (2011): 123–129.

Miller, Char. *Gifford Pinchot and the Making of Modern Environmentalism*. Washington, DC: Island, 2001.

Morag-Levine, Noga. *Chasing the Wind*. Princeton: Princeton University Press, 2003.

Newmyer, Kent. "John Marshall, McCulloch v. Maryland and the Southern States' Rights Tradition." *John Marshall Law Review* 33 (2000): 875–934.

Nie, Martin, et al. "Fish and Wildlife Management on Federal Lands: Debunking State Supremacy." *Environmental Law* 47 (Fall 2017): 797–932.

Novak, William. *The People's Welfare.* Chapel Hill: University of North Carolina Press, 1996.

Novick, Sheldon. "Introduction." In *Collected Works of Justice Holmes*, edited by Sheldon Novick. Vol. 1. New York: Dover, 1991.

Novkov, Julie. *Constituting Workers, Protecting Women.* Ann Arbor: University of Michigan Press, 2001.

O'Brien, David. *Constitutional Law and Politics*, 10th ed. 2 volumes. New York: W. W. Norton, 2017.

Olson, Revel. "Legal Problems in Colorado River Development." *Annals of the American Academy of Political and Social Science* 135 (1928): 108–114.

Orren, Karen. *Belated Feudalism.* Cambridge: Cambridge University Press, 1991.

Pearson, Susan. *The Rights of the Defenseless.* Chicago: University of Chicago Press, 2011.

Peck, Robert. "The Renaissance of the Beaver." *Forest and Stream* 111 (April 1921): 152.

Penick, James. *Progressive Politics and Conservation.* Chicago: University of Chicago Press, 1968.

Percival, Robert. "The Clean Water Act and the Demise of the Federal Common Law of Interstate Nuisance." *Alabama Law Review* 55 (2004): 717–774.

———. "The Frictions of Federalism." University of Maryland Working Research Paper 2002–2003 (2003).

———. "Greening the Constitution: Harmonizing Constitutional and Environmental Values." *Environmental Law* 32 (2002): 809–871.

Phelps, Earle. "Stream Pollution by Industrial Wastes and Its Control." In *A Half Century of Public Health*, edited by Mazÿck Ravenel. New York: American Public Health Assoc., 1921.

Phillips, Sarah. *This Land, This Nation.* Cambridge: Cambridge University Press, 2007.

Pierson, Paul. *Politics in Time.* Princeton: Princeton University Press, 2004.

Pinchot, Gifford. *The Fight for Conservation.* New York: Doubleday, Page, 1911.

Pisani, Donald. *To Reclaim a Divided West.* Albuquerque: University of New Mexico Press, 1992.

———. *Water, Land, and Law in the West.* Lawrence: University Press of Kansas, 1996.

Power, Garrett. "Advocates at Cross-Purposes." *Journal of Supreme Court History* 2 (1997): 79–87.

Reid, Charles. "America's First Great Constitutional Controversy." *University of St. Thomas Law Journal* 14 (2018): 105–192.

Reiger, John. *American Sportsmen and the Origins of Conservation.* New York: Winchester, 1975.

Reitz, Arnold. *Air Pollution Control Law: Compliance and Enforcement.* Environmental Law Institute, 2001.

Roosevelt, Theodore. *The Rough Riders: An Autobiography* [1913], Library of America ed. New York: Penguin, 2004.

———. *The Works of Theodore Roosevelt*, edited by Hermann Hagedorn. Vol. 18. New York: Charles Scribner's Sons, 1925.

Runte, Alfred. *National Parks*. Lincoln: University of Nebraska Press, 1979.

Sawyer, Logan. "Grazing, Grimaud, and Gifford Pinchot: How the Forest Service Overcame the Classical Nondelegation Doctrine to Establish Administrative Crimes." *Journal of Law & Politics* 24 (Spring 2008): 169–208.

Schieffen, William. "Work of the Committee of One Hundred on National Health." *Annals of the American Academy of Political and Social Science* 37, no. 2 (1911): 77–86.

Sherow, James. *Watering the Valley*. Lawrence: University Press of Kansas, 1990.

Skocpol, Theda. *Protecting Soldiers and Mothers*. Cambridge, MA: Belknap, 1992.

Skowronek, Stephen. *Building a New American State*. Cambridge: Cambridge University Press, 1982.

Smith, Kimberly. *Governing Animals*. Oxford: Oxford University Press, 2012.

Stark, Jack. "A History of the Internal Improvements Section of the Wisconsin Constitution." *Wisconsin Law Review* 1998: 829–839.

Stradling, David, ed. *Conservation in the Progressive Era*. Seattle: University of Washington Press, 2004.

———. *Smokestacks and Progressives*. Baltimore, MD: Johns Hopkins University Press, 1999.

Szymanski, Ann-Marie. "Wildlife Protection and the Development of Centralized Governance in the Progressive Era." In *Statebuilding from the Margins*, edited by Carol Nackenoff and Julie Novkov. Philadelphia: University of Pennsylvania Press, 2014.

Tarr, Joel, James McCurley, and Terry Yosie. "The Development and Impact of Urban Wastewater Technology." In *Pollution and Reform in American Cities, 1870–1930*, edited by Martin Melosi. Austin: University of Texas Press, 1980.

Tober, James. *Who Owns the Wildlife?* Westport, CT: Greenwood, 1981.

Treanor, William. "Jam for Justice Holmes." *Georgetown Law Journal* 86 (1998): 813–847.

Urofsky, Melvin, and Paul Finkelman. *A March of Liberty*. 2nd ed. 2 vols. Oxford: Oxford University Press, 2002.

Vig, Norman, and Michael Faure. "Introduction." In *Green Giants*, edited by Norman Vig and Michael Faure. Cambridge, MA: MIT Press, 2004.

Wellington, Raynor. *The Political and Sectional Influence of the Public Lands, 1828–1842*. Cambridge, MA: Riverside, 1914.

Wells, Philip. "Philip Wells in the Forest Service Law Office." *Forest History Newsletter* 16 (April 1972): 23–29.

White, Adam. "Infrastructure Policy: Lessons from American History." *New Atlantis* 35 (Spring 2012): 3–31.

Widner, Ralph, ed. *Forests and Forestry in the American States.* National Assoc. of State Foresters, 1968.

Wilkins, David. *American Indian Sovereignty and the U.S. Supreme Court.* Austin: University of Texas Press, 1997.

———. "Indian Treaty Rights: Sacred Entitlements or 'Temporary Privileges'?" *American Indian Culture and Research Journal* 20 (1996): 87–129.

Williams, Michael. "Industrial Impacts on the Forests of the United States, 1860–1920." *Journal of Forest History* 31, no. 3 (July 1987): 108–121.

Wolf, Michael. *The Zoning of America.* Lawrence: University Press of Kansas, 2008.

Woolhandler, Anne, and Michael Collins. "State Standing." *Virginia Law Review* 81 (1995): 387–520.

Young, Christian. *In the Absence of Predators.* Lincoln: University of Nebraska Press, 2002.

Index

Fifteenth Amendment, 11
Fifth Amendment, 193, 210
Fischel, William, 211, 295n128
fish and game. *See* fish conservation;
    game laws, state; hunting; wildlife
    conservation
Fish Commission, US, 22, 42–43
fish conservation
    and *The Abby Dodge*, 43–44, 53, 222
    in constitutional debate, 41–46, 53
    and *Corfield v. Coryell*, 29–30, 31, 43
    and *Cottrill v. Myrick*, 28–29
    and *McCready v. Virginia*, 31–32
    property rights and, 28–30, 31–32, 46
    public trust doctrine and, 28, 29
    and *Smith v. Maryland*, 43
    state authority over, 21, 28–36, 40–41,
        43, 44–46, 222, 286n55
    state failure argument and, 40–44
    treaty power and, 44–46
    See also *Geer v. Connecticut* (1895);
        water pollution control
Flathead Forest Reserve, 106, 107
Flathead Indian Reservation, 147–148
Forest and Stream, 26, 29, 33–34, 43
forest conservation
    Adirondacks and, 37–38, 76, 77, 81–86
    Appalachian-White Mountain forest
        reserve and, 60, 129–130, 131–131,
        142–148, 279n78
    Commerce Clause and, 60–61, 132, 142,
        144–145
    and constitutional change, 72, 80–81,
        98–99
    in constitutional debate, 86–89, 89–96
    constitutional framework for, 78–81
    and equal footing doctrine, 108–115,
        117, 118, 119, 120, 121, 126
    federal authority over, 101–105, 221
    federal irrigation projects and, 128–129,
        135, 137, 138–139
    and forest conservation movement, 37,
        73–75, 82, 83
    and forest reserves from public lands,
        97, 99–101, 105, 113–115, 128–129,
        143–144, 145, 149–150, 153
    and game laws, 59–60, 126, 164–165,
        170

and game refuge debate, 164–169
and grazing regulations, 112–113, 114,
    117–118
and "internal improvements" debate,
    89–96
National Park Service and, 97,
    104–105, 129
policy rationales for, 75–81, 101–105
Property Clause and, 79–80, 97–98,
    105, 107–108, 112, 128, 129, 150,
    168–169, 176–179
USDA and, 74, 97, 98–99, 102–103,
    112–114, 117–118, 151–153, 157,
    180–181, 182
See also Forest Service, US; *Light v.
    United States* (1911); *United States v.
    Grimaud* (1911)
Forest Service, US
    and *Chalk v. United States*, 170, 181–182,
        289n117
    and forest reserves, 105, 113–115,
        143–144, 145, 149–150, 153
    Franklin Hough and, 74, 77, 78–80,
        82, 99
    Gifford Pinchot and, 97, 98, 113, 124,
        128, 142, 153, 157, 256
    and grazing law, 7–8, 54, 113–115
    and *Hunt v. United States*, 156, 169–180,
        181, 182, 233, 288n90
    and 1905 Transfer Act, 97
    and wildlife management, 59–60,
        169–170
    See also *Light v. United States* (1911);
        United States v. Grimaud (1911);
        Weeks-McLean Act (1913)
The Forging of Bureaucratic Autonomy
    (Carpenter), 8–9, 16, 98
Fort Leavenworth Railroad Co. v. Lowe
    (1885), 159–160, 162, 163, 286n55
Foster, James, 179
Fourteenth Amendment, 11, 17, 21, 27, 29,
    42, 86–87, 190, 191, 207
Frankfurter, Felix, 248
Franklin, Benjamin, 14
Free Timber Act (1878), 99
Frierson, William, 65
Fuller, Melville, 85, 120, 207, 229, 230,
    232, 234, 299n68

and federal authority over navigation, 55, 144, 222
in *Hudson County Water Co. v. McCarter*, 239
in *Light v. United States*, 119
Property Clause and, 55, 121, 154
and state and federal authority over water resources, 5, 141–142, 144–145, 222, 234–235
and state water rights, 116, 234–235, 239, 251–252, 278n58, 295n123
Kansas v. McCullagh and Savage (1915), 58
Kersch, Ken, 11–12
Kidd v. Pearson (1888), 33
King, Alex, 65
Knaebel, Ernest, 120
Knapp, George, 154
Knox, Philander, 45, 155, 157–161, 162, 163, 164–165, 166, 168, 173, 180
Kohler Act (1921), 210, 211
Kohl v. United States (1875), 95, 144

Lacey, John, 22–23, 48, 155, 157–158, 161, 164, 167, 256
Lacey Act (1900), 22–23, 36, 46, 48–49, 155, 173, 178, 269n31
Lake Michigan, 224, 233
Lake Union, 222–223
Lamar, Joseph, 120–121, 124–126, 166–167
Land and Water Conservation Fund, 152
Landis, James, 248
Laramie River, 242, 249
Leighton, M. O., 218
Leopold, Aldo, 2, 59–60, 176–177
Leshy, John, 4, 109
Levenstein, Harvey, 35
Levinson, Sandford, 263n34
Lewis and Clark Forest Reserve, 106
Light, Fred, 118–120, 126
Light v. United States (1911), 98, 117–121, 126–127, 154, 166–167, 168–169, 178, 182
"Lochner era," 5–6, 147, 183, 201–202
Lochner v. New York (1905), 5–6, 37, 186, 200
Lone Wolf v. Hitchcock (1903), 286n56
Louisiana, 80, 108, 109, 191, 205, 225, 229. See also *Louisiana v. Texas* (1900)

Louisiana v. Texas (1900), 229–231, 232, 243, 299n68
Lucas v. South Carolina Coastal Council (1992), 272n121
Lurton, Horace, 120

Madison, James, 14
Maine, 58, 86–88, 92, 93
Maine v. Sawyer (1915), 58
Malheur National Wildlife Refuge, 1–2, 3, 18, 257
Man and Nature (Marsh), 73–74, 77
Manchester v. Massachusetts (1891), 222
Marine Hospital Service (MHS), 216–217, 218, 220
Mariposa Big Tree Grove, 75
Marsh, George Perkins, 73–74, 77
Marshall, Louis, 14, 66–67, 69, 136, 188, 215
Marshall, Roujet, 90, 91, 92–94, 275n81
Martin v. Waddell (1842), 25, 144–145
Maryland, 13, 43, 243–244, 246–247
Massachusetts, 28–29, 33, 80, 202–205, 242
Massachusetts v. Mellon (1923), 242
Mather, Stephen, 147, 172, 174, 284n6
Maxwell, George, 134, 138
Maysilles, Duncan, 238–239
MBTA. See Migratory Bird Treaty Act (MBTA)
McCarthy, Michael, 111
McCready v. Virginia (1876), 31–32, 44
McCulloch v. Maryland (1819), 143, 144
McKenna, Joseph, 120, 235, 300n110
McLean, George, 47–48, 53. See also Weeks-McLean Act (1913)
McLean, John, 225, 227, 298n59
McNab v. Board of Park Commissioners (1923), 94
McQuillin, Eugene, 200, 292n64
McReynolds, James, 209, 242–243
Meidinger, Errol, 84, 274n46
Melosi, Martin, 185, 186
Merriam, C. Hart, 23
Metropolitan Board of Health v. Heister (1869), 190–191, *192* (table), 194
Michigan, 55, 92, 93, 224
Migratory Bird Conservation Act (1929), 148, 156, 170

Public Health Service (PHS), 220–221
public nuisance doctrine, 184–185,
    187–188, 190, 197, 211, 212, 225–228,
    231–232

Railroad Fire Line Law (1909), 88
Reclamation Service, 141–142, 247
Reeder, Robert, 177
Reiger, John, 33–34
Richards, John, 123
Rio Grande. See United States v. Rio
    Grande Dam and Irrigation Co.
    (1899)
River Rendering Co. v. Behr (1882), 194–195
Rivers and Harbors Act (1899), 215, 221,
    222–223, 228
Roosevelt, Franklin D., 263n34
Roosevelt, Robert, 42–43
Roosevelt, Theodore
    conservation movement and, 41,
        49–50, 113
    and federal irrigation authority,
        138–139, 141
    and forest conservation, 87, 113, 155
    Grand Canyon Game Preserve created
        by, 171
    "inherent powers" doctrine of, 49–51,
        116, 141, 255
    1908 Conference of Governors address
        by, 13, 117
    Republican Party split and, 97
    wildlife refuges created by, 3, 50–51, 156
Root, Elihu, 41, 44–45, 61, 224
Runte, Alfred, 104
Rupert v. United States (1910), 49
Rutledge, R. H., 174

Sand County Almanac, A (Leopold), 2
San Jacinto Forest Reserve, 106
Sawyer, Logan, 122–123, 124, 126
Sawyer v. Davis (1884), 203
Schaite v. Senior (1922), 206
Schuster v. Metropolitan Board of Health
    (1867), 192 (table), 194
Shauver. See United States v. Shauver (1914)
Sherman, E. A., 174
Shiras, George, Jr., 51, 95, 231–232, 233,
    234, 236, 299n75

Shiras, George, III, 51–52, 219–220
Shoemaker v. United States (1892), 95
Skowronek, Stephen, 6–7, 8
Slaughterhouse Cases, 185, 189–190,
    191–194, 192 (table), 196
Smith, George Otis, 219, 220
Smith v. Maryland (1855), 43
smoke abatement movement, 196–198, 199
    (table), 200, 292n65
Soil Conservation and Domestic
    Allotment Act (1936), 283n95
Soil Conservation Service, 286n67
South Dakota, 55, 58, 277–278n50
Sporhase v. Nebraska (1982), 240
Standing Rock Sioux Reservation, 1,
    18, 257
Stanislaus Forest Reserve, 106
Stark, Jack, 89
State ex rel. Civello v. New Orleans
    (1923), 205
State ex rel. Jones v. Froehlich (1902), 91
State ex rel. Lachtman v. Houghton
    (1916), 205
State ex rel. McCue v. Sheriff of Ramsey
    County (1892), 292n65
State ex rel. Owen v. Donald (1915), 90
State v. Burk (1921), 178
State v. Magner (1881), 27
State v. Robb (1905), 195
State v. Towessnutte (1916), 286n55
St. Louis (MO), 34, 35, 194–195, 196, 231
St. Louis v. Heitzeberg Packing & Provision
    Co. (1897), 197, 199 (table)
Story, Joseph, 150, 226
Stoughton v. Baker (1808), 25–26
Stradling, David, 196–197, 198, 200
Supremacy Clause, 44. See also treaty
    power
Sutherland, George, 179, 207, 208–209,
    242, 259, 301n122
Swamp Land Act (1850), 134
Swift v. Tyson (1842), 226, 235
Szymanski, Ann-Marie, 36

Taft, William Howard, 45, 61, 120, 142,
    220, 244
Taney, Roger, 16, 25, 225, 226–228, 233,
    244, 277n46, 284n11, 298n59

Yellowstone National Park, 76, 77–78, 101, 156, 268n3
Yellowstone Reservation Act (1871), 99
Yellowstone Reserve, 101
Yosemite National Park, 76, 78, 99
Yosemite Valley, 75, 76
Young, Christian, 176–177

zoning, 200–207, 293n73, 294n104. See also *Euclid v. Ambler Realty* (1924); urban planning